Study and Critical Thinking Skills in College

Fifth Edition

Kathleen T. McWhorter

Niagara County Community College

Longman

New York   San Francisco   Boston
London   Toronto   Sydney   Tokyo   Singapore   Madrid
Mexico City   Munich   Paris   Cape Town   Hong Kong   Montreal

VICE PRESIDENT AND EDITOR-IN-CHIEF:	Joseph Terry
SENIOR ACQUISITIONS EDITOR:	Steven Rigolosi
DEVELOPMENT MANAGER:	Janet Lanphier
DEVELOPMENT EDITOR:	Leslie Taggart
SENIOR MARKETING MANAGER:	Melanie Craig
SUPPLEMENTS EDITOR:	Donna Campion
MEDIA SUPPLEMENTS EDITOR:	Nancy Garcia
PRODUCTION MANAGER:	Douglas Bell
PROJECT COORDINATION, TEXT DESIGN, AND ELECTRONIC PAGE MAKEUP:	Elm Street Publishing Services, Inc.
COVER DESIGN MANAGER:	John Callahan
COVER DESIGNER:	Kay Petronio
COVER PHOTOS:	Courtesy of PhotoDisc
PHOTO RESEARCHER:	Photosearch, Inc.
MANUFACTURING BUYER:	Al Dorsey
PRINTER AND BINDER:	Courier Corporation
COVER PRINTER:	Phoenix Color Corporation

For permission to use copyrighted material, grateful acknowledgment is made to the copyright holders on pp. 405–408, which are hereby made part of this copyright page.

Library of Congress Cataloging-in-Publication Data

McWhorter, Kathleen T.
    Study and critical thinking skills in college / Kathleen T. McWhorter.—5th ed.
        p. cm.
    Includes bibliographical references and index.
    ISBN 0-321-08923-5
        1. Study skills. 2 Thought and thinking. 3. Critical thinking. I. Title.

LB2395 .M445 2003
378.1'70281—dc21

2002025093

Please visit our website at http://www.ablongman.com/StudySkills

ISBN 0-321-08923-5

2 3 4 5 6 7 8 9 10—CRW—05 04 03

Brief Contents

Detailed Contents

Preface

Over the past several decades, educators have become increasingly aware of the need to teach students how to learn and study. Many two- and four-year colleges offer learning and study skills courses, "how to study" manuals are readily available, and even prestigious graduate and professional schools provide instructional or tutorial services in study skills. The field of study skills, once relatively unknown, now enjoys wide acceptance and academic legitimacy.

Another relatively new discipline—the field of critical thinking skills—has experienced similar growth and acceptance. Critical thinking skills have become an important part of the college curriculum, and many institutions include critical thinking skills requirements as part of their general education programs. Consequently, instruction in critical thinking skills has become a rapidly expanding frontier within higher education.

Although these two fields, study skills and critical thinking, have evolved independently of each other, they are integrally connected. This text represents a unique endeavor: to integrate study skills and critical thinking and to provide a unified instructional sequence for skills development.

Goals

Study and Critical Thinking Skills in College was written to enable students to become academically competitive and to prepare them for success in the workplace. It aims to achieve the following goals:

Active Learning

A primary purpose of the text is to approach study as an active thinking process. For many students, learning is a passive assimilation process, and their goal is to acquire as many facts and as much information as possible. This book encourages students to take an active role in learning by thinking critically about and interacting with text and lecture material. It focuses on sorting, interpreting, synthesizing, and evaluating ideas and information. It provides students with a repertoire of active study and thinking strategies that will enable them to handle college course work confidently and effectively.

Critical Thinking

A basic assumption of this book is that students can learn how to learn and can be taught to think critically. The second major purpose of this book, then, is to teach specific learning and thinking strategies. Learning is approached as a highly versatile and adaptive process. Students are encouraged to analyze learning tasks and to choose appropriate strategies that suit the nature of the task and their prior knowledge and experience. Critical thinking is presented as an integral part of all learning and study tasks. The text presents six levels of thinking based on Bloom's taxonomy: knowledge, comprehension, application, analysis, synthesis, and evaluation. Students are also encouraged to analyze the level of thinking each learning task requires and to adapt their approaches accordingly.

Attitudes Toward Learning

While a major emphasis is on cognitive skills, skills in the affective and behavioral domains that shape and control learning are also introduced. Developing positive attitudes toward learning, taking charge and accepting responsibility for one's own learning, analyzing one's own learning style, using effective organizational and time management skills, and managing stress are discussed.

Workplace Applications

All of the skills taught in this text have immediate academic application. Many of the skills, however, are also applicable to and contribute to success in the workplace. A secondary purpose of the text, then, is to promote students' success in the workplace as well as in the classroom.

Metacognitive Skills

The final purpose of this book is to apply current research findings in the areas of metacognition, schema theory, and writing as learning. Metacognitive strategies are built into specific learning and study techniques. Academic thought patterns, emphasized throughout, function as schema that provide students with overriding concepts or blueprints with which to organize text, research, and lecture material, and to approach assignments, exams, and term papers. Writing as a learning process is also incorporated into various study and review techniques.

Content Overview

Study and Critical Thinking Skills in College presents a unique integration of study and critical thinking skills. Study and learning are approached as cognitive processes that require various levels and types of thinking. Students are taught to become active learners by analyzing tasks, selecting appropriate learning strategies, and monitoring and revising their strategies to suit the nature of the tasks. Metacognition, the learner's awareness and control over his or her cognitive processes, is, then, a central focus here. A secondary focus is the use of academic thought patterns as thinking and organizing strategies, providing students with a thread that can tie together seemingly divergent courses.

◆ **Part One introduces students to college learning and thinking and establishes a focus on student success.** These chapters encourage students to develop specific success strategies. They learn to become familiar with the college system, take responsibility for their own learning, establish goals, manage their time, reduce stress, communicate effectively in the classroom, and think critically to solve problems. Specific strategies for success as well as organizational and time management skills are presented. Students also learn life skills, including managing finances, health, jobs, and relationships.

◆ **Part Two teaches students fundamental approaches to the learning process and to essential critical thinking strategies.** In Chapter 8 students analyze their own learning style, consider how to use their learning style to choose study methods, and discover how to adapt to various teaching styles. Chapter 9 discusses principles of learning and memory and their application to academic tasks.

◆ **Part Three shows students how to apply skills to various academic disciplines.** Techniques for approaching the social sciences, natural sciences, mathematics, arts and humanities, and career fields are discussed. The importance of learning specialized and technical vocabulary is stressed, and specific learning strategies are suggested.

◆ **Part Four offers students skills and strategies for mastering course content.** The section begins with a chapter on academic patterns of thought, emphasizing their predominance and use across various academic disciplines. The remaining chapters discuss techniques and strategies for lecture note taking, textbook reading and study, and organization and synthesis of course content, and discuss academic thought patterns as organizing features. The SQ3R reading-study system is also introduced.

◆ **Part Five equips students with the skills and strategies needed in preparing for and taking exams.** Students learn to organize their review, use thematic study, and develop study strategies for specific academic disciplines. They learn specific strategies for answering objective test questions, writing essay exams, and controlling test anxiety.

These part divisions were designed to give the user of this text the greatest possible flexibility. The opening chapters provide a basic framework and introduction to study and critical thinking; the remaining units and chapters may be rearranged according to instructor preference. This flexible organization allows instructors to maximize their ability to meet specific course objectives and to accommodate the needs of their students.

Special Features

The following features significantly enhance the text's effectiveness as a motivational teaching tool:

◆ **Focus Questions.** Each chapter begins with a brief list of questions that identifies key chapter topics and provides students with purposes for reading. The questions can also serve as a means of checking recall after reading the chapter.

◆ **Thinking Critically . . . About.** These boxed inserts relate critical thinking skills to chapter content and offer practical suggestions and tips for developing critical thinking skills.

◆ **How Do You See It?** Each chapter contains an activity based on a photo or cartoon that stimulates critical and creative thinking and encourages students to view chapter content from new perspectives.

◆ **In-Chapter Exercises.** Numerous exercises within each chapter provide students with opportunities to immediately apply and evaluate techniques. While the exercises take a variety of forms, their focus is the practical application of skills in realistic college course situations, and they often require the use of the students' own textbooks or course materials.

◆ **Working Together Activity.** Each chapter contains an exercise designed for group interaction. Its purpose is to promote collaborative learning, allowing students to listen to and learn from the thinking processes of other students.

◆ **Interactive Chapter Review.** The final part of each chapter includes one or more activities for each of the six levels of thinking. These activities reinforce chapter content while ensuring that students apply, analyze, synthesize, and evaluate their learning.

◆ **Further Analysis.** Each chapter includes a practical reading/study problem that is an application of chapter content. Students are directed to analyze the situation and to offer possible solutions.

◆ **The Work Connection.** This activity, appearing near the end of each chapter, encourages students to explore workplace applications of chapter content. By extending chapter skills to the workplace, students realize the long-term benefits of the skills they are learning.

◆ **The Web Connection.** Each chapter concludes with a list of Web sites containing additional information on topics covered in the chapter. A brief description of each Web site is included, along with its URL. The sites may provide helpful tips, offer alternative viewpoints, or contain useful study aids such as worksheets, questionnaires, or checklists.

Changes in the Fifth Edition

The fifth edition of *Study and Critical Thinking Skills in College* adds four important topics to its already comprehensive instruction that will help students strengthen their learning and study skills.

◆ A new Chapter 4, "Managing Your Life," discusses how to stay physically, mentally, and emotionally healthy while experiencing the lifestyle changes of college.

◆ A new chapter feature, "How Do You See It?", stimulates critical and creative thinking through the use of photographs and cartoons.

◆ A new feature at the end of each chapter, "The Web Connection," helps students find additional resources for improving learning and study skills at respected academic Web sites.

◆ A new emphasis on reading informs Chapter 14, which now includes the SQ3R reading/study system to encourage students to learn as they read.

New Chapter 4, "Managing Your Life"

Mental and physical health are prerequisites for academic success. "Managing Your Life" shows students how to manage the new and unique demands placed upon them at college. College students are faced with lifestyle changes, in addition to more challenging and stringent academic requirements. College students may have new living arrangements, new financial obligations, new social relationships, and a new schedule all of which can affect levels of exercise, nutrition, and sleep. This chapter discusses four keys to a successful college lifestyle: finances, health, jobs, and relationships. This new chapter and the chapter on managing stress that first appeared in the previous edition provide students with a well-integrated and well-rounded approach to mental agility and physical health.

New "How Do You See It?" Feature

"How Do You See It?" is a new feature in each chapter that presents students with novel tasks designed to spark critical and creative thinking. Students view a photograph or cartoon and then respond to a specific question that encourages them to offer unique and thoughtful perspectives.

New "Web Connection" Feature

Students are encouraged to explore additional resources to improve their learning and study skills. "The Web Connection" is an annotated list of URLs of respected academic Web sites that provide helpful advice, activities, and suggestions to enable students to extend and apply chapter content. Each entry is annotated so that students can that students can preview the list and decide which sites will be most helpful.

New Section on the SQ3R Reading/Study System

Chapter 14 now includes instruction on the SQ3R reading/study system. The new section lists the steps, guides students in its application, and discusses adapting the system to suit various academic disciplines and the students' own learning styles.

The Teaching and Learning Package

Each component of the teaching and learning package has been crafted to ensure that the course is a rewarding experience for both instructors and students.

The **Instructor's Manual and Test Bank** provides many suggestions for using the text, including how to structure and organize the course and how to approach each section of the book. The manual also contains a 10-item multiple-choice quiz for each chapter of the text. 0-321-08924-3

Also be sure to visit our Study Skills Web site at **http://www.ablongman.com/ StudySkills.** In addition, a series of other skills-based supplements is available for both instructors and students. All of these supplements are available either free or at greatly reduced prices.

For Additional Reading and Reference •

The Dictionary Deal. Two dictionaries can be shrink-wrapped with this text either free or at a nominal fee. *The New American Webster Handy College Dictionary* is a paperback reference text with more than 100,000 entries. *Merriam-Webster's College Dictionary,* 10th edition, is a hardback reference with a citation file of more than 14.5 million examples of English words drawn from actual use. For more information on how to shrink-wrap a dictionary with your text, please contact your Longman sales representative.

The Longman Textbook Reader. This supplement, for use in developmental reading courses, offers five complete chapters from Addison Wesley Longman textbooks: computer science, biology, psychology, communications, and business. Each chapter includes additional comprehension quizzes, critical thinking questions, and group activities. Available free with the adoption of this Longman text. For information on how to bundle *The Longman Textbook Reader* with your text, please contact your Longman sales representative. Available in two formats: with answers and without answers.

***Newsweek* Alliance.** Instructors may choose to shrink-wrap a 12-week subscription to *Newsweek* with any Longman text. The price of the subscription is 57 cents per issue (a total of $6.84 for the subscription). Available with the subscription is a free "Interactive Guide to *Newsweek*"—a workbook for students are using the text. In addition, *Newsweek* provides a wide variety of instructor supplements free to teachers, including maps, Skills Builders, and weekly quizzes. For more information on the *Newsweek* program, please contact your Longman sales representative.

Electronic and Online Offerings

Longman Reading Road Trip Multimedia Software, CD Version and Web Version. This innovative and exciting multimedia reading software is available either on CD-ROM format or on the Web. The package takes students on a tour of 15 cities and landmarks throughout the United States. Each of the 15 modules corresponds to a reading or study skill (for example, finding the main idea, understanding patterns of organization, and thinking critically). All modules contain a tour of the location, instruction and tutorial, exercises, interactive feedback, and mastery tests. To shrink-wrap the CD or the access code to the Web site with this textbook, please consult your Longman sales representative.

Longman Study Skills Web Site. For additional study skills-related resources, visit Longman's free Study Skills Web site at **http://www.ablongman.com/StudySkills.**

The Longman Electronic Newsletter. Twice a month during the spring and fall, instructors who have subscribed receive a free copy of the Longman Developmental English Newsletter in the e-mailbox. Written by experienced classroom instructors, the newsletter offers teaching tips, classroom activities, book reviews, and more. To subscribe, visit the Longman Basic Skills Web site at **http://www.ablongman.com/ BasicSkills,** or send an e-mail to **BasicSkills@ablongman.com.**

For Instructors

Teaching Online: Internet Research, Conversation, and Composition, Second Edition. Ideal for instructors who have never surfed the Net, this easy-to-follow guide offers basic definitions, numerous examples, and step-by-step information about finding and using Internet sources. Free to adopters. 0-321-01957-1

[NEW] The Longman Instructor's Planner.   This all-in-one resource for instructors includes monthly and weekly planning sheets, to-do lists, student contact forms, attendance rosters, a gradebook, an address/phone book, and a mini almanac. Ask your Longman sales representative for a free copy. 0-321-09247-3

[NEW] The Longman Guide to Classroom Management.   Written by Joannis Flatley of St. Philip's College, the first in Longman's new series of monographs for developmental English instructors focuses on issues of classroom etiquette, providing guidance on dealing with unruly, unengaged, disruptive, or uncooperative students. Ask your Longman sales representative for a free copy. 0-321-09246-5

For Students

Research Online, Sixth Edition.   A perfect companion for a new age, this indispensable new supplement helps students navigate the Internet. Adapted from *Teaching Online,* the instructor's Internet guide, *Researching Online* speaks directly to students, giving them detailed, step-by-step instructions for performing electronic searches. Available free when shrink-wrapped with text. 0-321-11733-6

Learning Together: An Introduction to Collaborative Theory.   This brief guide to the fundamentals of collaborative learning teaches students how to work effectively in groups, how to revise with peer response, and how to coauthor a paper or report. Shrink-wrapped free with any Longman Basic Skills text. 0-673-46848-8

Ten Practices of Highly Successful Students.   This popular supplement helps students learn crucial study skills, offering concise tips for a successful career in college. Topics include time management, test taking, reading critically, stress, and motivation. 0-205-30769-8

The Longman Reader's Journal, by Kathleen T. McWhorter. This reader's journal, free with any textbook by Kathleen McWhorter, offers students a space to record their questions about, reactions to, and summaries of materials they've read. Also included is a personal vocabulary log, as well as ample space for freewriting. For an examination copy, contact your Longman sales consultant. 0-321-08639-2

The Longman Writer's Journal.   This journal for writers, free with any Longman English text, offers students a place to think, write, and react. For an examination copy, contact your Longman sales consultant. 0-321-08639-2

The Longman Researcher's Journal.   This journal for writers and researchers, free with this text, helps students plan, schedule, write, and revise their research project. An all-in-one resource for first-time researchers, the journal guides students gently through the research process. 0-321-09530-8

The Longman Planner.   This daily planner for students includes daily, weekly, and monthly calendars, as well as class schedules and a mini-almanac of useful information. It is the perfect accompaniment to a Longman reading or study skills textbook, and is available free to students when shrinkwrapped with this text. 0-321-04573-4

Acknowledgments

I wish to acknowledge the contributions of my colleagues and reviewers, who have provided valuable advice and suggestions over the course of many editions:

Sue Burdette, Wichita State University

Doris Burgert, Wichita State University

Chris Butterill, University of Manitoba

Nancy Cannon, Cecil Community College

Deborah Ceppaglia, Medaille College

Julie Colish, University of Michigan, Flint

Ray DeLeon, California State University–Long Beach

Barbara Doyle, Arkansas State University

Peter Geller, Inter-Universities North

Janet Griffin, Howard University

Orlando E. Katter, Jr., Winthrop University

Trish LaFlamme, Community College of Southern Nevada

Seana Logsdon, Medaille College

Rose Manzer, Sir Sanford Fleming College

Cheryl McLean, Edmonds Community College

Patricia I. Mochnacz, University of Manitoba

Jayne Nightengale, Rhode Island College

Mary Parish, Minneapolis Community and Technical College

Jim Roth, Spokane Community College

Cecilia Russo, St. John's University

Gladys Shaw, University of Texas–El Paso

Barbara Smuckler, College of Mount St. Vernon

Helene Stapleton, Cayuga Community College

Sharon Stevens, Oklahoma City Community College

Gail Watson, County College of Morris

Carolyn J. Wilkie, Indiana University of Pennsylvania

Donna Wood, Southwest Tennessee Community College, Macon

I am particularly indebted to Leslie Taggart, my developmental editor, for her creative talent, sound advice, and expert guidance and to Steven Rigolosi, Senior Editor, for his careful attention, enthusiasm, and strong support of this project.

Kathleen T. McWhorter

Quick Guide to the Book

Study and Critical Thinking Skills in College teaches students a full range of cognitive and affective strategies for succeeding in their college studies and participating in campus life. The text provides step-by-step directions for mastering specific study skills such as time management, lecture note taking, class participation, and exam preparation. At the same time, it integrates comprehensive and careful development of critical thinking skills in multiple contexts: in solving study problems, responding to images, evaluating learning, and thinking ahead to the world of work. In addition to skill-based exercises within chapters, each chapter of *Study and Critical Thinking Skills in College* ends with a full range of interactive applications for students.

Study Skills

Critical Thinking Development

Attitudes and Behaviors for Success in College

Discipline-Specific Strategies

Learning Styles

Electronic Media and Online Resources

Interactive Applications

Thinking Critically . . . About Feature Boxes: for example, page 92, 103–104
How Do You See It? for example, page 185, 318, 361
Interactive Chapter Review: for example, page 95, 187, 339
Working Together: for example, page 107, 320, 362
Further Analysis: for example, page 109, 188, 220
Discussion: for example, page 95, 109, 294
The Work Connection: for example page 96, 321, 402
The Web Connection: for example, page 82–93, 189, 364

Chapter 1

The College System: An Orientation

DO YOU KNOW?

How can you find the information you need about college?
What college services are available on your campus?
How can you learn from the people you will meet in college?
How are different courses organized?
How does the grading system work?
How can you succeed in the classroom?

College is very different from any other place you have studied or worked. It has its own way of operating, its own set of rules and regulations, and its own procedures. To function effectively within any new environment, you have to learn how it works and how to make it work to your advantage. For example, when you started a new part-time job, it may have felt strange at first; you weren't sure who was in charge, what was expected of you, and how best to get tasks accomplished. Then, once you learned how the business operated, who was who, and what was expected of you, the job became routine and comfortable. College, too, may seem strange and uncomfortable until you learn how it works and how to function within it.

Most colleges invite new students to attend college orientation sessions in which campus services, academic policies, financial aid, and campus life are discussed. Some students mistakenly choose not to attend; some attend but do not realize the importance of such sessions until it is too late. Others feel overwhelmed and confused by the barrage of information. The purpose of this chapter is to provide a general orientation to college—one you can refer to as needed and reread whenever you like. This chapter cannot, however, provide detailed information about your particular college. Sources of detailed information about your college are suggested below.

Before continuing with the chapter, assess your knowledge of your college by completing the questionnaire shown in Figure 1.1, p. 2.

Figure 1.1

Rate Your Knowledge of Your College

Answer each of the following questions about your college.

1. What are the hours of the college library?
2. What is the last date by which you can withdraw from class without a penalty?
3. Where do you go or whom do you see to change from one major (or curriculum) to another?
4. How is your grade point average (GPA) computed?
5. Where is the student health office located?
6. Who is your advisor and where is he or she located on campus?
7. Does your college use pluses and/or minuses as part of the letter grading system?
8. Where are computer labs located on campus?
9. How would you contact each of your instructors if it should be necessary?
10. What assistance is available in locating part-time jobs on campus?

Information Sources

Important official sources of information include the college catalog, the college's Web site, one's academic advisor, and the student newspaper. An important part of learning the college system is knowing where to find needed information, as you can see from the following situation.

A student is considering dropping his psychology class because he realizes he was overly ambitious in registering for 18 credit hours for his first college semester. Unsure of how and when to drop a course, the student consults a friend in his math class who tells him not to worry about it until after midterm week. Later, this student learns that the deadline was the fifth week of classes. This student, mistakenly, relied solely on a friend for information and failed to check official or authoritative sources.

Using the College Catalog

The college catalog is your primary source of information for staying in and graduating from college. Be sure to obtain a current edition. It is your responsibility to know and work within the college's regulations, policies, and requirements to obtain a degree. Although faculty advisors are available to provide guidance, you must be certain that you are registering for the right courses in the right sequence to fulfill requirements to obtain your degree. Furthermore, be sure to obtain a complete catalog, not a preadmissions publicity brochure. Keep the catalog that is in effect during your freshman year. It is considered the catalog of record and will be used to audit your graduation requirements. A complete catalog usually provides several types of information:

Academic rules and regulations	Course registration policies, grading system, class attendance policies, academic dismissal policies
Degree programs and requirements	Degrees offered and outlines of degree requirements for each major
Course descriptions	A brief description of each course, the number of credits, and course prerequisites (Note: Not all courses listed are offered each semester.)
Student activities and special services	Student organizations, clubs and sports, student governance system, and special services

Your College's Web Site

Many colleges have a Web site on the Internet that contains useful general information about the college, as well as information about degrees, programs, and services. Figure 1.2 on p. 4 shows an excerpt from Spokane Community College's home page (a directory of information contained on the Web site). Notice that it contains such valuable information as campus maps, an academic calendar, course and program information, and employment opportunities.

You can locate your college's Web site by using a search engine or by calling the college's admissions office and asking for the Web site address.

Many Web sites have links (references to other Web sites) to sites that offer grammar hot lines, study skills workshops, library research assistance, term paper writing tips, and so forth.

Exercise 1.1

Use your college catalog or Web site to answer the following questions.

1. Does the college allow you to take courses on a Pass/Fail or Satisfactory/Unsatisfactory basis? If so, what restrictions or limitations apply?

2. What is the last date on which you can withdraw from a course without academic penalty?

3. On what basis are students academically dismissed from the college? What criteria apply to readmission?

4. What is the institution's policy on transfer credit?

5. What rules and regulations apply to motor vehicles on campus?

6. List five extracurricular programs or activities the college sponsors.

7. Describe the health services the college provides.

8. What foreign languages are offered?

9. Is a course in computer literacy offered?

10. What courses are required in your major or curriculum? Are any general education courses required?

Figure 1.2

A Sample College Web Site

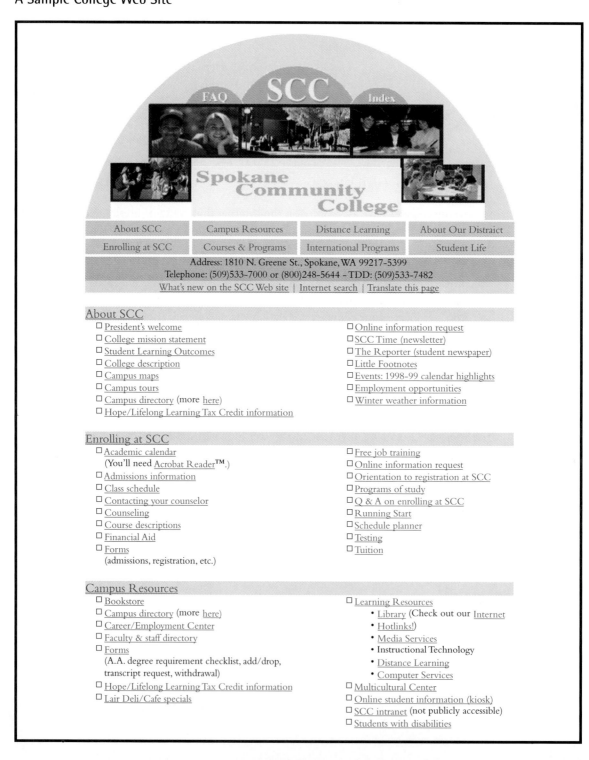

Your Academic Advisor

In most colleges, each student is assigned an academic advisor. Your advisor's primary function is to help you select appropriate courses and make certain that you meet all requirements for your degree. Meet with your advisor early in the semester and get to know him or her. Many advisors on campus have e-mail addresses. Often you can use e-mail to schedule an appointment with him or her or to ask a quick question. Your advisor's primary function is to help you select appropriate courses and make certain that you meet all requirements for your degree. Be sure to consult with your advisor before adding or dropping courses or making other important academic decisions. Your advisor can also give valuable advice, put you in touch with sources of assistance, and help you learn the college system. Sometimes he or she can help you resolve a problem by "cutting through the red tape" or knowing whom to call. Your advisor is an important source for a letter of recommendation, which you may need for college transfer, graduate school, or job applications, so it is important to develop and maintain a positive relationship with him or her.

Student Newspaper

The student newspaper is another useful source of information. It provides a student perspective on issues, problems, and concerns on campus. It may also contain important announcements and list upcoming events. The paper's advertising will help you learn what is available in the surrounding community.

College Services

A large portion of your tuition is spent to provide a wide range of academic, social, recreational, and health services. Since you are paying for these services, you should take advantage of them. Table 1.1 on p. 6 lists the most common services offered on college campuses. Check to see exactly what services are offered on your campus.

Exercise 1.2	Answer the following questions about college services on your campus.

1. What services does the student health office offer?
2. List five student organizations sponsored by the college.
3. Where would you go to find out if tutoring is available for mathematics courses?
4. In what intercollegiate sports does the college participate?
5. Where is (are) the computer lab(s) located?

Table 1.1

College Services

Office	Services offered
Student Health Office	Handles illnesses and injuries; may dispense over-the-counter drugs
Student Activities Office or Student Center	Offers a range of recreational activities; sponsors social events; houses offices for student organizations
Counseling and Test Center	Provides personal and career counseling and testing
Financial Aid Office	Offers assistance with loans, grants, and scholarships
Placement Office	Lists job openings (full time and part time); establishes a placement file that records student references and transcripts
Library	Lends books, records, and films; provides listening, typing, and study rooms; has photocopy machines; offers assistance in locating reference material; obtains books and research materials from other libraries through interlibrary loans
Learning Lab/Academic Skills Center	Offers brush-up courses; individualized instruction or tutoring in study skills; reading, writing, math, and/or common freshman courses

Campus Diversity

For many students, college is an opportunity to meet people unlike themselves: students and instructors from different social, cultural, and national backgrounds. This means you are likely to encounter people whose beliefs, values, and experiences differ significantly from your own. If you consider this diversity as an opportunity to broaden your horizons and think from different points of view, you will benefit more than if you socialize only with other students who come from backgrounds similar to your own.

Look for opportunities to meet students from diverse backgrounds who share your interests. Get involved with sports activities and clubs, for example. Most colleges present many opportunities for students with common interests to meet and think about matters of concern at the local, national, and even international levels. Don't restrict your activities to those that include only others of your own background.

Share your experiences and background when relevant in class discussions. Most students are interested in the customs, traditions, and viewpoints of others. You possess a unique body of information based on your life experiences. Sharing it adds depth and texture to relevant class discussions.

Consider study and research projects that will give you a chance to learn about unfamiliar cultures. Take advantage of any course-related opportunities to study unfamiliar cultures, whether in the library, on the Internet, or by conducting person-to-person research on campus. Use academic assignments as a way to move beyond familiar territory and into contact with new people and new ideas.

Twenty years ago, first-year college students typically were 18-year-olds who lived on campus in dorm rooms. Today, the average age of college students is 24, and well over 50 percent are commuters who travel to and from campus daily. As a result of these and other changes in the college population, many colleges and universities now offer services for students with different needs. Be sure to check what services are available on your campus, as well as using the following suggestions.

Commuter Students

Check to see if your campus offers special services for commuter students. Your college may coordinate "ride boards" for sharing rides; it may offer commuter lounges; it may loan laptops to commuters who do not have ready access to the college's computer labs. Table 1.2 identifies common problems commuting students experience and offers suggestions for coping with each.

Table 1.2

Tips for Commuting Students

Problem	Suggestions
1. You are trying to balance responsibilities of family, job, and college.	• Time management skills are essential. Pay particular attention to Chapter 3. • Establish your priorities. Once you list what is most and least important to you, you won't feel guilty about choices you must make.
2. Family and friends don't understand your new commitment to college.	• Explain the new demands college has placed on you. • Make clear when you have reserved times for study. • Learn to say "no" to friends and family who expect you to be able to live as you did before you began college.
3. Commuting takes time.	• Use your commute time for learning. • If driving, play tapes of lectures. • If riding, work on assignments.
4. It's difficult to meet other students; you don't feel as if you belong.	• Talk to others; don't wait for them to talk to you. • Get to know one person in each of your classes. Exchange phone numbers. • Join clubs and attend student activities on campus. • Spend extra time on campus; don't leave immediately after your last class.

Adults Returning to College

The many adults returning to education have boosted the average age of college freshmen to 24. This means that if you are an adult beginning or returning to college, you are not alone. Many other students on your campus face the same concerns and problems as you do. Get in touch with these students; they can offer moral support, serve as sounding boards, and provide valuable advice for succeeding in college. Your college's activities office may sponsor a club or offer workshops. At Niagara County Community College, for example, the student organization is called the Comeback Club. It has regular weekly meetings, but students soon find themselves meeting other members almost daily for coffee or for lunch.

Use the following suggestions to make your transition back to education a smooth one.

1. **Make sure your family understands and supports your decision.** You may need to ask them to pick up part of the household workload that you had previously carried.

2. **Do not study all the time.** Many adults feel they are behind or out of touch and, consequently, study nonstop. Instead, develop a realistic study plan and stick with it. (See Chapter 3 for specific suggestions.)

3. **Start slowly.** Do not take four or five different courses your first semester. Instead, ease yourself into college. Take courses that will strengthen your self-confidence and at the same time build your skills.

4. **Recognize that your first semester will be the hardest.** During your first semester you are not only working on each of your courses, you are also working on developing a new lifestyle.

5. **Contact your faculty advisor.** Your advisor can be very helpful in suggesting how and where to solve academic problems.

Cultural Diversity

College offers you an incredible opportunity to meet students from many different cultural, ethnic, and religious backgrounds. If you actively seek them out, you'll learn as much about different ways of seeing and being in the world from other students as you will in your college classes. The rich variety of cultural and spiritual practices represented by diverse students and instructors can help you see your own culture from a very different point of view.

Many colleges organize student groups that enable students of color to get in touch with one another and discuss problems, and sponsor activities that encourage students to share their cultural and ethnic heritage with others. At Niagara County Community College, for instance, the African-American Student Group is active in recruiting students from the local community and in fund-raising for scholarships for other African-American students. At Worcester Polytechnic Institute, Asian students formed the Asian Club, whose two main goals are to increase knowledge and awareness of Asian culture and to help Asian students adjust to college life. Among the 23 cultural organizations for students at the University of California, Los Angeles, are Mujeres Unidas, with a focus on women's issues, and Club Italiano, one of whose main goals is to encourage people of all races and ethnicities to celebrate the Italian culture. If your college does not sponsor such student clubs or activities, consider starting your own group or club or see what is available in the larger community. Also, check for Web sites sponsored by cultural organizations in order to find out about services and resources and activities at the national level. For example, Movimiento Estudiantil Chicano de Aztlan has Web sites at 41 college campuses around the country, and Hillel is a national Jewish student organization that promotes unity among the members of the Jewish community.

No matter what your background, the following tips can help you get off to a successful start in college.

1. **Consult with a campus mentor frequently.** Try to find a person—either a student or a faculty, or staff member—who is familiar with the college and who is willing to guide you through your first semester and offer advice.
2. **Find a role model from your community.** Talk to a relative, friend, or acquaintance who has attended college to find out what strategies helped them succeed. Use their experiences and expertise as a guide to develop your own.
3. **Once you become familiar with college expectations, become a mentor to a younger person from your community.** Define your academic and personal goals (see Chapter 3) and then share them with a junior-high or high-school student who wants to attend college. Share both the problems you encounter and the successes you experience. Doing so will help reinforce a continuing tradition of success in your community.

Students with Disabilities

College is becoming increasingly accessible to students with physical or learning disabilities. Federal laws mandate that colleges provide specific services to disabled students. Most colleges have an office or counselor designated to assist students with disabilities, as well as a full range of services and equipment, including interpreters for hearing-impaired students, writers, note takers, books on audiotape, and so forth. Student organizations for disabled students may provide social networks or peer counseling, for example. If you are a student with a disability, here are a few suggestions to help you succeed.

1. **Communicate with your instructors.** Meet with each of your instructors. Explain any kind of assistance or special accommodation you may require or certain preferential treatment you want them to avoid. Most instructors are anxious to assist; it is your job to let them know *how* to help.

2. **Take advantage of available facilities and accommodations.** Some students who have special needs try not to use the services available to them unless absolutely necessary. They do not want to be given an unfair advantage or seem privileged to other students. Your goal is to succeed in college; take advantage of whatever services are available.

3. **Get to know other students in each of your classes.** Many students are genuinely interested in you, but they are unsure of how to initiate a conversation. Help them along; introduce yourself to them.

Multilingual Students and ESL (English as a Second Language) Students

If you are an international student or from a family or community in which English is usually not spoken, you face the challenge of reading, listening to lectures, writing papers, and participating in class discussions in a language that is not your first, native language. Here are a few suggestions.

1. **Take ESL courses, even if they are not required.** These are taught by specialists in second-language learning; you will learn more quickly and easily than if you try to teach yourself.

2. **Use a good dictionary.** Acquire a comprehensive two-language dictionary (English-Spanish, English-Japanese, etc.) and use it regularly. Carry it with you to classes; refer to it as needed during lectures.

3. **Consider tape-recording lectures.** You can play back the lectures and catch ideas you missed during the lecture.

4. **Discuss problems or limitations with your professors.** Once they are aware of your special needs, most will be eager to assist.

Exercise 1.3	Working with a classmate, brainstorm a list of potential problems—academic, social, or personal—that a student may encounter while attending college. For each problem, identify a source of help.

Course Organization

No two college courses are conducted in exactly the same manner. Each course is tailored by the instructor to best express his or her approach to the subject matter, teaching style, and educational objectives. Two sections of the same course offered the same semester may be structured entirely differently from one another. One instructor may require a text; the other may assign readings. One instructor may lecture; the other may conduct class discussions. One instructor may give exams; the other may assign papers. The key to success in college courses, then, is to understand and work within the instructor's course organization. On the first day of class many instructors distribute a *syllabus* that explains their organization and approach. These, too, vary according to instructor, but they usually list the following:

- ◆ the required text
- ◆ the attendance policy
- ◆ the grading system
- ◆ the course objectives
- ◆ weekly assignments or readings
- ◆ dates of exams or due dates for papers

An excerpt from a syllabus for a human anatomy and physiology course is shown in Figure 1.3. One of the most important parts of the syllabus is the course objectives. Objectives state, in general terms, what the instructors intend to accomplish and what they expect you to learn through the course. Objectives can provide valuable clues about what the instructor feels is important and how he or she views the subject matter. Objectives state what you are to learn; exams, then, are built to measure how well you have learned it. For example, in the sample syllabus shown in Figure 1.3, objective 2 states "demonstrate familiarity with the terminology." Consequently, you can anticipate exams that contain questions measuring your mastery of definitions and terminology.

Figure 1.3
A Sample Course Syllabus Excerpt

DEPARTMENT OF LIFE SCIENCES
BIO 131: HUMAN ANATOMY & PHYSIOLOGY 1
INSTRUCTOR: Dr. Paul Eberhardt

Course Description
This course is the first semester of a two-semester study of the topics involved in Human Anatomy and Physiology. The major emphasis in the course is bodily structure and function. A molecular-cellular approach will be used in the course.

Course Objectives
Upon completion of this course, students will

1. demonstrate an understanding of bodily structure and function.
2. demonstrate familiarity with the terminology used to describe bodily structure and function.
3. perform laboratory activities for collection analysis of experimental data.

Exercise 1.4	Study the syllabus for one of your courses and answer as many of the following questions as possible.

1. What types of thinking are emphasized? (Refer to Chapter 2, p. 34.)
2. How is the subject matter of the course divided?
3. Summarize the grading system.
4. Predict three topics that might be asked in a final exam consisting entirely of essay questions.

HOW DO YOU SEE IT?

*"Now you're probably all asking yourselves,
'Why must I learn to read and write?'"*

Telling people what they "must" do often triggers anger or anxiety. Think of something that would be difficult for you to learn (X) and say to yourself, "I *must* learn to X." Then, say to yourself, "I *want to* learn to X." Last, say to yourself, "I *can* learn to X." Write a paragraph identifying which of these three statements would best encourage you to learn to X, and why.

Grades and the Grading System

Most colleges use a letter grade system in awarding final grades. Each college has its own variations, special policies, and unique designations, so be sure to read the section in your college catalog on grading policies. Specifically, find out about the following:

Pass/Fail Options

Some colleges allow you to take certain courses on a Pass/Fail basis. You earn the credit but receive only a Pass or Fail grade on your record. The Pass/Fail option, if available, allows you to take courses without competing for a letter grade. You might consider electing a Pass/Fail option for a difficult course. If, for example, you are required to take one math course and math has always been difficult for you, then consider taking that course on a Pass/Fail basis. Be sure to check your college catalog and with your advisor to be certain that required courses can be taken on a Pass/Fail basis and how to initiate the process. The instructor's permission may be required. Also, there may be a restriction on the number or types of courses that may be elected using this option.

The Pass/Fail option also provides an opportunity to take interesting elective courses without worrying about grades. Suppose you are interested in taking a history of modern music course but know that it is a difficult course taken mostly by students majoring in the arts. A Pass/Fail option would allow you to enjoy the course without competing for a letter grade.

Course Withdrawal

Most colleges have a provision by which you can withdraw from a course up to a given deadline in the semester without academic penalty. Be sure to check the college catalog for the deadline for course withdrawal. If you withdraw, you receive neither credit nor a grade. A letter code such as W may appear on your transcript following the course number. If you know you are doing poorly in a course, discuss the possibility of course withdrawal with your instructor. Some students who think they are in danger of failing learn otherwise by speaking with their instructor. Also, consult your advisor and the financial aid office to learn what impact, if any, course withdrawal will have on your academic and financial aid status.

Incomplete Grades

Many grading systems have a provision for students who are unable to complete a course for which they are registered. This grade, often called an Incomplete, is awarded at the discretion of the instructor when he or she feels the student has a legitimate reason for being unable to complete the course. Instructors may award an Incomplete if you are injured during the last week of classes or if a death of a close relative prevents you from taking the final, for example. Be sure to contact your instructor as soon as possible; offer to provide the instructor with verification of your reason. Many colleges have a deadline by which an Incomplete must be converted to a grade. This means you must arrange with your instructor to complete whatever course requirements he or she specifies by a given date. Be sure it is clear what assignments must be done, how to do them, and when they must be completed.

Grade Point Average (GPA)

Each semester an average is computed using the individual grades you received that semester. This average is computed by assigning numerical values to letter grades. An A may be assigned four points, a B three points, a C two points, a D one point, and an F zero points, for example. Consult your college catalog to discover what numerical values are used at your school and specifically how they are calculated. Find out if pluses and minuses are considered.

A cumulative GPA is computed over successive semesters by averaging all the grades you have received since you began attending college. Many colleges require a specific cumulative GPA for admission to an academic department and for graduation. Grade point average may also influence financial aid eligibility and your academic status. You may be required to maintain a minimum GPA to receive financial aid or to remain in good academic standing. Check your college catalog to learn about these policies.

Exercise 1.5   Answer each of the following questions about the grading system at your college.

1. What is the deadline for course withdrawal?
2. Is the Pass/Fail grading option available? If so, is there a limit to the number of courses you may elect using this option?
3. Is there a time limit by which the work for Incomplete grades must be completed?
4. Are pluses and minuses considered part of your grading system?
5. What is the point value of D grades in your college's grading system?

Thinking Critically
... About Grades

Grading is an important part of most college courses. Successful students learn to use the grading system to their advantage. Here are a few questions to consider:

1. **How can you use the grading system to help you organize your study?** Suppose, for example, biweekly quizzes on textbook chapters in your business marketing class constitute 50 percent of your grade. How should you schedule your study?

2. **How can the grading system help you decide what is important to learn?** Suppose that 40 percent of your grade in sociology is based on weekly summaries and critiques of films shown in class. What can you do while watching the film and immediately after each film to improve this portion of your grade?

3. **How can the grading system help you make choices?** Suppose, for example, you have the choice of taking a final exam or writing a paper for your history class. What factors would you consider in making your decision?

Classroom Success Tips

The following suggestions will help you be successful in each of your courses.

Attend All Classes

Even if class attendance is optional or not strictly monitored by your instructor, make it a rule to attend *all* classes. For most students, class time totals 12 to 15 hours per week, except for laboratory and studio courses. This amounts to less than 10 percent of your time each week! If you say you don't have enough time to attend all classes, you are not being honest with yourself. Remember, class instruction is a major part of what your tuition is paying for. You are cheating yourself if you don't take advantage of it. Seldom is a class taught in which you do not learn something new or gain a new perspective on already familiar ideas.

Get Acquainted with Faculty

Get to know your professors; you will find your classes more meaningful and interesting, and you will learn more. Challenging and stimulating conversations often result, and you can gain new insights into the subject matter that you might never obtain by merely attending class. Don't hesitate to talk with your professor or ask questions. Talking with your instructors is an opportunity to apply and connect the course with your academic interests and goals. Getting to know your instructor will also help you establish yourself as a conscientious and interested student.

Keep Up with Assignments

It is tempting to delay work on projects and assignments until you feel like doing them or until you have an exam or quiz on them. This approach is a mistake and can lead to a failing semester. Students who procrastinate end up with an impossible amount of reading to do within a short time. As a result, they don't do the reading at all or read the assignments hurriedly and without careful thought.

Form a Study Group

Choose several classmates and form a study group. Schedule a regular meeting time and place. Use the sessions to review, quiz each other, and study for exams.

Project a Positive Image

Be sure to approach each class positively and demonstrate that you are a serious student. Unfortunately, some students do act thoughtlessly or rudely in class. The unspoken message they send is that the class is unimportant and uninteresting, and instructors are quick to perceive this. Work on establishing a positive image by

◆ arriving at class promptly
◆ participating in class discussions
◆ asking or answering questions
◆ sitting in the front of the room
◆ making eye contact with the instructor
◆ completing assignments on time
◆ reading assigned material before class
◆ saying "hello" when you meet your instructor on campus

Take Action If You Are in the Wrong Class

You may find yourself in a course that is either too easy or too difficult. Courses in which this most often occurs are mathematics, foreign languages, the sciences, and skills courses such as typing or athletics. If you suspect you are in the wrong course, talk with your instructor immediately. If he or she confirms that you are misplaced, ask for advice. Also consult with your advisor. Generally, it is inadvisable to continue in a course that is too difficult; dropping the course, if possible, is a reasonable alternative. Be certain, however, that dropping the course does not reduce your course load to below the minimum if you are a full-time student. If you make your decision to drop a course early enough in the semester, you may be able to add another course in its place.

Purchase Recommended Materials

While most instructors require a textbook, some make the purchase of other materials optional. These materials include review books, workbooks, dictionaries, or other reference books, manuals, or style sheets. Your instructor would not recommend the materials unless he or she feels they would be helpful. Therefore, make sure you purchase these optional materials. Often you will find that these materials make review easier and/or are helpful in completing required assignments or papers.

Take Action When You Miss an Important Exam or Deadline

Hopefully you will never have to miss an important exam or deadline for a paper. However, if you should wake up with the flu on the morning of a midterm exam, for example, you may have to miss the exam. Be sure to contact your instructor *before* the exam. Leave a phone message in the department office if you are unable to contact him or her directly. Explaining the situation ahead of time is preferable to making excuses later. If a paper is due and you are ill, ask a friend or fellow student to deliver it for you.

Get Involved with College Life

Academic course work is, of course, the primary reason for attending college. However, if all you are doing on campus is taking courses and studying, you are missing an important part of college life. College is more than textbooks, exams, and lectures. The academic environment is a world of ideas, a place where thought, concepts, and values are of primary importance. It is a place where you can discuss and exchange ideas, explore new approaches to life, and reevaluate old ones. College also provides an opportunity for you to decide who you are (or who you want to be) and how you would like to spend the rest of your life.

Considerable research indicates that students who become involved with college activities tend to be more successful in college than those who do not. Activities provide an opportunity for you to get involved and to feel part of a group with similar interests. On large campuses, where it is easy to feel lost, involvement is especially important. If you are preparing for a career, getting involved with college life is important. Most employers are interested in hiring well-spoken, interesting people who are aware of the world around them and can interact with others effectively. College can help you become well rounded, if you take advantage of it.

To get involved with college life, find out about activities and issues on campus. Many interesting lectures, debates, films, and concerts are sponsored weekly. Make it a point to meet someone in each of your classes; you will feel better about going to class, and a worthwhile friendship may develop. Find out if there is a student group that shares your interests, and join it. You may meet interesting people in the ski club, chorus, nursing students' association, or black students' union, for example.

If You Plan to Transfer

If you are attending a two-year college and plan to transfer to a four-year school after completing your associate's degree, plan accordingly. Do not assume that any course you take at one institution will be accepted for a degree at another. Each college and each academic department has its own policies and guidelines for the acceptance of transfer credit.

To ensure that most or all your credits will transfer, be sure to do the following:

- ◆ Obtain the college catalog of the institution to which you intend to transfer and read about degree requirements and transfer credit policies and procedures.
- ◆ Contact an admissions counselor to answer any questions.
- ◆ Make your current academic advisor aware of your plans. He or she can assist you in determining and selecting appropriate courses for transfer.

Working Together

Form groups of two or three students and compile a list of success tips not included in this chapter that could be included in a tip sheet to be distributed to first-year students. Also include pitfalls to avoid. Include advice on things you've learned so far this semester (hints: registration, parking, dorms, food service, bookstore, add-drop procedures).

Interactive Chapter Review

Throughout this book, the Interactive Chapter Reviews will ask you questions designed to increase your ability to think critically about study skills topics. (You will read about the levels of critical thinking in Chapter 2.)

Knowledge	Name three sources of information about courses and degree requirements that are available on your campus.
Comprehension	What does an academic advisor do? When should you seek out your academic advisor, and why?
Application	Introduce yourself to another student who seems to come from a background different from your own.
Analysis	Compare the syllabi from two different courses. How are they different? How are they the same?
Synthesis	Based on the information in this chapter and your own experience in college so far, what have you learned?
Evaluation	Reread the list of Classroom Success Tips on pp. 15–17. Which tip do you think will be most difficult for you to apply? Why? What can you do to be sure you will successfully address this issue?

Further Analysis

Analyze the following situation and answer the questions below.

A private four-year college does not award grades to first-semester first-year students. Instead, all grades are given on a Pass/Fail basis. The college implemented this policy to reduce stress on beginning students. It was intended to de-emphasize competition and to place greater emphasis on learning.

1. Discuss the advantages and disadvantages of this grading policy.

2. Do you feel the policy encourages students to learn? If so, how?

3. Although your college probably does award grades, what can you do to lessen the pressure they impose?

Discussion

1. What should a student do if he or she finds the academic advisor frequently unavailable or not helpful?

2. What additional college services do you feel should be offered on your campus?

3. Should the student newspaper be able to print articles critical of the college, of its faculty, or of its administration?

The Work Connection

The workplace of the 21st century, researchers agree, will be quite different from the workplace of the past. Corporate mergers, acquisitions, downsizing, new technologies, and global competition are only a few of the factors that are causing a shift in the qualities, skills, and capabilities that employers will expect of successful employees. Research also suggests that the average person will make three to five major career changes in the course of his or her work life. Now is the time to start considering how the decisions you make in college are likely to affect your future employment. Begin by thinking about the following questions:

1. What are three careers that you might enjoy pursuing during your lifetime?

2. What skills will you learn in this course that relate to your career and life goals? List four or five skills.

3. What college courses might you consider taking that will make you versatile and employable in a variety of career settings?

The Web Connection

Each chapter ends with a list of Web sites that include information helpful to college students. Visit them when you need more assistance with particular topics, strategies, or skills.

1. How to Flunk Out with Style and Grace

   http://www.iue.indiana.edu/Departments/aca_advis/flunkwithstyle.htm

   This site from Holyoke Community College uses humor and irony to tell students how to succeed by telling them how not to succeed.

2. Three Credits and a Baby

   http://www.rwuniversity.com/articles.cfm?id=44&action=show

   From the Real World University site, this brief article describes one young woman's struggle as a single mother going to college.

3. How to Avoid the Freshman 15

   http://exercise.about.com/c/ht/01/09/How_Avoid_Freshman_150999710278.htm?terms=Freshman+15

   Many students find themselves gaining weight during their first year of college. This piece from About.com offers tips for keeping off unwanted pounds.

4. Commuters and College Life

   http://www.wealtheffect.com/icampusa/ic-commuters.htm

   Some tips for commuters are presented here as part of a larger guide to starting college.

Go Electronic!
For additional readings, exercises, and Internet activities, visit the Longman Study Skills Web site at:
http://www.ablongman.com/StudySkills
If you need a user name and password, please see your instructor.

Chapter 2

Taking Charge of Your College Career

DO YOU KNOW?

What is expected of you in college?
How can you take charge of your college career?
What are the early warning signs of academic difficulty?
How can you take an active approach to learning?
Why is critical thinking the key to college success?

You are now a college student. Reaching this point may have required years of hard work, preparation, and planning. Now that you are here, you are ready to begin the challenging, exciting tasks that college involves. At this point it is only natural for you to be wondering, "How successful will I be?" or "How well will I be able to meet these new challenges?" The answers to these questions depend on how well you can take charge of your college career. Two major tools you will need throughout college are the ability to study effectively and the ability to think critically. The degree to which you sharpen and polish these skills will largely determine your success. Therefore, developing and refining your study and critical thinking skills are the primary purposes of this book. Before we consider specific techniques, it is helpful to know what college learning involves. This chapter describes the new demands of college, offers numerous success strategies, teaches you *how* to learn, and shows you *how* to become an active, involved learner. It also introduces you to critical thinking skills and shows their importance in college success.

Coping with New Expectations

College is a unique learning experience. Whether you have just completed high school or are returning to college with a variety of work experiences or family responsibilities, you will face new demands and expectations in college. The following section discusses how to cope with these demands.

Set Your Own Operating Rules

College is very different from lower levels of education and from jobs you may have held because it imposes few clear limits, rules, or controls. There are no defined work hours except for classes; your time is your own. Often, you face no threats or penalties for missing classes or failing to complete assignments. You do *what* you want, *when* you want, *if* you want to at all. For many students, the lack of structure requires some adjustment; at first, it is often confusing. Some students feel they should spend all their free time studying; others put off study or never find quite the right time for study.

One of the best ways to handle this flexibility is to establish your own set of operating rules. For example, you might decide to limit yourself to two absences in each course. Here are examples of rules successful students have set for themselves:

◆ Study at least three hours each day or evening.
◆ Start studying for a major examination at least a week ahead.
◆ Complete all homework assignments regardless of whether you get credit for them.
◆ Make review a part of each study session.
◆ Read all assigned chapters *before* the class in which they will be discussed.

You may feel more committed to the rules you set if you write them down and post them above your desk as a constant reminder.

Take Responsibility for Your Own Learning

In college, learning is completely up to you. Professors function only as guides. They define and explain what is to be learned, but *you* do the learning. Class time is far shorter than in high school; there is not enough time to provide numerous drills, practices, and reviews of factual course content. College class time is used primarily to introduce what is to be learned, to provoke thought, and to discuss ideas. Instructors expect you to learn the material and to be prepared to discuss it in class. When, where, and how you learn are your decisions.

The course textbook is your main source for learning in each subject. Instructors expect you to read the text independently. Often, on the first day of class, instructors distribute a course syllabus, outline, or set of requirements that lists the topics to be covered each week and the corresponding textbook chapters to be read.

Develop New Approaches to Learning

College requires new attitudes and approaches toward learning.

Focus on Important Concepts

Each course you take will seem to have endless facts, statistics, dates, definitions, formulas, rules, and principles to learn. It is easy, then, to become a robot learner—absorbing information from texts and lectures, then spewing it out automatically on exams and quizzes. Actually, factual information is only a starting point, a base from which to approach the real content of a course. Most college instructors expect you to go beyond facts to analysis: to consider what the collection of facts and details *means*. Many students "can't see the forest for the trees." They fail to see the larger, overriding concepts of their courses because they get caught up in specifics. Too concerned with memorizing information, they fail to ask, "Why do I need to know this?" "Why is this important?" or "What principle or trend does this illustrate?" Here are a few examples of details from a course in American government and the more important trend, concept, or principle they represent:

Topic	Detail	Importance
Voting Rights Act of 1965	Federal registrars were sent to southern states to protect blacks' right to vote.	This was the beginning of equality in voter registration.
Supreme Court case: Roe v. Wade	Court ruling forbade state control over abortion in first trimester of pregnancy; permitted states to limit abortions to protect the mother's health in the second trimester; permitted states to protect fetus in the third trimester.	Established policy on abortions; opened questions of "right to privacy" and "right to life."

Exercise 2.1	Choose one of your textbooks and turn to a section of a chapter you have already read. List six consecutive headings that appear in that text. After each heading, explain why each topic is important. In other words, indicate its significance and the concept or principle it illustrates.

Focus on Ideas, Not Right Answers

Through previous schooling, many students have come to expect their answers to be either right or wrong. They assume that learning is limited to a collection of facts and that their mastery of the course is measured by the number of right answers they have learned. When faced with an essay question such as the following, they become distraught:

Defend or criticize the arguments that are offered in favor of legalized abortion. Refer to any reading you have done.

You can see that there is not *one* right answer; you can either defend the argument or criticize it. Instead, the instructor who asks this question expects you to think and to provide a reasoned, logical, consistent response using information acquired through readings. Here are a few more examples of questions for which there are no single correct answers:

◆ Do animals think?
◆ Would you be willing to reduce your standard of living by 15 percent if the United States could thereby eliminate poverty? Defend your response.

◆ Imagine a society in which everyone has exactly the same income. You are the manager of an industrial plant. What plans, policies, or programs would you implement that would motivate your employees to work?

◆ Is the primary purpose of an artist to represent his or her own feelings?

Exercise 2.2	Examine two or three newspapers or magazines to identify controversies—issues people disagree about—currently in the news. Based on what you read, compose a list of five questions for which there are no single correct answers—questions for which different viewpoints or opinions exist.

Evaluate New Ideas

Throughout college you will continually encounter new ideas; you will agree with some and disagree with others. Don't make the mistake of accepting or rejecting a new idea, however, until you have really explored it and have considered its assumptions and implications. Ask questions such as these:

◆ What evidence is available in support of this idea?
◆ What opposing evidence is available?
◆ How does my personal experience relate to this idea?
◆ What additional information do I need in order to make a decision?

Considerable research has been conducted on readers' comprehension of ideas. Results of these studies indicate that comprehension is lower for ideas with which the reader disagrees. Readers seem to shut off their attention or subconsciously block out information that conflicts with their beliefs or values. With this evidence in mind, you may need to devote additional effort to material on controversial issues or on values and beliefs about which you have strong negative feelings.

Thinking Critically
. . . About Course Content

To become an active learner, get in the habit of asking critical questions. Critical questions are questions that help you analyze and evaluate what and how you are learning. As you work through this book, you will learn to ask many critical questions. Here are a few to help you get started:

◆ Why was this material assigned?
◆ What am I supposed to learn from this assignment?
◆ How does this assignment relate to today's class lecture?
◆ What is the best way to learn this information?
◆ How will I know I have learned the material?
◆ What levels of thinking does this assignment or exam require?

Working Together

Form small groups (three or four students) and complete the following steps:

1. List the courses taken by each group member. Each group should identify courses that

    a. require new approaches to learning.
    b. focus on ideas and concepts.
    c. focus on logical thinking.
    d. require reaction and discussion.
    e. require evaluation of new ideas.
    f. involve creative thinking.
    g. require problem solving.

2. Each group should present its lists to the class; then the class should compare the lists in each category.

Taking Charge

People who make plans and decisions are more successful than those who do not. People without definite plans and goals drift through life passively, letting things happen and allowing others to control their lives. Active decision makers, on the other hand, know what they want and plan strategies to obtain it. Here's how to take charge.

Accept Responsibility for Grades

Certainly you have heard comments such as, "Dr. Smith only gave me a B on my last paper" or "I got a C on my first lab report." Students often think of grades as rewards that teachers give to students. Thinking this way is avoiding responsibility, blaming the instructor instead of owning up to the fact that a paper or exam failed to meet the standards set by the instructor.

Be honest; you will not always earn the grades you want and you will not always score as well as you expect to on every exam. Try to avoid making excuses and blaming others. If you fail an exam, it is easy to say that the questions were too detailed, that the exam covered material not emphasized in class, or that you did not study for it because you were upset about a recent argument with a friend. The fact is that you did not *earn* a passing grade. Analyze what you could have done to improve that grade, and put this to work in preparing for the next exam.

Don't Make Excuses

Studying is not easy; it requires time and conscious effort. Although the remainder of this book will show you many valuable shortcuts, studying is often a demanding, challenging task. Try not to make it more difficult than it really is by avoiding

HOW DO YOU SEE IT?

"This place reeks of education."

Someone once joked that education is a business where customers are happy when they don't get their money's worth. Write a paragraph from the opposite point of view. How can you secure the most value from your college experience?

it. Some students avoid studying by following a variety of escape routes. Here are a few common ones:

◆ I can't study tonight because I promised to drive my sister to the mall.
◆ I can't study for my physics test because the dorm is too noisy.
◆ I can't finish reading my psychology assignment because the chapter is boring.
◆ I didn't finish writing my computer program because I fell asleep.

Do any of these excuses sound familiar? Each is a means of escaping the task at hand.

If you find yourself making excuses to avoid studying, step back and analyze the problem. Consider possible causes and solutions (see Chapter 7). For example, if the dorm really is too noisy to study, could you study at a different time or find a new place to study? More likely, the problem is that you were just not in the mood to study. Be honest! Before you quit and go on to something else, make a definite commitment to finish the assignment later; be specific about when and where. Postponing study may be better than avoiding it completely, but bear in mind that it probably will not be much easier after it has been postponed.

Exercise 2.3	Analyze your past study performance by answering the following two questions honestly.

1. What excuses have you used to avoid study?
2. Whom have you blamed when you could not study or did not earn the grade you expected?

Develop Essential, Marketable Skills

Many students enter college with a rigid, narrowly defined, and often limiting academic self-image. They make choices and decisions based on an image they express with comments like these:

"I'm not good with math."

"I've never done well in writing."

"If I have to speak in front of a group, forget it."

If you think you are weak in math, then majoring in accounting may not be a good idea. However, avoiding all courses that involve mathematics or calculations is not realistic. In almost any job, you will sooner or later need to work with numbers. Potential employers will look for and expect at least minimum competency.

Work on expanding and modifying your skills by taking courses to strengthen your weaknesses (elect a Pass/Fail grade, if you are worried about grades) and to acquire basic competencies in a variety of areas. Decide to become computer literate, even if it is not required in your curriculum. An elective course in public speaking will boost your confidence in your ability to present yourself effectively. Build a marketable package of skills that will place you in a competitive position to land that all-important job after graduation.

Exercise 2.4	Define your current strengths and weaknesses as a student. If you find that your strengths and weaknesses vary in different courses, make your list specific for each course you are taking. Chart a course of action to address each weakness.

Early Warning Signals of Academic Difficulty

A major part of getting ahead academically and staying there is monitoring your progress in each course and then adjusting your study strategies accordingly. In courses with weekly quizzes or frequent assignments, it is easy to assess how well you are doing. In other courses, knowing how well you are doing is more difficult. Some instructors give only two or three exams per semester; others may require only a term paper and a final exam. Such courses offer no grades during the term for you to determine if you are doing well; instead, you will have to be alert for the early warning signals of academic difficulty.

Questions That Predict Academic Difficulty

Here are some questions that will indicate whether you are on the right track in a course.

Are you falling behind on assignments?   Do you put off studying by saying, "I'll wait until this weekend to work on calculus; then I'll have enough time to really concentrate on straightening this out"? Meanwhile, you fall further behind as the week goes by. It is human nature to do what is pleasant and rewarding and to avoid what is unpleasant and difficult. If you are behind on assignments, you may be avoiding them because they are difficult and unrewarding. This is a signal that something may be going wrong with the course.

Have you missed several classes recently?   Most instructors agree that student attendance is a good predictor of success in a course; students who attend class regularly tend to earn good grades. If you have missed several classes in a course without a legitimate reason for doing so, this may be another form of avoidance. It isn't pleasant to attend a class for which you are not confident and well prepared; cutting class is an avoidance technique.

Do you feel lost or confused in any course?   If you are having trouble making sense of what the instructor is doing day to day or cannot see how various topics and assignments fit together, you may be in academic difficulty. The course may be at the wrong level for your current academic background or you may lack an overview or perspective on the course.

Are you relying heavily on a friend for help in completing assignments?   Depending regularly on a classmate for help suggests that you are not able to handle the course alone. Remember, your friend won't be much help when it comes to the final exam.

Do you feel restless and listless, as if something is wrong but you're not sure what it is?   If you feel anxious and depressed, most likely something is wrong. Look for patterns and discover where and when you feel this way.

Do you feel constantly tired or spend a lot of time sleeping?   Overtiredness may be a reaction to a general feeling of stress. It, too, may be a signal that something is wrong. Find out what it is.

How to Handle Academic Problems

If you are like many college students, discovering and admitting that you are having trouble with a course can be difficult and traumatic. The possibility that you may fail a course is a shock and a threat to your self-image. "Could this really be happening to me?" is a very common feeling. Here is some advice to follow if you should have this feeling.

Maintain your self-confidence.   Don't lose your confidence just because you are having trouble with one course. Remind yourself of the successes you have experienced in other courses. Don't start thinking differently about yourself; realize that you are merely gaining additional experience that will help you learn more.

Remember that you are not alone.   The first semester of college is the most difficult one for most students. A review of students' grade point averages throughout their college experience confirms this. The first semester or quarter grades are the lowest; grades gradually rise as students develop skills and acquire experiences in handling college courses. Keep on striving and you will improve.

Take immediate action.   As soon as you suspect you are having trouble in a course, take immediate action. Things seldom improve on their own. In most cases the longer you wait, the further behind you will fall and the more difficult it will be to catch up.

Talk with your instructor.   Before things get too bad, talk with your instructor. Most instructors have office hours each week, times when they are available to talk with students. They are also available by phone. When you talk with your instructor, try to define topics, areas, or skills that are troublesome. Have specific questions in mind. State the steps you have already taken and ask for advice. Your instructor may recommend additional reading to fill in gaps in your background knowledge or suggest a new approach to follow as you read and study.

Many instructors also have e-mail addresses and encourage you to use e-mail to ask questions about specific assignments or to discuss your progress in the course.

Explore sources of help.   Many colleges and universities have sources of academic assistance. Find out if there is an Academic Development Center or Learning Center on your campus. Such centers offer brush-up courses and sponsor peer tutoring programs for popular freshman courses. Check to see if the library or media center has videotapes, computer programs, or self-instructional workbooks that deal with the subject matter of your course. For a troublesome course, if free tutoring is not available, consider hiring an upperclass student as a tutor. Ask your instructor to recommend someone. Although this may be expensive, consider what you will lose if you fail and have to retake the course.

Consider withdrawing from the course.   If you and your instructor feel you cannot handle the course or if you have fallen so far behind that it is nearly impossible to catch up, consider withdrawing from the course. (Your college catalog explains policies and deadlines for course withdrawal.) While it is painful to admit that you were not able to handle the course, withdrawal will free your mind from anxiety and enable you to concentrate and do well with the remaining courses.

If you decide to withdraw from a required course and you must reregister for the course in a subsequent semester, consider taking the course from another instructor whose approach and teaching style may work better for you. Since course withdrawal is an expensive option, use it only as a last resort.

Active versus Passive Learning

A freshman who had always thought of herself as a good student found herself getting low Cs or Ds on her first quizzes and exams. She was studying harder and spending more time but was not earning the grade she expected. After discussing the problems with her professors, she realized that, although she was studying, she was not studying *in the right way.* She was using the same study methods she had always used: She read and reread her text and notes and conscientiously completed all homework assignments. However, these methods were no longer effective for the kinds of learning expected by her instructors.

Her approach was essentially a passive one. She did what her instructors requested. She read what was assigned, completed assignments as required, and followed instructions carefully. To be more successful, this student needed to develop a more active approach. She should have interacted with the material she read: asked questions, sorted out what was important to learn, and decided how to learn it. Table 2.1 lists characteristics of the two types of learners. As you read through the list, determine which type you are.

Why Become an Active Learner?

Becoming an active learner is the key to getting the most from your college experience as well as the key to advancement in many careers and professions. For responsible positions, employers are interested in someone who can think and act without being told precisely what to do, and they are willing to pay for such self-direction. As preparation for an active career that you control, start now to develop skills that will be an asset to you throughout college and later in your career.

Think about the many types of learning you have experienced. How did you learn to ride a bike, make pizza, or play tennis? In each case, you learned by doing, by active participation. While much of what you will learn in college is not as physical as riding a bike or playing tennis, it still can be learned best through active participation. Studying and thinking are forms of participation, as are making notes, speaking up in class discussion, or reviewing chapters with a friend. Active involvement, then, is a key to effective learning. Throughout this text, you will learn strategies to promote active learning. Assess your active learning strategies by completing the questionnaire shown in Figure 2.1 on p. 32.

Table 2.1

Characteristics of Passive and Active Learners

	Passive learners	Active learners
Class lectures	Write down what the instructor says	Decide what is important to write down.
Textbook assignments	Read	Read, think, ask questions, try to connect ideas.
Studying	Reread	Make outlines and study sheets, predict exam questions, look for trends and patterns.
Writing class assignments	Carefully follow the professor's instructions.	Try to discover the significance of the assignment; look for the principles and concepts it illustrates.
Writing term papers	Do what is expected to get a good grade.	Try to expand your knowledge and experience with a topic and connect it to the course objective or content.

Figure 2.1

Rate Your Active Learning Strategies

Respond to each of the following statements by checking "Always," "Sometimes," or "Never."

	Always	Sometimes	Never
1. I try to figure out *why* an assignment was given.	❏	❏	❏
2. While reading I am sorting important information.	❏	❏	❏
3. I think of questions as I read.	❏	❏	❏
4. I try to make connections between reading assignments and class lectures.	❏	❏	❏
5. I attempt to see how a newly assigned chapter in my text relates to the previously assigned one.	❏	❏	❏
6. I try to see how my instructor's class lectures fit together (relate to one another).	❏	❏	❏
7. I think about how the information I am reading can be used or applied.	❏	❏	❏
8. After writing a paper or completing an assignment, I think about what I learned from doing it.	❏	❏	❏
9. I review a returned exam to discover what types of questions I missed.	❏	❏	❏
10. I react to and evaluate what I am reading.	❏	❏	❏

Each item that you marked as "Sometimes" or "Never" identifies skills you need to work on to become a more active learner. Review the checklist, then gradually introduce the skills into your daily reading and study methods.

Become a More Active Learner

When you study, you should be thinking about and reacting to the material in front of you:

Ask questions about what you are reading. You will find that this helps to focus your attention and improve your concentration.

Discover the purpose behind assignments. Why might a sociology assignment require you to spend an hour at the monkey house of the local zoo, for example?

Try to see how each assignment fits with the rest of the course. For instance, why does a section titled "Consumer Behavior" belong in a retailing textbook chapter titled "External Retail Restraints"?

Relate what you are learning to what you already know. Use your background knowledge and personal experience. Connect a law in physics with how your car brakes work, for example.

Exercise 2.5	Consider each of the following learning situations. Suggest ways to make each an active learning task.

1. Revising a paper for an English composition class
2. Reading an assignment in a current newsmagazine
3. Studying a diagram in a data processing textbook chapter
4. Preparing a review schedule for an upcoming major exam
5. Looking up synonyms in a thesaurus for a word for your sociology term paper
6. Reading the procedures in your chemistry lab manual for the next laboratory session

Critical Thinking: The Key to College Success

To be a successful student, you must be able to take in information, think critically about it, reason with it, and apply it. Knowing a large number of facts and ideas is not as important as knowing how to use them—how to interpret, evaluate, and apply them to solve problems, create new ideas, or approach ideas in unique ways.

Critical thinking is an essential part of many academic activities. Common learning activities involve a variety of thinking skills.

The ability to think critically is a key ingredient of college and career success. The ability to think critically is a marketable, desirable quality sought by many employers. By polishing your critical thinking skills, you will be preparing not only for a successful college experience but also for success in the career you choose.

Critical thinkers exhibit a valuable and important set of characteristics. A critical thinker

1. **Constantly asks questions.** Ask critical questions about why things are as they are, how they became such, and what would happen if circumstances changed.

2. **Keeps an open mind.** Do not make up your mind about an issue until you have seen all the facts and evidence. Be willing to change preconceived notions or opinions if you find evidence to support a different position.

3. **Recognizes other viewpoints.** A critical thinker readily admits that others have the right to disagree and to hold viewpoints that seem wrong.

4. **Approaches issues systematically.** A critical thinker collects and weighs evidence in a systematic, organized fashion. In particular, a critical thinker examines other viewpoints and logically considers their implications.

5. **Uses writing to explore ideas.** Writing crystalizes ideas and is an excellent means of testing critical thinking.

Critical thinking is not a single skill; instead it is a collection of skills that enables you to use, interpret, analyze, and evaluate information. Critical thinkers question, challenge, and respond with interest to new ideas and information.

Activity	Critical Thinking Skills
Taking lecture notes	Identifying what is important, organizing information, working with various lecture styles, anticipating the speaker's thought patterns
Reviewing for an exam	Classifying and synthesizing information, making generalizations
Writing papers	Using thought patterns to organize ideas supporting a thesis, judging the relevance and importance of ideas

Levels of Thinking

To give you a better understanding of the variety of thinking skills involved in academic learning, a model is shown in Table 2.2 on p. 36. This model, developed by Benjamin Bloom, describes a hierarchy, or progression, of thinking skills. These levels of thinking will help you master textbook material, prepare for exams, and predict exam questions. Notice that the levels move from basic literal understanding to more complex critical thinking skills. The first two levels describe information-gathering skills—the ability to recall and understand information. The remaining four are critical thinking skills.

When college instructors write exams, most assume that you can operate at each of these levels. Table 2.3 on p. 36 shows a few items from an exam for a sociology course. Notice how the items require different levels of thinking.

| Exercise 2.6 | Read the following excerpt from an interpersonal communication textbook and then answer the questions that follow. Use each level of thinking to understand and evaluate the excerpt. |

Forms of Nonverbal Communication

Nonverbal elements, as already noted, sometimes work separately from verbal communication; that is, we may receive a nonverbal message without any words whatsoever. But usually the nonverbal domain provides a framework for the words we use. If we think of nonverbal communication as including all forms of message transmission *not* represented by word symbols, we can divide it into five broad categories: emblems, illustrators, affect displays, regulators, and adaptors.

In their early work in this area, Jurgen Ruesch and Weldon Kees outlined just three categories: sign, action, and object language. Sign language *includes gestures used in the place of words, numbers, or punctuation.* When an athlete raises his index finger to show his team is "Number One," he is using sign language. Action language *includes all those nonverbal movements not intended as signs.* Your way of walking, sitting, or eating may serve your personal needs, but they also make statements to those who see them. Object language *includes both the intentional and unintentional display of material things.* Your hairstyle, glasses, and jewelry reveal things about you, as do the books you carry, the car you drive, or the clothes you wear.[1]

1. *Knowledge*	What is the definition of "object language"?
2. *Comprehension*	What does object language include?
3. *Application*	Give an example of object language.
4. *Analysis*	Analyze and describe the object language used by a friend.
5. *Synthesis*	What objects are important means of communication among your group of friends? Rank them in order of importance.
6. *Evaluation*	Do you agree or disagree with Ruesch and Kees's categorization of nonverbal communication? Explain your answer.

The various categories of thinking are not distinct or mutually exclusive; they overlap. For example, note taking during a lecture class involves comprehension, but it also involves analysis, synthesis, and evaluation. Taking an essay exam may involve, at one point or another, all six levels.

Throughout this book you will learn strategies for improving each level of thinking.

Table 2.2
Levels of Thinking

Level	Description	Examples
Knowledge	Recalling information; repeating information with no changes	Recalling dates; memorizing definitions
Comprehension	Understanding ideas; using rules and following directions	Explaining a law; recognizing what is important
Application	Applying knowledge to a new situation	Using knowledge of formulas to solve a new physics problem
Analysis	Seeing relationships; breaking information into parts; analyzing how things work	Comparing two poems by the same author
Synthesis	Putting ideas and information together in a unique way; creating something new	Designing a new computer program
Evaluation	Making judgments; assessing the value or worth of information	Evaluating the effectiveness of an argument opposing the death penalty

Table 2.3
Test Items and Levels of Thinking

Test Item	Level of Thinking Required
Define "stereotype."	Knowledge
Explain how a stereotype can negatively affect a person.	Comprehension
Give an example of a stereotype that is commonly held for a particular age group.	Application
Study the two attached interviews. Which of the interviewers reveals a stereotypic attitude?	Analysis
Construct a set of guidelines that might be used to identify a stereotypic attitude.	Synthesis
Evaluate the film shown in class, discussing how a stereotypic attitude was revealed and approached.	Evaluation

Exercise 2.7   For each activity or situation described below, indicate the levels of thinking that are primarily involved.

1. Answering the following short answer test question: Give an example of defensive behavior.
2. Solving a math problem
3. Taking notes on a college lecture

4. Translating into English a poem written in Spanish

5. Studying a famous painting for an art history course

6. Selecting a topic for a term paper in a criminal justice class

7. Revising a composition to make its thesis clearer and to improve its organization

8. Completing a biology lab in which you dissect an insect

9. Writing a computer program for a class assignment in a data processing course

10. Answering the following essay exam question: Most people would probably be outraged if someone sprayed them with poisonous air or fed them dangerous chemicals. In effect, this is what industrial polluters and many of their products are doing. Why, then, are people not outraged?[2]

Interactive Chapter Review

Knowledge	What does the word "analysis" mean?	
Comprehension	What are three ways you can take charge of your college career?	
Application	Right before you start your next assignment in another course, reread the points on p. 33 in the section "Become a More Active Learner." Take 10 minutes before your study session to apply each of the points.	
Analysis	Do you currently demonstrate the characteristics of a critical thinker? Describe your usual habits according to the 5 points on p. 33–34, and then decide how to improve your critical thinking ability.	
Synthesis	What characteristics do active learning and critical thinking have in common?	
Evaluation	In what areas of your life do you have solid experience in setting your own operating rules (if any)? How can you use this other experience as a guide to setting your own operating rules in college?	

Further Analysis

Analyze the situation described below and answer the questions that follow.

A political science professor has just returned graded midterm exams to her class. One student looks at the grade on the first page, flips through the remaining pages while commenting to a friend that the exam was "too picky," and files it in her notebook. A second student reviews his exam for grading errors and notices one error. Immediately, he raises his hand and asks for an adjustment in his grade. The instructor seems annoyed and tells the student that she will not use class time to dispute individual grades. A third student reviews her exam blue book to identify a pattern of error; on the cover of the blue book she notes topics and areas in which she is weak.

1. Compare the three students' responses to the situation.

2. What does each student's response reveal about his or her approach to learning?

3. Analyze the student's response to the instructor's error in grading. What alternatives might have been more appropriate?

Discussion

1. To what extent do you feel your performance as a student is shaped by what you think of yourself as a student?

2. Discuss the following hypothetical situation by answering the questions that follow.

   A student completed four years of study and received a bachelor's degree in accounting from a prestigious major university. After several months of searching for a job, he was finally hired by a small accounting firm. After six months on the job, he was fired for incompetence. The student sued the university for accepting his tuition but failing to provide him with the knowledge and skills to handle the job of accountant.

   a.   Do you think the student's claim is legitimate?

   b.   How does this situation draw upon the distinction between teaching and learning?

   c.   What questions does this hypothetical situation raise?

3. Which type of thinking is most important for college success? Might your answer vary depending on your major?

4. List five careers or professions you have considered and identify the thinking skills essential to each.

5. Explain why you agree or disagree with each of the following statements:

   a.   Getting good grades depends on spending enough time studying.

   b.   The amount of material you learn makes the biggest difference in the grade you get.

   c.   Academic success is guaranteed if you are able to memorize enough information.

   d.   Learning from college lectures is simply a matter of focusing your attention.

The Work Connection

What workplace skills will you develop in college? Carolyn Corbin, founder and director of the Center for the 21st Century, has coined a new word for the successful worker of the future: "indipreneur."™ An indipreneur is a person who is independent and entrepreneurial, even when working for a corporation. Indipreneurs are self-reliant, flexible, and experience change as a challenge rather than as a threat.[3] Corbin identifies the top three skills most important to a person's workplace success: "Know how to think, how to get along in the workplace with other people, and how to stay current in skills and technology."[4]

1. How will developing active learning skills in college aid you in the workplace of the 21st century? List eight to ten ideas.

2. What steps can you take now to ensure that you will have the top three skills Corbin considers most important for career success? List at least five steps.

The Web Connection

1. How Realistic Are Your College Expectations?

   http://sdcl.wayne.edu/uac/hndbk/expect.html

   This true/false quiz will help you determine how you view college life.

2. Great Expectations

   http://www.publicagenda.org/specials/highered/highered.htm

   Browse the findings of a recent study on the public's opinion of higher education. How do these findings compare with your own ideas about the role of college in your life?

3. A Point-By-Point Comparison of High School and College

   http://www.umt.edu/ucoll/newfreshmen/pointbypoint.htm

   The University of Montana presents this site which shows two dozen very specific differences between high school and college life.

4. College Lifestyle Assessment

   http://www.byu.edu/stlife/cdc/Learning_Strategies/lifestyle/lifeassm.htm

   Brigham Young University offers this weekly worksheet for students to keep track of their tasks and accomplishments.

Go Electronic!
For additional readings, exercises, and Internet activities, visit the Longman Study Skills Web site at:
http://www.ablongman.com/StudySkills
If you need a user name and password, please see your instructor.

Chapter 3

Establishing Goals and Managing Your Time

DO YOU KNOW?

How can you decide what you want out of life?
How can you organize your life for success in college?
How can you analyze your existing time commitments?
How can you build a study plan?
How can you make better use of your time?
How can you concentrate to make the most of your study time?

Being a college student is difficult and demanding, but it need not overwhelm you. Certainly, a great deal is expected of you, and at times you will wonder if you can handle the workload. Assignments, papers, and exams seem to keep coming, and just when you feel as if you've gotten things under control, another assignment or examination is announced. But you can learn to cope with the tremendous workload of college if you organize your life for success in college and learn to manage your time effectively.

Time management is a highly marketable skill in career and professional fields as well as in college. Handling the pressures of the workload of a responsible, fulfilling job also requires time management skills. If you develop and apply these skills to college life, you will be able to make an easy transition to career or professional life.

Time management is the skill of taking charge or control of your life and your time. Just as the manager of a store makes certain that the store operates efficiently, effectively, and profitably, so you must manage the various facets of your life in order to become a productive, successful person. Time management involves goal setting, organizing, planning, conserving time and resources, and maintaining peak efficiency.

Establishing Life Goals

In order to manage your time effectively, you must first decide what things in your life are more important and which are less so.

Let's begin, then, by defining some life goals. Life goals are what you want out of life. They should be statements of where you are headed. They represent focal points of your life and can help you stay on track when life gets confusing, frustrating, or overwhelming.

How to Discover What Is Important

1. Make a list of the 10 most joyous moments in your life. A phrase or single sentence of description is all that is needed.

2. Ask yourself, "What do most or all these moments have in common?"

3. Try to write answers to the above question by describing why the moments were important to you—what you got out of them. (Sample answers: helping others, competing or winning, creating something worthwhile, proving your self-worth, connecting with nature, and so forth.)

4. Your answers should provide a starting point for defining life goals.

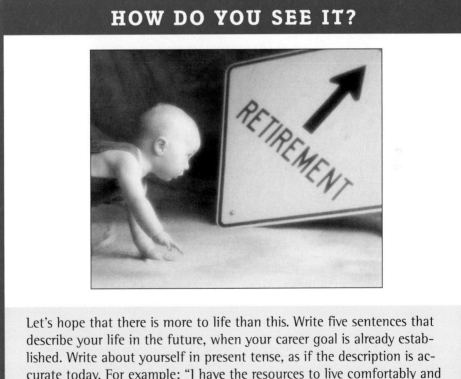

HOW DO YOU SEE IT?

Let's hope that there is more to life than this. Write five sentences that describe your life in the future, when your career goal is already established. Write about yourself in present tense, as if the description is accurate today. For example: "I have the resources to live comfortably and provide opportunities for my family." "I go to work each day anticipating interesting challenges."

Defining Life Goals

In defining your life goals be specific and detailed. Use the following suggestions.

◆ Your goals should be positive (what you want) rather than negative (what you want to avoid). Don't say, "I won't ever have to worry about credit card balances and bill collectors." Instead, say, "I will have enough money to live comfortably."

◆ Your goals should be realistic. Unless you have strong evidence to believe you can do so, don't say you want to win an Olympic gold medal in swimming. Instead, say you want to become a strong, competitive swimmer.

◆ Your goals should be achievable. Don't say you want to earn a million dollars a year; most people don't. Set more achievable, specific goals, such as, "I want to buy my own house by the time I am 30."

◆ Your goal should be worth what it will take to achieve it. Becoming an astronaut or a brain surgeon takes years of training. Are you willing to spend that amount of time?

◆ Your goal should include a time frame. The goal "To earn a bachelor's degree in accounting" should include a date, for example.

◆ Don't hesitate to change your goals as your life changes. The birth of a child or the loss of a loved one may cause you to refocus your life.

Exercise 3.1	Write a list of five to ten life goals.

How a College Education Contributes to Your Life Goals

College can help you achieve many of your life goals. College can provide you with the self-awareness, self-confidence, knowledge, skills, practice facilities, degrees, friendships, business contacts, and so forth that can help you achieve your life goals.

Try to make the connection between college and life goals clear and explicit. College demands hard work and a "stick-with-it" attitude. You will be more motivated to work hard if you can see directly how that hard work will pay off in helping you fulfill your life goals.

Exercise 3.2	For each of your life goals, explain how attending college will help you achieve that goal.

Organizing Your Life for Success in College

Now that you see how doing well in college can help you achieve important goals, you are ready to work on organizing your life so that you can be successful in college. Specifically, you need to organize space, courses, work, family, finances, and your health.

Organize a Place to Study

A first step in managing time successfully is to assess your living arrangements, determine if they are conducive to study, and, if necessary, make changes. If you live on a floor of a dorm where parties occur frequently, then you are going to have difficulty studying. If you share an apartment or live at home, you may find studying at busy times nearly impossible. If you find your situation intolerable (your dorm roommate is entertaining friends in your room every evening, for example), then make a change as soon as possible. In the meantime, make temporary adjustments; alter the time or place you study. Consider alternatives such as the library, student lounge, or designated campus study areas.

It is usually beneficial to study in the same place each day, where all the materials you need (pens, calculator, paper) are readily at hand. There is also a psychological advantage to studying in the same place each day: You build a mental association between an activity and the place where it occurs. If you become accustomed to studying at a particular desk, you will build up an association between the place (your desk) and the activity (reading and studying). Eventually, when you sit down at the desk, you expect to read or study, and the expectation makes getting started much easier. Be sure not to select a place you already associate with a different activity. Don't try to study in your TV chair or stretched out across your bed; you already have built associations with your chair and bed as places to relax or sleep. Assess your organizational skills by completing the questionnaire shown in Figure 3.1 on p. 44.

Organize Each Course

For each course you are taking, some preliminary organizational strategies can help you make the most of your time.

Become familiar with each textbook.   Even though the lines in the bookstore may be long, purchase your textbooks as soon as possible in each new term. Be certain to buy new rather than used texts. Used textbooks that are already marked or underlined are distracting and make learning more difficult. You may not have an assignment right away, so spend time becoming familiar with each of your texts. Find out how each is organized and identify what learning aids it contains.

- Read the preface or introduction and study the table of contents.
- Choose a chapter at random and examine its format. What special features does it contain? How does the author emphasize what is important to learn? Does it contain review questions and vocabulary lists?
- Check the end of the book. Does it have an index, glossary (minidictionary of important words), bibliography, or appendix? If so, check to see what each contains. (The appendix often contains useful tables, charts, documents, or reference material to which you may frequently need to refer when using the text.)

Figure 3.1

Rate Your Organizational and Time Management Skills

Respond to each of the following statements by checking "Always," "Sometimes," or "Never."

	Always	Sometimes	Never
1. Do you use a pocket calendar or assignment notebook to record due dates of assignments and exams?	❏	❏	❏
2. Do you study at your peak periods of concentration?	❏	❏	❏
3. Do you study difficult subjects first?	❏	❏	❏
4. Do you avoid studying in front of the TV?	❏	❏	❏
5. Do you use lists to keep organized?	❏	❏	❏
6. Do you assign priorities to your assignments?	❏	❏	❏
7. Do you give yourself deadlines or establish time limits by when assignments should be completed?	❏	❏	❏
8. Do you know when you are losing concentration and recognize when your attention span is weakening?	❏	❏	❏
9. Do you plan out what needs to be done each week?	❏	❏	❏
10. Do you plan to study at least two hours outside of class for every hour spent in class?	❏	❏	❏

If you answered "Sometimes" or "Never" to three or more of the questions, your time management skills need improvement.

Previewing a text in this way will give you a working knowledge of it, and when the first assignment is made, you will be able to put your texts to work for you immediately.

Organize a notebook for each class.   Decide what type of notebook best suits each of your courses. For lecture classes with few or no supplementary materials, a spiral notebook works well. A loose-leaf notebook works best for courses in which numerous handouts, outlines, and supplementary materials are distributed. Date and organize these day-to-day class handouts, and place them next to the lecture notes with which they correspond. Handouts are important when studying and reviewing for an exam. Include all class homework assignments and returned quizzes, exams, and written assignments.

Use a pocket calendar.   College professors frequently give long-term assignments and announce due dates for papers, assignments, and exams far in advance. Many do not feel that it is their responsibility to remind students as the dates approach. Consequently, you will need to organize a system for keeping track of what assignments need to be done and when each is due.

Many students keep pocket diaries or calendar notebooks in which they record all their assignments as they are given, as shown in Figure 3.2. These allow you to see at a glance what assignments, tests, and quizzes are coming up. Most useful are the monthly calendars that display a full month on one page. These allow you to anticipate work requirements easily without flipping pages.

Figure 3.2
A Week in a Calendar Notebook

March						
Sun	Mon	Tue	Wed	Thu	Fri	Sat
2	3	4	5	6	7	8
	English comp due Math H.W.	Speech- draft	Psych Quiz Math H.W.	Speech- give edit computer program	Topic for term paper due Math H.W.	

Exercise 3.3

Assess your organizational skills by answering each of the following questions.

1. When an instructor makes an assignment during class, where do you record it?

2. Do you have a specific place to keep returned quizzes, completed homework, and graded papers for each course?

3. Are you familiar with each of your textbooks?

   a. Have you previewed each of your texts to learn if each contains a glossary, appendix, and answer key?

   b. Have you read the preface or introduction in each and studied the table of contents?

   c. Have you reviewed a random chapter in each text and become familiar with its format?

4. What is the average cost of books per semester or quarter at your college? (Estimates often appear in college financial aid brochures.)

5. Have you chosen and organized a place to study? If you do not live on campus, have you found a place on campus to study during free hours?

6. Do you have a filing system (envelopes, folders) for keeping both college paperwork (transcripts, financial aid agreements) and everyday documents (car insurance, registrations, licenses, checking account statements)?

Organize Your Job to Work for You

Many students hold part-time jobs while attending college; others work full time and attend college part time. A job can be either a refreshing break from the routine of studying or a source of additional stress, depending upon how you organize and approach it. If you are a full-time student, here are a few suggestions for managing your part-time job.

Keep work hours to a minimum. The number of hours you work should not take needed time away from study. If you are unsure of how much time you will need for study, underestimate rather than overestimate the number of hours you can spend on the job. Many college-sponsored work-study programs limit students to a maximum of 15 hours per week; use this number as a guide.

Choose a job with a regular work schedule. Unless you know in advance when and how long you will work each week, the job may turn your life into a nightmare of confused commitments, missed classes, and uncompleted assignments.

Make sure your employer understands your college commitments. If an employer or supervisor knows you are working toward a degree, he or she is often helpful and supportive.

Choose a job that provides a break or diversion from the task of studying. A job that is physically active or involves working with people may be refreshing.

If you have a full-time job, either as an employee or within your home, and are a part-time student, use the following tips:

Try to schedule your class(es) early in the week.   You are more energetic at the beginning of the workweek than toward its end.

Plan to use part of your weekend for study.   Reserving a block of time on the weekend usually works better than trying to sandwich in study during the workweek.

Use spare time during the workweek to handle routine tasks and to get organized. During the week, for example, you might reorganize a set of history lecture notes or prepare a set of vocabulary flash cards for biology.

Do not overload yourself with classes.   If you try carrying too many credit hours, you will feel overwhelmed and will not enjoy your classes. You run the risk, too, of not earning the grades you deserve.

Organize Your Family Responsibilities

If you are an adult returning to college, you may have family responsibilities in addition to those of college and a part-time or full-time job. Try the following suggestions to maintain a "happy" household as you start back to college.

Make sure family members understand how college will help you achieve your life goals. Explain to everyone, including young children, why you are returning to school. Discuss how you may have less time for family activities, while reassuring everyone that spending less time does not mean that you care less about them.

Reserve special times for family members most affected by your decision.   Children are often most directly affected by your absence. They may also fail to understand why you must be alone to study. Designate a special time or activity each week that will be that child's exclusive time with you.

Make children part of the process.   Try to involve your children with your return to college. Take them for a brief campus visit so they can see where you attend classes. When studying at home, give them a job to do that will let them think they are helping. For example, one student asked her six-year-old to use a highlighter to color code vocabulary flash cards by chapter. Another gave her nine-year-old a list of words to check for correct spelling in a dictionary.

Redistribute household responsibilities.   Now that you are back in school, you probably do not have time to complete all the tasks you did previously. Assign responsibilities to other family members. Remember, your family wants to help you succeed in college, but often they do not know how to do so. Children, for example, depending on their age, can be asked to unpack groceries, put away dishes, vacuum, and mow the lawn.

Organize a message center and purchase an answering machine.   Designate a place where family members should look for notes and messages. Use an answering machine to leave messages for family members while you are away.

Organize Your Finances

Unless you are fortunate enough to have access to unlimited funds, organizing your finances, often for the first time in your life, is an important task. Worrying about money can be a major source of distraction and can interfere with your ability to concentrate on your course work. Budgeting, then, is essential; be sure to allow a "cushion" for hidden and unexpected expenses. These costs, especially if you are living away from home, may include local transportation, laundry and dry cleaning, phone calls, toiletries, and higher clothing costs in small college towns. Check with the college's financial aid office to be sure you are taking advantage of all sources of aid.

Exercise 3.4	Discuss with a classmate the various responsibilities you have for school, work, and home. Identify any organizing you need to do to keep your life running smoothly this term.

Analyzing Your Time Commitments

Time is one of our most valuable resources. Time management is a skill few people have but most people need. Many large companies pay consultants generous fees to conduct time management seminars to encourage their employees to make better use of their time. These seminars demonstrate how to accomplish more in less time.

Effective time management can make the difference between being a mediocre student and being an excellent one. Your management of time can also determine whether you feel as if you should spend every waking moment studying or whether you are confident about your courses and know you can afford time for fun and relaxation.

A first step in managing your time more effectively is to analyze your commitments and determine the time each requires. In time management seminars sponsored by corporations, employees are first asked to identify required tasks and responsibilities—travel time, weekly meetings, reading and responding to memoranda, supervising subordinates, and so forth—and then to estimate the time each involves. You can profit from doing the same. To determine how much of your time is already committed, estimate the amount of time various activities require per week.

Apply the "2-for-1" Rule

To estimate study time, use the "2-for-1" rule. Most professors assume the 2-for-1 rule of student time management: Students should spent two hours studying outside of class for every hour spent in class. If you spend 12 hours per week attending classes, you should spend 24 hours outside class reading text assignments, doing research or experiments, studying for exams, or writing papers. This explains why carrying 12 credit hours is usually considered full-time study.

Depending on your familiarity and expertise in a given discipline, adjust the 2-for-1 rule. If you are an excellent math student, you may need less than two hours per class hour for math courses. On the other hand, if mathematics is a weak area, you may need to spend three or 3 ½ hours of study per class hour.

Many students find it motivating to set their sights on a particular grade and to work toward earning it. Allot more time for study for higher grades. The 2-for-1 rule estimates the time the typical college student will need to earn an average passing grade (a C).

Consider each of your courses—its workload, your expertise in the field, and the grade toward which you are working—to estimate the amount of time per week each will require by completing the following chart.

Course Title	Desired Grade	Study Hours per Week

Determine If You Are Overcommitted

Many students take on extra work hours, make commitments to family and friends, or join sports, as the following case example shows.

Maria was majoring in accounting and had several difficult courses including business law and business management. Yet when her boss asked her to add Friday nights to her work schedule at TGI Friday's she agreed. Her best friend convinced her to join a ski club and her sister signed her up for an aerobics class. Without realizing it, Maria was overextended; she had more commitments than she could handle.

To find out if you are overcommitted, fill out the following Time Analysis chart.

Time Analysis

Activity	Hours per week
Classes and labs	_____
Study	_____
Sleep	_____
Breakfast, lunch, dinner	_____
Part-time job	_____
Transportation (driving, walking to class)	_____
Personal care (showering, dressing)	_____
Other commitments (sports, activities)	_____
Total	_____

After you have totaled your time commitments, subtract that total from 168, the number of hours in a week:

$$168 \text{ hours} - (\text{committed time}) = \underline{\hspace{3cm}}.$$

The remainder represents the number of hours of uncommitted time you have available. If you find you have very little or no uncommitted time or if your total time commitment exceeds 168 hours, you are overextended. There are several possible solutions. You may need to revise your goals to settle for a B instead of an A in English composition, reduce the number of hours you work at your part-time job, or drop one or more activities. You can also become more efficient and spend less time completing required tasks by applying the principles of effective time management described in the following sections.

Exercise 3.5	Refer back to the life goals you developed in Exercises 3.1 and 3.2. Compare your time analysis and your life goals. Are you spending most of your time actively pursuing your goals? Use your comparison to decide how you wish to spend your time.

Building a Study Plan

You have already estimated your total study hours per week and identified other weekly time commitments. The next step in successful time management is to display these commitments on a semester plan.

Develop a Semester/Term Schedule

Begin by blocking out class time and scheduled work hours. Also include other commitments that will remain unchanged throughout the semester or term. Sports team practice, regular baby-sitting on Tuesday evenings, and morning exercise routines are examples. Include your part-time job hours if they do not change from week to week. Use the blank schedule in Figure 3.3 on p. 51 as a worksheet. Alternately, use an electronic calendar to develop a schedule. You will use this semester/term worksheet to develop a weekly study schedule.

Develop a Weekly Study Schedule

Once you have constructed a semester/term plan, the next step is to use the plan as a basis for developing a more specific, detailed weekly schedule. If you have access to a photocopy machine, make enough copies of your semester plan for each week of the semester. Before each week begins, preferably on Saturday or Sunday, review upcoming assignments, papers, and examinations. For each course, identify what needs to be done or reviewed; list specific chapters and pages along with assignments to complete. A sample list is shown in Figure 3.4, p. 52.

Figure 3.3

A Semester/Term Plan Worksheet

	Sunday	Monday	Tuesday	Wednesday	Thursday	Friday	Saturday
7:00							
8:00							
9:00							
10:00							
11:00							
12:00							
1:00							
2:00							
3:00							
4:00							
5:00							
6:00							
7:00							
8:00							
9:00							
10:00							
11:00							

Figure 3.4

A Weekly To-Do List

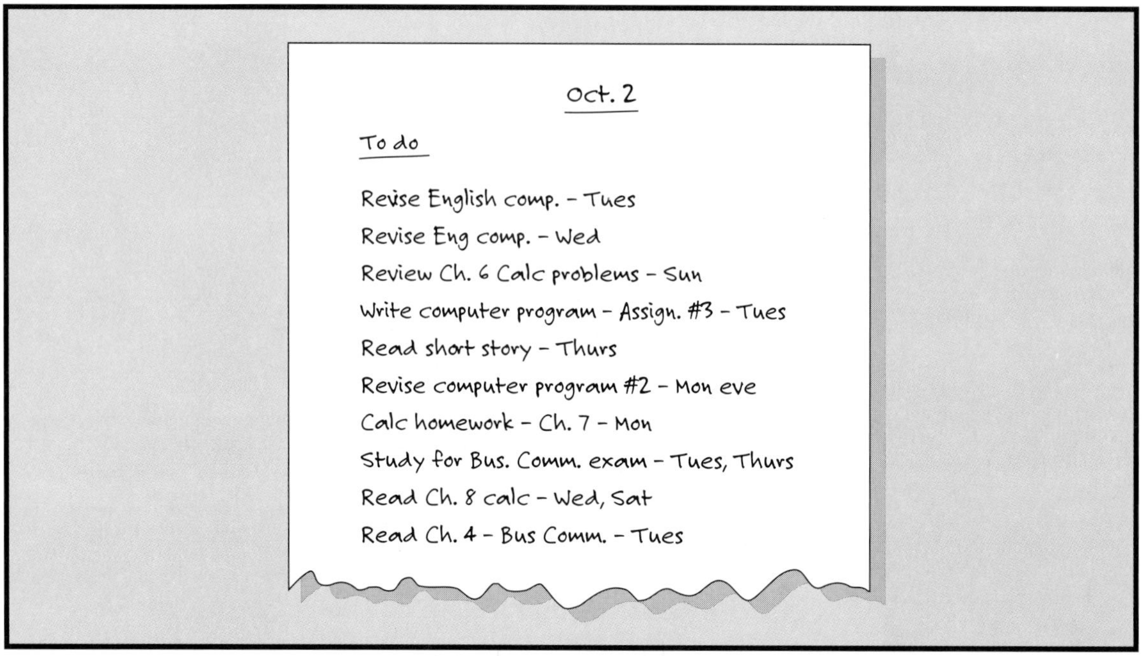

Oct. 2

To do

Revise English comp. – Tues
Revise Eng comp. – Wed
Review Ch. 6 Calc problems – Sun
Write computer program – Assign. #3 – Tues
Read short story – Thurs
Revise computer program #2 – Mon eve
Calc homework – Ch. 7 – Mon
Study for Bus. Comm. exam – Tues, Thurs
Read Ch. 8 calc – Wed, Sat
Read Ch. 4 – Bus Comm. – Tues

Once you have constructed your weekly list, identify when you will accomplish these tasks and write them on a copy of your semester/term plan. Use the following guidelines in selecting specific study times.

1. **Use peak periods of concentration.** Everyone has high and low periods of concentration and attention. First, determine when these occur for you; then reserve peak times for intensive study and use less efficient times for more routine tasks such as recopying an assignment or collecting information in the library. Use the lowest concentration times for nonacademic tasks: errands, laundry, phone calls, and so forth.

2. **Study difficult subjects first.** While it is tempting to get easy tasks and short, little assignments out of the way first, do not give in to this approach. When you start studying, your mind is fresh and alert and you are at your peak of concentration. This is the time you are best equipped to handle difficult subjects. Thinking through complicated problems or studying complex ideas requires all the brainpower you have, and you are able to think most clearly at the beginning of a study session.

3. **Schedule study for a particular course close to the time when you attend class.** Plan to study the evening before the class meets and soon after the class meeting. If a class meets on Tuesday and Thursday mornings, plan to study Monday evening

and Tuesday afternoon or evening and again Wednesday. By studying close to class time, you will find it easier to see the connections between class lectures or discussions and what you are reading and studying, and so reinforce your learning.

4. **Include short breaks in your study time.** Take a break before you begin studying each new subject. Your mind needs time to refocus—to switch from one set of facts, problems, and issues to another. Short breaks should also be included when you are working on just one assignment for a long period of time. A 10-minute break after 50 to 60 minutes of study is reasonable.

5. **Use distributed learning and practice.** Learning occurs more effectively when it is divided and spaced over time, rather than done all at once. Distributed practice means that you should spread out your study sessions. For example, try to study a subject for an hour each of three nights rather than three hours in one evening. Distributed practice is effective for several reasons. First, research evidence suggests that after you stop studying, your mind continues to work on the material and learning continues for a brief time. If, then, you study over several blocks of time, this aftereffect occurs several times rather than once, as illustrated below. Second, distributed practice prevents mental fatigue and keeps you working at peak efficiency. Third, distributing the material over several sessions allows you to approach it in reasonable pieces that can be mastered more easily.

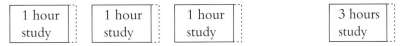

6. **Be generous when estimating needed time.** It is better to overestimate than underestimate how much time you need to complete your study. If you overestimate, the free time you have left will function as a reward for hard work; however, if you underestimate you will feel pressured, rushed, and dissatisfied.

A computer science major designed a weekly plan using the worksheet shown in Figure 3.5. Since calculus was this student's most difficult course, he planned to devote nine hours per week to it. The class met Monday, Wednesday, and Friday; he decided to study the day before each class since the instructor spent most of the class reviewing difficult problems assigned as homework. He also planned to work on Saturday and Sunday afternoons, reviewing the week's assignment and reading new material. Because English was his strongest subject, he scheduled five hours weekly for English, but six hours each week for business communications and computer programming logic.

Planning Long-Term Assignments

When a term paper or semester project is assigned, draft a timetable for its completion. Since assignments such as these usually constitute a major portion of your final grade, you want to be certain to meet each deadline. It may be necessary to add additional hours to your weekly plan to work on such projects.

Figure 3.5
Sample Weekly Schedule

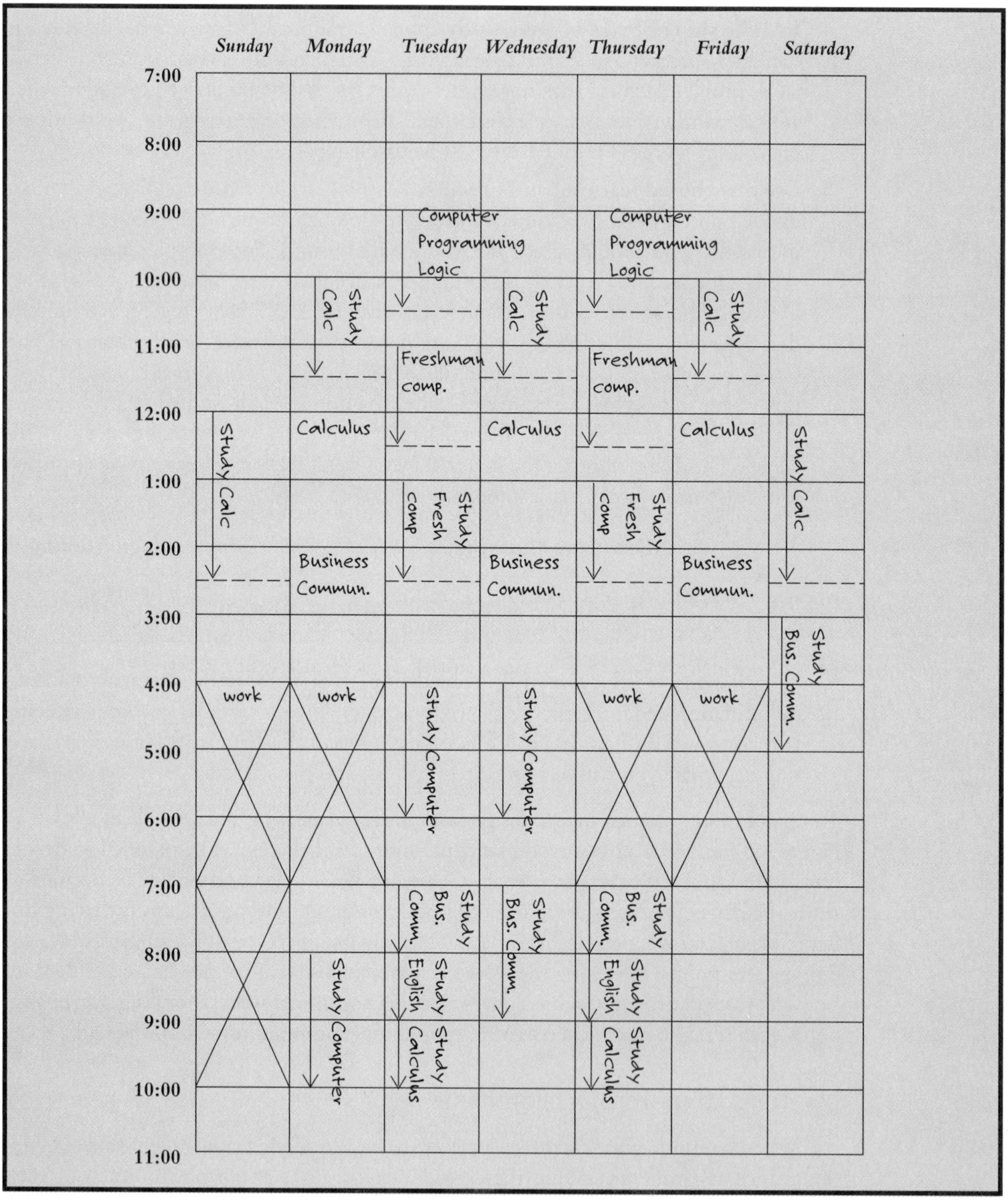

Exercise 3.6	Build a semester study plan, using the guidelines given above. Work with the plan for a week and then analyze its effectiveness. Revise it so it becomes more effective.

Exercise 3.7	For each of the next several weeks, prepare a weekly to-do list. After each week, stop and analyze whether the list helped to improve your efficiency.

Making Better Use of Time

Here are a few suggestions that will help you make the best use of your time.

Assign priorities to your work.   There may be days or weeks when you cannot get every assignment done. Decide what is most important to complete immediately and which assignments could, if necessary, be completed later.

Spending valuable time doing relatively unimportant tasks and making routine decisions can create unnecessary stress. Chapters 4 and 5 discuss strategies to help you avoid these time traps.

Use lists to keep yourself organized and to save time.   A daily reminder list is helpful in keeping track of household tasks and errands as well as course assignments. As you think of things to be done, jot them down. Then, each morning look over the list and figure out the best way to get everything done. You may find, for instance, that you can stop at the post office on the way to the bookstore, thus saving yourself a trip.

Combine activities.   Most people think it is impossible to do two things at once, but busy students soon learn that they can combine some daily living chores with more routine kinds of class assignments. For example, you might outline a history chapter while waiting for your wash to finish at the laundromat. Or you might mentally review formulas for math and science courses or review vocabulary cards for a foreign language course while walking to class.

Use spare moments.   Think of all the time that you spend waiting. You wait for a class to begin, for a ride, for a friend to call, for a take-out order to be ready. Although you should take advantage of some of these times to relax or take a break, other times you can use them to review a set of lecture notes, work on review questions at the end of a chapter, or review a set of problems. If you always carry with you something you can work on in empty moments, then you will always have a choice between relaxing and studying.

Use the telephone.   When you need to get information or make an appointment, phone rather than visit the office. For example, to find out if a book you have requested at the library has come in, phone the circulation desk.

Don't be afraid to admit you are trying to do too much.   If you find your life is becoming too hectic or that you are facing pressures beyond your ability to handle them, consider dropping a course. Don't be concerned that dropping a course will put you behind schedule for graduation; more than half of all college students take longer than the traditional four years to earn their degrees. (Do remember, however, to find out how dropping a course may affect your financial aid status.) You may be able to pick up the course during a summer session or carry a heavier load another semester. Time pressures are often a basic cause of failure in college. Unless you relieve some of the pressure, your performance in all your courses may be affected.

Time Management in the Electronic Age

Be sure to take advantage of new technology to help you save time. Overall, electronic devices are great time-savers. Answering machines, cellular phones, beepers, and computers can all make your life run smoothly and efficiently, but they also can interrupt you and cause undue pressure and stress if misused.

Answering machines allow you to study uninterrupted, without worrying that you are missing important calls.   Be sure to turn off the volume so you do not hear any incoming messages while you are studying.

Cellular phones and beepers allow you to be available to friends and family, regardless of where you are.   They can be particularly valuable as a way to stay in touch with your children. However, if you are constantly available, you can be constantly interrupted and distracted. Discuss with family and friends what types of calls you want to take.

Computers.   The word processing capacity of computers is a huge time-saver in completing course work. Other functions may be useful as well. Many computers offer electronic calendars, for example, that will keep track of important dates and appointments. Many also have electronic address/phone lists, to-do lists, and notepads that allow you to write yourself reminders and brief notes. E-mail is a fast and efficient way to communicate and is a great time-saver.

Time Management Tips for Returning Adult Students

Returning adult students face unique time management problems. Younger students who move into dorms are beginning an entirely new lifestyle. Everything—where they eat, where they sleep, where they work—is different. They know they must adjust their habits to succeed in their new environment. Returning adults face a different challenge. They often do not realize that they, too, must adjust their lifestyle. Even a well-organized lifestyle usually must change. Here are some useful tips.

1. **Make a new schedule to reflect your new priorities.** Don't try to fit college into your old way of getting through the week; succeeding in college takes too much time for this to work well.

2. **Make a household schedule.** Just as you have planned a weekly study schedule, develop a weekly household schedule. Instead of hoping that all jobs will get done, plan when you or a family member will tackle each. Designate specific times for laundry, shopping, errands, and so forth.

3. **Increase your efficiency by doing things at off-peak times.** Don't go to the grocery store or laundromat on a busy Saturday morning; instead choose a weekday early morning or later evening.

4. **Delegate jobs to others.** Because you are in college, you cannot possibly do everything you did before you returned. Don't hesitate to ask others for help.

5. **Use weekends for study.** Take care of household responsibilities during the week by "sandwiching" them in between work and school. This will free up larger blocks of time on the weekend for study.

6. **Consider remaining on or returning to campus to study.** Many adult students find their households too distracting for concentrated study and work better in the college library or at a local public library.

Time Management Tips for Commuters

Commuting to and from campus costs time, possibly several hours each day. Here's how to use your valuable time effectively.

1. **Use your commuting time.** If you are driving, listen to tapes of class lectures or mentally review material you studied recently. If you are riding, you may be able to read or complete routine assignments.

2. **Find a place on campus to study.** Most likely you will have open hours between classes. Find a quiet place on campus where you can use these hours for study; be sure to avoid the cafeteria and snack bar during study periods.

3. **Plan your next semester's schedule to cut down on commuting time.** Consider, for example, registering for both day and evening classes on three or four days, instead of driving to campus five days a week. Use your noncommuting day for assignments requiring concentrated blocks of time.

4. **Do not do things when everyone else does.** If you are spending valuable time hunting for a parking space, get to campus earlier. Use your early arrival time to get organized, review, and prepare for the day's classes. If you are wasting time standing in a cafeteria line, pack your lunch or plan to eat early or late to avoid crowds.

5. **Avoid the morning mad rush.** Your day begins earlier than most students, especially if you have an early class. Get organized the day and night before; fill your gas

tank on the way home, select clothing, and pack your books and materials the night before.

6. **Buy a large backpack so you can comfortably carry books and notebooks.** Carry enough supplies (highlighters, index cards, etc.) so you can work between classes. Think of it as your portable desk away from home.

Thinking Critically
. . . About Procrastination

Procrastination is the tendency to postpone tasks that need to be done. If you know you should review your biology notes but decide to do something else instead, you are procrastinating. Many people tend to put off tasks that are difficult, dull, or unpleasant. Procrastination can serve as an early warning signal that something is going wrong in a course. For example, frequently putting off assigned math problems is a signal that you are having or will have trouble with your math course.

If you find yourself procrastinating in a particular course, ask yourself the following questions:

1. **What tasks am I avoiding?** Make a list of all the tasks you are avoiding.

2. **Why am I avoiding these tasks?** Think honestly about *why* you have avoided them. Perhaps they are boring, or too difficult.

3. **When, realistically, can I start each?** If you have avoided these tasks because they are dull, divide each task into manageable pieces and set up a schedule in which you do a small part each day. Dividing the task will make it seem less burdensome.

4. **Are the tasks too difficult?** If so, you should seek further information or assistance. You might:
   - consult a classmate
   - talk with your instructor
   - get a tutor
   - visit the academic skills center
   - obtain a more basic text and read it first

Concentration Tips

Regardless of how effectively you plan your time, if you are not able to concentrate when you *do* study, you are not using your time efficiently. Spending time studying is not sufficient; time must be spent productively. Results are what counts. The key to concentration is monitoring—always staying aware of your concentration level. You must continually check to make certain that you are focusing your attention and operating at peak efficiency.

Focus Your Attention

Concentration is focusing attention on the task at hand while shutting out external distractions such as noises, conversations, and interruptions.

Vary your activities.   Avoid working on one type of activity for a long period of time; instead, alternate between several types of study. For example, you might plan your study schedule so that you read sociology for a while, then work on math problems, and finally switch to writing an English paper. This plan would be much more effective than doing all reading activities in the same study session, say, reading sociology, then reading chemistry, then reading an essay for English. The change from one skill or mental process to another will be refreshing and make concentration easier.

Write and highlight as you read.   Have you ever read an entire page and then not remembered anything you had read? One way to solve this problem is to write or highlight. After reading a section, write or highlight what is important to remember. This activity forces you to think—to identify what is important, to see how ideas are related, and to evaluate their worth and importance.

Approach assignments critically.   Keep active as you read. Instead of trying to take in large amounts of information, read critically, looking for ideas you question or disagree with. Look for points of view, opinions, and statements that are not supported. Try to predict how the author's train of thought will develop. Make connections with what you have already learned about the subject, with what you have read previously in the course, and with what the instructor has said in class. If you are able to maintain an active, critical point of view, you will find distraction to be minimal or nonexistent.

Challenge yourself with deadlines.   If you have difficulty maintaining concentration, try setting deadlines for completion of various tasks. Give yourself 1½ hours maximum to draft a one-page English composition; allow only two hours for working on your computer program. Establishing a deadline will force you to stick with the assignment. You also will be motivating and conditioning yourself to work within time limits on exams.

End on a positive note.   When you stop working on a project or long-term assignment for an evening, stop at a point at which it will be easy to pick up again. If you end on a positive note, then you will be starting with that same positive note when you return to it.

Techniques for Self-Monitoring

An important part of strengthening your concentration is increasing your own awareness of your levels of concentration. Once you are aware of your concentration level and can recognize when your focus is beginning to blur, then you can take action to control and improve the situation. Here is some advice on how to monitor, or assess and control, your concentration.

Check your own concentration.   Keep track, for a half hour or so during a particular study session, of how many times you are distracted. Each time you think about something other than what you are studying, make a mark on a piece of paper. Total up your marks at the end of the specified time. You probably will be surprised to see how many times your concentration was broken. Work on decreasing the tally. Do not keep this tally every time you read or study anything. Instead, use it once a week or so as a check on your concentration.

Learn to read your symptoms of distractibility.   When you find that your concentration is broken, stop and analyze the situation. Why did you lose your concentration? Was it an external distraction? Did an idea in the text trigger your memory of something else? Look for patterns in loss of concentration: At what time of day are you most easily distracted? Where are you studying when distractions occur? What are you studying? Use this information to adjust your semester study plan.

Keep a list of distractions.   Often, as you are reading or studying, you will think of something you should remember to do. If, for example, you are trying to remember a dental appointment you have scheduled for the next afternoon, you will find that a reminder occasionally flashes through your mind. To prevent these mental reminders from disrupting your study, keep a distractions list on a separate sheet of paper. You will find that by writing this list, you will temporarily eliminate the distractions from your memory. Use the same paper to record other ideas and problems that distract you. A list of distractions might look like this:

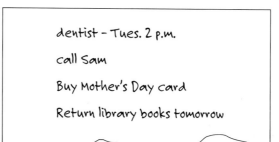

Interactive Chapter Review

Knowledge	What is distributed study?
Comprehension	Why is distributed study effective?
Application	Which five tasks are your top priorities this week? How long will each one take to accomplish? (Remember to allow a generous amount of time.) Schedule a time period in which to do each one.

Analysis	What is your best time of day to concentrate easily? How do you normally spend that time period each day? Are there any changes you need to make so that you can take full advantage of your best concentration time? If you can't make that change right now, when can you make it?
Synthesis	Set a goal for yourself that you want to accomplish in the next year. (It might relate to college or it might not.) Write four shorter-term goals that will help you achieve it. Make all your goal statements detailed and specific.
Evaluation	Is it important to you personally to have a match between your life goals and your semester schedule? Why or why not?

Further Analysis

Analyze the following situation and answer the questions below.

Shellie is a student returning to college after eight years of staying at home to raise her children. Her children attend school from 8:15 to 3:00, and they have the following after-school activities: Coltan, in third grade, has soccer practice on Mondays, Wednesdays, and Fridays from 3:15 to 5:00, and typically wants to play with his friends on the other days. Sarah, a second grader, has joined a chorus that practices on Mondays from 4:30 to 5:30. She makes play dates about twice a week. Shellie's husband, Cyrus, works from 9:00 to 5:00 each weekday and is not available to take the children to their after-school activities. Shellie wants to figure out when she can take three courses this semester and when she can put in an additional 15 hours of study outside of class time.

1. Evaluate the situation overall. What time management problems related to school and home is Shellie likely to face this semester? What suggestions would you give her for organizing how to prevent time management problems later?

2. Make a weekly schedule for Shellie to demonstrate when she can take classes, when she can devote three or four hours at a time to concentrated study, and when she can do more routine course assignments. Block out how she should spend her time each day.

3. Are there any additional resources Shellie will need in order to succeed in her first semester back to college? Be creative in considering what kinds of help she may need.

Discussion

1. What advice would you give to a student who says he cannot work productively because his concentration is frequently broken by thoughts of problems with his two girlfriends, one from his hometown and the other on campus?

2. Analyze the following situation: A student is failing her 8:00 A.M. western civilization class. She misses, on average, one class per week. She says she just cannot wake up that early. What advice would you offer?

3. What timesaving tips, not mentioned here, have you found that help to increase your efficiency?

The Work Connection

Are you working a part-time job while you attend college? A part-time job can be more than just a way to earn money for tuition and books—it can also help you gain experience related to your career goals. For example, you can gain hands-on experience related to your classroom studies, get practical advice on career planning from on-the-job mentors, and even gain entrance to a company you'd like to work for after college. Here are two Web sites that allow you to search for part-time jobs:

On-Line Career Center (Its Internet address, or URL, is: http://www.occ.com)—the On Campus page links to a list of college placement centers, corporate recruiters, and job search services.

Jobtrak (Its URL is http://jobtrak.com)—connects to 600 colleges and universities; type in your school's name and receive listings of part-time jobs and internships in your area.[1]

1. What would be an ideal part-time job for you based on your work or life goals? List at least three ways you could find such a job.

2. Visit one of the sites mentioned above, or your campus career resources center, and evaluate its usefulness to you in your part-time job search.

The Web Connection

1. Where Does the Time Go?

    http://www.ucc.vt.edu/stdysk/TMInteractive.html

    Try this online inventory prepared by Virginia Polytechnic Institute and State University to find out how you spend your time each week.

2. Study Environment Analysis

   http://www.ucc.vt.edu/stdysk/studydis.html

   Also from Virginia Tech., this site helps you evaluate the places where you study most often.

3. Seven Day Procrastination Plan

   http://www.uiowa.edu/~shs/stress4.htm

   From the Student Learning Center at the University of California at Berkeley, these tips will help you rid your life of procrastination.

Go Electronic!
For additional readings, exercises, and Internet activities, visit the Longman Study Skills Web site at:
http://www.ablongman.com/StudySkills
If you need a user name and password, please see your instructor.

Chapter 4

Managing Your Life

DO YOU KNOW?

How do you manage your finances?
How do you maintain your health?
How do you make your job work for you?
How do you manage relationships?

College is a new experience; it creates new and different demands on your lifestyle. Your schedule is different than before you began college. You face new and more challenging academic requirements and expectations. You may have new living arrangements, a new apartment or dorm, for example. You are surrounded by new, unfamiliar people, both students and professors, and possibly roommates, as well. Because you have a new schedule, you may find yourself readjusting meals, work, exercise, and sleep habits. Your social life may change, too, as you meet new friends and lose touch with old ones. Many important aspects of your life, then, are affected by college. You can make these changes work for you, or you can let them pull you down and work against your college success. This chapter discusses four keys to a successful college lifestyle: finances, health, jobs, and relationships.

Managing Your Finances

Money is always a problem; no one seems to have enough, and nearly everyone wants more. In fact, one of the primary reasons many students attend college is to get a better, more financially and personally rewarding job. Money is a major worry for many students, and financial crises can destroy concentration and limit the ability to succeed. Overwhelming financial problems are a key reason many students must drop out of college. Time spent worrying about money is time that can be better spent studying or earning needed income. The keys to getting control of your finances are assessment and planning.

Assessing Your Needs and Spending Patterns

The first step in money management is to assess your financial obligations and spending patterns. You need to find out how much money you need per month and whether your current spending patterns are sensible and realistic. Use the following chart to analyze and summarize your minimum financial needs. Estimate your costs for an entire semester or term. Be sure to list only essentials, not "would-like-to-buy" items.

Income Needed per Semester/Term

Tuition and Fees	$_____
Housing (include utilities such as the telephone, etc.)	$_____
Food	$_____
Books and Supplies	$_____
Insurance (health, car, etc.)	$_____
Transportation	$_____
Clothing/Personal Care Items	$_____
Other Essentials (child care, laundry, etc.)	$_____
Total	$_____

Now, estimate your sources of income, again for the entire semester or term. Be sure to include as savings money you earned in summer jobs.

Sources of Income per Semester/Term

Savings	$_____
Part-Time Job	$_____
Scholarships/Grants	$_____
Student Loans	$_____
Parental Support	$_____
Total	$_____

If your total income and your total expenses from the above charts do not meet, you have only two choices: you can either decrease your spending or increase your income.

Decreasing Your Spending

Decreasing your spending may be easier than it seems. Start by keeping track of everything you spend in a week, especially cash purchases. Be sure to include small items, as well as more costly ones. Keep track of parking meter fees, library fines, photocopy costs, cups of coffee purchases, and vending machine snack purchases. At the end of the week draw a line through everything that was nonessential. Did you really need that one-dollar can of soda? Could you read the recent issue of your favorite magazine in the library or bookstore rather than purchase it?

Here are some other ways to reduce your spending:

Do things yourself instead of paying others.   Do your laundry yourself instead of sending it out. Change the oil in your car yourself, or ask a friend to do it. Look for repairs and maintenance duties that you can assume responsibility for.

Prepare your own food.   Make a pizza instead of ordering one. Pack your lunch instead of buying it. Pack a snack and soda instead of purchasing them from vending machines.

Use coupons; shop for sales.   You can save considerable money using coupons for groceries and buying food and clothing when they're on sale.

Reconsider your housing arrangements.   Can you move to a less expensive apartment, even if it is farther from campus? Consider finding a roommate to share living expenses. Offer to make repairs or do maintenance (painting, shoveling snow, etc.) in exchange for reduced rent.

Avoid credit card finance charges.   Pay cash for your purchases. If you cannot afford an item, do not buy it. Avoid charging items on your credit card when you may incur hefty finance charges if your payment is late or you do not pay the balance in full.

Walk instead of drive or ride.   Bus fares, cabs, and automobile operating expenses can add up. Walk to nearby destinations or consider car pooling. If you own a car, consider whether you can sell it and use public transportation.

Seek free forms of entertainment.   Many campus activities are free, as are community-sponsored events.

Exercise 4.1	Identify at least three ways you can reduce your spending.

Increasing Your Income

The alternative to decreasing your spending is to increase your income. Here are a few sources to explore:

Student loans.   Check with the college's financial aid office to find out if you are eligible for student loans. Be sure to use them sparingly. You do not want excessive debt after graduation.

Student grants and scholarships.   Check to see if you are eligible for state, federal, or private grants and scholarships. Various social organizations, corporations, and fraternal organizations offer funding to eligible students. Check with a financial aid counselor to learn what is available.

Part-time jobs.   If you do not already have a part-time job, consider finding one. Many jobs are available on campus that allow you to schedule work hours around your class meeting times. If you already have a part-time job, consider finding a better paying one or adding additional weekend hours to your current job.

Check with your employer.   Many corporations offer tuition reimbursement programs or tuition assistance plans.

Selling possessions. Although selling your possessions should be a last resort, you can raise money from a garage sale or by selling a car, musical instrument, or sporting equipment.

Develop a Budget

Once you have equalized income and expenses, develop a weekly budget to maintain your income/expense balance. Decide exactly how much you will spend on each category: clothing, food, entertainment, and so forth. In fact, some students find it helpful to create and label envelopes for each expense category. If you have allotted 10 dollars for entertainment per week, place a 10-dollar bill in the envelope marked "Entertainment." When you have spent the 10 dollars, do not borrow from other envelopes. Instead, seek free entertainment or postpone to the following week the activity you cannot afford.

Use Credit Cards Cautiously

Credit cards are the downfall of many students. Credit card companies make it easy for college students to obtain credit cards, and they offer generous lines of credit. They also have high finance charges and penalties for late payments. It is easy to overspend using credit cards. In fact some students find themselves hopelessly in debt after applying for and freely using numerous credit cards for a semester. Here is some advice:

Apply for only one or two credit cards.   If you have more, you will be tempted to use them.

Do not carry your credit card unless you plan to use it.   This strategy will prevent impulse buying or charging small items when you run out of cash.

Pay your balance in full every month to avoid finance charges.   You can end up paying interest rates of 18 percent or higher if you do not pay the balance in full.

Protect your credit rating by paying on time.   Your credit rating is valuable; a bad credit rating can seriously impact your ability to buy a home, finance a car, or obtain additional credit cards when needed.

HOW DO YOU SEE IT?

This photo both attracts and repels the viewer. Write a paragraph that describes both responses to the image.

Exercise 4.2	Write a plan for improving your financial well-being. Include at least four actions you can take.

Maintaining Your Health

Your health is one of your most valuable assets, and you should strive to protect it. Because college requires a new schedule, it is easy to skip meals, munch too many snacks, and eat unhealthy fast foods. It is also easy to skip an exercise routine and cut yourself short on sleep. Due to the pressures of college, some students get heavily involved with drugs and alcohol abuse, as well. This section of the chapter will offer suggestions for staying healthy.

Eat Sensibly

You are what you eat. This is an old saying, but it holds much truth. What you eat most directly influences how you feel and how healthy you are. Many students are unaware that their eating habits change upon beginning college. Some students who live on campus must get accustomed to cafeteria food. Others who live in apartments must begin cooking for themselves. Still others with no change in living arrangements find themselves just too busy to think about what they eat. Eating sensibly involves analyzing what you eat, choosing healthy foods, and avoiding unhealthy habits.

Analyze Your Eating Habits

To be sure that you are eating sensibly, analyze your eating habits. It is easy to forget how many handfuls of potato chips you grabbed on your way out the door or how many candy bars you consumed during a week. And then there are those cans of soda, that midnight pizza you ordered, and those french fries you could not resist ordering. Many students think they are eating sensibly until they actually start keeping track of what they eat.

Once you are well into your schedule for the semester or term, keep track of what you eat for a week. At the end of each day, write in a log everything you ate and the approximate time you ate it. Do not forget to include vending machine purchases, midday snacks, soft drinks, etc. At the end of the week, analyze your eating patterns and answer the following questions:

- When do you tend to snack?   _____
- Are your snack foods healthy or just crunchy?   _____
- What types of foods dominate your diet?   _____
- When do you eat the most?   _____
- How frequently do you eat?   _____
- Are certain types of foods absent from your
  diet (fruits, vegetables, for example)?   _____
- Do you tend to eat when you are stressed or
  when you are studying?   _____
- What portion of your diet is fast food?   _____
- Do you eat only when you are hungry?   _____
- Is eating usually a social activity?   _____
- Is eating often a nervous activity?   _____

Eat a Balanced Diet

Different nutrition experts offer different interpretations of what it means to eat a healthy diet. Most agree, however, that all the basic food groups should be represented, in varying proportions. The basic food groups are shown in the food guide pyramid on p. 70. Developed by the U.S. Department of Agriculture, the pyramid indicates visually the recommended proportions of various food groups.

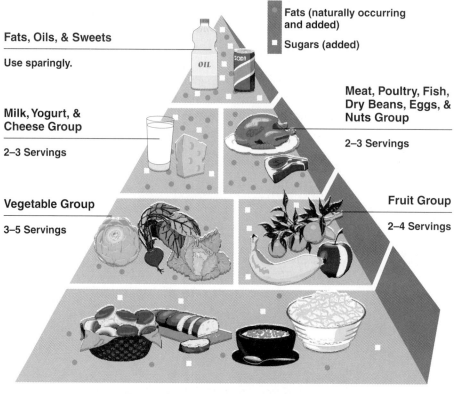

As you plan meals or select foods, keep the food pyramid in mind. If you are eating mostly fats and sweets, for example, you should consider making changes in your diet. Here are a few guidelines to follow in choosing a more healthy diet:

Use sugar and salt sparingly or moderately.   Sugar is a major source of calories, and salt is sometimes linked with high blood pressure in some individuals.

Choose foods low in saturated fats.   Choose fat-free or low-fat products (milk, yogurt, cheeses, etc.).

Drink plenty of water.   Experts recommend six to eight glasses per day, although individual needs vary, depending on the amount of foods consumed that contain water.

Include fiber in your diet.   Fiber is roughage, or bulk, and refers to the undigestible parts of plant foods that help move foods through the digestive system. Fiber may offer some protection against some forms of cancer as well as heart disease, obesity, and diabetes.

Do not depend on vitamin pills or dietary supplements to stay healthy.   It is better to eat foods that contain essential vitamins and minerals than to take supplements.

Avoid foods with empty calories.   Some foods have high nutritional value, while others, although high in calories, have very little nutritional value. Milk, for example, has a higher nutritional value than beer, and fish is more nutritionally valuable than a hot dog.

Avoid a fast-food diet.   Fast foods are convenient, tasty, and inexpensive, but many fast foods, such as fried chicken, french fries, shakes, and hamburgers, are also high in calories. Eat fast food as a special treat or as a break in your routine, rather than as a regular diet.

Eat Regularly

Because class schedules vary from day to day, it is sometimes difficult to get into a routine of having regular meals. You may have classes at noon some days, but not others. You may have an early morning lab one day a week, but not others. Try not to skip meals. Instead, try to make accommodations in your schedule. On those mornings that you have an early class, for example, take some healthy food with you, such as a granola bar and an apple, and eat them as you walk to class. Whenever possible, try to eat at the same time each day. Your body will begin to expect food at those times and you will avoid hunger pangs at other times. If you cannot develop a schedule that is the same each day of the week, then develop a separate plan for each day, and follow it consistently from week to week. For instance, if you have an evening class on Tuesday nights, then plan to have a light meal before class and a healthy snack afterward. Follow this plan every Tuesday night throughout the semester or term.

Avoid Fads: Diets, Pills, and Programs

If you find yourself gaining weight, avoid fad diets. There are many diets that claim to help you shed pounds quickly. The Zone diet and the Atkins diet are examples. Many students find that the diets work for a while, but are not a substitute for developing new and healthy eating habits. Once dieters stop following the diet, they often begin regaining the weight they lost. Medical doctors, too, caution against fad diets, warning that they may place undue stress on bodily systems. Many diet pill products claim to facilitate weight loss, but their safety and effectiveness are questionable. Take diet pills only if they are prescribed and supervised by your medical doctor. Also be cautious about diet programs or systems that provide prepackaged food. Many are quite expensive and once you return to selecting and preparing your own food, the likelihood of maintaining weight loss diminishes.

| Exercise 4.3 | Write an evaluation of your eating habits. What is healthy? What needs to change? Use the remaining sections to correct any unhealthy patterns you observed. |

Get Adequate Exercise; Focus on Physical Fitness

If you feel as if you need exercise, you probably do. Unfortunately, much of what is expected of you as a college student—attending classes, reading, writing, studying, doing homework, and researching on the Internet or in the library—requires low levels of activity. Most tasks are sedentary, requiring little or no physical activity.

Physical activity is important to your mental as well as your physical well-being. Exercise reduces the risks of heart disease and high blood pressure. It contributes to immunity from diseases, improves bone mass and weight control, and may even contribute to longevity. Exercise has other benefits as well. It may help "burn off" stress, increase mental clarity, reduce tension, and improve self-esteem. Most experts agree that an exercise routine is one of the best ways to become and stay physically fit. Here is how to develop a fitness program.

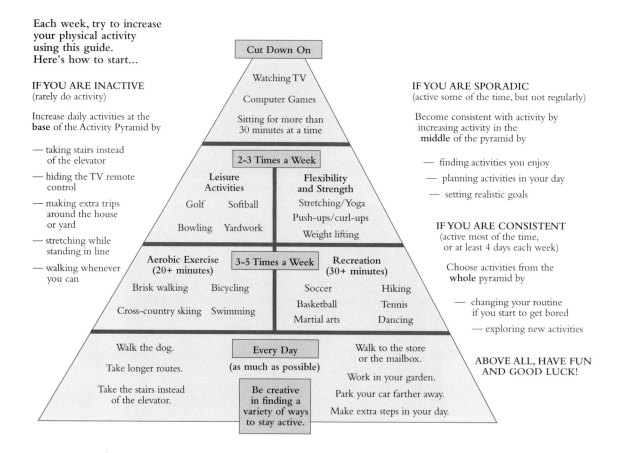

Each week, try to increase your physical activity using this guide. Here's how to start...

IF YOU ARE INACTIVE (rarely do activity)

Increase daily activities at the **base** of the Activity Pyramid by

— taking stairs instead of the elevator
— hiding the TV remote control
— making extra trips around the house or yard
— stretching while standing in line
— walking whenever you can

Cut Down On
Watching TV
Computer Games
Sitting for more than 30 minutes at a time

2-3 Times a Week
Leisure Activities
Golf   Softball
Bowling   Yardwork

Flexibility and Strength
Stretching/Yoga
Push-ups/curl-ups
Weight lifting

Aerobic Exercise (20+ minutes)
Brisk walking   Bicycling
Cross-country skiing   Swimming

3-5 Times a Week

Recreation (30+ minutes)
Soccer   Hiking
Basketball   Tennis
Martial arts   Dancing

Walk the dog.
Take longer routes.
Take the stairs instead of the elevator.

Every Day
(as much as possible)

Be creative in finding a variety of ways to stay active.

Walk to the store or the mailbox.
Work in your garden.
Park your car farther away.
Make extra steps in your day.

IF YOU ARE SPORADIC (active some of the time, but not regularly)

Become consistent with activity by increasing activity in the **middle** of the pyramid by

— finding activities you enjoy
— planning activities in your day
— setting realistic goals

IF YOU ARE CONSISTENT (active most of the time, or at least 4 days each week)

Choose activities from the **whole** pyramid by

— changing your routine if you start to get bored
— exploring new activities

ABOVE ALL, HAVE FUN AND GOOD LUCK!

Analyze your limitations, likes, dislikes, and daily schedule of work, study, and classes. Consider your limitations. If you have weak ankles, avoid ice-skating, for instance. Consider your preferences. Don't join a volleyball team if you are not competitive or do not enjoy being part of a team. On the other hand, if being part of a team will motivate you to participate, then do consider team sports. Consider what is feasible and practical within your time limitations. Teams have regular practice times; if you do not want to add another commitment to your already busy life, then choose an activity that can be done at your own convenience.

Set fitness goals.   Decide whether you want to improve your cardiovascular fitness, build strength and agility, or lose weight, for example.

Build an exercise program.   The chart shown on p. 72 provides guidelines for improving physical fitness through a variety of activity levels. Use it to get ideas of the level and types of exercise that are appropriate for you.

Begin slowly and stick with your program.   Many students make the mistake of undertaking a program that is too demanding and find themselves unable to keep up. It is best to start slowly and work up gradually to higher levels of performance. If you decide to start jogging, don't try to jog three miles the first day. Set a reasonable goal that you know you can achieve and gradually increase your distance each week. It will be helpful to choose a specific time to exercise each day, rather than to exercise whenever you have time or whenever you feel like it. If you have not chosen a team sport, try exercising with a friend; partners can motivate each other.

Get Enough Sleep

Sleep deprivation, or the lack of sleep, is a common problem among college students. Sleep has two biological functions: It conserves energy so you can perform well when awake, and it restores the body by resupplying materials that were depleted during waking hours. If you do not get enough sleep, your body and your mind do not work well. If you are sleep deprived, you may decrease your abilities to concentrate, to learn and remember, to solve problems, and to think flexibly, all essential skills for college students.

The amount of sleep needed varies among individuals. Some people need 10 hours each night; others can function well on 7 or 8 hours per night. If you feel drowsy during class, doze during class, or fall asleep while studying, these are serious warning signals that you are sleep deprived. Take action immediately to get more sleep. If you feel tired, cranky, or irritable, or if you are having trouble concentrating, you may not be getting enough sleep. Try increasing your sleeping time, and see if you notice a difference.

Some students suffer from sleeplessness: they have difficulty falling asleep. Sleep insomnia—difficulty falling or staying asleep or waking too early—is common among 20 to 40 percent of Americans. Here are a few suggestions to overcome insomnia:

Avoid eating heavy meals late in the evening before bedtime.   An active digestive system may keep you awake.

Don't drink alcohol or smoke before bedtime.   Both can keep you awake.

Relax before retiring.   Watch TV, listen to music, or chat with friends, but do not study up until the minute you want to fall asleep.

If you can't fall asleep, get up and do something.   If after a half hour or so you cannot fall asleep, get up. Return to bed a short time later.

Get some exercise.   Exercise may make you feel physically tired and may help you fall asleep. Do not exercise just before bedtime.

Avoid Substance Abuse and Addictions

Substance abuse refers to the overuse of drugs, alcohol, and tobacco. Substance abuse often leads to addictions. Addictions come in many forms, chemical or behavioral: There is drug addiction, alcohol addiction, Internet addiction, exercise addiction, money addiction (gambling, excessive shopping), and so forth. Addiction, broadly defined, is the continued involvement with a substance or activity despite negative effects. All types of addictions have four common characteristics: (1) the behavior is compulsive—an individual has an overwhelming need to perform it; (2) there is a lack of control, and the individual cannot judge when to stop; (3) the behavior always produces harmful, negative consequences such as bodily damage or academic problems; (4) the individual does not see that the behavior is responsible for the negative consequences.

Three common types of substance abuse and addictions among college students are the abuse of tobacco, drugs, and alcohol.

Tobacco

Smoking cigarettes is harmful because it may cause lung cancer, heart disease, and other illnesses. Although smoking is banned in most public places, many students still smoke. If you smoke, analyze why you smoke. What does it do for you? Weigh the benefits versus the risks. If you decide to quit, seek help from a medical doctor who can offer assistance in overcoming the addiction.

Drugs

Illegal drugs used by college students include marijuana, cocaine, heroin, amphetamines, and LSD. Because drugs stimulate the brain's neurochemistry, including its pleasure centers, they often produce a temporary high, or feeling of elation or relaxation. Often the high is followed by a "low" which may lead to further drug use. Drugs are addictive, both physically and psychologically, and once you are dependent on a drug, it is very difficult to break the habit. Addiction has serious, long-term consequences including death from an overdose, arrest, academic failure, and broken relationships with friends and family.

The best way to avoid drug addiction is to stay away from drugs completely. Do not experiment or agree to try a drug once. Also avoid socializing with classmates who do use drugs. They may encourage you to join them in substance abuse.

Alcohol

Alcohol is a legal drug, but that does not mean it is not dangerous. It is important to use alcohol responsibly, if you use it at all. Binge drinking (having numerous drinks in a short period of time) or becoming intoxicated can lead to serious illness, even death. Before you decide to drink, understand the motivation behind it. Why do people drink? Reasons include peer pressure, escape from problems and pressures, rebellion against rules, and so forth. If you do decide to drink, use the following suggestions to do so responsibly:

Be sure to eat before or while drinking.   Food slows the rate at which alcohol is absorbed into the circulatory system.

Get your own drinks.   That way you can be sure of what you are drinking, how strong your drinks are, and that no one has slipped a drug into your drink.

Do not drink if you are pregnant or think you may be pregnant.   Drinking may endanger the unborn baby and result in physical disabilities, learning problems, or intellectual impairment.

Avoid drinking games.   It is easy to lose track of how much you are drinking, and you may ingest alcohol at a rate faster than you are accustomed.

Know your limits.   Stop before you feel as if you have had too much.

Never drink and drive.   Choose a designated driver, and do not agree to ride with anyone who is drunk.

Thinking Critically
. . . About Drinking

Easy, legal access to alcohol can lead to a casual attitude toward drinking. How can you know if you are drinking too much? The relatively safe use of alcohol, sometimes referred to as social drinking, can be defined as *the infrequent, planned use of a small amount of alcohol to enhance an already positive experience,* where "infrequent" means weekly or less and "small amount" means two to three 12-ounce beers or their equivalent.

If you drink more than "socially," consider stopping for one week (while continuing your usual activities where drinking occurs) as you think about the following questions:

1. **Do the people you drink with try to pressure you into drinking?** Alcohol promotes an artificial sense of familiarity or connection among people who may not have much in common besides the drinking.

2. **Do the activities and settings where you drink seem as interesting and attractive to you when you are sober as they do when you are drinking?** People can develop a reliance on alcohol to put them at ease in awkward situations.

3. **Do you have effective ways to manage your day-to-day emotions without using alcohol?** Since life has its ups and downs, using alcohol to feel better can lead to habitual use.

4. **Do you notice changes in your energy level, motivation, alertness, or clarity of thought?** The physical and mental effects from excessive alcohol use develop so gradually that many people don't notice the changes until it is too late.

Exercise 4.4	Write a plan for improving your health. Include at least three strategies.

Managing Your Part-Time Job

Many students hold part-time jobs while attending college, usually out of necessity. They need the income to afford college. So the question is not whether you need to have a job. Instead the question becomes: Do you have the right job? Is it a job that works for or against pursing a college degree? Is it a job that will be useful after graduation in obtaining a career position?

Evaluating Your Job

The following questionnaire can be used for your current job or for any job you are considering accepting. It will help you determine whether your job is an asset or a liability.

Job Questionnaire

1. **Do work hours fit easily with your class schedule?** If you find yourself hurrying from class to your job or worrying about being late for class because of your job, your job is creating added stress and pressure. Try to change your hours to create a less hectic schedule. If you are unable to do so, consider finding another job.

2. **Are your work hours the same each week?** It is helpful to have the same work schedule each week, just as you have a class schedule that does not change, week to week. If you are working different hours each week, it is difficult to know when to study and how to arrange other commitments.

3. **Can you reduce your hours if needed with little difficulty?** If an important exam comes up or if you get behind because of the flu, for example, can you get someone to work for you? A job that is flexible enables you to pay more attention to academic priorities when necessary.

4. **Does your employer appreciate and support your college goals?** An employer who values college attendance is often more accommodating and supportive than one who does not.

5. **Is your job physically or mentally draining?** If you leave your job feeling physically tired, consider finding a job that is less demanding. A job performed in a loud, noisy, hectic environment may be more stressful than one that is not. A job in which you are constantly pressured to produce may leave you mentally exhausted. Evaluate your work environment and determine if it is draining your energy. If it is, consider finding a job that is less taxing.

6. **Does your job cost you time in travel or preparation?** If you have to commute a distance to reach your part-time job, it is costing you time and money. Or if you have to launder uniforms, or perform other tasks in preparation for your job, then you must factor that time into your consideration of whether the job is workable for you. If your job is inconvenient, consider searching for one closer to where you live or closer to campus, or that requires less of your time in preparation.

7. **Are you working during peak study times?** Most people have a time of day or evening when they are most alert and can concentrate most easily. Are you wasting those precious hours working instead of studying? If so, try to rearrange your work hours.

Finding a Job That Will Advance Your Career

Even though you may be working at a fast-food restaurant, for instance, it probably is not something you plan to do for the rest of your life. You are in college to get a better, more rewarding job. It makes sense to hold part-time jobs that will help you land a job in the career for which you are preparing. If you plan to become a nurse, why not work in a hospital or a nursing home? You will learn a great deal about how a medical facility operates and have plenty of opportunities to observe nurses at work. Your part-time job would be an asset in getting your first job as a nurse. You would possess experience that other candidates lack, giving you a competitive advantage.

To find a job related to your field of study, check with your college placement office, other students, and your professors. Also consider internships—supervised work experience in your field of study. Often, these are not well paying, but they are a definite asset when applying for a full-time job in your field.

Balancing Work and School

Regardless of the type of job you have, you have to divide your time between work and school. Use the following suggestions to balance these two segments of your life.

◆ Make sure your supervisor knows you are attending college and that your job helps pay for it. He or she may be more understanding and helpful if he or she knows you are a serious student.

◆ Try to find a coworker who may be willing to switch work hours or take your hours if you need extra time to study.

◆ If possible, try to build a work schedule around your class schedule. For example, if you have an eight-o'clock class on Tuesday mornings, try not to work until midnight on Monday night.

◆ Allow study time for each class. Make sure you have time between class sessions to do homework and complete assigned readings. For example, if you have a Tuesday/Thursday class, make sure you have some study time between the two sessions.

Exercise 4.5	Write an evaluation of your part-time job. Conclude with a sentence indicating whether it is beneficial in preparing you for your intended career.

Managing Relationships

College means new and changing relationships. You will develop new relationships with classmates, professors, and campus personnel. Your relationship with your family and existing friends may change as well. Managing new and changing relationships often requires new skills. This section of the chapter will offer advice on developing new friendships, improving your communication skills, managing conflict, and managing online relationships.

Seek New Friendships

College provides a wonderful opportunity to get to know people from new places and unknown cultures. Make a deliberate effort to get to know your classmates. Commuter students, in particular, tend to insulate themselves from those around them with friends from high school, their neighborhood, or their community. In doing so, they miss the chance to broaden their horizons and make new friendships. One of the best ways to build new friendships is to get to know someone in each class. Another way is to participate in campus activities. Join a club, help out in a silent auction to support a local charity, or participate in a walkathon, for example.

Improve Your Communication Skills

Relationships depend on communication. Communication can occur through words, body language, gestures, posture, and so forth. To become a better communicator, focus on becoming a better listener, learning to share information, and using "I" messages.

Becoming a Better Listener

To be a good friend, parent, partner, or employee, you have to know how to listen. Listening means more than paying attention: it means responding. Use the following suggestions to become a better listener in your interpersonal relationships:

Don't just listen—respond verbally or nonverbally.   Let the speaker know you are listening by reaffirming what has been said, asking questions, or showing interest through facial expressions.

Maintain eye contact.   It is easy to let your mind wander when someone else is talking, especially if the person is long-winded or talking about something not of high interest to you. Maintaining eye contact will force you to pay attention and will reassure the speaker that you are paying attention.

Pay attention to the emotional message, as well as to the intellectual one.   Observe how the speaker is feeling about what he or she is saying. If appropriate, respond with an emotional message. You might say, "That sounds so frustrating" or "You must have been very disappointed," for example, if you sense that the speaker is expressing frustration or disappointment.

Learn to Share Information About Yourself with Others

To get along well with others and to develop new relationships, you have to be willing to share information about yourself with others. If you want to get to know another person, you have to allow him or her to get to know you. You certainly do not want to share your innermost beliefs and feelings with everyone immediately, but you can start slowly, first by sharing facts about yourself—family history, background, career goals, and so forth. As a relationship develops, trust builds, and you will feel more comfortable sharing more personal information.

Use "I" Messages

You can improve your communication with others by using "I" messages—messages that directly express your feelings. If a friend disappoints you, you may be tempted to say, "You disappointed me." It is more effective to use an "I" message—"I am disappointed." "You" messages place the listener on the defensive and make it seem as if you are blaming him or her. "I" messages, on the other hand, allow you to accept responsibility for your feelings. "I" messages should be specific and direct and, when appropriate, include reasons. Here is an example: If you are annoyed at a friend who is always late, you might say, "When you are late, I get upset because I end up wasting valuable time waiting."

Exercise 4.6	Evaluate your communication skills, identifying both your strengths and weaknesses.

Managing Conflict

Conflicts occur when the behavior or intentions of one person interfere with those of another. A conflict may occur if a classmate dominates the discussion, not allowing other students to participate. A conflict may occur with a roommate who leaves her clothes all over the floor, preventing the other roommate from being neat and organized. When individuals discuss a conflict, an argument may occur. Conflicts and arguments involve issues, but they also often involve emotions and feelings. Since conflicts can destroy relationships, it is important to learn to deal with conflicts and arguments. Use the following suggestions:

Avoid hasty judgment.   It is best to think through a conflict and approach the individual when you are calm and collected.

Allow the issues to become clear.   It is often wise to wait until a conflict is obvious, apparent, and recognized by both parties. Both are more likely to be willing to discuss the conflict and seek solutions when it is clear that there is a problem.

When you initiate a discussion to resolve a conflict, identify the issue.   Make it clear exactly what behaviors you want to discuss. Be as specific as possible about your criticisms.

Avoid angry, hostile outbursts.   If a discussion escalates to anger and hostility, stop the discussion. Postpone it until a later time.

If you have second thoughts about saying something, don't say it.   You can never take back what you have said. It is better to wait than to be sorry.

Managing Online Relationships

The Internet has become an important part of our lives. It is a primary source of information, but it is also a way to communicate and develop new relationships. Here are a few tips for managing online relationships:

Don't reveal confidential information online.   It is sometimes possible for others to access your e-mail messages. As a general rule, do not write anything in an e-mail message or contribute anything to an online discussion group or message board that you would not want published in your campus newspaper, for instance.

Be cautious about online friendships.   Many people falsely represent themselves. Although you may think you are exchanging e-mail with a student on another college campus, you may actually be communicating with a teenager, a criminal, or even a child. If you agree to meet someone you have met online, be sure to do so in a public place.

Do not use your employer's online account for personal e-mail.   Some employers routinely screen e-mail, and it is not considered confidential.

Use proper netiquette (etiquette for the Internet).   There are numerous rules and conventions that you are expected to follow in online communications. For example, typing a message in all capital letters is considered inappropriate and is similar to shouting when talking with another person. For more information on netiquette, consult the following Web site: http://www.fau.edu/netiquette/net/elec.html.

Don't respond immediately to e-mail that angers you or is disturbing. Take time to cool down. If you respond immediately, you may say things you later wish you had not said.

Working Together

Two students should role-play an argument. Two other students should critique the argument techniques used.

Interactive Chapter Review

Knowledge	Name at least five strategies you can use to improve your financial well-being.
Comprehension	Explain why credit cards can be dangerous.
Application	Write a list of everything you ate today. Identify the position of each item on the food pyramid.
Analysis	Refer to the diagram on p. 72. List the suggestions that seem feasible. Which seem unworkable for you?
Synthesis	List three similarities between drug and alcohol abuse or addiction.
Evaluation	List five ways that attending college has altered your lifestyle. Evaluate how well you have coped with each change.

Further Analysis

Analyze the following situation and answer the questions that follow.

Shawn has never been physically active. In high school he didn't enjoy physical education classes because he didn't have the fitness level or skills needed for competitive activities like basketball and soccer. Now 20 years old and a sophomore in college, Shawn typically drives his car to campus rather than walks the 10 blocks from his apartment. His idea of a complete meal is a large pepperoni pizza delivered to his door, washed down with a large soda. To relax, he plays computer games. Recently Shawn heard about the adverse health effects of a sedentary lifestyle and he no longer wants to be a couch potato.[1]

1. Now that Shawn wants to have a more active and healthy lifestyle, how should he begin?

2. What types of activities should he consider?

3. Make suggestions for improving his diet.

Discussion

1. How do you define physical fitness? What criteria would you use to measure a person's physical fitness?

2. What are the major obstacles that college students face in deciding to eat the right foods?

3. If someone is 75 years old and eats a high-fat, high-sugar diet, but has never been sick or had major surgery, should the person change his or her eating habits?

4. What could public schools do to encourage children to develop a more healthy lifestyle?

The Work Connection

Employers recognize the relationship between problems employees have on the job and at home. Accidents, decreased productivity, friction between employees, lateness, and absenteeism are considered possible indicators that problems outside the workplace are affecting job performance. Many companies have set up Employee Assistance Programs, programs that provide workers with guidance in finding the right professional help for problems with family and relationships, finances, legal issues, emotions, substance abuse, and health. The EAP services are usually provided free of charge because employers have found that they actually save money when their workers are able to focus on the job. A Web site at http://interlock.org/whateap.html provides an overview of EAP programs.

1. Visit the site mentioned above or find out through the Student Assistance Program (SAP) at your college about the resources offered. Are there resources available that might help you or that might have been helpful to you or your family at some point in your life?

2. Employee and Student Assistance Programs guide people to a wide range of helpful services. How might someone in your chosen career field provide services for employees or students referred by an EAP or SAP?

The Web Connection

1. Success and Happiness Attributes Questionnaire

   http://front.csulb.edu/success/shaqCares.htm

   Try this online assessment from California State University, Long Beach. It could lead you to success in school, your job, and life.

2. Health 101

   http://www.intelihealth.com/IH/ihtIH?t=14198&p=~br,IHW|~st,24479|~r,WSIHW 000|~b,*|

   Health information especially geared to college students is presented on this trusted medical site.

3. Ten Ways to Save Money

   http://www.savvystudent.com/page14.html

   From The Savvy Student, great ideas on how to save and budget your money.

Go Electronic!
For additional readings, exercises, and Internet activities, visit the Longman Study Skills Web site at:
http://www.ablongman.com/StudySkills
If you need a user name and password, please see your instructor.

Chapter 5

Managing Stress

DO YOU KNOW?

What is stress?
How do you know if you are feeling stress?
What causes stress?
How can you change your thinking to reduce stress?
How can you change your habits to reduce stress?

Do you often feel worried and upset about your classes, your job, or your family? Do you often have headaches or feel tired? Do you feel that there is more to do than you can handle? If so, you are probably experiencing stress. Stress is a common problem for college students because college represents a dramatic change in lifestyle—socially, economically, and academically—and changes in lifestyle often affect people psychologically, emotionally, and even physically. Many college students feel pressure to earn good grades, to keep their part-time jobs, and to meet family obligations. These pressures also contribute to stress.

What Is Stress?

Stress can be defined as a natural response to the expectations, demands, and challenges of life. When you are asked to perform more (or better) than you think you can, stress may result. For example, stress can occur when you don't have enough time to study for an upcoming exam (you are expected to study but you cannot find enough time). Stress occurs when your boss wants you to work for her on the weekend so she can take it off. (She expects you to work, but you cannot give up study time to work extra hours.) You can respond to stressful situations (called stressors) either positively or negatively. You can use stress to motivate yourself to get started on a project and to focus on using your skills and talents to meet the goals you have set. In fact, some people thrive on pressure; they perceive it as a challenge. Others perceive stress as a threat. Experienced this way, stress can interfere with the ability to function mentally, emotionally, and physically.

Everyone can learn to handle stressful situations more effectively. The purpose of this chapter is to learn to recognize the symptoms and causes of stress and learn methods of reducing and preventing stress.

Symptoms of Stress

The first step in controlling stress is to recognize its symptoms. A symptom is a sign or signal that stress exists. Usually it is not the cause (source) of stress. Overall, stress is an attitude that you are "losing it"—that you can't keep up. There are both emotional and physical symptoms of stress:

Emotional Symptoms:

◆ Feeling rushed or mentally exhausted
◆ Difficulty concentrating
◆ Short-temperedness
◆ Feeling listless, unfocused

Physical Symptoms:

◆ Headaches
◆ Fatigue
◆ Queasiness or indigestion
◆ Weight loss or weight gain

The Stress Questionnaire on page 86 will help you identify symptoms of stress you may be experiencing. Complete the questionnaire now before continuing with the chapter.

Causes of Stress

In order to harness stress to work for you, you need to recognize which situations provoke a stressful response. Ask yourself: "What events or situations in my life today am I responding to with a feeling of stress?" In some cases, the situations are obvious. If so, write them on paper. Seeing them in print is the first step to making them manageable. Other times, however, you may be unable to point to specific situations. Following are some common stressors to consider.

Common Stressors

Any single event or situation by itself may not cause stress, but if you experience it at the same time as several other mildly disturbing situations, all of a sudden you may be under stress. For instance, getting a low grade on a biology lab report by itself may not be stressful, but if it occurs the same week during which your car "died," you argued with a close friend, and you discovered your checking account is overdrawn, then it may contribute to stress. Here are a few common sources of stress.

Major Life Changes.   Every time you make a major change in your life you are susceptible to stress. Major changes include a new job or career, marriage, divorce, birth of a child, or the death of someone close. Beginning college is one major life change. Try

Stress Questionnaire

Respond to each of the following statements by checking Yes, No, or Sometimes on the lines provided and then adding up the total for each column.

	Yes	No	Sometimes
1. I feel as if I don't have enough time in a week to get everything done.	❑	❑	❑
2. Having at least one healthy meal per day at which I can sit down and relax is unusual.	❑	❑	❑
3. I worry about money regularly.	❑	❑	❑
4. I have recently begun to smoke or use alcohol, or I have increased my use of either.	❑	❑	❑
5. I have more conflicts and disagreements with friends than I used to.	❑	❑	❑
6. I am having difficulty staying involved with social or religious activities.	❑	❑	❑
7. I seem to get colds and other minor illnesses (headaches, upset stomachs) more frequently.	❑	❑	❑
8. I find myself confused or listless more than usual.	❑	❑	❑
9. I resent the time I have to spend with routine chores.	❑	❑	❑
10. My usual level of physical activity or exercise has decreased.	❑	❑	❑
11. I am losing or gaining weight.	❑	❑	❑
12. I seldom get six to eight hours of sleep at night.	❑	❑	❑
13. I am having difficulty staying in contact with friends and family.	❑	❑	❑
14. I seldom find time to confide in friends.	❑	❑	❑
15. Small problems seem overwhelming.	❑	❑	❑
16. I seldom find time to do some fun things each week.	❑	❑	❑
17. I find myself unable to meet deadlines and am losing track of details (appointments, chores, promises to friends, and so on).	❑	❑	❑
18. I have difficulty concentrating on my assignments.	❑	❑	❑
19. I spend time worrying about grades.	❑	❑	❑

	Yes	No	Sometimes
20. I am more short-tempered or more impatient than I used to be.	☐	☐	☐
Total	———	———	———

If you answered "Yes" to more than four or five items, or "Sometimes" to more than six or seven items, you may be experiencing more stress than you realize. Evaluate the pattern of your responses. Look at the questions to which you answered "Yes" or "Sometimes." Some questions deal with physical habits; others focus on organizational skills. By checking your answers, you will get an idea of your own stress indicators.

HOW DO YOU SEE IT?

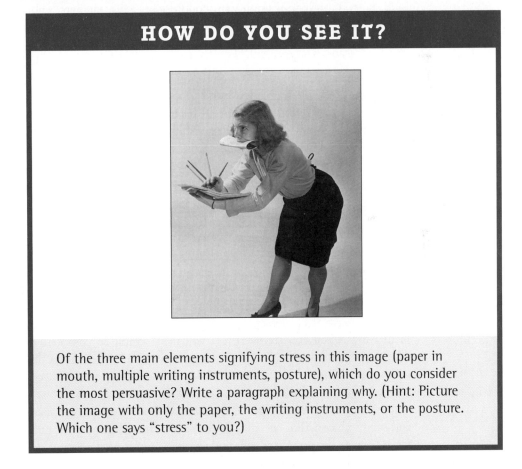

Of the three main elements signifying stress in this image (paper in mouth, multiple writing instruments, posture), which do you consider the most persuasive? Write a paragraph explaining why. (Hint: Picture the image with only the paper, the writing instruments, or the posture. Which one says "stress" to you?)

not to create multiple life changes, which multiply the potential for stress, especially during the semester.

Academic Course Work.   Your college classes may provoke stress, especially if you don't have enough time to prepare for each adequately. If you attend a class knowing you are not prepared or that you are underprepared, you are likely to experience stress. If you follow a time schedule, as suggested in Chapter 3, you can be sure to get all assignments done on time.

If you find that you have overestimated the number of courses you can handle in one semester, consider dropping or withdrawing from one. Colleges have different deadlines for these procedures. If you receive financial aid, be sure to consult the Financial Aid Office before making changes in your course schedule.

Jobs.   Because you probably depend on your job to pay part or all of your college expenses, your job is important to you and you feel pressure to perform well in order to keep it. Some jobs are more stressful than others. Those, for example, in which you work under constant time pressure tend to be stressful. Jobs that must be performed in loud, noisy, crowded, or unpleasant conditions—a hot kitchen, a noisy machine shop, and so forth—with coworkers who don't do their share can be stressful. Consider changing jobs if you are working in stressful conditions.

Relationships.   Family, friends, and spouses can all be sources of stress if your relationship with them is troubled. Overly directive parents, self-centered or demanding friends, or insensitive spouses can all become sources of stress. In particular, the demands of college may test some relationships, especially if the time demands are not understood or if the family member does not share your commitment to college. To alleviate as much stress as possible in personal relationships, be sure to communicate to those close to you your commitment to college and the time demands involved.

Financial Problems.   Paying your tuition bill, meeting car payments, and paying rent and credit card bills create stress for many of us. Developing a weekly and monthly budget and sticking to it may help eliminate stress in this category.

Lack of Sleep.   Lack of sleep, usually caused by existing time pressures, can increase stress. Small problems may seem insurmountable when you are overtired or suffering from long-term sleep deprivation. Actually, you may even waste time trying to complete a task when you are overtired; you may be able to complete it in half the time when your mind is fresh. Try to get enough sleep each night. You can't save up sleep for when you will need it and you cannot regularly make up for lost sleep.

Health, Fitness, and Nutrition.   Poor health or poor nutrition can increase existing stress and can produce additional stress. If you're not eating regular meals of healthy, nutritional foods, you are not providing your body with the fuel it needs to remain alert and active.

Try the following suggestions:

◆ Eat balanced meals. Avoid heavy doses of fats and sugars. They may cause you to feel stuffy and lethargic.
◆ Don't skip meals.

◆ Use healthy snacks as a midafternoon "pick-me-up" when you feel your energy faltering.

◆ Avoid empty calories. Foods that have a high calorie count but little nutritional value are usually not healthy.

◆ Include regular exercise in your daily schedule. Even a brief, brisk walk will restore your energy level and clear your mind.

◆ For more information on health, fitness, and nutrition, refer to Chapter 4, pp. 68–76.

Exercise 5.1	Rate each of the following causes of stress as High, Medium, or Low.

Source	Rating
Job	_____
Friends	_____
Family (spouse)	_____
Academic Coursework	_____
Health, Fitness, and Nutrition	_____
Financial Problems	_____
Sleep	_____

Compare your ratings with those of a classmate. Discuss means of eliminating or controlling each stressor.

Changing Your Thinking to Reduce Stress

While some people struggle with the kinds of situations listed as common stressors, others respond resourcefully to them. They don't feel daunted or overwhelmed by the challenge of getting things done. Instead, they feel motivated and even determined to succeed. What makes the difference? The people who rise to the challenge think differently about the situation. *The situation is the same;* it is the individual's response to the stressors that is different. For example, one student who has three midterm exams in one week may feel stressed, pressured, and anxious. Another student, however, faced with the same situation may regard it as a week of focused, intensive study which will leave her freer in following weeks to pursue other activities. You may not be able to change your environment in order to relieve stress, but you can always change how you think.

Accept Responsibility

People who are motivated by potentially stressful situations accept responsibility for completing a task—but only if the responsibility is actually theirs. Sometimes it isn't. To figure out whether you are responsible for a task, you can ask yourself these questions:

◆ Do I agree that this task is necessary?
◆ Am I the right person to perform this task?
◆ Do I have (or can I get) the resources I need to succeed in this task?

For example, suppose you are organizing a study group before final exams. Ask yourself:

◆ Is it necessary? *Yes, I want to do well on the exam and we all can benefit when we compare notes and exchange information.*
◆ Am I the right person? *Yes, I haven't organized a group this year although I've been invited to several.*
◆ Do I have the resources? *Yes, I can contact people during class. My living room is large enough for six people to work comfortably.*

When you can answer "yes" to all three of these questions, you have accepted responsibility for completing the task. This first step is crucial before considering the next thinking patterns. If you answer "no" to any question, you can discuss your reservations with the person who assigned the task and figure out a solution. Or, as is sometimes the case, you may find that although the responsibility really isn't yours, you agree to do the task anyway for various reasons: to preserve a relationship, to avoid potential complications or consequences, to move on to more important things, and so on. Coming to understand that you are making a *personal choice* to take on the responsibility for doing a task will then allow you to use the next three strategies to help change your stress responses.

Focus on Doing the Best You Can

People who respond well to stressors focus on doing the best they can, not on how they might fail. It's not that the potential problems have disappeared, it's that successful people believe in the possibility of success. Once success is seen as possible, you can focus your attention on completing the task to the best of your ability. For example, instead of saying, "I cannot do this assignment on time," leave out the word "not." Ask yourself: "How *can* I finish this assignment on time?" and "How well *can* I do this assignment?"

Before beginning an assignment or before you walk into an exam room, stop, close your eyes, and imagine yourself beginning, successfully working on, and then completing the task. By visualizing success, you will give yourself a positive frame of mind in which to begin work. If you get discouraged midway through a task, stop and visualize yourself successfully completing the task. Sports psychologists encourage athletes to visualize themselves making successful plays, earning points, and winning the game. Use visualization to help you win the study game!

Focus on the Benefits of Achieving the Goal

People who handle stressors well focus on the benefits of achieving the goal, not the consequences of failing to achieve it. Instead of asking, "What's going to happen if I can't work this weekend? Will my boss be mad at me? Am I going to lose my job?" consider "What can I gain from working this weekend?" (Remember, if you really couldn't work this weekend, you would not have accepted responsibility for doing so. You would have talked to your boss about it and worked out a solution together.) Sometimes the benefits will be for other people, as in "How will my coworker benefit if I work this weekend while the boss is away?" Notice that by considering benefits, you focus on the positive consequences of completing the task.

Exercise 5.2	Complete each of the following steps to analyze your response to stress.

1. Choose a three-day period. At least one day should be a class day, and one a weekend day without classes.

2. Six or seven times throughout the day, stop and jot down hassles, annoyances, aggravations, conflicts, worries, and upsets that just occurred and the situations in which they occurred. Often, your answer may be "none." At other times, however, you will begin to identify stressors.

3. After the third day, look over your list for patterns. In what situations did you experience stress? You may, for example, discover that most stress occurred on the job, or that most stress occurred while studying or while attending classes.

4. Once you have identified your current stressors, choose one. Write brief answers to the following questions:

> Do I accept responsibility for the task? Explain your thinking.

> How can I focus on doing my best?

> What are the benefits of achieving the goal?

Then think about how you will respond more effectively to a similar situation in the future.

Exercise 5.3	Compare your three-day stress log described in Exercise 5.2 with that of a classmate. Exchange logs and look for patterns. What stressors do you share?

Changing Your Habits to Reduce Stress

This section describes a number of different strategies for reducing stress by changing your habits. Experiment to discover which will work for you.

Leave Work Problems at Work

Do not bring on-the-job problems home with you. If you bring a problem home with you it becomes part of your whole life and it tends to magnify in importance. Instead, discuss the problem with a coworker or with your boss before you leave; then leave the problem at work. Face it again, if necessary, when you return.

Similarly, do not study during breaks at work; you need the breaks to relieve the stress of the job. Do not make a habit of making work-related phone calls during breaks between classes. Doing so only creates more pressure to use every spare moment productively.

Thinking Critically
... About Accomplishing Tasks

When you feel overwhelmed about the number of tasks you have to accomplish, take five minutes to think through the following questions. Your responses will form a plan to eliminate the stress you are experiencing.

- How many different activities or concerns am I thinking about right now? If there are five or more, make a list of all your concerns. If there are four or fewer, just list them mentally.

- Which activities or tasks can be done later? Jot yourself a note to relieve your mind about these.

- Of the activities that need to be done now or today, which one is the most crucial to the priorities I have set for myself? (Your priorities may be for this week, this term, or your life goals. It depends on your situation.)

- How much time will this task take, approximately? Be generous in your estimate. Then take that much time to do the task.

Control Your Own Time

Take charge of your time; do not permit friends, roommates, or neighbors to consume it. Make clear when study times are planned, and don't allow interruptions. If people call or visit during those times, be brief and firm; insist that you must get back to work. If friends call to invite you to a movie, explain that this is a study hour and suggest a time that is convenient for you. Stay in control of your time. Apply the same firmness to family members who want you to drive them somewhere or to parents who want you to run errands. Suggest an alternate time when you can fulfill their requests.

Use a yearly calendar or computer organizer to keep track of appointments and other commitments. Getting control of your time will help you feel in control of your life. For more suggestions on time management, refer to Chapter 3.

Give Yourself a Break

Constantly pushing yourself compounds stress. Take a break; give yourself some downtime or personal space in which you can just be you. During your break you are not a student, not an employee, not a parent, not the one who cooks dinner. Just be yourself. Think of something you enjoy—a special song, a favorite place, a friend whom you miss. Your break can be brief: Between one and five minutes is often sufficient to slow you down, provide relief from your routine, and reduce stress.

Interact with Others

Sharing your concerns and problems with others and listening to their concerns will help you put your problems in perspective and realize that others experience similar problems. Problems seem smaller and more manageable once you talk about them. Sometimes just a brief phone call to a friend is all that is needed to allow you to refocus.

Learn How to Say "No"

Friends, family, and employers often place numerous demands upon you. Try to protect your valuable time and energy by saying "no" to unreasonable requests and expectations.

Help Someone Out

If you spend all your time thinking about yourself and the amount of work you have, your problems will grow out of proportion. Refocus your attention occasionally on others. Spend time helping someone else when you can afford the time. You might shop for an elderly relative, tutor a classmate, or volunteer at a soup kitchen or animal shelter. Once your mind is off yourself and you see others with problems, your problems will seem more manageable.

Get Some Exercise

Build an exercise routine into your weekly schedule. Exercise can reduce stress by enabling your body to release the hormone norepinephrine, which promotes increased awareness, and endorphins, which give you a sense of well-being. Fresh air is also helpful in reducing stress. It stimulates your mind and body and gives you a sense of well-being. Take a brisk walk outdoors when you feel stress mounting.

Make Fewer Choices

Stress tends to increase when you are responsible for making a large number of decisions. To reduce stress, eliminate some of the daily decisions that consume your time and energy. For example, instead of having to decide each evening what time to set your alarm clock for, get up at the same time each weekday. Instead of having to decide what to cook, eat, or order for dinner each night, decide the menus for the whole week all at once. Alternatively, make every Monday pasta night, every Tuesday chicken night, and so forth. If you have fewer decisions to make, you'll feel less pressured and will have more time to think about important decisions you must make.

Control Your Environment

Arrange your living and study environments so that you experience as little stress as possible. First, reduce the clutter. Get organized and keep everything in its place. You will feel as if you are in more control of your life and you won't waste time looking for misplaced objects or devoting hours to cleanup blitzes. Second, create a study area. Equip it with everything you need to complete assignments: stapler, pens, blank disks, dictionary, a bottle of water, and so forth. Since you have created this area, you will feel in control of it.

Change Your Study Habits

To reduce stress, you may need to change some of your study habits. For example, if you tend to go to classes unprepared—without having finished all the required reading, for example—you are creating stress for yourself. You will feel guilty and worry during class that the instructor may ask you a question you cannot answer. Make it a rule that you will always complete reading assignments before the class for which they are due. Successful study habits are explained throughout this book; think about which habits you need to change to stay on top of your course load.

Seek the Help of Others

If you are unable to manage the stressors you face, seek the help of counselors in the Campus Counseling Center. Often a skilled counselor can ask you the right questions to help you solve a stressful situation or help you examine a problem from a number of different perspectives.

Working Together

Working with a classmate, prepare individual plans for the next two weeks to identify the sources of stress you are most likely to encounter. Plan how you can respond more effectively to stressful situations. Your plan should include both changes to thinking and changes to habits. Then analyze each other's plans and offer suggestions for improvement.

Interactive Chapter Review

Knowledge	List at least four different symptoms of stress.
Comprehension	What are three important ways to think that will help reduce or eliminate stress?
Application	Reread the headings in the section "Changing Your Habits to Reduce Stress" on pp. 91–94. Think about two to three habits you can change to reduce or eliminate stress in your life. What will you do to change them?
Analysis	If you knew a person who often feels overwhelmed by the number of tasks to be accomplished, what course of action would you recommend to him or her?
Synthesis	What time management techniques from Chapter 3 can help reduce or eliminate stress? How can these techniques help with stress?
Evaluation	As this chapter has indicated, some people experience stress as a real problem, and others experience it as an interesting challenge. How do you tend to experience stress? Give three examples from your life to back up your statement.

Further Analysis

Analyze the following situation and answer the questions below.

A freshman business student is returning to college after eight years of working full time and is taking the following courses: writing, mathematics, economics, and introduction to business management. She has recently started her own business, a manicure shop which she opens two evenings a week and weekends. She is the single parent of a six-year-old son who has just begun kindergarten. This student is frustrated with college and feels constantly under stress. When she is working in her shop, she worries about her classes. When she studies, she finds herself thinking about how to get more clients for her shop. She feels guilty about not spending enough time with her son.

1. Analyze this student's source(s) of stress.

2. Is her return to college well-timed?

3. What time management strategies would you suggest she use?

4. How can she reduce the stress she feels?

Discussion

Students who must work 20 to 30 hours per week in order to afford college often experience academic difficulty. They face a catch-22 situation: If they reduce their work hours, they cannot pay their tuition, and if they reduce their course load, they lose their financial aid. What stress reduction techniques might these students explore?

The Work Connection

Employers find the ability to manage stress so important to job success that they have devised ways to measure this ability. One method is through different kinds of job interviews. Among the techniques used by human relations managers, two types are the *behavior interview* and the *stress interview.* The behavior interview involves asking the job candidate to describe how he or she has handled particular stressful situations in the past. The stress interview is designed to see how candidates handle an interviewer who deliberately creates a stress-provoking interaction. The first type focuses on how the potential employee has handled stress in the past, and the second on how the candidate handles stress in the present.[1]

1. Think about a stressful experience you handled well. Describe this experience as if talking to a potential employer about a demonstration of your ability to manage stress.

2. Think about someone you know who seems particularly good at handling stressful situations. What strategies do they use to remain calm and reasonable? (If you're not sure, ask them.) Make a list of at least three strategies you can develop.

The Web Connection

1. Online Screening for Anxiety

   http://www.med.nyu.edu/Psych/screens/anx.html

   Sometimes what seems like stress can really be anxiety. Check your symptoms with this online questionnaire prepared by the New York University School of Medicine.

2. Strategies for Coping with Stress

   http://www.twu.edu/o-sl/counseling/SH007.html

   The Texas Women's University Counseling Center offers some excellent tips for dealing with stress.

3. Top 10 Strategies for Wildy Effective Stress Management

   http://www.unc.edu/depts/unc_caps/MStress.html

   Another great list of tips for coping with stress from the University of North Carolina at Chapel Hill.

Go Electronic!
For additional readings, exercises, and Internet activities, visit the Longman Study Skills Web site at:
http://www.ablongman.com/StudySkills
If you need a user name and password, please see your instructor.

Chapter 6

Communication Skills for the Classroom

DO YOU KNOW?

How can you listen carefully and critically?
How can you participate effectively in class?
How can you ask and answer questions effectively?
What should you do to work productively with classmates on projects?
How can you make effective oral presentations?

Success in college depends on your ability to read, write, and think effectively, but it also depends on your ability to communicate with others. In many of your classes you participate by listening to and responding to classmates in class discussions. You must ask intelligent questions in class and be prepared to answer those asked by your instructor. You must also be able to communicate with classmates in both formal and informal situations. Finally, you must be able to make oral presentations. While each of these skills is important for college success, they are also important for career success. Research studies have demonstrated that listening and speaking are our primary means of communication. One study concluded that listening occupies 53 percent of college students' communication time and speaking occupies 16 percent (reading and writing, together, then, occupy 31 percent).[1]

In most jobs, you must be able to express your ideas clearly, listen and respond to the ideas of coworkers and supervisors, and work together productively in small groups, discussing problems and brainstorming solutions.

Listening Critically

As you listen to class lectures and class discussions, one task is to absorb and learn the information presented. See Chapter 13 for information on taking lecture notes and developing recall clues to learn them. However, another equally important task is to think critically about what your instructor presents and what other students say in class.

Common Pitfalls in Critical Listening

Avoid the following barriers to critical listening:

Avoid Closed Mindedness

In college you will hear many ideas that you disagree with and you will meet people who have different values than you do. What others may feel is right, wrong, or important in life may not be the same as what you feel. Avoid prejudging a speaker or his or her announced topic. Keep an open mind. Delay your judgment until the speaker has finished and you understand fully the speaker's message and intentions.

Avoid Selective Listening

When listening to ideas with which they disagree, some listeners hear only what they want to hear. That is, they pay attention to ideas they agree with and may misinterpret or even ignore ideas with which they disagree. Selective listening often occurs when discussing ethnic, national, religious, or moral issues. To avoid selective listening, first recognize your own biases; be aware that you feel strongly about an issue. Make a deliberate effort to understand the speaker's viewpoint even though you disagree with it. Distract yourself from your feelings by taking notes or writing an outline.

Avoid Oversimplifying Difficult or Complex Ideas

While it is tempting to ignore details or to simplify complicated ideas, try to get the full picture, including details, reasons, and supporting evidence. For example, if you were listening to an argument advocating the use of force to control world terrorism, the speaker's details would be extremely important. You would need to know when, why, how much, and by whom such torture would be performed in order to evaluate the argument.

Avoid Judging the Speaker Instead of the Message

Be sure to focus on the message, not the person delivering the message. Try not to be distracted by mannerisms, dress, or the method of delivery (pauses, tone of voice, grammatical errors, and so forth).

Exercise 6.1	Working with a classmate, identify at least three or four topics of class discussion for which it would be important to keep an open mind and avoid selective listening.

Evaluating the Message

Once you have completely understood a speaker's message, use the following suggestions to evaluate it:

1. Identify the speaker's main point or position on an issue. The speaker may identify it by using key phrases such as "The issue is . . ." or "What I am trying to say is . . ."
2. Develop a mental outline of the speaker's message.

3. Identify whether the speaker has supported his or her main point or position with reasons and evidence.

4. Identify unanswered questions or opposing viewpoints.

Exercise 6.2	For a class discussion in one of your other courses, identify each of the following. a. Main point or issue b. Reasons and evidence c. Unanswered questions or opposing viewpoints

---

Participating in Class

Participation in class means more than being interested, prepared, and alert in class. To participate you must ask and answer questions and be involved in class discussions. Participating in class, even if it is not required, has a number of advantages. First, participation will help you concentrate and stay focused. It will also make the instructor notice you and identify you as a serious, thoughtful student. Participating will help you learn; you will remember concepts and ideas that you have spoken about. Finally, participation gives you practice in speaking before groups—a skill you will definitely need in the workplace.

Class participation requires planning and preparation. Useful participation usually involves much more than offering an idea that comes to mind during a class discussion.

Preparing for Class Discussions

Preparing for a class discussion demands more time and effort than does getting ready for a lecture class. In a lecture class, most of your work comes *after* the class, editing your notes and using the recall clue system to review them. The opposite is true for discussion courses, where most of your work is done *before* you go to class. You must spend considerable time reading, evaluating, and making notes. The following suggestions will help you get ready for a discussion class.

Read the Assignment

Usually a class discussion is about a particular topic. Frequently, instructors give textbook or library reading assignments that are intended to give you some background information. The reading assignments are also meant to start you thinking about a topic, show you different points of a view about an issue, or indicate some aspects of a problem. Read carefully the material assigned. Do not just skim through it as you might for a lecture class. Instead, read the assignment with the purpose of learning all the material. Mark and highlight important ideas as you read.

Ask Critical Questions

Class discussions seldom center around factual information. Instead, they usually focus on the application, analysis, synthesis, and evaluation of ideas and information. To prepare for discussions, then, start with the following critical questions:

- ◆ How can I use this information? To what situations is it applicable?
- ◆ How does this information compare with other information I have read or learned on the same topic?
- ◆ What is the source of the material?
- ◆ Is the material fact or opinion?
- ◆ What is the author's purpose?
- ◆ Is the author biased?
- ◆ Is relevant and sufficient evidence provided?

These questions will provoke thought and provide a base of ideas to use in discussions.

Review: Make Notes for Discussion

After you have read the assignment, review it with the purpose of identifying and jotting down the following:

1. **Ideas, concepts, or points of view you do not understand.** Keep a list of these; you can use the list as a guide to form questions during class.

2. **Ideas and points with which you disagree or strongly agree.** By jotting these down, you will have some ideas to start with if your instructor asks you to react to the topic.

3. **Good and poor examples.** Note examples that are particularly good or particularly poor. These will help you react to the topic.

4. **Strong arguments and weak arguments.** As you read, try to follow the line of reasoning, and evaluate any arguments presented. Make notes on your evaluations; the notes will remind you of points you may want to make during the discussion.

Getting Involved in Class Discussions

Discussion classes require greater, more active involvement and participation than do lecture classes. In lecture classes, your main concern is to listen carefully and to record notes accurately and completely. In discussion classes, your responsibility is much greater. Not only do you have to take notes, but you also have to participate in the discussion. The problem many students experience in getting involved in discussions is that they do not know what to say or when to say it. Here are a few instances when it might be appropriate to speak. Say something when

- ◆ you can ask a serious, thoughtful question.
- ◆ someone asks a question that you can answer.

- you have a comment or suggestion to make on what has already been said.
- you can supply additional information that will clarify the topic under discussion.
- you can correct an error or clarify a misunderstanding.

To get further involved in the discussion, try the following suggestions:

1. **Even if you are reluctant to speak before a group, try to say something early in the discussion.** The longer you wait, the more difficult it becomes. Also, the longer you wait, the greater the chance someone else will say what you were planning to say.

2. **Make your comments brief and to the point.** It is probably a mistake to say too much rather than too little. If your instructor feels you should say more, he or she will probably ask you to explain or elaborate further.

3. **Try to avoid getting involved in direct exchanges or disagreements with other class members.** Always speak to the group, not to individuals, and be sure that your comments relate to and involve the entire class.

4. **Announce change of topics.** When you feel it is appropriate to introduce a new idea, clue your listeners that you are changing topics or introducing a new idea. You might say something like, "Another related question . . . ," or "Another point to consider is . . ."

5. **Make notes.** If, as the discussion is going on, you think of comments or ideas that you want to make, jot them down. Then when you get a chance to speak, you will have your notes to refer to. Notes help you organize and present your ideas in a clear and organized fashion.

6. **Organize your remarks.** First, connect what you plan to say with what has already been said. Then state your ideas as clearly as possible. Next, develop or explain your ideas.

7. **Watch the group as you speak.** When making a point or offering a comment, watch both your instructor and others in the class. Their responses will show whether they understand you or need further information, whether they agree or disagree, and whether they are interested or uninterested. You can then decide, based on their responses, whether you made your point effectively or whether you need to explain or defend your argument more carefully.

Making Effective Contributions to the Discussion

Some students' participation in class can be distracting and disruptive. Use the following tips to be certain that you make a worthwhile contribution to the class discussion.

- Do not interrupt other speakers; wait until other speakers have finished. Signal to your instructor that you would like to be recognized to speak, if necessary.
- Avoid talking privately with or making comments to another student while the discussion is going on.

- ◆ Do not tell lengthy personal anecdotes; make sure that what you say is relevant to the ideas under discussion.
- ◆ Try not to monopolize the discussion; give others a chance to express their ideas.
- ◆ Be sensitive to the feelings and viewpoints of other class members.
- ◆ Try not to be bullying, argumentative, or overly emotional. These tactics detract from your effectiveness as a speaker.

Exercise 6.3	For a reading assignment in one of your other courses, prepare a set of notes that would help you get involved in a class discussion on that topic. (Do not choose a highly factual assignment.)

HOW DO YOU SEE IT?

"Please, Ms. Sweeney, may I ask where you're going with all this?"

Meaningful questions often help instructors as well as students clarify their thinking. Write a paragraph describing a situation where you believe that your question was helpful to others.

Asking and Answering Questions

Asking clear, direct questions is a skill you can develop and improve. Framing clear, direct answers to questions asked by your instructors or by fellow students is also a skill worth developing. Effective questioning is important in college classes, but it is also an important workplace skill. Use the following suggestions to strengthen your questioning and answering skills.

1. Conquer the fear of asking questions. Many students are hesitant to ask or answer questions, often because they are concerned about how their classmates and instructor will respond. They fear that their questions may seem dumb or that their answer may be incorrect. Asking questions is often essential to a complete and thorough understanding, and you will find that once you've asked a question, other students will be glad you asked because they had the same question in mind. Answering questions posed by your instructor gives you an opportunity to evaluate how well you have learned or understood course content as well as to demonstrate your knowledge.

2. To get started, as you read an assignment, jot down several questions that might clarify or explain it better. Bring your list to class. Refer to your list as you speak, if necessary.

3. When you ask a question, state it clearly and concisely. Don't ramble or make excuses for asking.

4. Remember, most instructors invite and respond favorably to questions: If your question is a serious one, it will be received positively. Don't pose questions for the sake of asking a question. Class time is limited and valuable.

5. In answering questions, think your responses through before you volunteer them.

6. Think of answering questions as a means of identifying yourself to the instructor as a serious, committed student, as well as a means of learning.

Exercise 6.4	Select a reading assignment from one of your other courses. Practice asking and answering questions with a student from that class. Take turns critiquing format, content, and delivery of both questions and answers.

Thinking Critically
. . . About Meaningful Questions

Use the levels of thinking (Chapter 2, pp. 34–37) to ask meaningful questions. In general, avoid basic knowledge and comprehension questions, unless they pertain to complicated material you do not understand. Instead, ask questions that will lead you to a fuller understanding of the topic. Here are some sample questions to ask at each of the higher levels of thinking.

Application: In what situations can this information be used?

Analysis: How do ideas fit together?
             How does it work?
             What are its parts?

Synthesis: How can this idea be combined with related ideas?
             What new and unique solutions or applications exist?

Evaluation: What standards or criteria exist?
             Of what value is this information?

Working with Classmates: Group Projects

Many assignments and class activities involve working with a small group of class-mates. For example, a sociology instructor might divide the class into groups and ask each group to brainstorm solutions to the economic or social problems of the elderly. Your political science professor might create a panel to discuss the private and collective consequences of voting. Group presentations may be required in a business course, or groups in your American history class might be asked to research a topic.

Group projects are intended to enable students to learn from one another by view-ing each other's thinking processes and by evaluating each other's ideas and approaches. Group activities also develop valuable skills in interpersonal communication that will be essential in your career. Some students are reluctant to work in groups because they feel that they are not in control of the situation; they dislike having their grade depend on the performance of others as well as themselves. Use the following suggestions to help your group function effectively:

1. Select alert, energetic classmates if you are permitted to choose group members.

2. Be an active, responsible participant. Accept your share of the work and expect oth-ers to do the same. Approach the activity with a serious attitude, rather than joking or complaining about the assignment. This will establish a serious tone and cut down on wasted time.

3. Because organization and direction are essential for productivity, every group needs a leader. Unless some other competent group member immediately assumes leader-ship, take a leadership role. While leadership may require more work, you will be in control. (Remember, too, that leadership roles are valuable experiences for your ca-reer.) As the group's leader, you will need to direct the group in analyzing the as-signment, organizing a plan of action, distributing work assignments, planning, and, if the project is long-term, establishing deadlines.

4. Suggest that specific tasks be assigned to each group member and that the group agree upon task deadlines.

5. Take advantage of individual strengths and weaknesses. For instance, a person who seems indifferent or is easily distracted should not be assigned the task of recording the group's findings. The most organized, outgoing member might be assigned the task of making an oral report to the class.

If your group is not functioning effectively or if one or more members are not doing their share, take action. Communicate directly, but try not to alienate or anger group members. Here are a few common complaints and possible solutions.

If a Group Member . . .	You May Want to Say . . .
Hasn't begun to do the work she's been assigned	"You've been given a difficult part of the project. How can we help you get started?"
Complains about the workload	"We all seem to have different amounts of work to do. Is there some way we might lessen your workload?"
Had missed meetings	"To ensure that we all meet regularly, would it be helpful if I called everyone the night before to confirm the day and time?"
Seems confused about the assignment	"This is an especially complicated assignment. Would it be useful to summarize each member's job?"
Is uncommunicative and doesn't share information	"Since we are all working from different angles, let's each make an outline of what we've done so far, so we can plan how to proceed from here."
Seems to be making you or other members do all the work	Make up a chart before the meeting with each member's responsibilities. Give each member a copy and ask, "Is there any part of your assignment that you have questions or concerns about? Would anyone like to change his or her completion date?" Be sure to get an answer from each member.

If the above suggestions do not help you correct problems with a nonparticipating group member, discuss with your instructor how to drop the person from the group.

Exercise 6.5	Suppose you are part of a five-member group that is preparing for a panel discussion on animal rights. One group member is very vocal and opinionated. You fear she is likely to dominate the discussion. Another group member is painfully shy and has volunteered to do double research if he doesn't have to speak much during the discussion. A third member appears uninterested and tends to sit back and watch as the group works and plans. How should the group respond to each of these individuals? List several possible solutions to each problem.

Planning and Making Oral Presentations

Oral presentations may be done in groups or individually. Groups may be asked to report their findings, summarize their research, or describe a process or procedure. Individual presentations are often summaries of research papers, reviews or critiques, or interpretations of literary or artistic works. Use the following suggestions to make effective oral presentations.

Understand the purpose of the assignment.   Analyze it carefully before beginning to work. Is the presentation intended to be informative? Are you to summarize, evaluate, or criticize?

Research your topic thoroughly.

Collect and organize your information.

Prepare outline notes.   Use index cards (either 3×5 or 5×8) to record only key words and phrases.

Consider the use of visual aids.   Depending on the type of assignment as well as on your topic, diagrams, photographs, or demonstrations may be appropriate and effective in maintaining audience interest.

Anticipate questions your audience may ask.   Review and revise your notes to include answers.

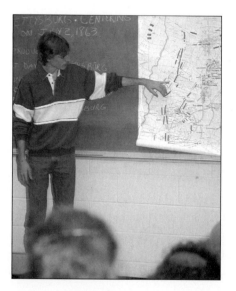

Practice delivery.   This will build your confidence and help you overcome nervousness. First, practice your presentation aloud several times by yourself. Time yourself to be sure you are within any limits. Then practice in front of friends and ask for criticism. Finally, tape-record your presentation. Play it back, looking for ways to improve it.

Deliver your presentation as effectively as possible.   Engage your audience's interest by maintaining eye contact; look directly at other students as you speak. Make a deliberate effort to speak slowly; when you are nervous, your speech tends to speed up. Be enthusiastic and energetic.

If you need additional information or help with making oral presentations, consult your college's learning lab or obtain a guidebook on public speaking from your campus library.

As a variation on oral presentations, some instructors might ask each student (or group) to lead one class discussion or form panel discussions. As in oral presentations, organization is the essential ingredient for these activities. Plan ahead, outlining topics to be discussed, questions to be asked, or issues to confront.

Figure 6.1 answers some commonly asked questions about making oral presentations.

Exercise 6.6	You are asked to make a three-minute oral presentation on how to study for a particular course you are taking this semester. Prepare a set of outline notes for your presentation, and practice delivery of your presentation. Then answer the following questions:

1. How did you organize your presentation?
2. Did preparation of your presentation force you to analyze how you learn in the course you chose?
3. How did you improve your presentation through practice?

Working Together

Five or six class members should volunteer to participate in a panel discussion on a current controversial issue. The panel members should convene to plan their panel discussion while the rest of the class forms groups of observers. The observer group should critique the panel group's planning, efficiency, and interaction. Your instructor may "plant" "problem" panel members.

Figure 6.1

Questions and Answers About Oral Presentations

Questions	Answers
1. How can I overcome the fear of public speaking?	• Be sure to practice delivering your speech several times before you actually make your presentation in front of the class. Practice speaking slowly and distinctly, taking deep breaths, and pausing.
2. How can I make sure my presentation is interesting?	• Vary the content. For example, you could start off by telling an interesting story or engaging the class's attention by posing a thoughtful question. • Use visual aids such as the chalkboard, an overhead projector, or a chart that you've designed to help you maintain the interest of your audience.
3. What if, during my presentation, the instructor and/or the class starts to show signs of boredom?	• Change the tone or pitch of your voice. • Maintain your audience's interest by engaging them in the presentation. Pose a question, for example. • Make eye contact with restless individuals.
4. What do I do if I "go blank"?	• Write notes on index cards. If you suddenly "go blank," all you need to do is look at your notes. • Ask whether there are any questions. Even if there aren't, this pause will give you time to think about what to say next.

Interactive Chapter Review

Knowledge	What are four barriers to effective listening?
Comprehension	What are three reasons it is important to develop listening and speaking skills?
Application	Prepare for one of your other classes as though it will take the form of a class discussion. Apply the critical questions on p. 100 to the reading you do before the class meets, and the four points on p. 100 to make notes for the discussion. Whether the class actually takes the format of a lecture or a discussion, afterward think about how preparing in this way aided you in comprehending the class.
Analysis	In one of your classes this week, pay attention to the types of questions and comments the students make. Which seem most helpful to the class as a whole? Which seem less important? Which seem to interrupt the class more than contribute to it? Why?
Synthesis	Would it be helpful to consider individual students' learning styles when making assignments for a group project? Why or why not?
Evaluation	Develop a checklist of five to ten different criteria that you could use to decide how effective an oral presentation is. The next time you are asked to make an oral presentation, use your checklist to evaluate a practice session.

Further Analysis

Martha is taking an interpersonal communication course in which the instructor allows students to select from a menu of activities that earn points that determine their final grade. Each student must choose at least three different activities. The activities include

Quizzes

Final exams

Oral reports

Group projects

Research papers

Panel discussions

Interviews with community leaders

Leading class discussions

Because Martha is not confident about her writing skills and gets nervous when taking exams, she selected oral reports, group projects, and panel discussions. Martha is a shy, quiet, self-directed person. She is well organized and feels most comfortable when she knows exactly what to expect and is in control of details.

1. Evaluate her choice of activities.

2. What advice would you give her for how to be successful with each of her choices?

Discussion

1. Discuss what members of a class should or should not do when one class member continually dominates the class discussion or fills class time with unimportant questions.

2. Discuss what classmates could do to help a student who is afraid to make a required oral presentation.

3. What courses of action might you take if you are a member of an assigned group that must prepare a group project and the group has chosen a topic that you are certain does not meet the instructor's requirements?

The Work Connection

How will learning oral presentation skills aid you in the workplace? Writing in the "Job Market" column that appears in each Saturday issue of the *New York Times,* Sabra Chartrand reports that even in technical jobs, communication skills are highly valued. In job interviews, the interviewer may be seeking to find out whether the candidate can "clearly and eloquently express his goals" and answer questions about solving technical problems in a way that is "well-expressed and easy to understand."[2] Working on group reports can also provide you with two other types of experiences that employers value: learning to work with a team and learning to take leadership roles within a group.

1. Which of your courses provide you with opportunities to give oral presentations? List four or five ways you learn the most from these experiences.

2. Aside from the course you are currently enrolled in, what other courses or campus activities would give you a chance to hone your oral presentation and team-building skills? Find and list about five different activities.

The Web Connection

1. Are You a Good Listener?

   http://www.effectivemeetings.com/productivity/communication/listener.asp

   Although this site is directed toward listening in meetings, it can still apply to the way students conduct themselves during class discussions and group work sessions.

2. Checklist for a Good Speaker

   http://www.artofspeaking.com/checklist.htm

   Look here for some straightforward tips on handling yourself in a public speaking situation.

3. Making Your Voice Heard: Classroom Discussions and Participation

   http://www.iss.stthomas.edu/studyguides/intstudy.htm

   From the University of St. Thomas, this site provides valuable advice on contributing to discussions in your classes.

Go Electronic!
For additional readings, exercises, and Internet activities, visit the Longman Study Skills Web site at:
http://www.ablongman.com/StudySkills
If you need a user name and password, please see your instructor.

Chapter 7

Thinking Critically and Solving Problems

DO YOU KNOW?

How can you make good decisions?
How can you specify a problem in a way that will help you solve it?
How do you analyze a problem?
Why should you identify a wide range of solutions to a problem?
How can you evaluate the possible solutions?
What factors should you consider in selecting a solution?

Each day as a college student you are faced with numerous decisions and problems. Some are more serious than others, and some are more difficult to solve than others. All require critical thinking—the careful analysis of the situation and ways to resolve it. Some of the decisions you face are academic—how to solve math problems, how to conclude an English composition, or which of two essay questions to answer. You also face nonacademic problems and decisions in day-to-day living—how to get to class if your car won't start, whether to buy a new compact disc player, or how to get that attractive person across the room to notice you. While these two types of decisions and problems seem quite different, the strategies for resolving them are very similar.

We have all made thousands of decisions and solved hundreds of problems in our lifetimes, but we may not have resolved them in the *best* possible ways. Nearly everyone can recall saying, "Why didn't I think of . . . ?" or "If only I had thought of . . . !" after the fact. The purpose of this chapter is to present systematic approaches to decision making and problem solving.

Thinking Critically about Decision Making

As a beginning college student you face a change in lifestyle: You face new surroundings, new courses and instructors, new friends, and new expectations. Consequently, you will have to make many decisions, some of which will affect the course of your life and career. Decision making is a critical thinking skill well worth developing.

Decision making is a process of thinking critically about choices. Each of us makes numerous choices each day: what to wear, which way to walk to class, which assignment to work on first, which essay question to answer. Many are relatively unimportant—

what to order for lunch, for example. Others, however, are of critical importance with far-reaching impact—what major to choose, for instance.

Decisions are different from hunches, wishes, or hopes. A decision means you will take a specific course of action. The statement "I would like to stop worrying about paying all my bills" is a wish. It is something you want to happen. To say, "I will develop a weekly budget to make sure I am able to pay all my bills," expresses a decision. Notice that it is action-oriented. It points toward an outcome.

The purpose of this section is to present strategies for effective decision making and to enable you to make those important choices in a reasoned, deliberate manner.

Types of Decisions

Let us consider several situations and analyze the type of decision making involved in each.

Situation 1:   You order a pizza with cheese, pepperoni, and mushrooms.

Situation 2:   On a spring afternoon you and a group of friends, at the last minute, decide to cut class and take a ride to the lake.

Situation 3:   You decide to register for child psychology next semester because you've just finished introductory psychology and child psychology is required in your major.

While each of the situations involves choice, each involves very different types of thinking. In ordering a pizza, you make a *routine decision* involving little or no thought; you usually or always order it that way. The trip to the lake is a last-minute, *impulsive decision*. The decision to register for child psychology is a *reasoned decision* based on evidence.

Routine decisions are usually safe, habitual choices that make your life run smoothly and eliminate the need to make choices constantly. Impulsive decisions on social occasions, for example when everyone decides to go bowling at midnight, can be fun and interesting. However, in other situations, since they are not well thought out, they can cause or lead to problems. Suppose, for example, that the day you impulsively decide to cut class, the instructor gives an unannounced quiz.

In new or important situations, the best type of decision to make is a reasoned one, in which alternatives are identified and weighed and outcomes are predicted.

Making Reasoned Decisions

Suppose your criminal justice instructor allows each student to elect, at the end of the third week of class, one of four grading options: (1) half the grade will be from your quiz average and half from the term paper, (2) half will be from the quizzes and half from the final exam, (3) half will be from the term paper and half from the final exam, (4) only the final exam will determine your grade. In analyzing the situation, you realize you must choose the option that best suits how you learn, so that you can earn the best possible grade. Since your instructor already identified all the alternatives, your next step is to weigh and compare them. Factors you must consider include how well you perform on quizzes and exams, how easily and how well you can write a term paper, and so forth. Then, in making a decision, you must consider risks and predict future outcomes.

An important part of decision making is to predict both short-term and long-term outcomes for each alternative. You may find that while an alternative seems most desirable in the present, it may pose problems or complications over a longer time period. For example, in choosing courses for next semester, suppose you decide against taking a public speaking course. You reason that it is not required, only recommended, and a mass media course would be more interesting. Your decision is reasonable for the short term. However, if you are considering a career in teaching, you may later find that a public speaking course would have been beneficial and that your decision was not effective in the long term.

To make reasoned decisions, use the following guidelines.

Recognize that not making a decision when one is called for is itself a decision. If you make no decision to act, you have decided not to act. For example, by not deciding to make a doctor's appointment to have an injured ankle checked, you have decided to ignore it.

Wait out a decision. Some decisions benefit from the perspective of time. If an immediate decision is not necessary, consider letting the decision rest. Often, circumstances change and the right decision becomes clear.

Focus on your life goals (see Chapter 3). Decisions should move you closer to attaining your life goals—what you want out of life. Suppose you need to decide whether to rent a larger, more expensive apartment or to make do with the one you are currently renting. If one of your life goals is to be able to afford to attend law school, then renting a more expensive apartment will not help you achieve that goal.

Talk with others. Talking about the problem will help you define it, and you may hear yourself saying things you never before consciously realized.

Play out the long-term consequences of a decision you are about to make. Create a mental movie; imagine the various possible consequences of the decision at various stages—in one month, three months, one year, or three years, for instance.

| Exercise 7.1 | For three of the following situations, identify several alternatives and then list factors that you would weigh in making a decision. |

1. Decide whether to attend summer session this year.
2. Decide what to do about a roommate who frequently interrupts you and distracts you from studying.

Continued

3. Decide which sports teams, campus organizations, or social groups to join.

4. Decide in which day-care center to enroll your child.

5. Decide when to buy a computer and which one to purchase.

Exercise 7.2	Make a list of important decisions that you face or will face in the next year. Compare your list with that of a classmate. You may discover that your lists contain similar items. Then discuss how you will reach a decision.

Problem-Solving Strategies

Problem solving is a critical thinking skill. While some people may have a natural aptitude for it, problem solving is a skill that you can and should develop. This means you must be willing to give up the comfort of such defenses or excuses as "I'm not good at problem solving" or "I'm not creative." It also means that you have to be willing to think in new ways, break old habits, and develop new approaches to solving problems. As you will see, problem solving involves making reasoned decisions.

The ability to solve problems is a valuable asset. It can make a substantial difference in your success in academic courses, in your future career, and in life. Many employers regard it as a necessary skill for holding positions of responsibility. Problem solving is a skill frequently assessed during a job interview. Questions that begin with,

"What would you do if . . . ?" or "Suppose you arrive at your desk one morning and you learn . . ." are designed to evaluate your problem-solving abilities.

A Model for Problem Solving

Put simply, a problem occurs when "what is" is not "what is desired." A problem exists when your grade in chemistry is not what you want it to be. A problem exists when you haven't finished your drawing for engineering, which is due tomorrow.

Let's call the "what is" your *present state* and the "what is desired" the *goal state*. Usually there are a number of ways to solve a problem, some more desirable than others. These various ways to solve a problem are called *solution paths*. A model for problem solving is shown in Figure 7.1.

Figure 7.1

Problem-Solving Model

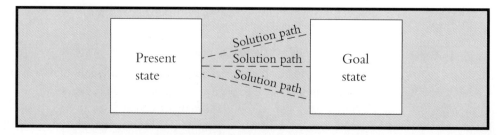

This model, when used as a basis for problem solving, forces you to identify existing circumstances (present state), the desired goal (goal state), and the various ways to achieve it (solution paths). Here's an everyday situation that fits the problem-solving model:

Present State:	You have earned B- and C+ grades on your presentations for your public speaking course.
Desired State:	Solid B or A grades.
Solution Paths:	1. Practice your presentations with friends and ask them to critique your performance.
	2. Ask your instructor for advice.
	3. Spend more time organizing your presentations.

Exercise 7.3

For each of the following situations, identify the present state and the goal state, and suggest several solution paths.

1. You are scheduled to address your speech communication class when you suddenly realize you left your note cards on the desk in your room. The class begins in 10 minutes.

2. Your political science instructor has asked you to declare a topic for your term paper by Friday. When you go to the library to select a topic, you discover that all the sources you want to consult have been checked out by other students.

3. You find your assigned lab partner in biology to be irresponsible and careless, more intent on finishing and leaving early than on following procedures and discovering principles.

Problem-Solving Processes

The best way to improve your problem-solving abilities is to develop a systematic approach and to use it consistently with all types of problems. While some problems are solved easily with a burst of insight, most require deliberate, step-by-step analysis. It is easy to panic and let your mind run wild, jumping rapidly from one possible solution to another. However, this random approach to problem solving may create more problems than it solves; some solutions may be partially evaluated, and the long-range consequences of others ignored. Here's a six-step approach to problem solving.

Step 1: Specify the Problem

A first step to solving a problem is to identify it as specifically as possible. Evaluate the present state and determine how it differs from the goal state. For example, instead of saying, "My problem is my mass media course," try to pinpoint the problem: "My problem is the low grades I'm getting on the reaction papers" or "I don't understand what my professor is talking about in her lectures." Use the following suggestions to pinpoint a problem:

State the problem.   The more specific you can be, the more likely it is that you will be able to identify workable solution paths.

Specify the problem in a way that allows you to solve it successfully.   For example, if the library is only open during hours when you are in class or working, specify the problem in terms of your class and work schedule rather than in terms of the library's business hours. It is more likely that you will be able to adjust your schedule, use the Internet, or locate an alternative library than get the library to change its hours.

Express the problem verbally or in writing.   This process often helps to define and clarify the situation by eliminating extraneous information, focusing your attention, and triggering alternative perspectives.

Focus on language.   Often, language further clarifies the problem. For instance, if you approach a professor to change a grade, is your problem how to *argue* for a higher grade, how to *persuade* him or her, or how to *request* a reevaluation of your paper? The more specifically you can state the problem, the more likely it is that you will be able to identify workable solution paths.

Step 2: Analyze the Problem

Once you have specified the problem, the next step is to analyze it. Let us suppose you identified low grades on papers in mass media as your main problem with the course.

Analyzing the problem involves learning as much as you can about it. You might begin by rereading each paper you have submitted and studying the professor's comments. Other possibilities include (1) arranging the papers from lowest to highest grades and analyzing the differences, (2) reading and comparing a friend's high-grade papers with yours, (3) asking a friend to criticize your papers, or (4) discussing the papers with your professor.

On occasion, in analyzing a problem, you may need to stretch your imagination and look beyond the obvious, surface situation for more creative options. For example, a nursing student was having difficulty establishing a trusting rapport with patients. She and her clinical supervisor discussed various communication breakdowns, but none seemed to pinpoint the problem. Finally, after thinking about and discussing her problem with a lifelong friend, she understood her problem. She was working in a geriatrics ward, and both her elderly grandparents, with whom she had been very close, had recently died. She realized she was emotionally blocking the establishment of any rapport with an elderly person. She discussed the problem with her supervisor and then identified several solution paths.

In analyzing a problem, use the following suggestions:

Seek other perspectives.   Discuss problems with professors, parents, or friends. Be sure to consider how knowledgeable, familiar, experienced, and successful the person is in handling similar problems. Weigh their opinions accordingly.

Be flexible in your analysis.   Do not eliminate possibilities because they do not "sound like you" or seem likely.

Consider various strands of impact.   Although a problem may seem economic (for example, how to afford a car for transportation), don't ignore social or emotional aspects (have you failed to consider public transportation because your friends do not use it?).

Brainstorm about all possibilities and implications.   Spend three to five minutes listing anything you think of that remotely relates to your problem. Sort through the list later, preferably the next day. Most likely you will discover seeds of new ideas or new ways of looking at the problem.

Research problems for which you lack complete information.   Libraries and the Internet contain a wealth of information, and reading in related areas can trigger your mind and lead you to a solution. For example, a student having problems arranging for the care of her infant son discovered a Web site for new parents; it outlined procedures for locating and hiring baby-sitters. She learned that she needed to actively seek and advertise—rather than to passively follow up advertisements and references from friends.

Exercise 7.4	Identify, as specifically as possible, the problem involved in each of the following situations, and suggest analyses.

1. A friend says she plans to drop out of school for the year—she has morning classes and now she realizes that her seven-year-old son needs supervision while walking to school: He fights with his peers and is picked on by older children.
2. A two-year college student is enrolled in a computer assisted drawing curriculum. He did not realize that the curriculum involves mathematics and technical skills. He wants to change his curriculum but doesn't know what area to transfer to.

Step 3: Formulate Possible Solution Paths

Once you have identified and analyzed the problem, you are ready to formulate possible solution paths. At this stage, your goal is to identify a wide range of possible solutions. Returning to the mass media problem, let's suppose that in analyzing your reaction papers you determined that your writing style and weak organization were causing low grades. Your ideas seemed adequate, but you were not expressing them in a manner acceptable to your professor. The next step is to identify all possible ways to correct the problem. You consider: (1) getting help from a classmate, (2) getting a tutor from the learning lab, (3) asking the mass media instructor for help, (4) visiting the writing lab on campus for tutoring, (5) having a friend who has superior English skills edit and proofread your papers, and (6) asking your English instructor to recommend a book on writing style.

When formulating possible solutions, use the following tips:

Try to think of all possible solutions.   For complicated problems, write down all possible solutions. At this stage, try not to evaluate a solution as you think of it. Just jot it down and continue thinking of others. Then reread your list; often it will help you think of alternative solutions.

Be creative.   Don't be afraid to think of crazy or outlandish solutions. Often, when wild solutions may in themselves be unacceptable, some aspect is workable or may trigger a solution that is.

Consider similar problems and how you have solved them.   You can learn from both your successes and your failures.

Exercise 7.5	For each of the problems described in Exercise 7.4, identify as many solution paths as possible. Then exchange your paper with a classmate. Did your classmate discover solution paths you had not thought of?

Step 4: Evaluate Possible Solution Paths

Once you have identified all possible solution paths, the next step is to weigh the advantages and disadvantages of each. To do so, you will need to think through each solution path in detail, considering how, when, and where you could accomplish each. Also consider whether you have the time, money, skills, knowledge, personal contacts, and so forth to pursue each solution path. Eliminate those that are impractical. For example, if you decided to get a tutor to help you write papers for the mass media course, you would need to consider practical details such as these:

◆   Do I have time to meet with a tutor?
◆   How will I feel working with a tutor?
◆   What will I do if I don't like my tutor?
◆   What if my tutor does not or cannot help me?

Table 7.1

Evaluating Solution Paths

	English	Communications	Psychology
Required credit hours outside major	0–16	24	0
Number of electives	24–48	35–45	64–74
Total credit hours in major	57	36	31
Graduation requirement	Thesis	No	Senior seminar
Foreign language requirement	Yes	No	No
Additional semester needed	Yes	No	No

Consider both immediate and long-term results of each solution. For instance, for the mass media problem, having a friend edit and proofread your paper may be a workable solution to correct the immediate problem. In the long term, however, it may not be the best solution because you will not have improved your writing style and organizational skills.

For complex problems with numerous solution paths, the technique of *mapping* is often useful. Mapping is simply drawing a picture that connects details for each solution path. (See Chapter 15, p. 307.)

For example, suppose you are majoring in business and your advisor is encouraging you to consider a double major. She has suggested English, communications, or psychology, but you cannot decide which to choose. To evaluate each, you might draw a chart such as the one shown in Table 7.1.

By studying the chart, you can more easily see the advantages of each alternative and make comparisons. While a map usually clarifies the situation, it seldom identifies clearly the best solution. (If the best solution were that obvious, you wouldn't need to make the map.) Instead, the map enables you to evaluate each alternative logically and systematically.

In solving some problems, you may realize that you need more information before you can evaluate various solution paths. For the mass media course problem considered throughout this chapter, you may need to know whether tutoring can be arranged conveniently before you can evaluate it as an alternative. Or, in choosing a double major, you may find that you want more information than is provided in the college catalog. You might talk with your advisor or meet with the department chairperson or do research in your career guidance and placement center or library to get information on job opportunities.

Exercise 7.6	Working in small groups, evaluate each of the solution paths you devised for the problems listed in Exercise 7.4.

Working Together

Most students face financial hardships and experience money problems while attending college. Some students "max-out" credit cards, others work as many as three part-time jobs. Working in groups of four or five students, select a real problem a group member faces or create a hypothetical financial problem that college students often face. Follow the first four steps in the problem-solving process to discover as many solution paths as possible.

Step 5: Choose a Solution

The fifth step in problem solving is the selection of one solution path. In weighing the various solution paths, there are three factors to consider.

Compatibility with your life goals and priorities. In choosing a solution, you must match the solution with what you have identified as most important to you. In the case of the mass media course papers, if an immediate improvement in grades is more important than improving your writing skills, some solutions are better than others. In evaluating majors, you will need to decide how convenient spending an additional semester is and whether it fits within your short-term and long-term goals.

Amount of risk. Some solutions involve more risk than others. For instance, working with a tutor from the learning lab may be a more reliable, controlled, and organized solution (and therefore less risky) than depending on the good nature of a classmate to help. The amount of risk you are willing to take depends on the seriousness of the problem and the consequences if the solution fails.

Practicality. The most logical of solutions won't work if it is not practical. Regardless how good a solution may seem, if you cannot carry it through, it is worthless. For instance, getting a tutor may seem the best solution to the mass media paper problem. However, if the tutor is only available at 8:00 in the morning and you know you'll have trouble keeping appointments at that time, then the solution is not practical.

Step 6: Evaluate Your Solution

Once you have chosen a solution path and have acted on it, check to be sure that it is working. Suppose you decided to work with a tutor to improve your grades on mass media assignments. If you get a higher grade on your next paper, you have evidence that your solution is working. If your grades are not improving, it is time to reconsider the problem and choose an alternative solution.

HOW DO YOU SEE IT?

" 'Give me liberty or give me death.' Now, what kind of person
would say something like that?"

Depending on your point of view, the quotation in this cartoon could
be inspiring or humorous. Write a paragraph that explains both possibilities.

Keys to Problem Solving

Here are a few tips to make the problem-solving process work for you. Use them in
conjunction with the problem-solving model just described.

Think aloud.   Problem solving is a cognitive (mental) process. For complicated problems, many people find it useful to think aloud or talk to themselves as they work
through the problem-solving steps. Hearing yourself think, so to speak, seems to facilitate the process. Sometimes, especially when solving academic problems, by thinking

aloud you catch yourself using the wrong rule or formula, or saying something that is contradictory to what you have read.

Allow time for incubation.   Archimedes, an ancient Greek, is said to have run naked through the streets shouting, "Eureka!" He was announcing that he had, while taking a bath, discovered the solution to a problem he had been studying for years, which is known today as Archimedes's principle. How and why was Archimedes able to arrive at a solution at a time when he wasn't even thinking about it? You may have had similar experiences when all of a sudden during an exam you know an answer you couldn't think of 10 minutes ago, or a new solution to a problem you have been wrestling with for days flashes in your mind without warning.

What happened to Archimedes and what happens to you when you get sudden flashes of insight illustrates a principle known as *incubation.* Just as chicken eggs are nurtured in the warmth and humidity of an incubator until ready to hatch, ideas, too, need incubation, until they are ready to hatch or come together to solve a problem. Even though you may not be consciously thinking about a problem, it is still there, in the back of your mind.

Time away from the problem allows ideas to gel or consolidate. It also provides a psychological distance and new perspective on the problem. The best advice, then, for when you cannot solve a problem is to wait. Give yourself time for the various solution paths to settle in. Distance from a problem also clears your mind, lessens the problem's importance, and often provides a fresh outlook.

Talk about the problem.   If you describe the problem to someone else and talk about it, the problem often crystallizes, becoming clearer and more defined, so that new solution paths sometimes surface. Talking to someone else externalizes the problem (takes it outside of you) and provides a measure of psychological distance.

Exercise 7.7   Study the two problems listed below and apply the six-step problem-solving approach to each. Keep a written record of the process. Generate as many solutions as possible, and then state which solution you would select. Justify your choice.

1. A major change has occurred recently in your family's financial situation, and you are not sure whether you will be able to afford to attend college next semester. Because it is near the end of the summer, you have heard that all of the college's financial aid funds have already been distributed for the next academic year.

2. It is the sixth week of a 15-week semester, and you have been hospitalized for complications resulting from bronchial pneumonia. Your doctor estimates you can return to classes in two to three weeks. You have already missed one week of classes.

Thinking Critically
. . . About Alternatives

An important step in both decision making and problem solving is weighing alternatives and selecting the one that is best for you. As you weigh decisions and possible solution paths, use the following questions to guide your thinking:

- What outcome is each alternative likely to produce, in both the short term and the long term?
- How easily can you accomplish each?
- What are the possible negative side effects of each?
- What risk, if any, is involved in each?
- Have I thought of all the alternatives?
- Which outcome will help me achieve my larger goals?

Interactive Chapter Review

Knowledge	Describe three types of decisions and give a brief example of each.
Comprehension	What are the six steps to solving problems?
Application	Write about a problem you are currently experiencing. Use these terms: present state, goal state, possible solution paths. Make sure you write about the problem in a way that will allow you to solve it successfully.
Analysis	Think about the problem you just described. Analyze the problem using at least three of the suggestions listed on pp. 116–117. If the problem is an important one, use all the suggestions.
Synthesis	Which possible solutions are compatible with your larger goals, involve an acceptable level of risk, and are practical?
Evaluation	For the problem you've been working with above, which solution is the best one? Why? Give at least three reasons.

Further Analysis

Analyze the following situation and answer the questions below.

A student has completed his freshman year at a community college. When registering in advance for his third-semester classes, he realizes that a normal course load would put him within six credit hours of graduation. He is considering registering for a six-hour overload and graduating a semester early. As an accounting major, he has consistently earned high C and B grades. Upon graduation, he intends to get a full-time job and pursue a four-year degree part time. One of his life goals is to become a certified public accountant. He works part time to earn living expenses.

1. What is the real problem this student faces? What solution paths are available?

2. List the advantages and disadvantages of each solution path.

3. What factors should he consider in evaluating various solution paths?

4. Project several different final outcomes, both short term and long term.

Discussion

1. How do you decide how much risk to take in making a decision? Give examples from your own experience.

2. In what situations, if any, do you feel routine, habitual decision making can limit or restrict your opportunities?

3. Consider your college and its surrounding campus. Identify current problems it faces. (Local or campus newspapers may serve as a reference point for the discussion.)

4. What problems and decisions do you feel college students typically face? Do they differ according to age? What other factors affect the level and type of problems students encounter?

5. Describe an instance in which incubation occurred in problem solving.

6. Describe an instance of ineffective problem solving that you have recently observed or read about.

The Work Connection

What do corporations look for in prospective employees? DeVry Institute of Technology conducted a survey to find out which skills and attitudes corporations value most highly. Here are the top 10 employee capabilities for workplace success:

1. Excellent verbal and written skills

2. Hands-on ability (ability to apply concepts)

3. Ability to work in groups, including working with people of different backgrounds

4. Flexibility to adapt to and use "new structures, programs, procedures"

5. Critical thinking and problem-solving abilities

6. Creative thinking that leads to "breakthrough solutions"

7. Having a balanced life, including activities outside the workplace

8. Effective time management and dependability

9. In technical fields, the willingness to fail and then try again to find solutions

10. Personal commitment to team and corporate goals[1]

1. Divide the 10 attributes listed above into two lists according to your current capabilities, one list for your strengths and another for weaker areas. Do this by considering specific examples from your school, work, and home life. Describe your strong points briefly as if talking to an interviewer. For your weak points, check through the table of contents of this book for suggestions.

2. Think about the courses you are enrolled in currently. What opportunities does each one present for you to become competent in the 10 skills defined above? List at least three opportunities each presents.

3. What elective courses might help you improve these skills? List at least three courses and use the problem-solving model from this chapter to decide which ones to take.

The Web Connection

1. Are You a Good Decision Maker?

   http://www.onlinewbc.gov/Docs/manage/decisions.html

   From the Online Women's Business Center at the Small Business Administration, this site offers decision-making tips, including the useful "Common Decision-Making Mistakes."

2. Universal Intellectual Standards

   http://www.criticalthinking.org/University/unistan.html

   The Foundation for Critical Thinking created this page to establish some basic questions students should ask in the process of thinking critically.

3. The World's Worst Decisions

   http://jewel.morgan.edu/~salimian/humor/humor_314.html

   From the Humor! Humor! Archives, an excerpt from David Frost's book that describes what turned out to be some pretty bad decisions.

Go Electronic!
For additional readings, exercises, and Internet activities, visit the Longman Study Skills Web site at:
http://www.ablongman.com/StudySkills
If you need a user name and password, please see your instructor.

Chapter 8

Learning Styles and Teaching Styles

DO YOU KNOW?

How can you discover your learning style?
How do you decide what you should learn?
How can an awareness of your learning style help you study better?
How can you adapt to different teaching styles?

Learning from both textbooks and lectures is the biggest challenge you face as a college student. Your success as a student depends almost entirely on your ability to learn. Often a student complains: "My instructor never tells us *how* to learn all this material!"

The reason instructors don't tell their students how to learn is simple. Students learn in many different ways. Advice offered to one student may not work for another. In this chapter you will discover how you learn best and then learn to choose study methods that suit how you learn. You will also find out how to adapt your study methods to different teaching styles.

Analyzing Your Learning Style

Have you found some types of learning tasks easier than others? Perhaps writing a term paper is easier than solving calculus problems; taking lecture notes may be easier than reading and marking textbook chapters. Essay exams may be more difficult than objective exams. Or perhaps you have found one instructor easier to learn from than another. Have you also noticed that tasks that may be easy for you may be difficult for others? Each person has his or her own approach to taking in and processing information. For example, some students learn best visually, seeing charts, diagrams, or models. Others are auditory learners; they learn best by listening. Such students would learn more quickly from an instructor's lecture than from a textbook chapter on the same topic. Such variations in how people learn are known as *learning styles.*

To begin to understand learning style, think of everyday tasks and activities that you have learned to do easily and well. Think of others that are always troublesome. For example, is reading maps easy or difficult? Is drawing or sketching easy or difficult? Can you assemble items easily? Are activities that require physical coordination (such as racquetball) difficult? Can you easily remember the lyrics to popular songs? Just as some everyday tasks are easy and others are difficult, so are some academic tasks easy and others more challenging.

The following questionnaire is designed to assist you in analyzing your learning style. Complete and score the questionnaire now before continuing with the chapter.

Learning Style Questionnaire

Each item presents two alternatives. Select the alternative that best describes you. In cases in which neither choice suits you, select the one that is closer to your preference. Write the letter of your choice on the line to the left of each item.

Part One

_____ 1. For a grade in biology lab, I would prefer to

    a. work with a lab partner.

    b. work alone.

_____ 2. When faced with a difficult personal problem, I prefer to

    a. discuss it with others.

    b. resolve it myself.

_____ 3. Many instructors could improve their classes by

    a. including more discussion and group activities.

    b. allowing students to work on their own more frequently.

_____ 4. When listening to a lecture or speaker, I respond more to

    a. the person presenting the ideas.

    b. the ideas themselves.

_____ 5. When on a team project, I prefer to

    a. work with several team members.

    b. divide up tasks and complete those assigned to me.

_____ 6. I prefer to shop and do errands

    a. with friends.

    b. by myself.

_____ 7. A job in a busy office is

    a. more appealing than working alone.

    b. less appealing than working alone.

Part Two

_____ 1. To solve a math problem, I would prefer to

    a. draw or visualize the problem.

    b. study a sample problem and use it as a model.

_____ 2. To remember things best, I

    a. create a mental picture.

    b. write it down.

_____ 3. Assembling a bicycle from a diagram would be

    a. easy.

    b. challenging.

_____ 4. I prefer classes in which I

    a. handle equipment or work with models.

    b. participate in a class discussion.

_____ 5. To understand and remember how a machine works, I would

    a. draw a diagram.

    b. write notes.

_____ 6. I enjoy

    a. drawing or working with my hands.

    b. speaking, writing, and listening.

_____ 7. If I were trying to locate an office on an unfamiliar university campus, I would prefer a student to

    a. draw me a map.

    b. give me a set of written directions.

Part Three

_____ 1. I prefer to

    a. learn facts and details.

    b. construct theories and ideas.

_____ 2. I would prefer a job involving

   a. following specific instructions.

   b. reading, writing, and analyzing.

_____ 3. I prefer to

   a. solve math problems using a formula.

   b. discover why the formula works.

_____ 4. I would prefer to write a term paper explaining

   a. how a process works.

   b. a theory.

_____ 5. I prefer tasks that require me to follow

   a. careful, detailed instructions.

   b. reasoning and critical analysis.

_____ 6. For a criminal justice course I would prefer to

   a. discover how and when a law can be used.

   b. learn how and why it became law.

_____ 7. To learn more about the operation of a high-speed computer printer, I would prefer to

   a. work with several types of printers.

   b. understand the principles on which they operate.

Part Four

_____ 1. I would prefer to follow a set of

   a. oral directions.

   b. written directions.

_____ 2. I would prefer to

   a. attend a lecture given by a famous psychologist.

   b. read an article written by the psychologist.

_____ 3. I am better at remembering

   a. names.

   b. faces.

_____ 4. It is easier to learn new information using

   a. language (words).

   b. images (pictures).

_____ 5. I prefer classes in which the instructor

   a. lectures and answers questions.

   b. uses films and videos.

_____ 6. To obtain information about current events, I would prefer to

   a. listen to news on the radio.

   b. read the newspaper.

_____ 7. To learn how to operate a fax machine, I would

   a. listen to a friend's explanation.

   b. watch a demonstration.

Part Five

_____ 1. To make decisions I rely on

   a. my experiences and "gut" feelings.

   b. facts and objective data.

_____ 2. To complete a task, I

   a. can use whatever is available to get the job done.

   b. must have everything I need at hand.

_____ 3. I prefer to express my ideas and feelings through

   a. music, song, or poetry.

   b. direct, concise language.

_____ 4. I prefer instructors who

   a. allow students to be guided by their own interests.

   b. make their expectations clear and explicit.

_____ 5. I tend to

   a. challenge and question what I hear and read.

   b. accept what I hear and read.

_____ 6. I prefer

   a. essay exams.

   b. objective (multiple-choice, true-false) exams.

_____ 7. In completing an assignment I prefer to

   a. figure out my own approach.

   b. be told exactly what to do.

To score your questionnaire, record the total number of choice *a*'s and the total number of choice *b*'s for each part of the questionnaire. Record your totals in the scoring grid provided below.

Scoring Grid

Parts	Total Number of Choice A	Total Number of Choice B
Part One	_____ Social	_____ Independent
Part Two	_____ Spatial	_____ Verbal
Part Three	_____ Applied	_____ Conceptual
Part Four	_____ Auditory	_____ Visual
Part Five	_____ Creative	_____ Pragmatic

Now, circle your higher score for each part of the questionnaire. The word below the score you circled indicates a dominant aspect of your learning style. The next section explains how to interpret your scores and describes these aspects.

Interpreting Your Scores

The questionnaire was divided into five parts; each part identifies one aspect of your learning style. Each of these five aspects is explained below.

Part One—Social or Independent Learners

This score reveals your preferred level of interaction with other people in the learning process. If you are a social learner, you prefer to work with others—both peers and instructors—closely and directly. Social learners tend to be people-oriented and enjoy personal interaction. If you are an independent learner, you prefer to work and study alone. You tend to be self-directed or self-motivated, and you are often goal-oriented.

Part Two—Spatial or Verbal Learners

This score reveals your ability to work with spatial relationships. Spatial learners are able to visualize or mentally see how things work or how they are positioned in space. Their strengths may include drawing, assembling things, or repairing. Verbal learners lack skills in positioning things in space. Instead they tend to rely on verbal or language skills.

Part Three—Applied or Conceptual Learners

This score describes the types of learning tasks and learning situations you prefer and find easiest to handle. If you are an applied learner, you prefer tasks that involve real objects and situations. Practical, real-life learning situations are ideal for you. Examples will often make an idea clear and understandable. If you are a conceptual learner, you prefer to work with language and ideas; practical applications are not necessary for understanding. You may enjoy working with theories and concepts and tend to work from rule to example.

Part Four—Auditory or Visual Learners

This score indicates through which sensory mode you prefer to process information. Auditory learners tend to learn more effectively through listening, while visual learners process information by seeing it in print or other visual modes including film, picture, or diagram. If you have a higher score on auditory than visual, you tend to be an auditory learner. That is, you tend to learn more easily by hearing than by reading. A higher score in visual suggests strengths with visual modes of learning.

Part Five—Creative or Pragmatic Learners

This score describes the approach you prefer to take toward learning tasks. Creative learners are imaginative and innovative. They prefer to learn through discovery or experimentation. They are comfortable taking risks and following hunches. Pragmatic learners are practical, logical, and systematic. They seek order and are comfortable following rules.

Evaluating Your Results

By responding to the questionnaire and analyzing the results, you should have discovered more about yourself as a learner. However, several words of caution are in order.

◆ The questionnaire is an informal indicator of your learning style. Other more formal and more accurate measures of learning style are available. These include *Kolb's Learning Style Inventory* and *Myers-Briggs Type Indicator.* These tests may be available through your college's counseling, testing, or academic skills center.

◆ Learning style has many more aspects than those identified through the questionnaire in this chapter. To learn more about other factors, one or both of the tests listed above would be useful.

◆ Learning style is *not* a fixed, unchanging quality. Just as personalities can change and develop, so can learning styles change and develop through exposure, instruction, or practice. For example, as you experience more college lectures, your skill as an auditory learner may be strengthened.

◆ People are not necessarily clearly strong or weak in each aspect. Some students, for example, may be able to learn equally well spatially or verbally. If there was very little difference between your two scores on one or more parts of the questionnaire, then you may have strengths in both areas.

◆   When most students discover the features of their learning style, they recognize themselves. A frequent comment is "Yep, that's me." If, for some reason, you feel the description of yourself as a learner is incorrect, then do not make changes in your learning strategies based on the information. Instead, discuss your style with your instructor, or consider taking one of the tests listed above.

HOW DO YOU SEE IT?

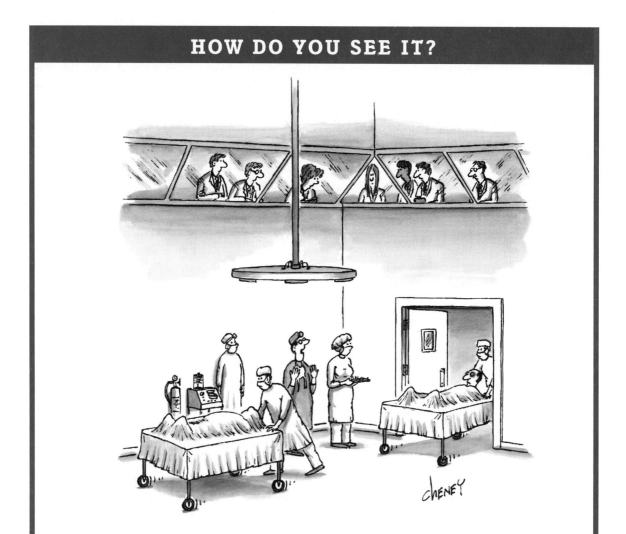

"Next, an example of the very same procedure when done correctly."

Do you learn best from being shown what to do or being shown what not to do? Write a paragraph that gives an example.

Exercise 8.1	Evaluate the results of the learning style questionnaire by answering the following questions.

1. How accurately do you think the results describe you? Identify aspects that you agree and disagree with. Explain why you disagree.

2. Evaluate your current study methods in light of the questionnaire's results. What are you doing that is effective? What changes are needed?

Working Together

Each class member should bring a week's worth of lecture notes for any course. Exchange your lecture notes with another student. Each of you should take about 10 minutes to study the notes your classmate prepared. You are looking for evidence that your partner is (1) a spatial or verbal learner, and (2) an applied or conceptual learner. Keep track of the evidence that you notice for each of these two aspects of your partner's learning style. When the study time is over, discuss your findings with your partner. Then your partner can share the results of his or her learning style questionnaire with you. Were you right on each count? Discuss what each of you, when taking lecture notes, can do differently to highlight the strengths of your particular learning style or to improve weaker areas.

Deciding What to Learn

Before you begin an assignment you should decide how you will approach it. Will you highlight it, outline it, prepare index cards, or tape-record it? Your decision depends on two factors: what you need to learn and your learning style.

Research on how people learn has clearly established that we remember only what we *intend* to remember. For example, take a moment to sketch the face of a dollar bill. Or draw the keypad on a telephone, indicating which letters correspond with each number.

Why did you have difficulty with each of these tasks? You certainly have seen each of these items many times. Most likely, you could not recall the needed information because you never *intentionally* learned it. This principle of intention strongly influences and controls your learning. Unless you select a given piece of information as important, and then consciously work on storing it in your memory, you will quickly forget it. Learning, then, is a sifting and sorting process in which you identify what is necessary and important to learn and remember. Here are a few suggestions on deciding what to learn:

Follow your instructor's emphases. Notice the topics the instructor emphasizes in lectures, spends a great deal of time discussing, or seems interested in or excited about; these are likely to be important.

Review previous exams and quizzes.   They indicate the type of information to learn.

Use the structure and organization of your text to identify key ideas and concepts.   Use the table of contents, chapter introductions, headings, summaries, and review questions as guides.

Use chapter objectives.   These usually indicate the most important topics in the chapter.

Use the end-of-chapter review questions.   These questions usually suggest what is important.

Talk with other students who have taken the course.   They may be able to tell you what kinds of information your instructor emphasizes.

Exercise 8.2	For a textbook reading assignment given by one of your instructors, use the suggestions given above to write a list of what you need to learn as you read the chapter.

Thinking Critically
. . . About the Intent to Learn

Intending to learn a piece of information is the first step to actually learning it. Two different meanings of the word *intention* can help you figure out ways to increase and heighten your intent to learn: (1) a plan of action, and (2) an aim or purpose to guide an action. Think about these definitions while answering the following questions.

- What actions can you take to strengthen your intent to learn?
- What personal purposes or reasons do you have for learning the course material?
- What do you aim to do with this material later that makes you want to learn it now?

The more specific your questions and answers are, the better you will be able to focus on your intent to learn.

Using Learning Style to Choose a Study Method

Once you have analyzed a learning task, you are ready to select the best techniques to accomplish it. Many students just jump into an assignment, only to find out midway through it that a different approach would have produced better results and saved valuable time. Here is an example:

Sarah, a spatial, social learner, was preparing for a midterm examination in human anatomy and physiology. As soon as the exam was announced, she began to prepare detailed outlines of each chapter. The day of the exam, in comparing notes with a classmate, she discovered that a system of testing herself by drawing and labeling diagrams and making tables and function charts would have been a more active means of learning. She also realized that studying with a classmate and testing each other would have been more effective.

Suppose you are faced with the task of reviewing several chapters in your mass media and communications text in preparation for an essay exam. What strategy would you use to learn and remember as much as possible? Some students would use the same strategy they use for every other reading assignment: reread and underline. A better approach is to choose a strategy that fits your learning style as well as the nature of the material to be read and the type of exam you anticipate. For example, you might predict possible essay questions and organize information to answer each.

Now that you are aware of some of the characteristics of your learning style, you can use that information in deciding how best to study. What is best for you may not be best for a classmate. Because your learning style is unique, you may need to approach a task differently from how others in your class do. In fact, two students with differing learning styles may study for the same exam in the same class in very different ways, as shown in Figure 8.1.

Figure 8.2 provides examples of learning methods that are suitable for each aspect of learning style in the learning style questionnaire. To use this chart, first go through and circle or highlight the five aspects of your learning style as identified in the scoring grid on p. 132, and then study the corresponding suggestions.

Here are a few suggestions to use in deciding how to approach an assignment:

Define the characteristics or nature of the task.   State as explicitly as possible what you are expected to accomplish.

Figure 8.1
Differing Learning Strategies

Course:	Anatomy and Physiology	
Type of Exam:	Multiple Choice	
	Student A	**Student B**
Learning Style:	Social, spatial, applied	Independent, verbal, conceptual
Learning Strategies:	1. study with classmate(s)	1. study alone
	2. draw diagrams, sketches	2. prepare index cards
	3. prepare charts	3. use summary sheets
	4. associate with practical situations	4. reorganize the information

Figure 8.2

Learning Strategies for Various Learning Styles

Applied

1. Associate ideas with their application.
2. Take courses with a lab or practicum.
3. Think of practical situations to which learning applies.
4. Use case studies, examples, and applications to cue your learning.

Auditory

1. Tape-record review notes.
2. Discuss/study with friends.
3. Talk aloud when studying.
4. Tape-record lectures.

Social

1. Interact with instructor.
2. Find a study partner.
3. Form a study group.
4. Take courses involving class discussion.
5. Work with a tutor.

Spatial

1. Draw diagrams, make charts and sketches.
2. Use outlining.
3. Use visualization.
4. Use mapping (see Chapter 15).

Creative

1. Take courses that involve exploration, experimentation, or discussion.
2. Use annotation to record impressions and reactions.
3. Ask questions about chapter content and answer them.

Conceptual

1. Use outlining.
2. Focus on thought patterns (see Chapter 12).
3. Organize materials into rules and examples.

Visual

1. Use mapping (see Chapter 15).
2. Use visualization.
3. Use computer-assisted instructions if available.
4. Use films and videos when available.
5. Draw diagrams, charts, maps.

Independent

1. Use computer-assisted instructions if available.
2. Enroll in courses using traditional lecture-exam format.
3. Consider independent study courses.
4. Purchase review books and study guides, if available.

Verbal

1. Record steps, processes, procedures in words.
2. Write summaries.
3. Translate diagrams and drawings into language.
4. Write your interpretation next to textbook drawings, maps, graphics.

Pragmatic

1. Write lists of steps, processes, and procedures.
2. Write summaries and outlines.
3. Use structured study environment.
4. Focus on problem-solving logical sequence.

Identify your options.   What strategies can you use? You will be able to answer this question more explicitly later, after you have worked through all the chapters of this book.

Try to match the strategy to the material.   As you will see in later chapters, not all learning strategies are equally effective in all situations. To strike the best match, ask yourself questions such as these: (1) What types of thinking and learning are required? For example, is the task primarily one of problem solving, or does it require creative thought? (2) What level of recall is required (facts and details or just major concepts)? (3) Am I expected to make applications? (4) Am I expected to evaluate and criticize? Review Table 2.2, "Levels of Thinking," on p. 36 to think of other useful questions.

Exercise 8.3	Discuss what learning strategies might be effective for each of the following students in each of the following situations.

Student A: strong visual, spatial learning style

Student B: strong social, applied learning style

Student C: strong auditory, conceptual learning style

Situation 1: Attending a city court trial as an assignment for a criminal justice class to learn about criminal trial procedures

Situation 2: Reading a chapter assignment in a book titled *The Intelligence Controversy* for a psychology course. The instructor plans a class discussion of the assignment.

Situation 3: Reading an assigned research report on North–South wage differences in the *American Economics Review* about which the student must write a synopsis

Situation 4: Watching a class demonstration in psychology designed to explain various forms of conditioning

---

Exercise 8.4	For the assignment you chose in Exercise 8.2, write a list of the learning strategies you intend to use as you read and study the chapter.

Adapting to Various Teaching Styles

Just as each student has his or her own learning style, so does each instructor have his or her own teaching style. Some instructors, for example, have a teaching style that promotes social interaction among students. An instructor may organize small group activities, encourage class participation, or require students to work in pairs or teams to complete a specific task. Other instructors offer little or no opportunity for social interaction. A lecture class is an example.

Some instructors are very applied; they teach by example. Others are more conceptual; they focus on presenting ideas, rules, theories, and so forth. In fact, the same five categories of learning styles identified on p. 132 can be applied to teaching styles as well.

To an extent, of course, the subject matter also dictates how the instructor teaches. A biology instructor, for instance, has a large body of factual information to present and may feel he or she has little time to schedule group interaction.

Comparing Learning and Teaching Styles

Once you are aware of your learning style and then consider the instructor's teaching style, you can begin to understand why you can learn better from one instructor than another and why you feel more comfortable in certain instructors' classes than others. When aspects of your learning style match aspects of your instructor's teaching style, you are on the same "wavelength," so to speak: The instructor is teaching the way you learn. On the other hand, when your learning style does not correspond to an instructor's teaching style, you may not be as comfortable, and learning will be more of a challenge. You may have to work harder in that class by taking extra steps to reorganize or reformat the material into a form in which you can learn it better. The following section presents each of the five categories of learning-teaching styles and suggests how you might make changes in how you study to accommodate each.

Social-Independent

If your instructor organizes numerous in-class group activities and you tend to be an independent learner, then you will need to spend time alone after class reviewing the class activity, making notes, perhaps even repeating the activity by yourself to make it more meaningful. If your instructor seldom structures in-class group activities and you tend to be a social learner, try to arrange to study regularly with a classmate or create or join a study group.

Spatial-Verbal

If you are a spatial learner and your instructor has a verbal teaching style (he or she lectures and writes notes on the board), then you will need to draw diagrams, charts, and pictures to learn the material. On the other hand, if you are a verbal learner and your instructor is spatial (he or she frequently uses diagrams, flowcharts, and so forth), then you may need to translate the diagrams and flowcharts into words in order to learn them more easily.

Applied-Conceptual

If your instructor seldom uses examples, models, or case studies and you are an applied learner, you need to think of your own examples to make the course material real and memorable to you. Leave space in your class notes to add examples. Add them during class if they come to mind; if not, take time as you review your notes to add examples. If your instructor uses numerous demonstrations and examples and you are a conceptual learner, you may need to leave space in your class notes to write in rules or generalizations that state what the examples are intended to prove.

Auditory-Visual

If your instructor announces essential course information (such as paper assignments, class projects, or descriptions of upcoming exams) orally and you are a visual learner, you should be sure to record as much information as possible in your notes. If your instructor relies on lectures to present new material not included in your textbook, taking complete lecture notes is especially important. If your instructor uses numerous visual aids and you tend to be an auditory learner, consider tape-recording summaries of these visual aids.

Creative-Pragmatic

Suppose your instructor is very systematic and organized in his or her lectures, and, as a creative learner, you prefer to discover ideas through experimentation and free-flowing discussion. Then you should consider creating a column in your class notes to record your responses and creative thoughts or reserving the bottom quarter of each page for such annotations. If your instructor is creative and tends to use a loose or free-flowing class format, and you tend to be a pragmatic learner, you may need to rewrite and restructure class notes. If he or she fails to give you specific guidelines for completing activities or assignments, you should talk with your instructor or ask for more information.

Exercise 8.5

Do an analysis of your instructors' teaching styles by completing the following chart for the courses you are taking this semester. List as many teaching characteristics as you can, but do not try to cover each aspect of each instructor's teaching style.

Course	Instructor's Name	Teaching Style Characteristics
1.		
2.		
3.		
4.		
5.		
6.		

Exercise 8.6

After you have completed the chart in Exercise 8.5, select one of your instructors whose teaching style does not match your learning style. Write a paragraph describing the differences in your styles. Explain how you will change your study methods to make up for these differences.

Evaluating Your Learning

You maintain an awareness or check on how well you are performing many daily activities. In sports such as golf, tennis, or bowling, you know if you are playing a poor game; you actually keep score and deliberately try to correct errors and improve your performance. When preparing a favorite food, you often taste it to be assured it will turn out as expected. You know whether your car is clean after taking it through the car wash.

A similar type of checking should occur as you learn and study. You should be aware of, or *monitor,* your performance. You need to keep track of whether the study method you have chosen is working. Here are a few questions that will help you decide whether you have chosen an effective study method.

1. **At what pace am I working?** If you are working extremely rapidly, you may not be spending enough time with the material. Consider adding additional steps to your chosen method. For example, if you have chosen to read and highlight, consider adding annotations or the preparation of flash cards. If your pace is so slow that you are inefficient, consider dropping a step. For example, perhaps you do not need to both highlight and outline a chapter.

2. **How much do I remember?** For textbook chapters, use the headings to test your recall. Turn each heading into a question and then answer it.

Heading	Question
Evaluating Storage and Retrieval Costs	How are storage and retrieval costs evaluated?
Multiple Uses of Stored Data	What are the uses of stored data?
The Database Concept	What is the database concept, and how is it used?

Since a heading announces the subject of the section that follows it, questions based on the heading will test your recall of the key ideas presented about that subject.

The best time to pose and answer these questions is *while you are reading.* As you finish each section, stop and take a moment to glance at the heading and recall the main points the section presented.

3. **How does this information fit with other material I have learned?** If you can draw connections between current and prior learning, your study method is working. If you can answer the following questions, you are probably on the right track.

   ◆ What does this topic have to do with topics discussed earlier in the chapter?
   ◆ How does this reading assignment fit with the topics of this week's class lectures?
   ◆ What does this chapter have to do with the chapter assigned last week?
   ◆ What principle do these problems illustrate?

These questions enable you to determine whether your learning is meaningful. They will help you check whether you are simply taking in information without much thought or whether you are thinking critically about the information and fitting it into the scheme of the course. The best time to ask connection questions is before you begin and after you finish the chapter or each major section.

Exercise 8.7	What questions would you ask when reading an economics textbook chapter titled "The Distribution of Income"?[1] The major headings of two sections are

Income Distribution in the United States

Historical Changes in Adjusted Income

Age Distribution and Income

Rags to Riches: Mobility

Some Characteristics of Income Distribution

Family Income Characteristics

Poverty

Poverty During Recession

Race and Sex Discrimination: Wages

Programs to Alleviate Poverty

As you evaluate your learning, you may, at times, find that a particular strategy is not working as well as it did in the past. You may find that an assignment is taking too long, that you do not seem to be making the right connections, or that you are not mastering the material as well as you feel you should. Perhaps the best way to describe this situation is to say that nothing has "clicked." It is best to stop, assess the situation, and modify your approach.

Often, a tried-and-true strategy that has always worked in the past fails when applied to a new type of learning. At first, the strategy may seem to be working as well as usual because you are so comfortable with it. Only later, when assessing your progress, do you realize that the strategy was not effective. For example, a student taking her first philosophy course approached the course by focusing on facts, as she had always done in other courses. She learned names and dates but found very few facts to learn. Eventually she realized her focus was too specific—she needed to focus on larger issues, theories, worldviews, and so forth.

The key to modifying your approach is to determine how the current situation differs from others in which you have used the strategy successfully. That difference pinpoints the problem. Next, you must alter your approach to accommodate that difference. Identify alternative approaches that are consistent with your learning style, evaluate each, and select the one most likely to work. It is also helpful to check with students who are doing well in the class to find out what learning strategies they are using.

Exercise 8.8	Complete the assignment you chose in Exercise 8.2. As you work, evaluate your learning, using one or more of the questions given on p. 143.

Interactive Chapter Review

Knowledge	Define the term *learning style*.	
Comprehension	List five strengths of your learning style based on the results of the Learning Style Questionnaire.	
Application	Examine the textbook of a course that you enjoy. In what ways, if any, does the textbook offer easy methods for you to learn, based on the various aspects of your learning style?	
Analysis	Compare two courses you are taking and describe in writing how they require you to rely on different strengths or aspects of your learning style.	
Synthesis	Think about how you learn most easily. Then describe what techniques the ideal instructor would use to teach you about the concept of learning styles. Discuss why these particular techniques would help you.	
Evaluation	Using the three questions on p. 143, evaluate one of your study sessions for a course you find difficult. Is your method of study effective? If not, make a list of at least three new and different ways you could study the course material. Then test these ideas the next time you study.	

Further Analysis

Analyze the following situation and answer the questions below.

In a course on intercultural communications, the topic this week is "Respecting the Boundaries of Personal Space." Instead of a textbook, the instructor uses a series of handouts to organize the course topics. The handouts, all of which include typed text only, are titled:

Personal Space: A Definition and Two Examples from Edward T. Hall

From North to South America: An Ever-Expanding Embrace

Italy, Germany, and Japan: Nonverbal Communications Problems in Cross-Cultural Interactions

African Cities Versus African Rural Areas: An Interesting Issue

Class time this week is divided like this: The instructor spends 15 minutes reading from the handouts and adding further examples from his own international business experience. Then he gives a group assignment, which students work on for about 20 minutes. For the last 25 minutes, everyone talks about what they learned from the handouts and the group activity, and students can ask questions.

1. What aspects of the instructor's teaching style can you determine from this scenario? Are there any aspects you are unsure of? Discuss evidence for your conclusions.

2. Suggest what type of student is going to have trouble learning in this class. Include information about at least two aspects of the student's learning style.

3. Describe for the instructor how he could revise his handouts to make them more useful to students who have a wide range of learning styles. Be as specific as you can.

Discussion

1. In college, a verbal learning style is very valuable. Why is this so? How might a student who wants to strengthen the verbal aspect of his or her learning style go about doing so?

2. Is a person's learning style the only factor to consider in how well he or she will do in a particular class? What other factors will determine a student's success?

The Work Connection

Your learning style is closely related to how you think and solve problems. As you approach a task or problem, you may tend to view it a certain way and overlook other ways that may lead to workable approaches and solutions. Pragmatic learners, for example, may tend to focus only on logical and systematic methods; applied learners may try to recall other practical situations in which a similar problem is solved. You can expand your ability to learn and thrive—at work, at school, and in your career—by broadening your perspective on a problem by asking all of these questions: "*Why* (should I know/do this)?" "*What* (do I need to know/do)?" "*How* (is it done/does it work)?" and "*What if* (x, y, or z happened)?" Seeking answers to all four of these questions, particularly in new or difficult situations, will stimulate your curiosity and help you find new solutions that may not have occurred to you if you had thought about a problem from only your usual perspective.

1. Think of a recent problem or challenge at work, home, or school. Write four complete questions using the samples above to broaden your thinking about this situation.

2. Answer as many of the questions as you can. For any you can't answer, what further information would you need to answer them? Write down the questions that would help you gather this information.

The Web Connection

1. Teaching Styles

   http://www.ntlf.com/html/lib/faq/ts-indiana.htm

   From the National Teaching and Learning Board, this site identifies five typical teaching styles and their advantages and disadvantages.

2. Best Teacher Description

   http://humanities.byu.edu/elc/teacher/bestteacher

   Compiled by a Brigham Young University faculty member, this site lists the characteristics of good teachers as described by students.

3. Quick Tips: Student-Instructor Differences

   http://www.lethbridgecollege.ab.ca/departments/learning/quicktip/stu_inst.html

   The Learning Centre at Lethbridge Community College in Canada offers these basic guidelines for student-instructor interaction.

4. Index of Learning Style Questionnaire

   http://www2.ncsu.edu:8010/unity/lockers/users/f/felder/public/ILSdir/ilsweb.html

   This online questionnaire from North Carolina State University will help you figure out what kind of learner you are and give you advice on learning strategies.

Go Electronic!
For additional readings, exercises, and Internet activities, visit the Longman Study Skills Web site at:
http://www.ablongman.com/StudySkills
If you need a user name and password, please see your instructor.

Chapter 9

Learning and Memory

DO YOU KNOW?

How do learning and memory work?
What are the three stages of remembering?
How can you improve your ability to learn?

Let's assume you have just finished reading a chapter in a data processing text; you read carefully and underlined important ideas. How much of that chapter are you likely to remember tomorrow? How much will you recall next week? The answers are surprising! Research evidence suggests that within one day, you will have forgotten more than half of what you read, and within a week, your recall will have dropped to less than 30 percent. These statistics have serious implications for you as a learner in college as well as later in your career. Despite all seriousness of purpose and good intentions, the rate of forgetting is rapid and dramatic *unless* you take specific steps to prevent it. This chapter briefly describes how learning and memory work. Once you become familiar with the learning process, you will learn numerous strategies for improving storage and retrieval of information and for overcoming forgetting.

How Learning and Memory Work

A popular but incorrect notion of memory is that it is a vast storage tank or a huge repository where information is deposited and retained. Rather, memory is a three-stage process involving encoding, storage, and retrieval. *Encoding* (or acquisition) is a process of acquiring information. Suppose you are unable to answer the question on a business exam, "Define a capital account." If you have never heard of a capital account, your memory broke down at the encoding stage; that is, you never acquired the information. The next stage of memory, *storage*, occurs when information is stored, briefly or permanently. A change in your nervous system occurs that allows storage to occur. This change is described as a neural or memory trace. If you once knew the term "capital account" and now cannot recall it, the memory trace may have faded or decayed. *Retrieval* is the process of getting at and using information held in storage. Another reason for your inability to remember the definition of capital account is retrieval failure. Although the information is stored, you are unable to retrieve it. Figure 9.1 is a visual

Figure 9.1
A Model of Memory

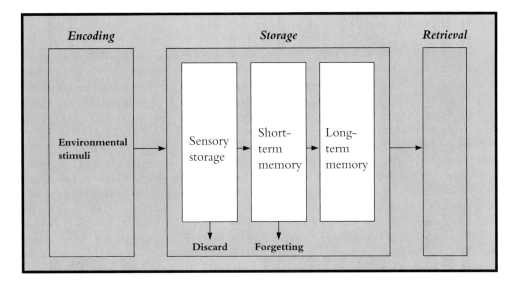

model of verbal learning and memory processes. Refer to it frequently as you read the sections below that explain each stage.

Stage 1: Encoding

Every waking moment your mind is bombarded with information and impressions of what is going on around you. Your five senses—hearing, sight, touch, taste, and smell—provide information about the world around you and your interaction with it. Think for a moment of all the signals your brain receives at a given moment. If you are reading, your eyes transmit not only the visual patterns of the words, but also information about the size and color of the print. You may hear a door slamming, a clock ticking, a dog barking. You may smell perfume or cigarette smoke; your sense of touch and feeling may signal that the pen you are using to underline will soon run out of ink or that the room is chilly. When you listen to a classroom lecture, you are constantly receiving stimuli—from the professor, from the lecture hall, from students around you. All these environmental stimuli are transmitted to your brain for a very brief *sensory storage* and interpretation.

Stage 2: Storage

Sensory Storage

Information received from your sense organs is transmitted through the nervous system to the brain, which accepts and interprets it. The information lingers briefly in the nervous system for your brain to interpret it. This lingering is known as *sensory storage.*

How does your mind handle this barrage of information from the senses? Thanks to *selective attention,* or *selective perception,* your brain automatically sorts out the more important signals from the trivial ones. Trivial signals, such as insignificant noises around you, are ignored or discarded. Through skills of concentration and attention, you can train yourself to ignore or discard other, more distracting signals, such as a dog barking or people talking in the background.

Although your sensory storage accepts all information, data are kept there only briefly, usually less than a few seconds. Then the information either decays or is replaced with incoming new stimuli. The function of sensory storage then is to retain information long enough for you to selectively attend to it and transmit it to your short-term memory.

Short-Term Memory

Short-term memory holds the information acquired from your sensory storage system. It is used to store information you wish to retain for only a few seconds. A telephone number, for example, is stored in your short-term memory until you dial it. A lecturer's words are retained until you can record them in your notes. Most researchers agree that short-term memory lasts much less than one minute, perhaps 20 seconds or less. Information can be kept or maintained longer if you practice or rehearse the information (repeating a phone number, for example). When you are introduced to someone, then, unless you repeat or rehearse his or her name at the time of introduction, you will not be able to remember it. New incoming information will force it out of your short-term memory.

Your short-term memory is limited in capacity as well as in time span. Research conducted by George Miller, a psychologist who studied memory, suggests that we have room in our short-term memory to store from five to nine chunks (or pieces) of information at a time, or on the average, seven.[1] Known as the Number Seven Theory, this finding has direct implications in both daily and academic situations. When you read a textbook chapter or listen to a lecture, for example, your short-term memory is unable to retain each piece of information you are receiving. To retain information beyond the limitations of short-term memory, it must be transferred to your long-term memory for more permanent storage.

Exercise 9.1	Answer the following items using your knowledge of the memory process.

1. Observe and analyze the area in which you are sitting. What sensory impressions (sights, sounds, touch sensations) have you been ignoring due to selective attention?

2. Can you remember what you ate for lunch last Tuesday? If not, why not?

3. Why are dashes placed in your social security number after the third and fifth numbers?

4. Explain why two people are able to carry on a deep conversation at a crowded, noisy party.

5. Explain why someone who looked up a phone number and then walked into another room to dial it forgot the number.

Learning: The Transfer from Short- to Long-Term Memory

To retain information beyond the brief moment you acquire it, you must transfer it to long-term memory for permanent storage. Several processes can help you store information in long-term memory: rote learning, rehearsal, and recoding.

Rote learning. Rote learning involves repetition of information in the form in which it was acquired in sensory storage. Learning the spelling of a word, memorizing the exact definition of a word, or repeating a formula until you can remember it are examples. Material learned through this means is often learned in a fixed order. Rote learning is usually an inefficient means to store information because, as you will see later, it is difficult to retrieve.

Elaborative rehearsal. Rehearsal, used at this stage, involves much more than simple repetition or practice. Elaborative rehearsal is a thinking process. It involves connecting new material with already learned material, asking questions, and making associations. It is a process of making the information meaningful and fitting it into an established category or relating it to existing memory stores. This form of rehearsal is discussed in more detail later.

Recoding. Recoding is a process of rearranging, changing, or grouping information so that it becomes more meaningful and easier to recall. For example, you could recode the following shopping list into three, easier to remember groups:

eggs, carrots, bleach, oranges, laundry soap, milk, onions, yogurt, cheese, plums, ammonia

Dairy	**Produce**	**Cleaning supplies**
eggs, milk, cheese, yogurt	carrots, onions, oranges, plums	laundry soap, ammonia, bleach

You could recode information from a reading assignment by outlining it. Taking notes from lectures is also a form of recoding.

Rehearsal and recoding are the underlying principles on which many learning strategies presented later in this book are based. Chapter 15, for example, discusses textbook highlighting and marking. Underlining is, however, actually a form of elaborative rehearsal. When you decide which information to underline, you are reviewing the information and sorting the important from the unimportant. When you make marginal notes, you are recoding the information by classifying, organizing, labeling, or summarizing it.

Exercise 9.2	Answer the following questions using your knowledge of the memory process. 1. On many campuses, weekly recitations or discussions are scheduled for small groups to review material presented in large lecture classes. What learning function do these recitation sections provide?

Continued

2. A literature instructor showed her class a film based on a short story that she had as-signed. What learning function(s) did the film provide?

3. Why might a text that contains pictures and diagrams be easier to learn from than one without them?

4. Two groups of students read the same textbook chapter. One group underlined key ideas on each page. The second group paraphrased and recorded the important ideas from each page. Explain why the second group received higher scores on a test based on the chapter than did the first group.

Long-Term Memory

Long-term memory is your permanent store of information. Unlike short-term memory, your long-term memory is nearly unlimited in both span and capacity. It contains hundreds of thousands of facts, details, impressions, and experiences that you have accumulated throughout your life.

Information is stored in long-term memory in three types of codes: (1) linguistic (language), (2) imaginal (mental or visual images), and (3) motor (physical). The linguistic code, which deals with verbal information, is the most important in academic learning. Ideas, concepts, and facts are encoded and often stored using language. Activities such as taking lecture notes, underlining texts, and writing outlines are forms of linguistic coding. Imaginal coding involves creation of mental or visual images. If, for example, you drew a diagram of a process or sketched the human ear in order to learn its parts, you would be using imaginal, or visual, coding. The third form of coding, motor, refers primarily to physical activities such as riding a bicycle, driving a car, or hitting a baseball. Significant research evidence suggests that dual coding—using more than one type of coding to store information—produces better recall than if only one code is used.

Stage 3: Retrieval

Think of retrieval as pulling stored information from your memory. Academic tasks requiring you to retrieve knowledge include math or science problems, quizzes and exams, and papers. Retrieval is integrally tied to storage. The manner in which information is stored in your memory affects its availability and the ease with which you can retrieve it. For example, suppose you have studied a topic but find that on an exam you are unable to remember much about it. There are several possible explanations: (1) you never completely learned (stored) the information at all, (2) you did not study (store) the information in the right way, (3) you are not asking the right questions or using the right means to retrieve it, or (4) you have forgotten it. Later this chapter suggests strategies for improving the effectiveness of both storage and retrieval.

**Exercise
9.3**

Use the principles of memory discussed so far in this chapter to explain each of the following situations.

1. A student does well on multiple-choice items on a test, but has difficulty with easy questions. What does this indicate about how he stored the information?

2. A student spends more time than anyone else in the class preparing for the midterm exam, yet she cannot remember important definitions and concepts at the time of the exam. Offer several possibilities that may explain her dilemma.

3. What form(s) of coding does each of the following situations involve?

   a. Replacing a ribbon in your printer or typewriter

   b. Drawing a blood sample from a patient's arm

   c. Plotting a graph to include in a term paper that shows the relationships among median income, sex, and educational level

   d. Interpreting a map

   e. Solving a problem in business math

4. You cannot state the sixth number of your social security number without repeating the first five.

**Exercise
9.4**

Identify the encoding, storage, and retrieval stages in each of the following tasks.

1. Learning to read a patient's chart

2. Learning the lyrics to a popular song

3. Learning to balance a ledger in accounting

4. Learning to operate a computer

Forgetting

Despite the vast capacity of human long-term memory, not all information remains there indefinitely. Forgetting does occur, and for newly learned material, it can occur at a dramatic rate. Table 9.1 summarizes the results of a research study[2] designed to measure the rate at which subjects forget previously learned verbal material.

These data have serious implications for you as a learner. They indicate that you will quickly forget a large portion of information you have learned *unless you take action to prevent this.*

Numerous theories have been offered to explain why forgetting occurs. One argues that the learned information fades from disuse. Fading may occur when the neural trace established when new learning occurs weakens from disuse, much as handwriting on a

Table 9.1
Rate of Forgetting

Time Lapse from Initial Learning	Amount of Material Remembered
1 day	54%
7 days	35%
14 days	21%
21 days	18%
28 days	19%
63 days	17%

piece of paper fades over time. Another, more popular theory suggests that interference with competing information causes forgetting. Two types of interference—proactive and retroactive—have been identified, as shown in Figure 9.2.

Proactive Interference

This situation occurs when old knowledge interferes with the recall of new, recently acquired knowledge. For example, you may have difficulty remembering a new formula in math if it is very similar to one you had learned last week. To combat this type of interference, make a conscious effort to examine similarities and differences between old and new learning.

Retroactive Interference

New learning sometimes interferes with the recall of old learning. You may be unable to recall a lecture from two weeks ago because the content of this week's lecture is blocking it. To overcome this type of interference, be certain to review previously learned material frequently, as well as to keep current with new material.

Figure 9.2
Types of Interference

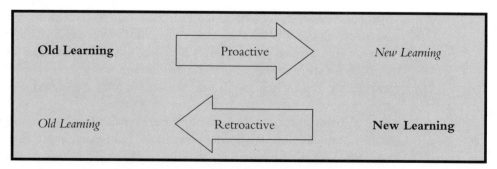

Exercise 9.5	Answer the following questions using your knowledge of memory and forgetting.

1. Someone who memorized a phone number before he left a party is unable to recall it the next evening. Why?

2. A victim of a robbery is unable to give a detailed, accurate description of the criminal to a police artist the morning after the robbery. What could the victim have done to improve his or her recall?

3. A student is taking an introductory course in Spanish and, at the same time, is completing several years of study of Hebrew as part of his religious training. What learning problems might he expect?

4. What learning problems would you expect if you were taking a British literature and an American literature course during the same semester?

Strategies for Improving Encoding, Storage, and Retrieval

Now that you have a notion of how memory works, you are ready to learn strategies that will both increase the effectiveness of your memory processes and retard forgetting.

Strategies for Improving Encoding

Use the following suggestions to improve encoding, which is the process of taking in information.

Exclude competing stimuli. Consciously exclude everything that does not relate to what you want to encode. For instance, if you are reading, do not sit where there are other competing visual stimuli, such as television.

Use various sensory modes. Use as many senses as possible to take in information. When listening to a lecture, for example, pay attention to visual clues the lecturer provides as well as to what he or she says.

Carefully and specifically define your purpose. As you filter incoming information, know clearly and specifically what types of information you need. If you are reading reference material for a research paper, you may need to pay attention to facts and statistics. If you are reading material to prepare for a class discussion, however, you might focus on controversial issues.

Use previewing. Since encoding involves accepting an incoming message, it is helpful to anticipate both the content and structure of that message. Previewing, discussed in Chapter 14, provides this preliminary information.

Strategies for Improving Storage

Use the following suggestions to improve how efficiently you store information.

Use immediate review. After working on a chapter for several hours (with frequent breaks) it is tempting, when you finish, to close the book and move on to something else. To quit, however, without taking five to ten minutes to review what you have read is a serious mistake. Since you have already invested several hours of time and effort, it is worthwhile to spend a few more minutes insuring that investment. Reviewing *immediately* following reading is an effective way of storing information and facilitating retrieval. A review of your notes immediately following a lecture is also effective.

Immediate review is effective because it consolidates new knowledge. Material that is meaningful and related to existing learning is more easily stored. As you read, you encounter a great deal of information that is not organized or focused. The relative importance of ideas is not completely clear until you establish the connections among ideas. Immediate review allows you to begin to see the big picture, to discover how individual portions of the chapter fit together and how they relate to prior learning.

To review a chapter you have just read, follow these seven steps:

1. **Begin as soon as you have finished reading the chapter.**
2. **Go back to the beginning of the chapter and review all the boldfaced text or major headings.**
3. **For each heading, form a question.** If a heading is "Causes of Hormonal Imbalance," ask, "What are the causes of hormonal imbalance?" For the heading "Treating Hormonal Imbalance," ask, "What are the treatments for hormonal imbalance?"
4. **Then look away from the page, or cover it up with a sheet of paper, and try to answer each question.** Try to recall the causes of hormonal imbalance and its treatment. You can answer mentally, aloud, or on paper.
5. **Check to see if you have answered the question completely by referring back to the text.** If you could not answer your question or only partially recalled information, check to see what you have missed and then retest your recall.
6. **Continue through the chapter in this manner, heading by heading.**
7. **When you have finished, stop and think.** Try to recall how the chapter was organized and how it progressed from idea to idea. Try to identify five to ten key points it discussed. Reread the chapter summary, if available, to verify these points.

Substantial research evidence supports the value of immediate review. Students who use immediate review consistently experience higher retention than those who do not review.

Use numerous sensory channels to store information.   Many students regard reading and studying as only a visual means of processing and reviewing information.

Learning can be enhanced, however, by using sight, sound, and touch, as well. If you can incorporate writing, listening, drawing or diagramming, and recitation or discussion into your study habits, storage will be more effective. Think of this technique as a means of reducing the burden on your linguistic processing systems by transferring some of the load to other forms of processing. Evidence suggests that each form of coding is distinct and that each creates its own path or trace. Using several forms of coding, then, creates several paths through which information can be retrieved.

HOW DO YOU SEE IT?

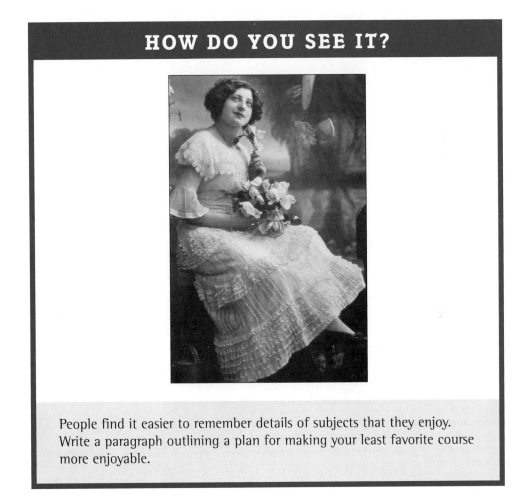

People find it easier to remember details of subjects that they enjoy. Write a paragraph outlining a plan for making your least favorite course more enjoyable.

Organize or recode information to be stored.   Remembering a large number of individual facts or pieces of information is often a difficult, frustrating task. *Recoding* is a primary means of storing information in your long-term memory. Recoding involves organizing or reducing information into groups or chunks. Instead of overloading your memory with numerous individual facts, you are inputting an organized, meaningful set of information that is stored as one chunk rather than numerous individual facts. Retrieval, then, is easier, too, because a chunk is retrieved as one piece and related information stays together. For example, a physics student used the chunking strategy to organize and connect the topics of speed, velocity, and acceleration into one topic, motion. A business student studying the differences among consumer markets used chunking to group the differences into three categories: geographic, demographic, and income differences.

To organize information, keep the following suggestions in mind:

◆   Discover how the material you are studying is connected. Search for some organizing principle.
◆   Look for similarities and differences.
◆   Look for sequences and for obvious divisions or breaking points within the sequences.

Exercise 9.6

Decide how you could organize or recode each of the following types of information for most effective storage.

1. The problems two-career families face
2. The effects of terrorism
3. The reasons for recycling garbage
4. Ecological problems of the future

Use elaboration.   Mere repetition of material is seldom an effective storage strategy. Studying a chapter by rereading it, for instance, would not be effective. Instead you must think about, or *elaborate* upon, the material—ask questions, make associations and inferences, think of practical applications, and create mental images. Elaboration makes the new material meaningful and easier to store. For example, a mechanical engineering student was studying the first law of thermodynamics: Whenever heat is added to a system, it transforms into an equal amount of some other form of energy. The student began by being certain she understood the law, so she expressed it in writing using her own words. She wrote: "Heat added = increase in internal energy and/or external work done by the system." Then she began to think of situations in which she had observed the law, in a steam engine's operation, for instance. She asked herself: What happens in the atmosphere when a body of air is heated? What external work is done?

Connect new learning with previous learning.   Isolated, unrelated pieces of information are difficult to store and also difficult to retrieve. If, however, you can link new learning to already stored information, it will be easier to store and retrieve since you have an established memory slot in which to hold it. For example, an economics student associated the factors influencing the supply and demand curves with practical instances from his family's retail florist business.

Exercise 9.7   Discuss techniques that might improve storage of the following tasks.

1. Learning to identify and distinguish various types of figurative language used in literature
2. Learning various bacterial forms and characteristics
3. Learning the environmental factors that affect entry of a product into a foreign market for a business marketing course
4. Learning the process of federal budget preparation for an American government course

---

Strategies for Improving Retrieval

Your ability to retrieve information is the true test of how accurately and completely you have stored it. The following strategies will improve your ability to retrieve information.

Use visualization.   As you read, study, and learn a body of information, try to visualize, or create a mental picture of, it. Your picture or image should be sufficiently detailed to include as much related information as possible. A student of anatomy and physiology found visualizations an effective way to learn the parts of the skeletal system. She would first draw it on paper and then visualize, or mentally draw, the system.

Visualization, a type of imaginal coding, makes retrieval easier because the information is stored in one unified piece, and, if you can recall any part of the mental picture, then you will be able to retrieve the whole picture.

Thinking Critically
. . . About Learning Strategies

In this chapter you encounter many learning strategies. Some will work better for you than others; a few may not work for you at all. Some may work for one course but not for another. The key to making information in this chapter work for you is to try to *critically evaluate* each strategy.

Begin by selecting two or three strategies that appeal to you. Decide which ones you will use for which course. Use them for a week. At the end of the week, do a preliminary evaluation. Rate the strategy as "Very Useful," "Somewhat Useful," or "Not Useful," and record your evaluation in the chart shown on p. 160.

Use the following questions to help you in rating each strategy:

1. Did the strategy seem to make a difference in how easily I was able to learn? (You may be able to answer this question more accurately after you take an exam or quiz.)
2. Was it easy to use?
3. Was it time consuming?
4. Did it help me see the information in a new way?
5. Did it improve my understanding of the material?

The next week, choose two or three more strategies to concentrate on and evaluate. *A word of caution:* Some strategies may take a little time to get used to. If a strategy seems to have potential but does not work right away, stick with it for a longer period of time.

Skill	Rating		
	Very Useful	Somewhat Useful	Not Useful
Encoding			
Exclude competing stimuli	❏	❏	❏
Use various sensory modes	❏	❏	❏
Define your purpose	❏	❏	❏
Use previewing	❏	❏	❏
Storage			
Use immediate review	❏	❏	❏
Use numerous sensory channels	❏	❏	❏
Recode information	❏	❏	❏
Use elaboration	❏	❏	❏
Connect new to previous learning	❏	❏	❏
Retrieval			
Use visualization	❏	❏	❏
Develop retrieval clues	❏	❏	❏
Simulate rehearsal tasks	❏	❏	❏
Learn beyond mastery	❏	❏	❏

Develop retrieval clues.   Think of your memory as having slots or compartments in which information is stored. If you can name or label what is in the slot, you will know where to look to find information that fits that slot. Think of memory slots as similar to the way kitchen cupboards are often organized, with specific items in specific places. If you need a knife to cut a pizza, you look in the silverware and utensils drawer. Similarly, if you have a memory slot labeled "environmental problems" in which you store information related to pollution—its problems, causes, and solutions—you can retrieve information on air pollution by calling up the appropriate retrieval clue. Developing retrieval clues involves selecting a word or phrase that summarizes or categorizes several pieces of information. For example, you might use the phrase "motivation theories" to organize information for a psychology course on instinct, drive, cognition, arousal, and opponent-process theories and the major proponents of each.

Simulate rehearsal tasks.   Practice retrieving learned information by simulating test conditions. If you are studying for a math exam, prepare by solving problems. If you know your exam in a law enforcement course will consist of three essay questions, then prepare by anticipating possible essay questions and drafting an answer to each. The form and process of practice, then, must be patterned after and modeled upon the event for which you are preparing.

Learn beyond mastery.   It is tempting to stop studying as soon as you feel you have learned a given body of information. However, to ensure complete, thorough learning, it is best to conduct a few more reviews. When you learned to drive a car, you did not stop practicing parallel parking after the first time you accomplished it correctly. Similarly, for a botany course you should not, at the moment you feel you have mastered it, stop reviewing the process of photosynthesis and its place within the carbon cycle. Instead, use additional review to make the material stick and to prevent interference from subsequent learning.

Exercise 9.8	What strategies would you use to learn (encode, store, and retrieve) each of the following types of information most efficiently?

1. Vocabulary words for a Spanish I course
2. The process of leaf development in plants for a botany course
3. A comparison between the Bill of Rights at the time it was written and in today's political and social climate
4. Types of nonverbal communication and their uses in communicating with an audience

Working Together

Form groups of four or five students and discuss causes of and solutions to each of the following situations:

1. A student frequently misplaces his car keys and wastes valuable time looking for them.
2. A friend has difficulty remembering names of new people he meets at a party.
3. A student's parents own a Mac computer, and he learned to use WordPerfect, a word processing program, to type his papers. Now that he lives on campus, he is trying to learn to use a new software program, Microsoft Word. He is having difficulty because he frequently confuses commands.

Interactive Chapter Review

Knowledge	Define each of the three stages of memory: encoding, storage, and retrieval.
Comprehension	Which stage of memory is affected by selective attention?
Application	What is an effective way to learn from a reading assignment?
Analysis	Think of two or three times recently when you have forgotten information you needed for a classroom discussion, homework, test, or research paper. Which of the two possible ways of forgetting (p. 154) does each seem to involve? Why do you think so?
Synthesis	Think about a course you are taking. What are two new techniques you could use at each stage of memory to learn the course material beyond mastery? When and how would you use them?
Evaluation	Evaluate how well you have learned the material in this chapter, using the seven steps for reviewing given on p. 156. For any information you haven't yet learned well, decide which learning techniques you can use to remember the information more thoroughly.

Further Analysis

Analyze the following situation and answer the questions that follow.

You are taking a course in mass media at the University of Alberta and you are studying techniques and effects of television advertising. Your instructor has given the following assignment:

Write a brief essay describing the principles of learning and memory that advertisers take advantage of when preparing and running an advertisement for television.

1. What do you think the instructor's purpose was in giving the assignment?

2. What do advertisers do to make sure that you encode their message rather than discard it?

3. What techniques do advertisers use to make sure you store the message in your long-term memory?

4. What do advertisers do to make sure that you are able to retrieve the ad's message?

Discussion

1. A student taking computer-assisted drafting said she felt that the storage and retrieval strategies presented in this chapter were of little use to her because her course required little factual learning. The focus of her course is labs, drawing assignments, and exams that require drawings. Do you agree with this student's assessment?

2. In what everyday situations do you use visualization?

3. Give several examples of situations where you have overlearned, or learned beyond mastery.

4. List the courses you are taking. Then review this chapter and indicate which storage and retrieval strategies would be useful for each.

5. Some researchers have proposed that human memory is structured and functions like a computer. Discover as many similarities and differences as possible.

The Work Connection

Read the following information and respond to the questions below:

If you are a student returning to college to learn new skills and attitudes that will help you succeed in today's high-performance workplace, congratulations! If you are just beginning to prepare for your first career, consider that you may need to refocus, retrain, or even change careers over the course of a lifetime. Never plan to stop learning. A commitment to lifelong learning is becoming a prerequisite for sound career planning in an ever-changing work environment. Indeed, a phrase that describes the attitudes of lifelong learners has been coined: "career self-reliance." Career self-reliance means taking responsibility for your own career: continually updating your skills, always seeking to improve your performance, and understanding how your skills are marketable both within and outside of your current company and industry. Lifelong learning is the "path to job security and career health."[3]

1. How will knowledge of the learning and memory processes help you become more self-reliant in college courses?

2. How do you think the skills and strategies taught in this chapter would help you refocus, retrain, or change careers, should it become necessary?

3. Rate your current level of self-reliance as a student. Give two examples that explain or justify your rating.

The Web Connection

1. Try these online memory experiments:

   http://www.essex.ac.uk/psychology/experiments/memtask.html

   http://www.exploratorium.edu/brain_explorer/memory.html

   http://www.dcity.org/braingames/pennies/

2. Improving Your Memory

   http://www.ctl.ua.edu/CTLStudyAids/StudySkillsFlyers/MemorySkills/improving memory.htm

   From the University of Alabama, this informative Web site discusses the "Four R's of Remembering."

3. Remembering

   http://www.ucc.vt.edu/stdysk/remember.html

   Virginia Tech. provides this site with memory information specifically geared to college students.

Go Electronic!

For additional readings, exercises, and Internet activities, visit the Longman Study Skills Web site at:

http://www.ablongman.com/StudySkills

If you need a user name and password, please see your instructor.

Chapter 10

Study Strategies for Academic Disciplines

DO YOU KNOW?

How can you get off to a good start in an unfamiliar field of study?
What are the characteristics of each academic discipline?
How should you adapt your reading and study strategies for each discipline?
What particular thought patterns can you expect in each discipline?
How should you take lecture notes for each discipline?

Each academic discipline is a unique system of study; each takes a specialized approach to the study of the world around us. To illustrate, let's choose as an example a popular house pet—the dog—and consider how various disciplines might approach its study.[1]

- An artist might consider the dog as an object of beauty and record its fluid, flexible muscular structure and meaningful facial expressions on canvas.
- A psychologist might study what human needs are fulfilled by owning a dog.
- The historian might research the historical importance of dogs—their use as guard dogs in warfare or their role herding sheep.
- A zoologist might trace the evolution of the dog and identify its predecessors.
- A mathematician might treat the dog as a three-dimensional object comprising planes and angles.
- An economist might focus on the supply of and demand for dogs and the amount of business that they generate (kennels, supplies, dog food).
- A biologist would categorize the dog as *Canis familiaris.*
- A physiologist would be concerned with the animal's bodily functions (breathing, heart rate, temperature).

Each academic discipline, then, approaches a given object or event with a different focus or perspective. Each has its own special purposes and interests that define the scope of the discipline. You will find that each discipline has its own methodology for studying topics with which it is concerned. Because each discipline is unique, each requires somewhat different study and learning strategies.

The purpose of this chapter is to show you how to modify and adapt your learning, thinking, and study strategies to five general academic areas: the social sciences, the life and physical sciences, mathematics, literature and the arts, and career fields. For each of these disciplines, unique approaches and characteristics are discussed, and then techniques for adapting textbook reading and lecture note taking strategies are described.

Approaching New Fields of Study

In your first few years of college, you are likely to encounter disciplines with which you have had no prior experience. Anthropology, political science, or organic chemistry may be new to you. In the beginning, these new fields of study may seem unfamiliar or foreign. One student described this feeling as "being on the outside looking in," watching other students participate in the class but being unable to do so himself. At first, you may feel lost, confused, or frustrated in such courses. These feelings may result from unfamiliarity with the specialized language of the discipline, with what types of learning and thinking are expected, and with conventions, approaches, and methodology of the discipline.

When approaching a new field of study, try the following:

Spend more time than usual reading and studying.   You are doing more than reading and studying: You are learning how to learn as well.

Learn as much as possible until you discover more about what is expected.   You will need as much information as is available to begin to fit information into patterns.

Since you do not know how you will eventually organize and use it, process the same information in several different ways.   For example, in an anthropology course, you might learn events and discoveries chronologically (according to occurrence in time) as well as comparatively (according to similarities and differences among various discoveries). In an accounting course, you might organize information by procedures as well as by controlling principles.

Use several methods of learning.   Since you are not sure which will be most effective for the types of learning and thinking that are required, try several methods at once. For example, you might highlight textbook information (to promote factual recall) as well as write outlines and summaries (to interpret and consolidate ideas). You might also draw diagrams that map the relations between concepts and ideas. (These learning strategies are discussed in detail in Chapter 15.)

Ask questions.   For example

◆ What is the logical progression or development of ideas?
◆ Are there any cause and effect relationships operating?
◆ What are the practical applications of this information?

Look for similarities between the new subject matter and other academic fields that are familiar to you.   If similarities exist, you may be able to modify or adapt existing learning approaches and strategies to fit your new field of study.

Establish an overview of the field.   Spend time studying the table of contents of your textbook; it provides an outline of the course. Look for patterns, progression of ideas, and recurring themes, approaches, or problems.

Obtain additional reference materials, if necessary.   Some college texts delve into a subject immediately, providing only a brief introduction or overview in the first chapter. If your text does this, spend an hour or so in the library getting a more comprehensive overview of the field.

◆ Read or skim several encyclopedia entries in your field of study, taking notes if necessary.
◆ Check the card catalog to see how the subject is divided.
◆ Locate two or three introductory texts in the field. Study the table of contents of each and skim the first chapter.

The Social Sciences and History

The social sciences are concerned with the study of people, their development, and how they function together and interact. Included are psychology, anthropology, sociology, political science, and economics. They deal with political, economic, social, cultural, and behavioral aspects of human beings. The term "science" is appropriate because each discipline concentrates on defining problems; observing, gathering, and interpreting information; and reporting measurable results. Some social science courses are required in most degree programs.

What to Expect

Courses in the social sciences tend to have the following characteristics:

◆ They are highly factual. Especially in introductory courses, an instructor's first task is to acquaint you with what is already known—principles, rules, and facts—so that you can subsequently use them in approaching new problems and unique situations.
◆ They introduce a vast number of new terms. Although each academic field has a language of its own, each social science has developed an extensive set of

terminology to make broad or largely subjective topics as objective and quantifiable as possible.

◆ They require large amounts of reading. Expect to read several textbook chapters per week. Additionally, your instructor may assign supplementary readings on a regular basis.

◆ They make use of graphics (maps, charts, tables, graphs).

◆ They are research oriented. Many texts describe or report research studies as supporting evidence. In introductory courses, the outcome of the research and what it proves or suggests are usually most important.

◆ They emphasize theories, and often the social scientists who developed them.

How to Read and Study the Social Sciences

Since social science texts tend to be highly factual, it is easy to get lost in detail and to lose sight of the general topics with which the discipline is concerned. Use the following guidelines when reading social science materials:

◆ Since large amounts of reading are usually required, be sure to keep up with assignments, reading a chapter section or two each day.

◆ Be certain to develop a course master file to record and learn new terminology (refer to Chapter 11).

◆ Plan time in your schedule for locating and reading supplementary reading assignments. Often these are on reserve in the library or you may be asked to access them on the Internet. Be certain to take summary notes on the material.

◆ Maintain a focus on large ideas: concepts, trends, and patterns. Previewing before and reviewing after reading will help establish this focus.

What Thought Patterns to Anticipate

Three thought patterns predominate in the social sciences: listing, comparison and contrast, and cause and effect. Table 10.1 describes their uses and includes several examples from specific disciplines.

Taking Lecture Notes

Use the following suggestions to improve your note taking in social science courses:

Take notes.   Regardless of whether the lecture supplements or covers material identical to your textbook, take thorough, complete notes. Recording information you have already read or will read in your text will reinforce your learning. Later, after checking the corresponding text closely, you may shorten and reorganize your notes to best fit with text material.

Summarize cases or examples.   Especially in sociology, psychology, and anthropology classes, a lecturer may use case studies (descriptions of a particular person, action, or

Table 10.1

Thought Patterns* in the Social Sciences

Pattern	Uses	Examples
Listing	To present facts, illustrations, findings, or examples; to list research	Sociology Types of white-collar crime Examples of institutional racism Characteristics of aerospace/defense industries Environmental abuses
Comparison and contrast	To evaluate two sides of an issue; to compare and contrast theories, groups, behaviors, events	Political science A comparison of ethnic groups' political power A study of various urban development strategies A discussion of types of consumer representation groups
Cause and effect	To study behavior and motivation; to examine connections among events, actions, behaviors	Psychology Sources of stress and how the body reacts to it The effects of drug therapy on schizophrenia The underlying causes of aggressive behavior Means of controlling and treating phobias

*See Chapter 12.

problem) to illustrate a concept presented in the text. In your notes, try to summarize the key information of the case study, recording enough facts to bring the example to mind again when you review.

Summarize films or videotapes.   Films and videotapes are often used to illustrate concepts, theories, and problems in psychology, sociology, and anthropology classes. While detailed notes are unnecessary, be sure to jot down the main points the film or videotape makes as well as your impressions and reactions.

Edit your notes.   In history lectures, editing your notes is particularly essential. Often an instructor will discuss numerous events, people, and laws simultaneously. Other instructors seem to switch between historical periods, discussing various trends or issues. As you edit, try to indicate the chronological sequence of events. Also, try to collect all facts about a particular person, event, or issue in one place.

Exercise 10.1	Analyze the following situation and answer the questions.

A psychology student has been assigned a 1,000-word paper on the founders of the field of psychology.

1. Analyze the purpose of the assignment.
2. How should the student approach the assignment?
3. Is research necessary? If so, what sources might he or she begin with?
4. What thought pattern(s) could he or she use to organize the paper?

The Life and Physical Sciences

Life sciences refer to the study of living organisms: anatomy and physiology, zoology, botany, and biology. The physical sciences are concerned with the function, structure, and composition of energy, matter, and substance in our environment and include physics, chemistry, and physical geology. Sometimes called the natural sciences, both types are primarily concerned with two questions: "Why?" and "How?" Scientists constantly ask these two questions and conduct experiments and research to learn the answers.

To work effectively in a science course, adopt a scientific way of thinking. The usual concerns, such as "What is important to learn?" and "How much supporting information do I need to learn?", may be of only secondary importance. Instead, to be most successful, you must adopt a scientific mind-set—you need to become comfortable with asking literal questions and seeking answers, or analyzing problems and seeking solutions or explanations.

To benefit most from your learning, ask practical questions. For example, if you are a nursing student studying organic chemistry, the question you must always keep in the back of your mind is "How does what I am learning apply to the field of nursing?"

Some students of science become too involved with fact and detail and fail to step back and look at the larger picture. Often, they fail to recognize connections and relationships between the subject matter at hand and its applications to various concerns and professions.

What to Expect

Scientific and technical material, both in lecture and in textbooks, has special characteristics.

Unfamiliar Subject Matter

While the social sciences present new concepts and principles, they often deal with subjects with which we are familiar and with which we function daily. Social groups, physical and emotional needs, and aspects of culture are examples. Scientific topics, on the other hand, are less familiar to most of us. For example, few of us have a background of everyday experience with molecular structure, mutant genes, or radioactive isotopes.

Because of the new, unfamiliar nature of scientific material, all science courses will require extra study time, perhaps even twice as much. Students should plan their schedules to allow for it. Even excellent students, to whom reading, studying, and learning have always come easily, find it difficult to admit that scientific study requires greater time, effort, and perseverance. Consequently, when learning does not occur as easily as in other subjects, they become frustrated and say that they cannot learn science or that the sciences are too difficult.

Active Participation Is Required

Most rigorous scientific courses require a weekly laboratory in addition to class lectures. Here the purpose is to test, apply, experiment with, or demonstrate the principles presented in lectures. Many students who are new or uncommitted to scientific study fail to recognize the importance of laboratory sessions. Consequently, they fail to approach the course with the necessary practical, testing, questioning attitude.

Factual Density

The pure sciences are even more factual than the social sciences. Introductory science courses leave little room for interpretation, debate, opinion, or conjecture. Texts and lectures appear formal, straightforward, and regimented (and to students who thrive on interaction and controversy—uninteresting).

How to Read and Study Scientific Material

Use the following suggestions when reading and studying scientific material:

Preview assignments.   Because scientific material is often unfamiliar, previewing the chapter before you give it a thorough reading is essential. Also preview the problems at the end of the chapter. Reading through these problems will provide clues about important principles emphasized in the chapter. Preview the vocabulary list to identify terms you will need to learn.

Do not skip anything.   Unlike with other, more familiar subjects, you cannot afford to skip anything. Never try to read quickly or settle for getting the gist of meaning. Facts and details are important, as are the connections among them.

Read carefully and thoughtfully.   Some students find it effective to read each section of a chapter at least twice: The first reading is intended to acquaint them with key ideas; the second reading is to fill in the details and grasp specific, detailed concepts.

Be alert for gaps in information.   Because information in a science course is presented sequentially and understanding depends on mastering earlier information, you may find that you lack background or specific information on a topic. It is your responsibility, if you should identify such a gap, to fill it through reading, researching, locating Internet sources, using a scientific encyclopedia, or checking with your instructor.

Focus on applications.   Though science courses contain a great deal of abstract theory and fact, they are also very concerned with applications. The end-of-chapter problems often focus on the use and application of information learned.

Make everyday connections.   To make the subject matter less abstract and easier to learn, try to relate facts, ideas, and principles to things with which you are familiar. In a human anatomy and physiology course, for example, when studying the bones in the skeletal system, try to feel your own bones. In chemistry, when studying various types of solutions, think of everyday liquids that are representative of each type.

Ask questions.   Do not look for facts—look for answers. Keep in mind constantly the questions "Why?", "How?", and "Under what conditions?". For each occurrence, be sure you understand how and why it happens.

Learn the notation system.   Each field uses its own version of shorthand, a series of signs, symbols, and characters that have become standard abbreviations or notations. To work within a given field, then, a first step is to learn its notation system. Make these notations a part of your course master file (see Chapter 11).

Translate formulas into words.   Most scientific fields express key relationships in abbreviated formulas. To be certain that you understand the relationship, try to express it in your own words. This will establish verbal connections and make storage and retrieval easier.

Develop a vocabulary master file.   The vocabulary of the sciences is exact and precise. In many of the sciences, learning depends on mastering a great deal of new terminology. Fortunately, the sciences rely more heavily on a common base of prefixes, roots, and suffixes than do most other disciplines. It is especially worthwhile, then, to develop a master file of word parts and learn them as soon as possible.

What Thought Patterns to Anticipate

The three most commonly used thought patterns (see Chapter 12) in scientific courses are cause and effect, process, and problem-solution. As you will see below, these three patterns often intertwine. Uses and examples of these patterns are shown in Table 10.2.

Taking Lecture Notes

Use the following guidelines to polish your lecture note taking in the sciences:

Don't get lost in detail.   Lectures in the life and natural sciences may involve experiments, demonstrations, or solving sample problems. For these activities, it is easy to get

Table 10.2

Thought Patterns* in the Sciences

Pattern	Uses	Examples
Cause and effect	Explain why natural phenomena occur	Biology An explanation of why trees shed their leaves A discussion of why plant cells divide (mitosis) The conditions under which plant fossil formation occurs An explanation of why domesticated plants were important in formulating the theory of natural selection
Process	Describe how events occur; present steps in experimental procedures	Anatomy and physiology How the liver functions How white blood cells function in the immune system Control of organ function by the endocrine system Transmittal of genetic code from parents to child
Problem-solution	Solve practical problems; study currently unexplained phenomena	Physics How sound waves transfer energy How refraction of light produces mirages Practical problems, such as calculating the work done by a woman who lifts a 13kg suitcase 5m upward, or estimating the time needed for an 850W coffeemaker to prepare 10 cups of coffee when the water used is 55°F.

*See Chapter 12.

lost in recording details, thus losing sight of the principles each is intended to emphasize. Do not try to record all the details of each step in a demonstration or experiment; instead, focus on organization and procedures with the intent to identify the overall purpose. For sample problems, frequently solved on the chalkboard, record what the instructor writes, leaving plenty of blank space. Then, as you edit your notes after the lecture, try to describe and fill in what occurred at each step.

Make quick sketches.   Diagrams and charts are often used as illustrations. When these are presented, draw a quick sketch, not a careful copy. You can redraw it later during editing, or a similar drawing may appear in your text. Concentrate on the process or point the diagram is intended to show. Label the steps if possible; if time is insufficient, simply number the steps in the process. Later, as you edit your lecture notes, be certain to write out the steps.

Outline or summarize notes briefly.   Since notes in the sciences tend to be highly factual, write a brief summary or outline of your notes each day. This will help you regain a perspective on key ideas and will force you to organize the details into meaningful groupings.

Use scientific notation.   Learn the scientific notation system and use it as you take notes. It is a shorthand system that will speed up your note taking significantly. At first, to help yourself get started, keep a list of common symbols and abbreviations close at hand for fast reference. As you edit your notes, build the habit of using symbols: Look for places where you could have used a sign or symbol instead of a word, and make corrections.

When You Are Having Difficulty

If the sciences are typically a difficult field of study for you, or if you suddenly find yourself not doing well in a science course, try the following survival tactics:

Make changes in your learning strategies.   Let's suppose you are a nonscience major taking your one or two required science courses; you may feel as out of place as if you were in a foreign country. As a first step to working with "foreign" fields of study, you *must* revise and alter your approaches and strategies. Many students mistakenly think they will get by in their one or two required science courses using the same reading, study, and thinking strategies that work in other fields. Plan on making the changes already described in this section. You cannot be even minimally successful unless you make them.

Learn from classmates.   Talk with and observe the strategies of students who are doing well in the course. You are likely to pick up new and useful procedures.

Obtain a tutor.   Many Academic Skills Centers offer peer tutors for specific courses.

Learn the metric system.   If the metric system is used, and you have not learned it, spend the time and effort needed to learn it. It is essential to most scientific fields.

Double your study time.   If you are having trouble with a course, first (if you have not done so already) make a commitment to spend more time and work harder. Use this added time to revise and try out new strategies. Never waste time on a strategy that is not working.

Purchase a review book, student practice manual, or other learning aid and work with it regularly.

Pull the course together:

- ◆ Review your notes and text assignments; discover how they work together and where they seem to be headed.

◆ As you review, make lists of topics you do understand and those you do not.

◆ Decide whether you are experiencing difficulty due to gaps in your scientific background. Ask yourself whether the instructor assumes you know things when you do not. If so, consider obtaining a tutor. Check with your college's learning assistance center on the availability of tutorial services.

◆ Ask for help from either your classmates or your instructor.

Exercise 10.2	Analyze the following situation and answer the questions below.

An English major is taking a required chemistry course to fulfill a general education requirement. A weekly three-hour laboratory is required, for which he must perform a series of experiments and submit a two-page report. The student complains about the lab: If he can find out the results of each experiment by looking them up in a book or by reading his text, he wants to know, why spend the three hours performing experiments for which the results are already known? He also complains about the lab and its required format, since it allows no creativity or self-expression.

1. What could you explain to this student to overcome his objections?

2. What does he fail to understand about science?

3. Evaluate the quality of his thinking about his chemistry course.

Mathematics

Mathematics is a very strict, regimented study that follows a prescribed order of events. Problems are solved using specified step-by-step procedures. Theorems are derived in a tightly logical, sequential order. Much of what you learn is dependent on skills that preceded it. Mathematics, then, is cumulative—skills build upon one another. For example, you cannot solve bank interest problems in financial accounting if you do not know how to work with percentages.

What to Expect

Mathematics is a discipline that requires regular, consistent, day-to-day study. Here are a few things you should expect in a mathematics course:

Expect every class to count.   Class attendance and participation are essential for learning math. Even if there is a "cut" policy, don't cut class. Because math learning is sequential, if you miss one specific skill, that gap in your understanding and competence may cause problems all semester.

Expect regular homework assignments.   Whether or not an instructor collects or grades homework, be sure to complete all assignments by when they are due.

Practice is an essential element in all mathematics courses. Never let yourself get behind or skip assignments. Because today's assignment will be used in the next section or chapter, skipping an assignment will create a gap in your knowledge and interfere with your ability to complete future assignments.

Expect to work independently.   Some introductory-level mathematics texts are "programmed," or self-instructional. You are expected to work through the chapter and then complete an in-class quiz demonstrating your mastery of the topic. Other texts are more traditional but also expect you to work on end-of-chapter problems on your own.

Accuracy and precision are important.   Many students, accustomed to flexible approaches to learning, have difficulty adjusting to the precise nature of mathematics. In particular, they are disturbed that "close does not count" and that knowledge of technique is not sufficient; rather, the technique must be precisely and accurately applied in order to be considered correct. Develop the habit of checking your work and focusing on accuracy.

How to Read and Study Mathematics Texts

Use the following guidelines for reading and studying mathematics:

Plan on spending more time.   Studying a mathematics textbook takes more time than reading textbooks in most other disciplines. As is also true of life and physical sciences, mathematics is concise and factually dense. Nearly everything is important.

Focus on process and procedure.   Be certain to understand *why* and *how* various procedures are used.

Pay attention to sample problems.   Usually, a textbook section that explains a procedure step-by-step is followed by a sample problem. The best way to read a section is to read a sentence or two and then refer to the sample problem to see how the information is applied. Then return to the text and read the explanation of the next step, and then refer to the sample problem again. The process of alternating between text and problem may seem confusing at first, but remember that your purpose is to see *how* the problem illustrates the process being described. Then practice solving the problem without referring to the text.

Learn to read mathematical language.   Mathematics, through use of notations, symbols, and formulas, expresses complicated relationships in a very brief, concise form. For example, the mathematical equation $c^2 = a^2 + b^2$ says that the square of the hypotenuse of a right triangle is equal to the sum of the squares of the two remaining sides. A large amount of information is packed into the smallest unit of mathematical language.

Study daily.   Never let your work pile up until the weekend. The principle of distributed learning (see p. 53) is especially important in mathematics.

Become adept at solving problems.   Quizzes and exams are made up almost exclusively of problems to solve. Here are a few tips to follow in solving mathematical problems:

- ◆ Be certain you understand what the problem is saying and what it is asking for. Try to express the problem in your own words.
- ◆ Identify the relevant information that is provided to solve the problem. (Some math problems may provide irrelevant or distracting information that is not useful in solving the problem.) Underline or circle essential information.
- ◆ Recall the formulas you have learned that relate to the problem at hand and select which you will work with.
- ◆ If you do not know or are unsure of how to solve a problem, look for similarities between it and sample problems you have studied.
- ◆ Be sure to check your work. Many students lose points, or sometimes full credit, due to arithmetic errors.

Study and practice variations of problems.   Explore the different forms in which a problem can be expressed, and identify variations of the same type of problem.

What Thought Patterns to Anticipate

Three thought patterns (see Chapter 12) predominate in the study of mathematics: process, problem-solution, and comparison and contrast, as shown in Table 10.3 below.

Taking Class Notes

Mathematics instructors seldom present formal lectures. Instead, they work through and explain procedures and problems. Here are a few suggestions for improving your note-taking skills in mathematics classes:

Table 10.3

Thought Patterns* in Mathematics

Pattern	Uses	Examples
Process	Describing steps to follow in solving problems or proving theorems	Algebra Solving quadratic equations
Problem-solution	Solving sample problems; homework problems	Business math Computing the interest on a $5,000 car loan at 5.5% add-on rate with monthly payments
Comparison and contrast	Recognizing how new problems are different from sample problems, how problem types differ; determining what operations are used in several types of problems	Basic mathematics Similarities between ratios and percentages

*See Chapter 12.

Focus on concepts and procedures.   Concentrate on understanding the concept or procedure the instructor is explaining, or the rationale he or she is giving. Then, once you understand it, write it down, either during the lecture or later, as you edit your notes.

Record sample problems.   As you edit your notes, try to identify and describe the steps followed in the problems.

Study the text before class.   Many instructors follow the textbook closely; consequently, it is useful to become familiar with the chapter before attending class. If you know, for example, that the instructor is working with a sample problem from the textbook, then you can make notes in the margin of your text.

Ask questions.   Most instructors are open to, and encourage students to ask, questions. Do not hesitate to ask a question; often several other people in the class have the same question, but are reluctant to ask it.

Exercise 10.3

Analyze the following situation and decide what advice you would offer this student.

A theater arts student is failing a required mathematics course. He has identified two difficulties.

1. He has trouble thinking in signs and symbols; the symbols and notations remain foreign and unfamiliar despite repeated attempts to memorize them.

2. Although he knows how to solve sample problems and those done in class, he cannot solve similar problems when they appear on an exam.

Literature and the Arts

Literature and the arts concentrate on the search for reasons, values, and interpretations in all areas of human interest and experience. Often, their focus is on subjective evaluation and interpretation of ideas expressed through literary or artistic works. Arts and humanities cover the full range of human experience. Many vehicles of expression are used to interpret the broad variety of topics covered: music, sculpture, painting, essays, poems, novels, and the body of information known as *criticism* that discusses, interprets, and evaluates each.

What to Expect

Courses in the arts and humanities are unique in the following ways:
They do not focus on a given body of information, sets of theories, facts, or principles to learn. This is unsettling to students who are accustomed to a defined, structured set of information to be learned. Instead, the focus is on ideas or their expression through various literary or artistic modes.

Most arts and humanities courses require and depend heavily on writing skills.   Analyses, interpretations, critiques, or reviews of critical essays (essays written about a given literary or artistic work) are often required and are the primary means of evaluation.

Often, there is no right answer or single, correct interpretation.   A literary work or philosophical theory can be interpreted in numerous ways. The interpretation, however, must be reasoned, logical, and consistent.

The instructor's own values, opinions, and perspective on life are necessarily revealed as he or she interprets and discusses a particular work.   Many students find this disturbing and mistakenly assume that they are forced to accept a given set of beliefs and attitudes. Actually, you are never forced to accept—but merely to understand and react to—a given philosophy.

To analyze and interpret art and literature, you must activate your feelings and imagination as well as your critical reasoning skills.   You must also define your values and hold them up for comparison with those expressed in various works and those of your instructor and your classmates.

How to Read and Analyze Literature

You will encounter two basic types of reading in the field of literature and criticism. *Original works* refer to literary pieces themselves: poems, articles, essays, philosophical treatises, short stories, plays, and novels. *Criticism* refers to all that has been written *about* a given original work and its author (book reviews, essays, biographies). In most introductory courses, the primary emphasis is on reading and interpreting original works. However, completing a paper or assignment sometimes requires you to consult secondary sources, to read what someone else thinks of the work you are studying. The suggestions listed below apply to reading original works.

Read slowly, carefully, and more than once.   Read a work the first time simply to establish its overall content and literal meaning: What is it about, or who is doing what, when, and where? Establish the main characters, basic plot, and setting. On your second reading, focus on interpretation. Find the writer's message and think about your reactions to the work.

Annotate as you read.   Jot down your reactions, hunches, insights, feelings, and questions. Mark or underline sections you feel are important—insightful statements by characters, or sections that provide clues to meaning. Circle repeated words or images, mark where characters are described, and look for unusual techniques or style. Table 10.4 lists features that often provide important clues to meaning.

Look for themes and patterns.   After you have read and annotated, inventory your annotations, looking for themes and patterns. Try to discover how ideas work together to suggest themes. Here are some possible themes in literature:

◆ Questions, issues, problems raised by the story: moral, political, philosophical, religious
◆ Abstract ideas: love, death, heroism, escapism
◆ Conflicting situations: appearance versus reality, freedom versus restraint, poverty versus wealth
◆ Common literary topics: self-realization, the inescapability of death, fall from innocence, search for the meaning of life

Table 10.4
Literary Clues to Meaning

Features of Language

Symbolism (objects or events that can be interpreted on several different levels)

Descriptive words (words that create a mental picture)

Emotionally charged words

Words and phrases with multiple meanings

Similes and metaphors (words that define by drawing a comparison)

Unusual or striking words

Repetition of words or phrases

Sarcastic or ironic statements (those that say one thing but mean another)

Characterization

What the characters say about their own thoughts, actions, motives

What the characters say about actions, motives of others (their perceptions of other characters)

What the characters actually do (compare this to what they say they do—often a character is self-deceived or naïve)

Contradictions or inconsistencies

How the writer describes the characters (to detect his or her attitude toward them)

Organization and Structure

How the work begins, including clues about what will happen next (foreshadowing)

The setting and how it changes

The mood (feeling) the writer creates

How the mood and setting compare the characters' actions

Complications or conflicts that arise

Resolution of these conflicts

Who is telling the story (narrator) and what he or she knows or does not know about the characters and their motives and actions

Whether the narrator is objective or biased

What Thought Patterns to Anticipate

In original works, the predominant thought patterns include chronological order, process, comparison and contrast, and cause and effect, as shown in Table 10.5.

How to Study and Analyze Art

Art is primarily a visual form of expression (with the exception of music). As is true in the study of literature, there are two main sources of study: the original work and criticism that discusses form, process, and style.

As you study and analyze original art forms, keep the following guidelines in mind:[2]

- ◆ Establish a first impression of and reaction to the work.
- ◆ Learn what background information is available. (Where and when was the work created? What is known about the artist? Where was the work originally shown?)
- ◆ Identify, if possible, the purpose of the work. Is it intended to portray a person, show respect, display a dilemma, make a religious statement, express feelings?
- ◆ Study the title and determine how it relates to the work.
- ◆ Examine the subject matter and the characteristics of the medium used and evaluate the techniques. In drawing and painting, for example, you would consider such factors as composition (color, lines, shape), depth, and scale (relative size).
- ◆ After carefully studying the work, ask yourself three questions: What is the artist trying to accomplish?

Table 10.5
Thought Patterns* in Literature and the Arts

Pattern	Uses	Examples
Chronological order	Sequence of events in fictional works; noting the development of various artistic or literary periods	Sequence of events in Crane's "The Open Boat"
Process	Studying the process through which writer or artist achieved his or her effect	Development of character in Thurber's "The Catbird Seat"
Comparison and contrast	Studying two or more artists, works, writers, or schools of thought	Comparing Steinbeck's and Hawthorne's use of symbolism
Cause and effect	Examining character motivation, studying effects of various literary and artistic techniques	Evaluating Hemingway's use of tone

*See Chapter 12.

Why did he or she do what was done? This type of question will force you to examine each feature of the work closely. *Examples:* In Michelangelo's *The Creation of Adam,* why is the creator's arm stretched toward Adam's? Why is the creator's body diagonal? Why is Adam's left leg supporting his arm?

What is my response to this work and why do I feel that way? *Examples:* Why do I feel sorry for the child in the photograph? Why does the portrait seem depressing? Why does that landscape seem inviting and relaxing?

Thinking Critically
. . . About Literature

Literature often makes use of imaginative or creative language to express meaning. Therefore, you must think critically and creatively in order to grasp the full meaning intended by the writer. Here are a few questions to ask that will focus your attention on the use of creative expressions in literature:

1. **Does the writer use descriptive language?** If so, what impact does it make? Descriptive language uses words that create a sensory impression or response. It is intended to help you create a mental picture of what the writer is describing. For example, to describe a stormy evening, a poet may write this:

Under the thunder-dark cloud, the storm mounts, flashes, and resounds.

These words give you a vivid picture of the storm and help you imagine its strength. When reading descriptive language, read slowly, allowing time for sensory impressions to register and for you to react to them.

2. **Does the writer use connotative language?** Connotative language suggests meanings beyond a word's primary, dictionary meaning. For example, the words *crowd, mob, gang,* and *audience* all mean a group of assembled people, but their connotative meanings are quite different. A crowd implies large numbers, a mob implies unruly or disorganized behavior, and so forth. Writers select words with particular connotative meanings to create a particular feeling or to evoke a particular response. Be sure to critically analyze a writer's use of connotative language to determine what effect he or she intends.

3. **What figurative expressions are used?** Figurative language is a way of describing something that makes sense on an imaginative or creative level but not on a literal or factual level. For example, the poetic lines

A sea
Harsher than granite

do not mean than the sea was a rock. Instead, they suggest that the sea shares some characteristics of granite: hardness, coldness, immutability. Two common types of figurative expressions are *similes* and *metaphors*. A simile makes a direct comparison by using the words *like* or *as* (her lips were as red as a rose). A metaphor makes a comparison by directly equating the two objects (her lips were a rose).

How to Read Criticism

As mentioned earlier, criticism refers to written materials that discuss, interpret, and evaluate a particular work. Some students erroneously assume that criticism is negative or limited to finding fault with a work. Actually, its primary purpose is to analyze and interpret. Criticism may include both positive and negative aspects. Film and book reviews are examples of criticism. Criticism also includes scholarly works that carefully research or examine a particular aspect, theme, or approach. Often, in order to complete a term paper, you will be required to consult several critical sources. In using these sources, follow these guidelines:

◆ Read and study the original work carefully and thoroughly before you consult critical sources.

◆ Make a preliminary interpretation of the work before reading criticism. Decide what you think the work means and why it was produced. Record these ideas in note form. If you consult sources before forming your own impressions, your judgment will be colored by what you read, and you will have difficulty separating your ideas from those you encountered as you read.

◆ Recognize that not all critics agree; you may encounter three critics who present three different interpretations of Leonardo's *Mona Lisa.*

◆ Although it is perfectly acceptable to revise your own interpretations based on your reading, do not immediately discard your own interpretation as soon as you encounter one that differs.

◆ Make notes on your readings, recording only key points.

Taking Lecture Notes

Lectures in literature and fine arts classes are primarily intended to guide and direct you in your interpretation of original works. Instructors provide essential background information and instruct you in the various themes, conventions, and characteristics of the particular art form. When taking notes, use the following suggestions:

◆ Make notes directly on the page where the poem, story, or art reproduction is printed. When an instructor discusses and interprets a poem, for example, the easiest way to record notes is to jot them in the margin next to the line or section of the poem to which they refer.

◆ After the lecture, try to summarize the instructor's main points; include the outstanding features of the work, various literary or artistic devices used, and predominant theme(s) identified.

Exercise 10.4	Analyze the following situation and answer the questions that follow.

An engineering student at the State University of New York at Buffalo is taking a required composition and literature course. He dislikes the course because he feels it has nothing to do with his major, and the readings do not address current issues. He feels uncomfortable in the course because he is not sure what he should learn. He has

Continued

not submitted several papers, each of which required him to explore a dominant theme in a specific literary work. He read each work several times but could not identify anything to write about.

1. What does this student fail to understand about literature?

2. What should he do to feel more comfortable and confident about the course?

3. What steps should the student take to solve his problem with writing assigned papers?

Career Fields

Career fields include many applied, currently popular fields such as computer science, criminal justice, computer-assisted drafting, physical therapy assistant, accounting, nursing, and technologies/engineering. Career fields are usually highly technical and specialized. They most closely resemble the life and physical sciences, and much of the advice given in the section on life and physical sciences (pp. 170–175) applies here. This section will present *only* information to supplement that contained in the earlier section.

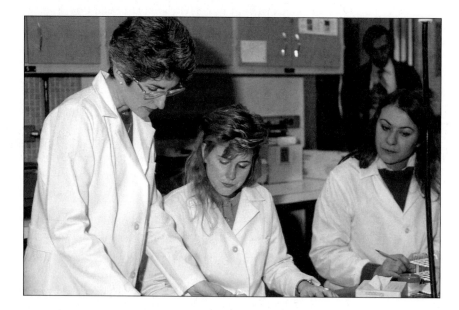

What to Expect

Career fields differ from pure sciences primarily in focus. While the emphasis in life and physical sciences is knowledge and theoretical problem solving, most career fields are concerned with direct, practical application of knowledge and skill. Expect the following:

◆ An emphasis on process and procedure

◆ More practical applications, in both textbook and lecture, of material taught

◆ Labs, practicums, clinical, or on-site work experience as an integral part of the course

◆ Grading and evaluation to be performance based. Your grade in an introductory accounting course, for example, will be based on your ability to balance a ledger.

◆ Exactness and precision. Develop systems of methodically performing tasks so you do not miss or overlook steps.

HOW DO YOU SEE IT?

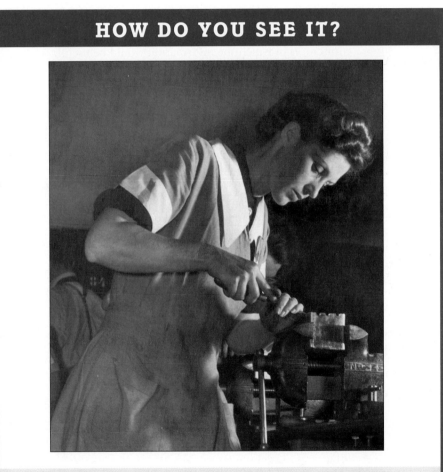

Cultural biases often influence whether a discipline or skill will be familiar or interesting to us or not. Write a paragraph explaining how expectations based upon your gender, economics, environment, race, religion, and so on may have influenced your choice of career goals.

How to Study Career Fields

In studying career fields, use the following suggestions:

Learn the language of the field.   Be certain to learn the specialized terminology and incorporate it into your own speech and writing. To communicate effectively on the job, you will need to speak the language of your field (see Chapter 11).

Maintain a practical focus.   Whenever you learn new information or procedures, ask, "How and when will I use this information?"

Note applications of what you are learning.   Since exams often test your ability to apply and use what is learned, as you read, make marginal notes indicating situations or circumstances in which the information would be useful.

What Thought Patterns to Anticipate

Process and problem-solution are the two predominant thought patterns (see Chapter 12) evident in many career fields, as shown in Table 10.6.

Taking Lecture Notes

Use the following suggestions to take notes most effectively:

◆ Lectures often involve practical demonstrations. Focus on the demonstration itself, not on taking notes. Afterward, record the purpose of the demonstration and the points it was intended to emphasize.
◆ Emphasize process and procedure in your notes.
◆ Pay attention to clues your instructor provides about the use and application of information presented.

Table 10.6

Thought Patterns* in the Career Fields

Pattern	Uses	Examples
Process	Learning and describing procedures	Nursing Obtaining a radial pulse Passing a nasogastric tube
Problem-solution	Practical applications; clinical or field situations	Computer science Modifying a program to suit job specifications Detecting a bug

---

*See Chapter 12.

Exercise 10.5	Analyze the following situation and answer the questions below.

A nursing student is earning A or high B grades in Nursing I and required courses in English composition, anatomy and physiology, and psychology. However, she is failing a clinical practicum that focuses on basic procedures of patient care. She is evaluated in this course by performing procedures, such as taking a blood sample from models in the clinic under close scrutiny by her clinical instructor. Although she memorizes each procedure, step-by-step, she can't recall them in practical situations. She says she gets nervous and freezes up during clinical evaluations.

1. How should this student revise her learning strategies for the clinical course?

2. What can she do to avoid freezing up during evaluations?

Working Together

Groups of four to six students should each select one of the following topics and identify how various academic disciplines might approach and study it:

1. Cloning
2. Television commercials
3. Senior citizens

Interactive Chapter Review

Knowledge	Choose one of the five general academic disciplines mentioned in this chapter and list three specific disciplines it includes.
Comprehension	What main thought patterns would you expect to find in a psychology course titled Child Development?
Application	Choose one course you are taking and reread the Table that notes the main thought patterns in that field. Consulting your text for that course, list one example of each thought pattern. (Hint: Use the headings in the table of contents to find general examples. Or, examine the chapter you have just read in that book to find more specific examples.)
Analysis	What steps can you take in one of your courses to improve your learning ability in that field? Write down at least three steps. Next to each step, write the date you will begin that step.
Synthesis	What is the most important lesson you have learned in this chapter?
Evaluation	Why is writing summaries of information a useful study skill? In general, what does writing a summary require in the way of thinking? In what course(s) do you think you should be doing more summarizing? Why?

Further Analysis

Analyze the following situation and answer the questions below:

A business major is taking a public speaking course. The primary course requirements include a midterm and final and seven speeches. Textbook chapters are assigned and discussed in class, and guidelines for each type of speech are distributed well in advance. The class and instructor critique each speech. This student is having difficulty organizing a systematic approach to learning and study. She claims the speeches involve on-the-spot performance and require little actual study, and she is unable to anticipate what type of exam questions may be asked. Other students in the class claim the course is an "easy A," but she doesn't agree.

1. What suggestions would you offer on how to succeed in this course?
2. What strategies would you recommend for taking class notes?
3. What thought patterns might the student anticipate and use?
4. How should this student prepare for each speech?

Discussion

1. Suppose you are interested in the topic of video games. How many different ways might you approach and analyze the topic? Consider how various disciplines might approach it.
2. At a certain college, a course titled Seminar in Interdisciplinary Studies is a first-semester requirement for all incoming students. The course is taught by four professors from the departments of philosophy, physics, fine arts, and sociology. The course is intended to explore relationships among traditional liberal arts disciplines. What would be your reaction to taking such a course? Of what value do you think it would be? What study and learning strategies might a course of this type require?
3. Suppose you are fulfilling a physical education requirement by taking a course in bowling. What general academic discipline area do you think the course most closely resembles? Justify your answer.
4. A student is studying a modern language, Spanish, for the first time. What should she expect? How should she approach the course? What thought patterns might help her learn the material?

The Work Connection

How does learning about new fields of study increase your ability to find a career you will enjoy? As you study new disciplines, you have an opportunity to figure out which types of thinking and learning you most enjoy. You can use this information to help choose a career that's right for you. Consider how you can combine your goals, your strengths, and your abilities with your interests in a particular academic field to choose a career that will allow you to stay flexible and employable in a changing economy.

1. Of the different subjects that you have studied so far, which ones do you enjoy the most? For each, list three or four particular aspects you find interesting.

2. When you envision your life five years from now, what do you see? Imagine that you are looking at yourself enjoying an ideal day at work. Are the aspects you wrote about in question 1 present in your ideal image of your future work life? If so, which ones?

The Web Connection

1. Examples of everyday item equivalencies for metric units of length, mass, volume, and temperature

   http://lamar.colostate.edu/~hillger/frame.htm

   Visit this site from the U.S. Metric Association to see visual comparisons of the metric system with the U.S. system of measurement.

2. American Mathematical Society

   http://e-math.ams.org/

   In exploring the AMS's site, you will discover how a field of study's professional society can lead a new student to important information about that subject.

3. Art Museum Network

   http://www.amn.org/

   Among other things, this site offers an extensive list of museums on the Internet. What a fabulous way to see art from around the world!

Go Electronic!

For additional readings, exercises, and Internet activities, visit the Longman Study Skills Web site at:

http://www.ablongman.com/StudySkills

If you need a user name and password, please see your instructor.

Chapter 11

Learning Specialized and Technical Vocabulary

DO YOU KNOW?

How is terminology a key to course mastery?
How do you use mapping to learn new terminology?
Why are core prefixes, roots, and suffixes important in learning new terminology?
What are course master files, and how can you create them?

Have you noticed that each sport and hobby has its own language—a specialized set of words with specific meanings? Baseball players and fans talk about slides, home runs, errors, and runs batted in. Wine enthusiasts may discuss a wine's tannin, nose, bouquet, and finish. Each academic discipline also has its own language. For each course you take, you encounter an extensive set of words and terms that are used in a particular way in that subject area. This chapter discusses how specialized terminology is tied integrally to course mastery and suggests approaches for learning it.

Terminology: The Key to Course Mastery

Each academic discipline has its own set of specialized words that enable accurate and concise descriptions of events, principles, concepts, problems, and occurrences. One of the first tasks you face in a new course is to learn the specialized language of that course. This task is especially important in introductory courses in which the subject is new and unfamiliar. In an introductory computer science course, for instance, you often start by learning how a computer functions. From that point, many new terms are introduced: *bit, byte, field, numeric characters, character positions, statements, coding, format,* and so forth.

Specialized Terminology in Class Lectures

Often, the first few class lectures in a course are devoted to acquainting students with the nature and scope of the field and introducing them to its specialized language.

Check your notes for the first few classes of the courses you are taking this semester. How many new or specialized terms were introduced?

You can see, then, that many disciplines devote considerable time to presenting the language of the course carefully and explicitly. Be sure to record accurately each new term for later review and study. Good lecturers give students clues to what terms and definitions are important to record. Some instructors make a habit of writing new words on the chalkboard, as a means of emphasis. Other instructors may emphasize new terms and definitions by slowing down, almost dictating so that you can record definitions. Still other instructors may repeat a word and its definition several times or offer several variations of meaning.

As a part of your note taking system (see Chapter 13), develop a consistent way of easily identifying new terms and definitions recorded in your notes. You might circle or draw a box around each new term; or, as you edit your notes, underline each new term in red; or write "def." in the margin each time a definition is included. The particular mark or symbol you use is a matter of preference; the important thing is to find some way to mark definitions for further study.

Exercise 11.1	Estimate the number of new terms that each of your instructors introduced during the first several weeks for each of your courses. Now, check the accuracy of your estimates by reviewing the first two weeks of your class notes for each course you are taking. How many new terms and definitions were included for each course?

Specialized Terminology in Textbooks

The first few chapters within a textbook are generally introductory, too. They are written to familiarize you with the subject of study and acquaint you with its specialized language. In one particular economics textbook, 34 new terms were introduced in the first two chapters (40 pages). In the first two chapters (28 pages) of a chemistry book, 56 specialized words were introduced. A sample of the words introduced in each text is given below. From these lists, you can see that some of the words are words of common, everyday usage that take on a specialized meaning; others are technical terms used only in the subject area.

New terms: Economics text	New terms: Chemistry text
capital	matter
ownership	element
opportunity cost	halogen
distribution	isotope
productive contribution	allotropic form
durable goods	nonmetal
economic system	group (family)
barter	burning
commodity money	toxicity

Textbook authors use various means to emphasize new terminology. In some textbooks, new vocabulary is printed in italics, boldface type, or colored print. Other texts indicate new terms in the margin of each page. Another common means of emphasis is the "New Terminology" list or "Vocabulary" list that appears at the beginning or end of each chapter.

Since textbook chapters (especially introductory ones) are heavily loaded with new, specialized vocabulary, you should develop a system for marking new terminology as it is introduced.

Occasionally in textbooks you may find a new term that is not defined or that is not defined clearly. In this case, check to see if the text contains a glossary: a comprehensive list of terms introduced throughout the text, found at the back of the text. If so, it may provide a thorough explanation of the word. Make a note of the meaning in the text margin.

The glossary is particularly useful at the end of the course when you have covered all or most of the chapters. Use it to test your recall of terminology; read an entry, cover up the meaning, and try to remember it; then check to see if you were correct. As you are progressing through a course, however, the glossary is not an adequate study aid. A more organized, systematic approach to learning unfamiliar new terms is needed.

Exercise 11.2   Review the first chapter from two of your texts and then answer the following questions.

1. How many new terms are introduced in each?

2. If your text contains a glossary, is each of these new terms listed?

3. Are most new words technical terms, or are they words from everyday usage to which a specialized meaning is attached?

4. How does each textbook author call your attention to these new terms?

Learning New Terminology

The following is a demonstration that makes an important point about learning new terminology. Follow the directions as listed.

Step 1

Read the following paragraphs from a computer science textbook; you will be able to refer back to the passage when completing the remaining steps.

7.4.1 Hash Functions

The hash function takes an element to be stored in a table and transforms it into a location in the table. If this transformation makes certain table locations more likely to occur than others, the chance of collision is increased and the efficiency of searches and insertions is decreased. The phenomenon of some table locations being more likely is called *primary clustering*. The ideal hash function spreads the elements uniformly throughout the table—that is, does not exhibit primary clustering. In fact, we would really like a hash function that, given any z, chooses a random location in the table in which to store z; this would minimize primary clustering. This is, of course, impossible, since the function h cannot be probabilistic but must be deterministic, yielding the same location every time it is applied to the same element (otherwise, how would we ever find an element after it was inserted?!). The achievable ideal is to design hash functions that exhibit pseudorandom behavior—behavior that appears random but that is reproducible.

Unfortunately, there are no hard and fast rules for constructing hash functions. We will examine four basic techniques that can be used individually or in combination. The properties of any particular hash function are hard to determine because they depend so heavily on the set of elements that will be encountered in practice. Thus the construction of a good hash function from these basic techniques is more an art than anything amenable to analysis, but we will present general principles that usually prove successful, pointing out their pitfalls as well.[1]

Step 2

Complete Quiz 1, referring to the passage as needed.

Quiz 1

1. Into what form does a hash function transform an element?
2. Define the term "primary clustering."
3. Describe an ideal hash function.
4. Why are the properties of a hash function difficult to determine?
5. What is "pseudorandom" behavior?

Step 3

Check your answers using the Answer Key on p. 199. No doubt you did quite well. But did you really *understand* what you read? Let's find out.

Step 4

Complete Quiz 2, referring to the passage as needed.

Quiz 2

1. Give an example of an element to be stored in a table.
2. Define the term "transformation."
3. Define z and h.
4. In what situations might "primary clustering" be important?

Unless you have already taken courses in computer programming, you probably could not answer these questions. Why not? You did well with Quiz 1; how is Quiz 2 different? Quiz 2 tested your *understanding* of the terms used in the passage. Quiz 1 only asked you to locate information in the passage; it measured your ability to find answers—not to understand their meaning.

The differences between Quiz 1 and Quiz 2 illustrate the difference between merely manipulating new terminology and really understanding it. Many students fall into the trap of convincing themselves that they have learned new terminology when, actually, all they have learned is how to find answers. Often, the answers lack real meaning to such students. You will know you have really mastered the terminology of a particular course when you begin to *think,* as well as speak and write, using those terms.

Exercise 11.3	Select a beginning chapter that you have already read from one of your textbooks. Make a list of 10 new terms it introduces. Without reference to the text, test your understanding of each by expressing its meaning in your own words. Whenever possible, include an example of how the term is used. Then check your understanding by examining the chapter again.

Working Together

Work with a partner for this activity. Each of you should take one chapter in this book that your class has already covered and do the following: Write a quiz of five questions that will test your classmate's understanding of the chapter's important terms. Make sure that your classmate will need to do more than merely repeat the definitions of the terms to get the right answers. Exchange questions. Take the other person's quiz. Then evaluate and discuss your results.

Using Subject Area Dictionaries

Many academic fields have specialized dictionaries that list most of the important words used in that discipline. These dictionaries list specialized meanings for words and suggest how and when to use the words. The field of nursing, for instance, has *Taber's Cyclopedic Medical Dictionary.* Other subject area dictionaries include *A Dictionary of Anthropology, The New Grove Dictionary of Music and Musicians,* and *A Dictionary of Economics.*

Find out whether there is a subject area dictionary for the disciplines you are studying. Most such dictionaries are available in hardback and are likely to be expensive. However, many students find them worth the initial investment. Most libraries have copies of specialized dictionaries in the reference section. You can also access numerous subject area dictionaries on the Internet.

Exercise 11.4	For each of the courses you are taking, find out if there is a subject area dictionary available. If so, record its title. Then determine whether or not your library has a copy or whether you can access it on the Internet. For dictionaries you can locate, be ready to share its call number or Internet address with your classmates.

Mapping Related Terminology

In most disciplines, you will be learning related groups of terms rather than separate, isolated words. For example, in a criminal justice course, you will learn a cluster of terms that describe the judicial process. In business marketing, you learn terms that describe marketing management: *market diversification, market-focus objective, opportunity forecasts,* and so forth. Mapping is an effective method to use when learning such related sets or clusters of words. Mapping, as discussed in Chapter 15, involves drawing a chart or diagram that maps or shows the connections among various terms.

A map can organize terminology to be learned by grouping related terms together and making them more meaningful by showing connections and relationships. Figure 11.1 shows a map that might be useful in organizing the terminology introduced in the first chapter of a physics text. It relates the various states and physical properties of matter. This map makes it easy to visualize how matter is classified and to understand the various external and internal properties used to describe matter.

Mapping can help you avoid the pitfall, described earlier, of using terms but not really understanding their meaning. Mapping forces you to think—to analyze how terms are related; by thinking, you are actively learning.

Figure 11.1

A Map of New Terminology

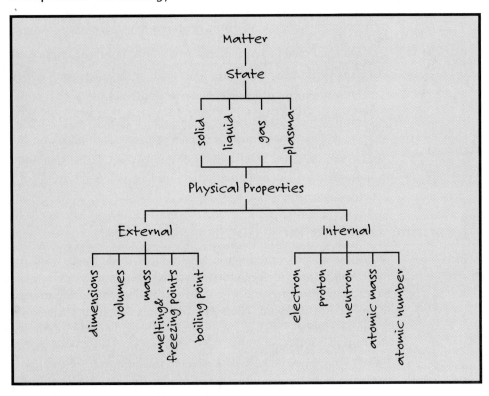

Exercise 11.5	Read the following paragraph from the first chapter of a business advertising text and draw a map relating the key terms introduced.

> Economists take a somewhat different approach, looking at marketing in terms of benefits to buyers. They suggest that consumers buy goods because they feel the goods will provide satisfaction, or utility. Economists identify four types of utility. *Form utility* is created when a producer manufactures, mines and refines, or grows and harvests a product. In addition to form utility you also buy *place utility:* you pay for the product being in a local store instead of in the producer's warehouse. You also buy *time utility:* you pay retailers to have swimwear and Christmas gifts in stock when you want to buy. Finally, you buy *possession utility:* you pay, as part of a sales, lease, or rental transaction, to have possession of a product transferred to you. Because the last three utilities are provided by marketing, marketing might be defined in terms of buyer benefits as the creation of time, place, and possession utilities.[2]

Exercise 11.6	Select a section of the first chapter from one of your textbooks and draw a map relating the key terms introduced in that section.

Thinking Critically
. . . About Vocabulary

As you learn new terminology for each of your courses, make sure you understand each new term. Use the following questions to evaluate your learning:

1. Can you explain a term in your *own* words, not those of the textbook author?
2. Can you explain a new term to a friend or classmate so that they understand it?
3. Can you explain differences between similar terms?
4. Can you think of examples or situations in which the term can be used?
5. Can you use newly learned terms in your speech, note taking, and writing?
6. Do you see terms as related sets of information, rather than individual pieces of information? Use mapping (p. 195) to help you organize sets of information.

Learning Core Prefixes, Roots, and Suffixes

Many words in the English language are made up of word parts called prefixes, roots, and suffixes, or beginnings, middles, and endings of words. These word parts have specific meanings and when added together can provide strong clues to the meanings of a particular word. The terminology in a particular academic discipline often uses a core of common prefixes, roots, and suffixes. For example, in the field of human anatomy and physiology, the prefix *endo* means "inner," and the root *derma* refers to "skin." Thus the word *endoderm* refers to the inner layer of cells in the skin. Numerous other words are formed using this root in conjunction with a suffix:

Root	Suffix	Example	Meaning
derma (skin)	*-itis* (inflammation)	*dermatitis*	Inflammation of skin
	-osis (abnormal or diseased condition)	*dermatosis*	Skin disease
	-logy (study of)	*dermatology*	Branch of medicine that deals with the skin

HOW DO YOU SEE IT?

"Very good, Gary: 'A hero is a celebrity who did something real.'"

"Gary" seems to believe that celebrities don't engage in "real" activities. Write a paragraph defining what you think he means by "real."

As you are learning new terminology for each course, make a point of noticing recurring prefixes, roots, and suffixes. Compile a list of these and their meanings, along with several examples of each. You will find these common word parts useful in learning other new terms that contain them. A sample list for the field of psychology follows on p. 198.

Prefixes	Meaning	Example
psych(o)-	Mind or mental processes	*psychoanalysis*
neur(o)-	Pertaining to nerves or nervous system	*neurosis*
super-	Above, over, outside	*superego*

Roots	Meaning	Example
somat(o)-	Pertaining to the body	*psychosomatic illness*
-phobia	Intense fear	*claustrophobia*
patho-	Indicates disease or suffering	*pathological*

Suffixes	Meaning	Example
-osis	Disorder or abnormal condition	*neurosis*
-ic	Pertaining to	*neurotic*
-ism	Indicates theory or principle of	*behaviorism*

For courses involving scientific measurement, be sure to learn prefixes that refer to the metric system. A partial list follows:

Prefix	Meaning
micro-	millionth
milli-	thousandth
centi-	hundredth
deci-	tenth
deca-	ten
hecto-	hundred
kilo-	thousand
mega-	million
giga-	billion

Exercise 11.7   For one of your courses, identify five commonly used prefixes, roots, and suffixes. If you have difficulty, review the glossary of the text to discover commonly used word parts.

Developing a Course Master File

For each course you are taking, set up a master file in which you include new terminology to be learned and a list of essential prefixes, roots, and suffixes you have identified as important. Also include lists of frequently used signs, abbreviations, symbols, and their meanings. In the sciences, numerous symbols are used in formulas. Some students resist making a special effort to learn the symbols; they assume that they will learn them eventually. This is a mistake because, until you do learn them, you will feel uncomfortable with the course, as if you are on the outside looking in rather than actively participating. You will save yourself time and avoid frequent interruptions if you learn them right away rather than having to refer to the text for translations of every sign or symbol.

You can construct and organize your master file in a number of ways:

Index cards.   Using a separate card for each entry, write the term (or symbol, abbreviation, etc.) on the front and the meaning on the back. Create separate packets of cards for prefixes, roots, and suffixes, new terms, abbreviations, and so forth.

Notebook sections.   Divide a small (6" × 9") spiral notebook into sections and create running lists of terms and meanings.

Computer files.   The computer's word processing capabilities allow you to add to, rearrange, and delete items easily. Using the cut-and-paste or copy functions, you can group similar terms for more effective study. A biology student, for example, grouped terms together according to the following categories: energy and life cells, biological processes, reproduction, biological systems, brain and behavior, and environmental structure issues.

An abbreviated version of a course master file for a nursing course in which students were studying laboratory assessment of blood is shown in Table 11.1 on p. 200.

Because each course deals with very different subject matter, your course master file will differ for each course you are taking. Table 11.2 lists tips for individualizing your course file to suit the requirements of particular academic disciplines. Check with your college's learning assistance center; it may offer lists of common prefixes and roots.

Exercise 11.8	Begin preparing a master file for one of your courses. Use both your text and corresponding lecture notes. Begin with the first chapter, and list new terms, prefixes, roots, and suffixes as well as symbols and abbreviations.

Answers to Quiz #1, p. 193

1. A hash function transforms an element to a location in a table.

2. Primary clustering refers to the situation in which some table locations being more likely than others.

3. An ideal hash function spreads the elements uniformly throughout the table.

4. The properties of a hash function are difficult to determine because they depend on the set of elements that will be encountered in the practice.

5. Pseudorandom behavior is behavior that appears to be random but is actually reproducible.

Table 11.1
Sample Course Master File

New Terminology

plasma—blood from which cellular material has been removed

platelets—photoplasmic disks; promote coagulation

bilirubin—orange-yellowish pigmentation in bile carried to the liver by the blood

Prefixes, Roots, and Suffixes

Prefixes	Meaning	Example
trans-	Across	*transfusion*
electro-	Indicates electricity	*electrophoresis*
hyper-	Abnormal, excessive	*hyperthyroidism*

Roots	Meaning	Example
hem-	Blood	*hematology*
thromb-	Clot	*thrombus*
cardi-	Heart	*cardiodynamics*

Suffixes	Meaning	Example
-lysis	Dissolution or decomposition	*hydrolysis*
-lyte	Substance that can be decomposed by a particular process	*electrolyte*
-stasis	Slowing or stoppage	*hemostasis*

Symbols and Abbreviations

CBC	Complete blood count
WBC	White blood count
RBC	Red blood count
HbF	Hemoglobin, fetal
ESR	Erythrocyte sedimentation rate

Table 11.2

Tips for Learning Specialized Vocabulary in Various Fields of Study

Sciences	Learn standard symbols.
	ex: F = force
	W = work
	Learn the metric system.
	ex: *deci* = tenth
	Learn notation systems.
	ex: $HNO_2 \nrightarrow N_2O_2 + H_2O$
	Consult data books and handbooks.
	ex: *Biology Data Book*
	Merck Index
	Handbook of Chemistry & Physics
	Van Nostrand's Scientific Encyclopedia
Mathematics	Learn words as well as the process they imply.
	ex: *average* (add, then divide)
	product (multiply)
	Learn symbols.
	ex: $>, <, \Sigma, \int$
	Learn abbreviations.
	ex: *quad., vol.*
	Consult: *Encyclopedia Dictionary of Mathematics*
Literature	Learn terms used to describe various features of literature.
	ex: *tone, mood, iambic pentameter*
	Learn terms that describe various styles of writing.
	ex: *informal, graphic, verbose*
	Learn terms that refer to particular parts of literary works.
	ex: *drama, interlude, finale, denouement*
	Learn terms that refer to techniques.
	ex: *flashback, monologue, soliloquy*
	Learn legendary/mythological figures.
	ex: *Midas, Venus*
	Consult: *Handbook of Literary Terms*
	A Dictionary of World Mythology
Arts	Learn terms that describe qualities, impressions, techniques.
	Learn terms that refer to mode of expression.
	ex: *design, form, structure*
	Consult: *The Thames and Hudson Dictionary of Art and Artists*

Continued

Table 11.2
(Continued)

Applied Sciences, Technical Courses, Computer Science	Learn terms that denote process; concentrate on steps in the process. Develop a working knowledge of the terminology; use the terminology in your speaking and writing. Draw diagrams to get the big picture and to show overall relationships. Connect terminology and processes with everyday experience, observable occurrences. Consult: *McGraw-Hill Dictionary of Scientific and Technical Terms*

Business	Learn terms that describe organization.
	        ex: *conglomerate, franchise*
	Learn abbreviations.
	        ex: *OTC, IBF, APR*
	Learn processes and procedures.
	        ex: *price, control, time study*
	Consult: *Dictionary of Business, Finance, and Banking*

Social Sciences	Learn words that describe general behaviors.
	        ex: *aggression, assimilation*
	Learn stages and processes.
	        ex: *oral stage, displacement*
	Learn laws, principles, theories.
	        ex: *late selection theory, Sapir-Whorf Hypothesis*
	Learn important researchers, theorists.
	        ex: *Maslow, Keynes*
	Consult: *International Encyclopedia of the Social Sciences*

History	Learn important historical figures.
	        ex: *Napoleon, Mao Zedong*
	Learn places of historical significance.
	        ex: *Sparta, Babylonia, Prussia*
	Consult: *Encyclopedia of World History*

Interactive Chapter Review

Knowledge	What is "terminology"? When, where, and why is terminology used?
Comprehension	Are the definitions for new terms all you need to know in order to understand the terminology in a course? If not, what else do you need to know? Why?
Application	Identify and map the relationships among the important terms introduced in Chapter 6 of this book.
Analysis	Suppose you are searching for the core prefixes, roots, and suffixes that are common in a field of study. How will you know which prefixes, roots, and suffixes are the important ones to know? List at least three ways to find out which terms are the important words.
Synthesis	Develop your own system for learning the terms you have placed in a course master file. Keep in mind your learning style (Chapter 8) and how people remember information (Chapter 9). Make sure your system has at least three separate steps for learning new terms.
Evaluation	After two weeks of using your system for learning new terms, evaluate it. How helpful was each separate step in learning the terms? What improvements, if any, do you need to make in your system?

Further Analysis

Analyze the following situation and answer the questions below.

A well-respected biology professor teaches her class from the first day using extensively the terminology of her field. Rarely does she explain or define a term. Some students say they are easily confused. Others complain among themselves, saying, "She assumes we know everything already; if we did, we wouldn't be taking the course!"

1. Do you agree or disagree with their complaints? Why?
2. Why do you think the professor chooses this approach?
3. How does this teaching style facilitate active thinking and learning?
4. What might students in this class do to prepare for the professor's lectures?
5. How should students adjust their lecture note-taking techniques to account for this lecture style?

Discussion

1. What tests or checking methods could you devise to be certain that you *understand* new terminology and have gone beyond memorizing definitions?
2. What system, other than a course master file, have you used to learn specialized terminology? Evaluate its effectiveness.

The Work Connection

How is learning new terminology linked to your career success? Forecasts of work in the digital age (the era of computers) suggest that many workers will do "knowledge work, . . . handl[ing] information rather than physical things."[3] In his book *The Work of Nations* (1991), Secretary of Labor Robert Reich called those who do knowledge work "symbolic analysts." Their jobs consist of identifying and solving problems through manipulating symbols: words, numbers, images."[4] As the workforce shifts to knowledge- and information-based work, your ability to learn new terminology will help you stay competitive.

1. In the current workforce, about 20 percent of employed people are knowledge workers.[5] List four or five types of work that you would consider to be primarily about handling information.

2. Consider the careers you may want. What aspects of these careers have to do with manipulating words, numbers, or images? List at least two or three ideas for each possible career.

The Web Connection

1. Vocabulary: An Ongoing Process

    http://www.ucc.vt.edu/stdysk/vocabula.html

    Virginia Tech. offers some simple tips for increasing your vocabulary.

2. Clues to the Meanings of New Words

    http://virtual.parkland.cc.il.us/studyskills/ActiveLearning&Studying/CollegeVocab. Clues.htm

    This site from Parkland College gives basic information and advice on building a college vocabulary.

3. A.Word.a.Day

    http://www.wordsmith.org/awad/index.html

    Sign up to receive a word a day in your e-mail or read a newsletter about words at this interesting language-lovers site.

Go Electronic!
For additional readings, exercises, and Internet activities, visit the Longman Study Skills Web site at:
http://www.ablongman.com/StudySkills
If you need a user name and password, please see your instructor.

Chapter 12

Thought Patterns of Academic Disciplines

DO YOU KNOW?

What are thought patterns?
How can recognition of thought patterns help you master your courses?
What are seven common academic thought patterns?
How can these thought patterns improve your memory and learning?

This semester or term you are probably taking courses in several disciplines simultaneously. You may study English composition, biology, psychology, and philosophy all in one semester. Many students find it difficult to manage such a diverse course load. During one day you may write a descriptive essay, learn how cells divide, and study early schools of psychology. These tasks become mind-boggling because you treat each course completely differently from every other. Consequently, you are forced to shift gears for each course, developing new approaches and strategies.

What few students realize is that a biologist and a psychologist, for example, think about and approach their subject matter in similar ways. Both may carefully define terms, examine causes and effects, study similarities and differences, describe a sequence of events, classify information, solve problems, and enumerate characteristics. While the subject matter and the language they use differ, the thought patterns are basically the same for each. Regardless of their field of expertise, then, researchers, textbook authors, and your professors all use standard patterns of thought to organize and express their ideas.

You might think of these patterns as learning blueprints. We have hundreds of blueprints, or preestablished operating instructions, that enable us to perform numerous everyday activities. These are sometimes referred to as *schema*. You may have a blueprint for riding a bicycle, swimming the crawl stroke, tying a shoelace, making pizza, or ironing a shirt. You have numerous academic blueprints as well: solving algebra problems, using the card catalog, or writing an English composition. These blueprints enable you to complete a task without analyzing it or rediscovering the best way to do it each time.

Thought Patterns: Guides to Learning

Familiarity with these basic thought patterns will enable you to approach all your courses more easily and effectively. You will find textbook chapters easier to read if you can identify the thought pattern(s) by which they are organized. Lectures will be easier to follow, and your notes will be better organized if you identify your professor's thought pattern.

Recognizing patterns will enable you to anticipate the author's or speaker's thought development. For example, from a heading or topic sentence alone, you often can predict the pattern of thought the section or paragraph will follow. If you read a heading "Types of Engineering Models," you might anticipate a classification pattern. Or suppose you read the following topic sentence:

> When you are viewing an online computer system in action, it is as if you are watching a science fiction movie.

Here, you would anticipate a comparison-contrast pattern of development in the paragraph. If a speaker announced, "Today we'll consider the impact of stress upon health," you could anticipate the speaker to use a cause-effect pattern of development. Patterns are useful learning tools:

Patterns provide a strategy or framework for comprehending a message. Thought patterns indicate how ideas are organized. Familiarity with patterns enables us to grasp meaning more easily. If, for example, you establish that a lecturer intends to contrast two forms of media advertising, then the lecture will be easier to follow.

Patterns facilitate storage and retrieval of information in memory. Information that is grouped, chunked, or organized is easier to store than single, unrelated bits of information. Also, the manner in which information is stored in memory influences the ease with which it is retrieved. Patterns provide a vehicle for organizing information and function as retrieval clues for subsequent recall.

Patterns provide a means of understanding and analyzing assignments. Often, an assignment seems difficult or confusing until you understand its function. Patterns provide a vehicle for organizing and expressing your ideas in a coherent, comprehensible form. As you write essay exam answers, class assignments, or term papers, patterns provide a base or structure around which you can effectively express your thoughts.

Academic Thought Patterns

Here are the commonly used thought patterns:

◆ Order or sequence
◆ Comparison and contrast
◆ Cause and effect
◆ Classification
◆ Problem-solution
◆ Definition
◆ Listing

The following section describes each pattern. In later chapters, you will see how these patterns are useful in taking lecture notes, reading textbooks, writing papers, and preparing for and taking exams.

Order or Sequence

If you were asked to summarize the plot of a film, you would mention key events in the order in which they occurred. In describing how to solve a math problem, you would detail the process step-by-step. If asked to list what you feel are your accomplishments so far this week, you might present them in order of importance, listing your most important accomplishment first, and so forth. In describing a building, you might detail the front, then the sides, then the roof. In each case, you present information in a particular sequence or order. Each of the above examples, then, illustrates a thought pattern known as order or sequence. Each form is described briefly below.

Chronology

Chronological order refers to the sequence in which events occur in time. This pattern is essential in the academic disciplines concerned with the interpretation of events in the past. History, government, and anthropology are prime examples, as are other disciplines for which historical background is provided. In various forms of literature, chronological order is evident: the narrative form, used in novels, short stories, and narrative essays, centers on chronological order.

Speakers and writers often provide substantial clues that signal that this thought pattern is being used. These signals may occur within single sentences or as transitions or connections between sentences. Several examples of these signals follow. (Clue words that occur in phrases are italicized here to help you spot them.)

In-sentence clues	*in* ancient times
	at the start of the battle
	on September 12
	the *first* Homo sapiens
	later efforts

Continued

Between-sentence transitions	then, later, first, before, during, by the time, while, afterward, as, after, thereafter, meanwhile, at that point

Process

In disciplines that focus on procedures, steps, or stages by which actions are accomplished, the process pattern is often employed. These include mathematics, natural and life sciences, computer science, and engineering. The pattern is similar to chronology in that steps or stages follow each other in time.

Clues and signals often used in conjunction with this pattern are similar to those used for chronological order.

Order of Importance

The pattern of ideas sometimes expresses order of priority or preference. Ideas are arranged in one of two ways: from most important to least important, or from least to most important. Here are some commonly used clues that suggest this pattern.

In-sentence clues	is *less* essential than . . . *more* revealing is . . . of *primary* interest
Between-sentence transitions	first, next, last, most important, primarily, secondarily

Spatial Order

Information organized according to its physical location or position or order in space uses a pattern that is known as spatial order. Spatial order is used in academic disciplines in which physical descriptions are important. These include numerous technical fields, engineering, and the biological sciences.

Diagramming is of the utmost importance in working with this pattern; in fact, often a diagram accompanies text material. For example, in studying the functioning of the various parts of the human eye, a diagram makes the process easier to understand. Lecturers often refer to a visual aid or chalkboard drawing when providing spatial description. Clue words and phrases that indicate spatial order include the following:

In-sentence clues	the *center,* the *lower* portion, the *outside* area, *beneath* the surface
Between-sentence transitions	next to, beside, to the left, in the center, externally

Exercise
12.1

Read each of the following opening sentences from a textbook reading assignment and anticipate whether the material will be developed using chronology, process, order of importance, or spatial order.

1. The rise of organizations of women both preceded and postdated the civil rights movements.[1]

2. As is common with all other cells, the neuron has a nucleus, a cell body, and a cell membrane, which encloses the whole cell.

3. As people move away from denial (they can no longer reject the fact that they are ill because their symptoms are growing so acute), anger (being angry is not helping symptoms), and bargaining (also ineffective; they are becoming worse, not better), they eventually arrive at a stage of really admitting to themselves that they are ill.[2]

4. Short fibers, dendrites, branch out around the cell body and a single long fiber, the axon, extends from the cell body.

5. The basic technique for input loop control involves using a flag to signal when the EOF record has been read.[3]

6. The battle for women's suffrage was fought mostly in the last years of the 19th and first years of the 20th century.[4]

7. A newborn needs careful assessment to be certain that his musculoskeletal and neurological systems are intact.

8. The key consideration in determining whether a college education is a good investment is the opportunity cost, the cost of choosing college over other alternatives.

Comparison and Contrast

The *comparison* pattern is used to emphasize or discuss *similarities* between or among ideas, theories, concepts, or events, while the *contrast* pattern emphasizes *differences*. When a speaker or writer is concerned with both similarities and differences, a combination pattern is used. Comparison and contrast are widely used in the social sciences, where different groups, societies, cultures, or behaviors are studied. Literature courses may require comparisons among poets, among several literary works, or among stylistic features. A business course may examine various management styles, compare organizational structures, or contrast retailing plans.

A speaker or writer may be concerned with similarities, differences, or both similarities and differences. In turn, this concern will affect the organizational pattern. For example, suppose a professor of American literature is comparing two American poets, Whitman and Frost. Each of the following organizations is possible:

◆ Compare and contrast the two; that is, discuss their similarities, then their differences.

◆ Discuss characteristics of Whitman, then discuss characteristics of Frost, then summarize their similarities and differences.

◆ Discuss by characteristic. For example, first discuss the two poets' use of metaphor, then their use of rhyme, and then their common themes.

Clues, words, and phrases that reflect these patterns are listed below:

Contrast	
Within-sentence clues	*unlike* Bush, Clinton . . .
	less rigid than . . .
	contrasted with
	differs from
Between-sentence transitions	in contrast
	however
	on the other hand
	as opposed to
Comparison	
Within-sentence clues	. . . *similarities between*
	is *as* powerful *as* . . .
	like Bush, Clinton . . .
	both Bush and Clinton . . .
	Clinton *resembles* Bush *in that* . . .
Between-sentence transitions	in a like manner
	similarly
	likewise
	correspondingly
	in the same way

Exercise 12.2   Read each of the following opening sentences from textbook reading assignments and anticipate whether a comparison, contrast, or combination pattern will be used.

1. Black Muslim religious practices closely follow those of Islam, a major religion of the Middle East and North Africa.

2. The majority of Americans will be better off in the year 2025 than we are today.

3. Two recent research reports have come to opposing conclusions about the dangers of hazardous waste pollution to the area's water table.

4. Both Werner (1994) and Waible (1995) focus on variability of genetic traces in pinpointing causes of cancer.

5. In the few areas on which they agree, the two authors dispute the credibility of each other's sources.

Cause and Effect

The cause and effect pattern expresses a relationship between two or more actions, events, or occurrences that are connected in time. The relationship differs, however, from chronological order in that one event leads to another by causing it. Information that is organized using the cause-effect pattern may

- explain causes, sources, reasons, motives, and action.
- explain the effects, results, or consequences of a particular action.
- explain both causes and effects.

The cause and effect pattern is used extensively in many academic fields. All disciplines that ask the question "why," all that involve research, and all that search for explanations for the operation of the world around us use the cause and effect thought pattern. It predominates in science, technology, and social science.

In its simplest form, cause and effect is straightforward and direct. In other situations, causes and effects, or reasons and consequences, although not directly stated, can be inferred. For example, consider the following sentence:

Because wages are decreasing, the pace of inflation is slowing.

Decreasing wages is the cause or reason, and the slowing of inflation is the result or consequence. Notice, however, that the relationship is not directly stated, only implied.

Many statements expressing cause and effect relationships appear in direct order, with the cause stated first and the effect following.

I couldn't find my keys, so I was late for class.

However, reverse order is sometimes used, as in the following statement:

I was late for class because I couldn't find my keys.

Exercise 12.3

Identify the cause and the effect in each of the following statements.

1. Your buying decisions influence the prices farmers receive for their products.

2. A computer program is easy or difficult to run, depending in part on the data entry system you choose.

3. Recently, the Justice Department investigated charges that some airlines were using their computerized reservations systems to gain a competitive edge over smaller airlines.

4. Computer users suffer when poor, incompletely designed error-checking systems are marketed.

5. The threat of nuclear war has been with us for so long—nearly two generations—that we are in serious danger of forgetting the real dangers it poses.

The cause and effect pattern, however, is not limited to an expression of a single one cause–one effect relationship. There may be multiple causes, or multiple effects, or both multiple causes and multiple effects. For example, both slippery road conditions and your failure to buy snow tires (causes) may contribute to your car's sliding into the ditch (effect). In other instances, a chain of causes or effects may occur. For instance, missing the bus may force you to miss your 8:00 A.M. class, which in turn may cause you to not turn in your term paper on time, which may result in a penalty grade.

Clue words or phrases that suggest the cause and effect pattern include the following:

Within-sentence clues	causes, creates, leads to, stems from, produces, results in
Between-sentence transitions	therefore, consequently, hence, for this reason, since

---

Exercise 12.4

For each of the following statements, determine whether it expresses single or multiple causes and single or multiple effects.

1. Acute stress may lead to an inability to think clearly, to organize, and to make decisions.

2. A mild stimulant, such as caffeine, appears to change a person's ability to maintain attention and concentration on relevant stimuli at hand.

3. Many people consider large families a blessing, or have religious objections to birth control, or are culturally ill-suited to the regular use of birth control methods.[5]

4. Regional conflict, then, is at the base of the huge military bill of the Third World, together with ideological competition, and sometimes revolution, between Western-oriented governments and Socialist movements.[6]

5. Geography and territorial position are among the most enduring determinants of national power and national defense.

Classification

Suppose a friend who had never used a microcomputer asked you to explain how it operates. You might start by describing the function of each major component: the monitor, the disk drives, the central processing unit, and so forth. By dividing a topic and discussing each of its components, you are using a pattern known as classification.

This pattern is widely used in many academic subjects. For example, a psychology text might explain human needs by classifying them into two categories: primary and secondary. Or in a chemistry textbook, various compounds may be grouped and discussed according to common characteristics, such as the presence of hydrogen or oxygen. The classification pattern divides a topic into parts, based on common or shared characteristics. Classification implies use of both the comparison and the contrast thought patterns, since it is on the basis of some similarity that items may be put into a class or category, and it is on the basis of some difference that individual members of a class remain distinct from one another.

Here are a few examples of topics and the classifications or categories into which each might be divided:

Cars: sports, luxury, economy
Energy: kinetic, potential
Diseases: communicable, noncommunicable

Clue words and phrases that indicate the classification pattern are as follows:

Within-sentence clues	There are several *kinds* of . . .
	There are numerous *types* of . . .
	can be *classified* as . . .
	is *composed* of . . .
	comprises . . .
Between-sentence transitions	finally, another, one type of . . .

Exercise 12.5

Divide each of the topics listed below into several categories.

1. Emotions
2. Music
3. Discrimination
4. Laws
5. Literature

Problem-Solution

Many scientific and technical fields are concerned with defining problems and conducting research to test possible solutions. In the social and behavioral sciences this approach is also used. This problem-solution pattern forms the basis of the scientific method, a process used throughout the sciences to ask questions, test hypotheses, solve problems, and acquire new knowledge.

Problem-solution is a complicated thought process, involving several other patterns as well. Cause and effect are also involved since the solution must have an effect on the problem. The "if . . . , then . . ." type of thinking involved in predicting possible solutions is basically a cause and effect relationship. Process, too, is involved, since problem solving involves step-by-step analysis of the problem.

In many texts, numerous forms of this pattern are found. Several solutions to a particular problem may be offered or various solutions may be discussed before the problem is fully defined, or various related problems may be discussed and numerous solutions offered. The clue words and phrases used within this pattern are as follows:

Within-sentence clues	since . . . , why . . . , would . . . , if . . . , then, why does . . .
Between-sentence transitions	since, whereas, consequently, as a result

Exercise 12.6	Predict which of the following textbook chapter headings is most likely to follow the problem-solution pattern.
	1. Types of Consumer Research
	2. Preventing the Spread of Infection
	3. Factors That Influence Food Choice
	4. Detecting Errors in Computer Programs
	5. Procedures for the Administration of Oral Liquid Medicine

Definition

Each academic discipline has its own specialized vocabulary (see Chapter 11). One of the primary purposes of basic textbooks is to introduce students to this new language. Consequently, definition is a commonly used pattern throughout most introductory-level texts.

Suppose you were asked to define the word *comedian* for someone unfamiliar with the term. First, you would probably say that a comedian is a person who entertains. Then you might distinguish a comedian from other types of entertainers by saying that a comedian is an entertainer who tells jokes and makes others laugh. Finally, you might mention, by way of example, the names of several well-known comedians who have appeared on television. Although you may have presented it informally, your definition would have followed the standard, classic pattern. The first part of your definition tells what general class or group the term belongs to (entertainers). The second part tells what distinguishes the term from other items in the same class or category. The third part includes further explanation, characteristics, examples, or application.

Here are a few additional examples:

	General Class	Distinguishing Characteristics
Opossum	animal	ratlike tail
		nocturnal habits
Prejudice	emotional attitude	involving a tendency to respond negatively to certain identifiable groups or group members

Exercise 12.7	Using the patterns described above, give a definition for each of the following.

1. Athlete
2. Cheating
3. Music
4. Internet
5. Discrimination

HOW DO YOU SEE IT?

"I thought it had a pretty good story and interesting characters, but I really didn't like the font."

Elements to evaluate in a book report generally include the story line and the character development, but not the typeface or the binding of the book. Write a paragraph describing an important academic thought pattern related to your favorite course.

Listing

If asked to describe an exam you just took, you might mention its length, its difficulty, the topics it covered, and the types of questions it contained. These details about the exam could be arranged in any order; each detail provides further information about the exam, but each has no specific relationship to any other. This arrangement of ideas is known as *listing,* the presentation of pieces of information on a given topic by stating them one after the other.

This pattern is widely used in college textbooks in most academic disciplines. The listing pattern is the least structured pattern, but it is used frequently in several ways. In its loosest form, the pattern may be simply a list of items: factors that influence light emission, characteristics of a particular poet, a description of an atom, a list of characteristics that define poverty. Step-by-step procedures may also be presented using this pattern. Somewhat more structured is the use of listing to explain, support, or provide evidence. Support may be in the form of facts, statistics, or examples. For instance, the statement "The newest sexually transmitted disease to come to public awareness, AIDS, was first documented in 1981 and has spread rapidly since that time" would be followed by details about its discovery and statistics documenting its spread.

The clue words or phrases used for this pattern include the following:

Within-sentence clues	the second . . .
	. . . and . . .
	also
	there are several . . .
	(1) . . . , (2) . . . , and (3) . . .
	(a) . . . , (b) . . . , (c) . . .
Between-sentence transitions	In addition,
	first, second, third
	finally
	another

Exercise 12.8

Identify the topics listed below that might be developed using the listing pattern.

1. Sources of Drug Information
2. Types of Computers
3. Problem-Solving Techniques
4. Two Famous 20th-Century Composers
5. Obstacles to Creative Thought

Mixed Patterns

Patterns are often combined. In describing a process, a writer may also give reasons why each step must be followed in the prescribed order. A lecturer may define a concept by comparing it to something similar or familiar. Let's suppose your political science professor opens a lecture by stating that the distinction between "power" and "power potential" is an important one in considering balance of power. You might expect a definition pattern, in which the two terms are defined, but you might also anticipate the difference or "distinction" between the two terms to be discussed using a contrast pattern.

Thinking Critically
. . . About Patterns

When you learn to identify patterns, you see the ideas in a piece of writing or a lecture as a coherent set rather than as unconnected facts. Patterns focus your attention on concepts, larger ideas, and issues rather than on small, individual details.

Patterns, then, help you decide what is important and what is not. Here's a list of patterns and what they emphasize:

Pattern	What Is Important
Chronology	• dates and events
Process	• steps or procedures
Importance	• priorities
Spatial	• physical location
Comparison	• similarities
Contrast	• differences
Cause and effect	• sequence, actions, relationships, consequences, motives
Classification	• characteristics and distinguishing features
Problem-solution	• causes, effects, solutions, outcomes
Definition	• terminology, examples

Exercise 12.9

For each of the following topic sentences, anticipate two patterns that are likely to be evident in the paragraph.

1. On balance, then, there appear to be four discernible reasons for nuclear weapons development: security, prestige, regional dominance or equilibrium, and reification of modern scientific development.[7]

2. Before examining the components of the balance of power, it will be useful to clarify five features about the international system that apply regardless of historical era or structural form.[8]

Continued

3. Industry, the second and more modern form of production, displaced feudalism.[9]

4. Like reinforcement, punishment comes in two varieties, positive and negative.[10]

5. The reasons for this huge increase in military expenditure in the Third World are many, and they go considerably beyond reasons of national grandeur. Perhaps most important is the degree to which the developing nations remain of interest to the superpowers.[11]

Exercise 12.10   For each of the following lecture topics, anticipate and discuss what pattern(s) the lecture is likely to exhibit.

1. Conducting an Interview

2. Why Computers Use Binary-Coded Information

3. Functions of Money

4. Classical Versus Instrumental Conditioning

5. Narrowing a Research Paper Topic

6. Assigning Data to a Two-Level Table

7. Adolescence: The Failure to Copy

8. Cures for Inflation

9. Phillips Curves: Hypothetical and Actual

10. Apartheid: Tradition or Discrimination?

Exercise 12.11   For each of the following topic sentences, anticipate what pattern(s) that paragraph is likely to exhibit.

1. Should terrorism and hostage-taking be controlled by an international response team? If so, what policies and procedures should govern its actions?

2. Unlike Japan and the Western European countries, Canada has been relatively removed from the balance of terror.

3. More recently, however, the Japanese outlook has shifted. American withdrawal from the mainland of Asia after the Vietnam War, together with the uncertainties introduced to national security by the Nixon Doctrine, necessitates a larger measure of self-dependence.[12]

4. We may agree in theory with the ringing words of the Declaration of Independence that "all men are created equal"; but in the concrete world of reality, the words are often obscured by conflicts.[13]

5. Writing in *Foreign Affairs* in 1947, foreign policy strategist George F. Kennan proposed a policy of containment. His containment doctrine called for the United States to isolate the Soviet Union, "contain" its advances, and resist its encroachments.[14]

6. Throughout the nuclear era much attention has been given to the various types of unintended nuclear war—war initiated by accident, error, or terrorist activity.

7. With the Doppler technique, high-frequency sound waves are "bounced off" body tissue; the rate and pitch at which they return demonstrate the movement and density of the underlying tissue.

8. The sections of a comprehensive history are introduction, chief concern, history of present illness, past medical history, family medical history, and review of systems.

9. In addition to nuclear devices and missiles and weapons for land, sea, and air warfare, arms designers have created a variety of weapons less well known but equally horrifying.[15]

10. Behaviorists see the individual as essentially passive, while cognitive psychologists maintain that the individual actively interacts with the environment.

Applying Your Knowledge of Thought Patterns

Now that you are familiar with the seven basic thought patterns, you are ready to use them to organize your learning and study and to shape your thinking. Chapter 10 discusses predominant patterns in each discipline. Subsequent chapters in this text will demonstrate the use of patterns in specific learning situations. In the next chapter, you will identify patterns in college lectures and use them to organize your note taking. In Chapter 14 you will see that they are helpful in interpreting graphs, tables, and diagrams. Patterns are used in Chapter 15 to describe various techniques of mapping (using drawings to organize ideas). When preparing for examinations (Chapter 17), you will need to organize thematic study as well as predict examination questions. Finally in Chapter 19 the thought patterns involved in various types of essay examination questions are discussed.

Working Together

While the thought patterns presented in this chapter are widely used in academic thinking, writing, and speaking, they also are important and frequent in our everyday lives. In groups of five or six, brainstorm a list of as many daily activities or decisions as you can that involve one (or more) of the seven thought patterns discussed in this chapter.

Interactive Chapter Review

Knowledge	What are four benefits of knowing the basic thought patterns?
Comprehension	Give an example for each of the four types of patterns having to do with order or sequence. Label each with the name of the pattern used.
Application	For one college lecture you attended this week, identify the thought pattern used to organize the lecture.
Analysis	Is figuring out the thought pattern in a lecture or textbook more like seeing the forest or the individual trees? Explain your answer.
Synthesis	Throughout this book, numerous ideas for being successful in college are given. Based on your reading, list at least 10 ideas for success, using a cause-effect statement to describe each. (For example, "Study two hours for every one hour of class in order to get a C grade.") Then analyze your list to answer the following question: Is the student, the instructor, the textbook, or the college most responsible for a student's success in a course?
Evaluation	Evaluate your mastery of thought patterns by examining a chapter you have already read in one of your textbooks. For one section of the chapter, examine each paragraph and label it according to the thought pattern it uses. (Note: There may be cases in which you need to look at several paragraphs in a row to find the overall pattern.)

Further Analysis

Analyze the following situation and answer the questions below:

A student attending the University of Toronto is given an assignment in art history class to write an essay discussing two paintings, one by Renoir, the other by Daumier. She has spent considerable time studying each painting, but she has no idea of how to begin the assignment. Although the paintings are obviously very different, she cannot seem to find an organizing principle on which to base her essay.

Feeling as if she is making no progress, she calls several friends and asks advice. One friend advises her to read some general background information on each artist. Another advises her to focus on her first impression of each painting and write about those impressions.

1. Evaluate the advice given by each friend.

2. What advice would you offer that would help the student complete this assignment?

3. What possible ways could the student organize her paper?

Discussion

1. Consider each course you are taking this semester. What thought patterns are predominant in each?

2. From your experience, do essay exam questions seem to use these thought patterns? Think of essay questions you have read and consider the types of responses they required.

3. What connections do you see between the patterns discussed here and the type of essays you have written or are writing in English composition classes?

4. Assume you must read and take notes on seven articles, one representative of each of the seven patterns discussed in this chapter.

   a. How would you modify your reading strategy for each?

   b. How would you organize your notes for each?

The Work Connection

The thought patterns you use in speech and writing will affect how your listener or reader thinks about a topic and about you, the speaker or writer. This is particularly true in that important work document, the resumé. Because your resumé needs to clearly highlight your best qualifications for a job, it's worth taking the time to think about how best to organize it. There are two basic patterns for successful resumés. The *chronological pattern* provides a list of your previous positions and accomplishments in reverse order (that is, the most recent job first). It is most useful when your job history shows progress and you are staying in the same career field. The *functional pattern*, similar to classification in this chapter, emphasizes the particular skills and abilities you have developed and downplays when you developed them. It is most useful when you want to emphasize skills you haven't used in recent jobs, when you are changing careers or reentering the job market, or when you want to show experience gained through courses or volunteer work.

1. Consider your own work and education history. Do you think a chronological or functional resumé would be more to your advantage? Why?

2. Imagine you have spent the last 10 years raising your children and running your household. What skills and abilities from your experience could you add to your functional resumé?

The Web Connection

1. Meet Melvil Dewey

   http://www.thrall.org/dewey/dewbio.htm

   The Dewey Decimal System is one of the most famous classification systems. Read about the man who created it at this site from the Middletown Thrall Library in New York State.

2. The Amazing Rube Goldberg

   http://rube.iscool.net/

   The machines in Rube Goldberg's cartoons depict cause and effect in a mechanical and humorous way. See some of his drawings as well as real inventions inspired by his imagination at this site dedicated to Goldberg.

3. Storyboarding

   http://wneo.org/video/storyboa.htm

   Filmmakers use storyboarding to lay out a sequence of shots. This site from PBS station WNEO shows an example of the use of storyboarding for television production.

 Go Electronic!

For additional readings, exercises, and Internet activities, visit the Longman Study Skills Web site at:

http://www.ablongman.com/StudySkills

If you need a user name and password, please see your instructor.

Chapter 13

Note Taking for Class Lectures

DO YOU KNOW?

Why should you learn a systematic approach to listening and lecture note taking?

What techniques can you develop to record the content and organization of lectures?

What are the various lecture styles, and how can you recognize them?

How can you identify and use instructors' thought patterns to take good notes?

How should you edit and review your notes?

Class lectures are a primary source of information. They are a personalized explanation or interpretation of course content, and note taking is your primary means of organizing and processing this material. Note taking is a means of thinking and reasoning about course content and of identifying and recording important information using thought patterns as organizing principles. This chapter discusses listening and note-taking techniques, describes various lecture styles, demonstrates how to anticipate and identify lecturers' thought patterns, and presents systems for editing and reviewing your notes.

Sharpening Your Listening Skills

During college lectures, listening is your primary means of acquiring information. Listening is also an essential skill in most careers. It is estimated that between 35 percent and 40 percent of a white-collar worker's day is spent listening. Yet research indicates that most adult students or employees do not listen efficiently. Rate the effectiveness of your listening skills by completing the questionnaire shown in Figure 13.1 on p. 224.

The Distinction Between Hearing and Listening

Have you ever found yourself not listening to a friend who is talking to you? Instead, perhaps you are thinking about something else entirely or about what you'll say next. Have you ever found yourself not listening to an instructor during class? In each case, the speaker's voice was loud and clear; you could *hear* but you were not *listening*. These two situations illustrate the distinction between hearing and listening. Hearing is a passive physiological process in which sound waves are received by the ear. In contrast, listening is an intellectual activity that involves comprehension and interpretation of incoming information. Listening is intentional—something you do deliberately and purposefully. It requires your attention and your concentration. Hearing, on the other hand, occurs without any thought or effort.

Figure 13.1

Rate Your Learning and Note-Taking Skills

Respond to each of the following statements by checking "Always," "Sometimes," or "Never."

	Always	Sometimes	Never
1. Do you tune in to a lecture before it begins by rereading previous notes or assigned material?	❏	❏	❏
2. Do you pay attention to the speaker's gestures, tone of voice, and body language?	❏	❏	❏
3. Do you reread and revise your notes after you have taken them?	❏	❏	❏
4. Do you use abbreviations instead of writing out long or frequently used words?	❏	❏	❏
5. Are you able to stay alert and focused throughout a lecture?	❏	❏	❏
6. Do you try to record only what is important in the lecture?	❏	❏	❏
7. Before attending the lecture, do you read the textbook assignment that is related to the lecture?	❏	❏	❏
8. Are you able to take notes on material that is boring, technical, or overly complicated?	❏	❏	❏
9. Do your notes reflect the lecturer's organization?	❏	❏	❏
10. Do you edit (review and revise) your notes after each class?	❏	❏	❏

If you answered "Sometimes" or "Never" to more than one or two questions listed above, your note-taking skills need improvement.

Tips for Effective Listening

Use the following suggestions to sharpen your listening skills:

Tune in.   Focus your attention on the lecture or presentation before it begins. Recall what you know about the topic. Review related reading assignments while you are waiting for the lecture to begin.

Maintain eye contact with the lecturer.   Except when writing notes, make eye contact with the lecturer. Eye contact improves communication; you will feel more involved and find it easier to stay interested in the lecture.

Stay active by asking mental questions.   Keep your attention focused on the lecture by asking yourself questions. Here are a few examples: What key point is the lecturer making? How does it fit with previously discussed key points? How is the lecture organized? How will the lecturer prove the point?

Anticipate what is to follow.   A good lecturer provides clues about his or her organization. Careful listeners, then, are able to predict or anticipate where the lecturer is leading up to or what topics will follow.

Stick with the lecture.   When a lecture becomes confusing, complicated, or technical, it is tempting to tune out, telling yourself you'll figure it out later by reading your textbook. Resist this temptation by taking detailed notes. These notes, when reviewed after the lecture, will be valuable as you try to straighten out your confusion.

Avoid emotional involvement.   If the lecture is on a controversial issue or the lecturer mentions a topic or word that has emotional meaning for you, it is easy to become emotionally involved. When this occurs, your listening sometimes becomes selective—you hear what you want to hear. Instead, try to remain objective and open minded. Your attention may be diverted by these topics unless you force yourself to concentrate on the speaker's position, not your own.

Use gaps and pauses in the lecture.   Use this time to organize or summarize your notes.

Focus on content, not delivery.   It is easy to become so annoyed, upset, charmed by, or engaged with the lecturer as a person that you fail to comprehend the message he or she is conveying. Force yourself to focus on the message, and disregard personal characteristics such as an annoying laugh or overused expressions.

Focus on ideas, not facts.   If you concentrate on recording and remembering separate, unconnected facts, you are doomed to failure. Remember, your short-term memory is extremely limited in span and capacity, so while you are focusing on certain facts, it is inevitable that you will ignore some and forget others. Instead, listen for ideas, trends, and patterns.

Listen carefully to the speaker's opening comments.   As your mind refocuses from prior tasks and problems, it is easy to miss the speaker's opening remarks, which may be among the most important. Here the speaker may establish connections with prior lectures, identify his or her purpose, or describe the lecture's content or organization.

Attempt to understand the lecturer's purpose.   If it is not stated explicitly, try to reason it out. Is the purpose to present facts, discuss and raise questions, demonstrate a trend or pattern, or present a technique or procedure?

Fill the gap between rate of speech and rate of thinking.   It is natural for your mind to wander while a friend is talking. Although you may be interested in what he or she is saying, you may think about other things while listening. This is natural, since the rate of speech is much slower than the speed of thought. To listen most effectively in class, use this gap to think about the lecture. Anticipate what is to follow, think of situations where the information may be applied, pose questions, or make the information fit with your prior knowledge and experience.

Treat listening as a challenging mental task.   We all know concentration and attention are necessary for reading, yet many of us treat listening as something that should occur without effort. Perhaps as a result of the constant barrage of the spoken word through radio, television, and social contact, we assume listening occurs automatically. Lectures, however, represent a concentrated form of oral communication that requires you to concentrate.

How to Start with an Advantage

Some students regard lecture note taking as a frustrating chore of handling an overwhelming rush of incoming information. Other students seem to approach it systematically, managing to process large amounts of information easily. Which it becomes for you depends largely on your approach. A few suggestions will enable you to approach lectures confidently and efficiently—with distinct advantages over students who just appear in class with a pen.

Get Organized

Organization is the key to handling many situations, and this is especially true of lecture note taking. Use the following tips to approach note taking in an organized, systematic manner:

Organize a notebook for each course.   Use standard size, $8\frac{1}{2} \times 11$ inches. Not enough information fits on a page in smaller notebooks, making review more difficult. Either spiral or loose-leaf notebooks are acceptable; loose-leaf types allow you to add class handouts, review sheets, and quizzes beside the notes to which they pertain.

Use ink.   Pencil tends to smear and fade.

Date your notes for later reference.

Get used to sitting in the same place, preferably near the front of the room.   You will feel more comfortable and less distracted if you have your own seat. Sitting near the front is especially important in large lecture halls. You will feel as if you are in more di-rect contact with the instructor and will be able to see as well as hear emphasis as you observe his or her facial expressions and gestures.

Make a point to attend all lectures, even if attendance is not mandatory.   Borrowing and copying a classmate's notes is not a substitute for attending the lecture, since it does not involve the key learning processes of identifying, organizing, and synthesizing in-formation. If it is absolutely necessary to miss a class, be certain to borrow and photo-copy several students' notes. Then, after you have reviewed each set, abstract from them your own set of notes. This procedure approximates the actual note-taking process by forcing you to think about, compare, and decide what is important.

Be Thoroughly Prepared for Each Lecture

Lecture note taking will be easier if you are familiar with the topic of a lecture, key points, key terminology, and basic thought patterns. If you approach a lecture "cold," without advance preparation, you must devote considerable time and effort focusing on the topic, determining its organization, and assessing its relationship to other course content.

To prepare in advance, read related text assignments. It is tempting to delay reading an assignment until after the lecture because a text assignment seems easier once you have heard the lecture on the same topic. However, reading the text in advance will im-prove your comprehension of the lecture. At first it may seem to be a toss-up as to which it is best to do first. Remember, however, that your text is always available for rereading, study, and review, while each lecture is a one-time opportunity.

If you are unable to read an assignment completely before a particular lecture, pre-view it using the procedure described in Chapter 14 to obtain a basic familiarity, and plan to read it after the lecture.

Overcoming Common Problems

Instructors present lectures differently, use various lecture styles, and organize their subjects in different ways. Therefore, it is common to experience difficulty taking notes in one or more courses. Table 13.1 on p. 228 identifies common problems associated with lecture note taking and offers possible solutions.

Table 13.1

Common Note-Taking Problems

Problem	Solution
"My mind wanders and I get bored."	Sit in the front of the room. Be certain to preview assignments. Pose questions you expect to be answered in the lecture.
"The instructor talks too fast."	Develop a shorthand system; use abbreviations. Leave blanks and fill them in later.
"The lecturer rambles."	Preview correlating text assignments to determine organizing principles.
"Some ideas don't seem to fit anywhere."	Record them in the margin or in parentheses within your notes for reassessment later during editing (see p. 233).
"Everything seems important." or "Nothing seems important."	"You have not identified key concepts and may lack necessary background knowledge. Locate a more basic textbook that discusses the topic.
"I can't spell all the new technical terms."	Record them phonetically, the way they sound; fill in correct spellings during editing (see p. 243).

Recording Appropriate Content and Organization

The worst mistake you can make when taking notes is to try to record everything the instructor says. While this may seem to be the safest, most thorough approach, it interferes with, and often prevents, learning. If you are constantly writing, you have little time to think—to understand, assimilate, or react to what is being said. The effectiveness of note taking as a learning strategy depends on active listening. Learning occurs as you evaluate the relevance and importance of incoming information and make connections with other information presented. The following sections offer some general suggestions on recording and organizing information.

Identifying Main Ideas

The main ideas of a lecture are the points your instructor emphasizes and on which he or she elaborates. They are the major ideas that the details, explanations, examples, and general discussion support. Frequently, instructors give clues such as the following to show what is important in a lecture.

Points repeated. When an instructor repeats a statement, he or she is indicating to you that the idea or concept is important. Look for signals such as "This, you will recall . . ." or "As we saw last week in a different framework . . ."

Change in voice. Some lecturers change the tone or pitch of their voices when they are trying to emphasize major points. A speaker's voice may get louder or softer or higher or lower as he or she presents important ideas.

HOW DO YOU SEE IT?

Reporter Taking Notes at Battle Scene of Modoc Indian War

Some note-taking situations are more demanding than others. What is the most difficult note-taking situation you have encountered so far? What could you do to improve that experience?

Change in rate of speech.   Speakers may slow down as they discuss important concepts. Sometimes a speaker goes so slowly that he or she seems to be dictating information. If, for example, a speaker giving a definition pauses slightly between each word or phrase, it is a way of telling you that the definition is important and you should write it down.

Listing and numbering points.   Lecturers often directly state that there are "three important causes" or "four significant effects" or "five possible situations" as they begin discussing a topic. These expressions are clues to the material's importance.

Writing on the chalkboard.   Some lecturers write key words or outlines of major ideas on the chalkboard as they speak. Although not all important ideas are recorded on the chalkboard, you can be sure that if an instructor does take the time to write a word or phrase on the chalkboard, it is important.

Use of audiovisuals. Some instructors emphasize important ideas, clarify relationships, or diagram processes or procedures by using audiovisual aids. Movies, filmstrips, videotapes, or photographs emphasize or describe important ideas and concepts.

Direct announcement. Occasionally, an instructor will announce straightforwardly that a particular concept or idea is especially important. He or she may begin by saying, "Particularly important to remember is . . ." or "One important fact that you must keep in mind is . . ." The instructor may even hint that such information would make a good exam question. Be sure to mark hints like these in your notes. Emphasize these items with an asterisk or write "exam?" in the margin.

Nonverbal clues. Many speakers provide clues to what they feel is important through their movements and actions as well as their words. Some lecturers walk toward their audience as they make a major point. Others may use hand gestures, pound the table, or pace back and forth as they present key ideas. While each speaker is different, most speakers use some type of nonverbal clue.

At the beginning of each course, be sure to analyze each professor's means of emphasis. Think of this analysis as a means of tuning in or getting on the same wavelength as your professor.

Exercise 13.1   Analyze the lecture technique of one of your instructors. Attend one lecture, and as you take notes, try to be particularly aware of how he or she lets you know what is important. After the lecture, analyze your instructor's lecture technique, using the following questions.

1. How does he or she emphasize what is important?
2. What nonverbal clues are evident?

Then analyze your note-taking skills.

1. What notetaking problems did you encounter?
2. What can be done to overcome these problems?

Recording Details and Examples

A difficult part of taking notes is deciding how much detail to include. You cannot record everything because the normal speed of speech greatly exceeds the normal speed of writing. Some lecturers speak as fast as 90–125 words per minute. Therefore, you will have to be selective and record only particularly important details. As a rule of thumb, record a brief phrase to summarize each major supporting detail.

If an instructor gives you several examples of a particular law, situation, or problem, be sure to write down in summary form at least one example. Record more than one if you have time. While at the time of the lecture it may seem that you completely understand what is being discussed, you will find that a few weeks later you really do need examples to help you recall the lecture.

Reflecting the Lecture's Organization

As you record the main ideas and details, try to organize or arrange them so that you can easily see how the lecture was organized and recall the relative importance of ideas. A simple way to show a lecture's organization is to use a system of indentation. Retain a regular margin on your paper. Start your notes on the most important of the topics at the left margin. For less important main ideas, indent your notes slightly. For major details, indent slightly farther. Indent even farther for examples and other details. The rule of thumb to follow is this: The less important the idea, the farther it should be indented. Use bullets or dashes to make your indentations easily distinguishable. Your notes might be organized like this:

Major topic
      Main idea
            Detail
            Detail
                  Example
      Main idea
            Detail
            Detail
            Detail
Major topic
      Main idea
            Detail
                  Example

Notice that the sample looks like an outline but is missing the roman numerals (I, II, III), capital letters (A, B, C), and arabic numerals (1, 2, 3) that usually enumerate an outline. This system of note taking accomplishes the same goal as an outline—it stratifies information to show, at a glance, the relative importance of the various facts or ideas listed. If the organization of a lecture is obvious, you may wish to use a number or letter system in addition to indenting.

Since not all instructor's lectures follow a tightly organized pattern, it is not always possible to develop an outline. Try not to spend too much time during the lecture thinking about the outline format. Be primarily concerned with recording ideas; you can always reorganize your notes after the lecture.

The notes in Figures 13.2 and 13.3 (pp. 232–233) were taken by two students on the same lecture. The notes in Figure 13.2 clearly indicate main ideas, important details, and examples and reflect the lecture's organization. The notes in Figure 13.3 are lengthy and do not emphasize key ideas. Read and evaluate each set of notes.

Figure 13.2

An Effective Note-Taking Style

```
        Marketing 101


                           Consumer Behavior

            How Buyers Buy
            2 factors involved:
      defs     1. product adoption = consumer's decision to buy
                2. product diffusion = rate of adoption by
                      consumers throughout market
            prod w/ quick diffusion = good chance of success
              "   "  slow        "         must sustain loss
            until diff. increases
            A. Types of Adopters – 5 classes, based on
                    speed of adoption
                1) innovators – 1st to buy   young, bit eccentric
                    rely on printed info rather than salespeople
                2) early adopters – socially, financially well-to-do.
                    if this group doesn't buy – product will fail
                3) early majority adopters – careful, cautious
                    – most influenced by sales people, ads
                4) late majority adopters – opinion followers
                    rely heavily on friends, family
                5) Laggards – fearful of new, older people, less
                    educated peers are primary source of info
            B. Factors affecting Diffusion
```

Taking Notes More Efficiently

If you record main ideas, details, and examples, using the indentation system to show the lecture's organization, you will take adequate notes. However, the following tips can help you make note taking easier, make your notes more complete, and make study and review easier.

Leave blank spaces.   To make your notes more readable and to make it easier to see the organization of ideas, leave plenty of blank space. If you know you missed a detail or definition, leave additional blank space. Fill it in later by checking with a friend or referring to your text.

Figure 13.3

An Ineffective Note-Taking Style

> <u>Marketing 101</u>
>
> What Makes Buyers Buy What They Do
>
> There are two factors involved: product adoption and product diffusion. Adoption – decision to buy. Diffusion means adoption throughout the market.
>
> There are 5 classes of buyers
>
> Innovators are the first to buy. They are young and eccentric and rely on printed information rather than salespeople. People who are socially and financially well off are early adopters. If this group doesn't buy the product will fail. Early majority adopters are most influenced by salespeople & ads.
>
> Late majority adopters are opinion followers who rely heavily on information from friends and family. Laggards are older people who are less educated and are the last to buy. Their peers are their primary source.
>
> There are several factors that affect diffusion.

Mark assignments.   Occasionally, an instructor will announce an assignment or test in the middle of a lecture. As you jot it down, write "Assignment" or "Test Date" in the margin so that you can find it easily and transfer it to your assignment notebook.

Mark ideas that are unclear.   If an instructor presents a fact or idea that is unclear, put a question mark in the margin. Later, ask your instructor or a classmate for a clarification.

Don't plan to recopy your notes.   Some students take each day's notes in a hasty, careless way and then recopy them in the evening. These students feel that recopying helps them review the information and think it is a good way to study. Actually, recopying often becomes a mechanical process that takes a lot of time but very little thought. Time spent recopying can be better spent reviewing the notes in a manner that will be suggested later in this chapter (see pp. 242–245).

Consider tape-recording lectures in special situations.   Students who lack confidence in their note-taking ability find it reassuring to tape lectures until they are certain they are able to take accurate and complete notes. Other students tape-record lectures from a particularly difficult course. Also, students who must spend large amounts of time commuting to campus listen to tapes during this time.

In using the tape system, you spend at least an additional hour in playback for every hour spent in class to complete your notes. Tape-recording, however, is usually time consuming and inefficient in terms of the time spent relative to the amount of learning that occurs.

Generally, tape-recording is not recommended. However, there are obvious exceptions. Students for whom English is not their first language often find the process valuable. If you do decide to tape a lecture, be certain to obtain the permission of your instructor.

Try not to write complete sentences.   Use as few words as possible. You will be able to record more information, and review will be easier.

Use abbreviations.   To save time, try to use abbreviations instead of writing out long or frequently used words. If you are taking a course in psychology, you would not want to write out p-s-y-c-h-o-l-o-g-y each time the word is used. It is much faster to use the abbreviation "psych." Try to develop abbreviations for each subject area you are studying. The following abbreviations, devised by a student in business management, will give you an idea of the possibilities and choices you have. Notice that both common words and specialized words are abbreviated.

Common Words	Abbreviation	Specialized Words	Abbreviation
and	+	organization	org.
with	w/	management	man.
compare	comp.	data bank	D.B.
comparison		structure	str.
importance	imp't.	evaluation	eval.
advantage	adv.	management by objectives	MBO
introduction	intro.	management information system	MIS
continued	cont'd.	organizational development	OD
		communication	comm.
		simulation	sim.

As you start to use abbreviations, be sure to begin gradually. It is easy to overuse abbreviations and end up with a set of notes that are almost meaningless.

Develop Creative Note-Taking Systems

Do not hesitate to create variations of the traditional lecture note-taking format. Here are a few possibilities; do not try to use them all in each course. Instead, choose those that fit your learning style and the individual courses you are taking.

◆ **Consider using color.** Either during the lecture or after it, use different colored pens or highlighters to distinguish particular types of information. For example, in psychology you might record or mark definitions in green and use blue to identify important research studies.

◆ **Create a response column.** Use it to record your own thoughts and reactions to the lecture.

◆ **Leave space for a summary.** Some students find it beneficial to write a brief summary at the end of each lecture.

◆ **Leave space for maps.** Especially if you are a spatial learner, you may find it helpful to draw or see diagrams or maps (see Chapter 15) that translate ideas from words to pictures.

◆ **Add an application column.** Consider adding a column or section of your notes in which you can add examples that illustrate lecture content. You might add these during the lecture as they come to mind, or do so later as you review your notes.

Working with Various Lecture Formats

Not all instructors lecture in the same way or for the same purpose. In fact, two instructors teaching the same course who use the same text may present very different lecture formats. Or a certain instructor may alternate among formats to achieve various purposes. Lectures may differ in focus, purpose, and organization, as well as content. While each instructor is unique, you will encounter four general lecture formats: factual, conceptual, analytical, and discussion.

The Factual Lecture Format

The factual lecture format centers around a straightforward presentation of information: facts, definitions, historical events, rules, principles, processes, and procedures. Many introductory-level course lectures fall into this category. The primary purpose of this type of lecture is to present and explain. As one psychology instructor tells his students: "You have to learn about psychology before you can think about and work within it." In other words, you must acquire a base of knowledge as you begin to study a new discipline. Here are a few examples of lecture topics using the factual style:

Course	Lecture Topic
Public speaking	Analyzing Your Audience
American government	The Structure of American Elections
Nursing	Fluid and Electrolyte Balance
Business communication	Strategies for Interviewing

Here are a few suggestions for taking notes from factual lectures:

◆ **Be as accurate and complete as possible.**
◆ **If you have difficulty recording all the needed information, leave blank spaces and fill in the information later.** Check with a classmate, if necessary.
◆ **Don't waste time rewriting information that duplicates what is contained in your text; jot down the topic and a page reference.**

The notes shown in Figure 13.2 on p. 232 were taken from a factual lecture.

Thinking Critically
. . . About Lectures

Although listening to a lecture is demanding, try to *think about* the lecture as well as take notes on it. Here are a few questions to ask:

Before the Lecture

1. What content and focus do you anticipate?
2. How does the lecture topic fit with the previous lecture?

During the Lecture

1. What are the most important ideas and concepts?
2. What examples from your own experience come to mind?
3. What information is unclear, if any?

After the Lecture

1. What did you learn from the lecture?
2. What levels of thinking (see p. 241) does the lecture require? Focus especially on application, analysis, synthesis, and evaluation.

The Conceptual Lecture Format

The conceptual lecture format focuses on the analysis and interpretation of information. It is concerned with ideas, trends, and concepts. Although factual information may provide the basis of this type of lecture, the focus is often on issues, policies, problems, and perspectives. This format is common in philosophy, special-issue classes such as "Environmental Problems," sociology, and economics. Here are a few examples of lecture topics that employ a conceptual format:

Course	Lecture Topic
Social problems	Welfare: Myths and Realities
Ecology	Solving the World Food Shortage
Marketing and advertising	Controlling Consumer Behavior

Figure 13.4

Conceptual Style Notes

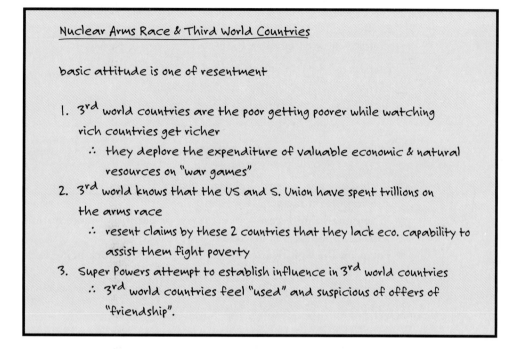

Use the following tips for taking notes on conceptual lectures:

Focus on concepts, or broad, organizing ideas. For example, it is much more important to record the concept that "impressionism, as an art form, dominated the last 20 years of the 19th century" than it is to record every fact your instructor gives you about impressionism.

Record only as much detail as you need to understand and recall the concept. Choose the most vivid details or those that provide the strongest evidence.

Record key details on which your instructor spends the most time. A sample set of notes from a conceptual lecture is shown in Figure 13.4 above.

The Analytical Lecture Format

The analytical format is used in courses that examine literary or artistic works, social issues, mathematical or scientific problems, and philosophical, moral, or religious issues. This style is evident in literature, art, mathematics, science, and philosophy courses, as well as in seminars that focus on a particular social issue, historical or literary period, or art form. In analytical lectures, close study followed by interpretation is the mode of presentation. Personal reaction is often important, as is assessment of value, worth, and aesthetic qualities. A search for reasons and interpretation of actions or published works is often involved.

Here are a few topics of lectures that use the analytical format:

Course	Lecture Topic
Literature	Steinbeck's Use of Symbolism
Philosophy	Mill's Theory of Utilitarianism
Business law	Antitrust Litigation: Three Illustrative Cases

To take notes on analytical lectures, use the following suggestions.

◆ **Record themes, essential characteristics, theories, significance of related events, and important facts.**
◆ **When analyzing a case, poem, story, or painting, make notes in the margin of your textbook as it is discussed.**
◆ **Focus on the significance or importance of the work being analyzed.**

Figure 13.5 on p. 239 shows a sample portion of notes taken on the analysis of Keats's poem "Ode on a Grecian Urn."

The Discussion Format

This form cannot be called a lecture format since the emphasis is not on the presentation of ideas but on their exchange. The purpose of class discussion is to involve students in thinking, reacting, and evaluating the topic at hand. Discussion-style classes are prevalent in disciplines that involve controversial issues or subjective evaluation.

For discussion classes, advance preparation is the key. In fact, you need to spend more time preparing for a discussion than you do studying your notes afterward. Plan to spend considerable time reading, making notes, and organizing your thinking about the topic. Make lists of questions, points with which you agree or disagree, good or poor examples, and strong or weak arguments. These lists will provide a basis for your input into the discussion.

When participating in class discussion, students often neglect to take notes. While careful, detailed note taking may not be as critical for class discussions as for lectures, try to keep a record of key points in the discussion. Not only will the notes be valuable for later review, they are also useful for immediate reaction and response during the discussion. If you have recorded someone's argument or objection, you are better prepared to defend or criticize it than to do so purely from memory.

You might also use your notes to outline or sketch a response before you present it. Writing is a vehicle that clarifies your thinking. By informally outlining or jotting down the points you intend to make, you will organize and focus your thoughts, thus improving your contribution.

Figure 13.5

Analytical Style Notes

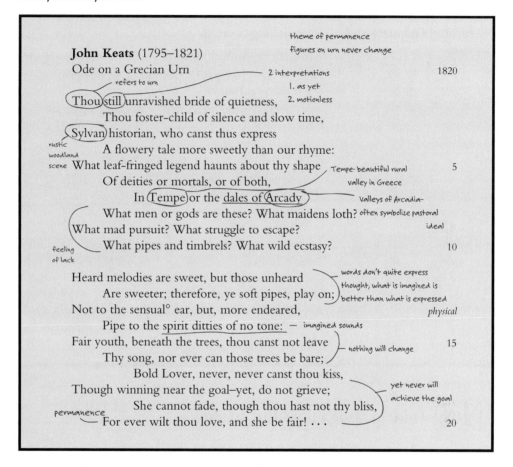

Discussion notes are much less detailed and reflect less organization than lecture notes. Think of them as a chronological record of the discussion, a list of ideas and topics discussed. After class, it is especially important to reread and edit discussion notes (see pp. 242–245).

Exercise 13.2	Each student should bring notebooks from two courses he or she is currently taking. Students should exchange notebooks and identify the predominant format used in several lectures.

Exercise 13.3	For each course in which you are currently enrolled, identify the predominant lecture style.

Table 13.2

Adapting Note Taking to Your Learning Style

Learning Characteristic	Note-Taking Strategy
Auditory	Take advantage of your advantage! Take thorough and complete notes.
Visual	Work on note-taking skills; practice by tape-recording a lecture; analyze and revise your notes.
Creative	Annotate your notes, recording impressions, reactions, spin-off ideas, related ideas.
Pragmatic	Reorganize notes during editing. Pay attention to the lecturer's organization.
Social	Review and edit notes with a classmate. Compare notes with others.
Independent	Choose seating in close contact with the instructor; avoid distracting groups of students.
Applied	Think of applications (record as annotations). Write questions in the margin about applications.
Conceptual	Discover idea relationships. Watch for patterns.
Spatial	Add diagrams, maps during editing.
Verbal	Record the lecturer's diagrams, drawings—but translate into words during editing.

Note Taking and Learning Style

Do you recall the learning style questionnaire you completed in Chapter 8? Refresh your memory by reviewing the results on p. 132–133. Your learning style influences your listening skills and your note-taking ability. Certain lecture formats, too, may be easier for you to work with due to your learning style. Auditory learners, of course, are well suited to listening and note taking, while visual learners are less inclined to learn by listening. Verbal learners find the lecture mode more appropriate than do spatial learners, who prefer a more concrete mode of presentation. Table 13.2 above offers suggestions for adapting your listening and note-taking abilities for various aspects of your learning style.

Using the Lecturer's Thought Patterns

If you approach lectures simply as a means of acquiring information, you are missing an important learning opportunity. Lectures provide you with the opportunity to understand how the instructor approaches the subject matter. They reveal how the instructor thinks: how he or she processes, organizes, and approaches the material. Understanding the lecturer's thought patterns will show you what to record and help you follow the lecturer's organization.

Understanding the instructor's thought processes is also an important advantage in completing assignments, taking exams, and writing papers. You will be better able to understand the purpose of an assignment, interpret exam questions accurately, or choose the appropriate focus for a paper. These skills will be discussed in greater detail in subsequent chapters.

Anticipating and Identifying Patterns in Lectures

The most common thought patterns used in lectures are those discussed in Chapter 12: order or sequence, comparison and contrast, cause and effect, classification, problem-solution, definition, and listing. Lecturers often use various devices to make their pattern of organization apparent.

Organizing Statements

At the beginning of a lecture, instructors frequently announce the topic and provide clues to their approach. For instance, a psychology instructor may open a lecture by saying:

This morning we will define behaviorism by studying two of its leading advocates—B. F. Skinner and Watson. Both believed that . . .

From this statement you can predict a comparison and perhaps contrast pattern between Skinner and Watson, as well as discussion of the characteristics of behaviorism (listing pattern).

Transitions

Good speakers and lecturers use transitions to assist their audiences in anticipating and following their train of thought. As they move from point to point, they often use a transitional word or phrase to signal the change. These transitions are similar to those used in writing, except that they tend to be more direct and frequent than in written language. If, for example, a lecturer says, "Consequently, we have . . . ," you can anticipate a cause and effect pattern.

Summary Statements

Similar to opening statements, summary statements provide strong clues about a lecture's organization. But since they come at the end of the lecture, the clues usually confirm patterns listeners have already identified.

Lecture Format

A lecturer's thought patterns are, to some extent, reflected in the format of lecture used. An instructor who uses a discussion format is more likely to employ cause and effect, comparison or contrast, or problem-solution patterns than to follow listing or sequence/order patterns, which seem more appropriate to a factual lecture format. For example, a political science class discussion on Third World countries might involve such topics as reasons for their growing importance or their effects on other countries.

Patterns as an Aid to Organizing Your Notes

Once you have identified a lecturer's predominant pattern, you can use that knowledge to organize your lecture notes. Note-taking tips for each pattern are presented in Table 13.3.

Table 13.3
Using Patterns in Lecture Note Taking

Pattern	Note-Taking Tips
Order or sequence	Record dates; focus on order and sequence; use time line for historical events; draw diagrams; record in order of importance; outline events or steps in a process.
Comparison and contrast	Record similarities, differences, and basis of comparison; use two columns or make a chart.
Cause and effect	Distinguish causes from effects; use diagrams.
Classification	Use outline form; list characteristics and distinguishing features.
Problem-solution	Record parameters of the problem; focus on nature of problem; record process of arriving at solution.
Definition	Record general group or class; list distinguishing characteristics; include several examples.
Listing	Record in list or outline form; record order of presentation.

Exercise 13.4   For each lecture topic, predict what pattern(s) might be used.

Course	Lecture Title/Topics
American government	The Bill of Rights—Then and Now
Speech communications	Ways to Research Your Topic
Nursing	Transfusion Reactions
Human sexuality	Components of Interpersonal Intimacy
Engineering/technology	The Rationale for the Use of Standard Parts

---

Exercise 13.5   Review your notes from each class lecture you attended last week, and identify the predominant patterns used in each lecture. Substantiate your answer.

Editing and Reviewing Your Notes

You should not assume that your lecture notes are accurate and complete or that simply by taking notes you have learned the information the notes record. Two more steps are necessary: (1) you must edit your notes, making them thorough and accurate, and (2) you need to develop and use a system for study and review.

Editing Lecture Notes

Even experienced note takers find that they often miss some information and are unable to record as many details or examples as they would like during a lecture. Fortunately, the solution is simple. Do not plan on taking a final and complete set of notes during the lecture. Instead, record just enough during the lecture to help you remember a main idea, detail, or example. Leave plenty of blank space; then, as soon as possible after class, review the notes. Fill in the missing information and expand the notes, adding any details or examples. The process of revising notes to make them more complete and accurate is called *editing.* Editing notes for a one-hour lecture should take no more than five or ten minutes. Some students find editing is easier when working with groups of two or three classmates. Group interaction and discussion provide a focus on the lectures, and one person may have recorded information that others did not.

The longer the time lapse between the note taking and the editing, the more facts and examples you will be unable to recall and fill in.

The sample lecture notes in Figure 13.6 have been edited. The notes taken during the lecture are in dark print; the additions and changes made during the editing are in the shaded areas. Read the notes, noticing the types of information added during editing.

Figure 13.6
Sample Edited Notes

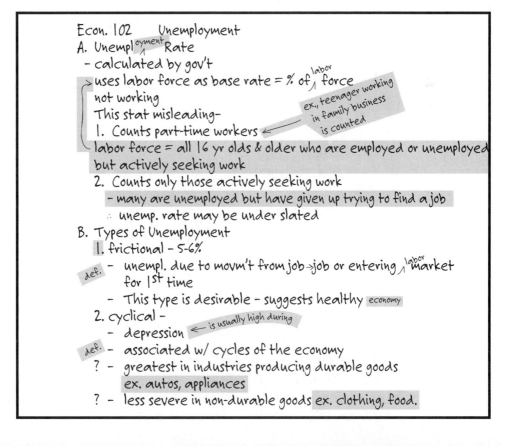

Use the Recall Clue System

The recall clue system helps make the review and study of lecture notes easier and more effective. It involves the following steps:

- Leave a two-inch margin at the left side of each page of notes.
- Keep the margin blank while you are taking notes.
- After you have edited your notes, fill in the left margin with words and phrases that briefly summarize the notes. These *recall clues* should be words that will trigger your memory and help you recall the complete information in your notes.

These clues function as memory tags. They help you retrieve information that is labeled with these tags. Figure 13.7 below shows a sample of notes in which the recall clue system has been used.

To study your notes using the recall clues, cover up the notes with a sheet of paper, exposing only the recall clues in the left margin. Next read the first recall clue and try to remember the information in the portion of the notes beside it. Then slide the paper

Figure 13.7

Recall Clue System

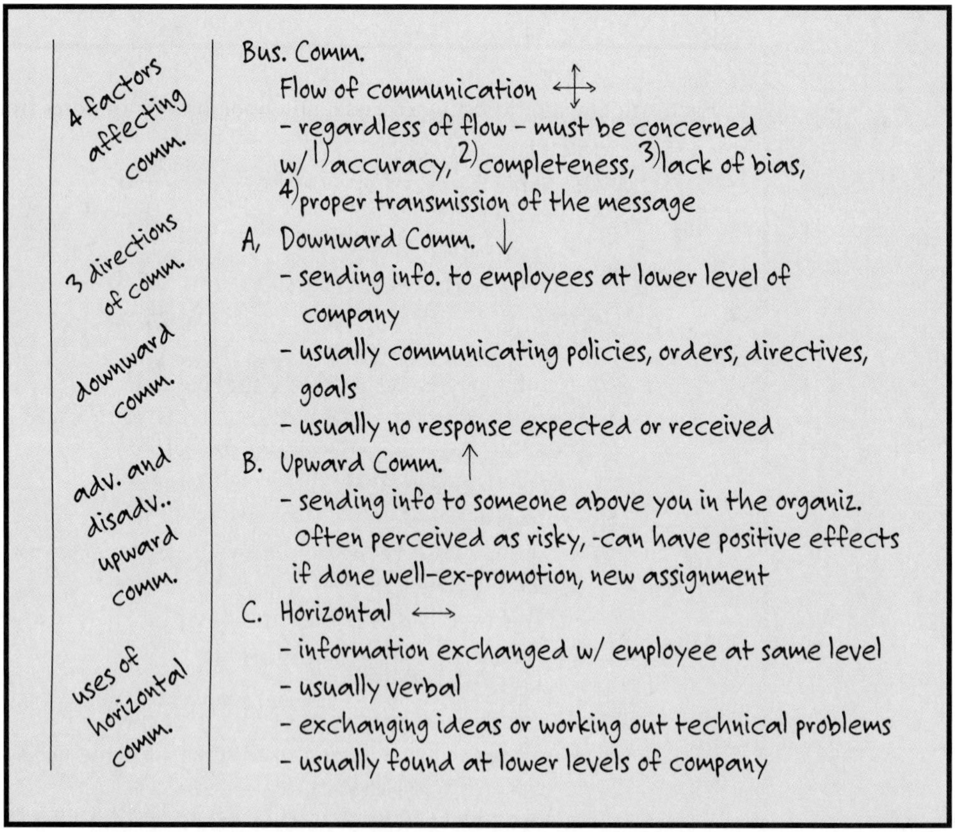
4 factors affecting comm.
3 directions of comm.
downward comm.
adv. and disadv.. upward comm.
uses of horizontal comm.

Bus. Comm.
Flow of communication
- regardless of flow - must be concerned w/ 1) accuracy, 2) completeness, 3) lack of bias, 4) proper transmission of the message
A, Downward Comm. ↓
- sending info. to employees at lower level of company
- usually communicating policies, orders, directives, goals
- usually no response expected or received
B. Upward Comm. ↑
- sending info to someone above you in the organiz. Often perceived as risky, -can have positive effects if done well-ex-promotion, new assignment
C. Horizontal ⟷
- information exchanged w/ employee at same level
- usually verbal
- exchanging ideas or working out technical problems
- usually found at lower levels of company

down and check that portion to see if you remembered all the important facts. If you remembered only part of the information, cover up that portion of your notes and again check your recall. Continue checking until you are satisfied that you can remember all the important facts. Then move on to the next recall clue on the page, testing and checking again.

A variation on the recall clue system that students have found effective is to write questions rather than summary words and phrases in the margin. The questions trigger your memory and enable you to recall the information that answers your question. With the questions you can test yourself, thereby simulating an exam. They also force you to think and actively respond to course content.

Working Together

Activity I:
Reading and listening are both receptive communication skills. Working in small groups of three or four students, discuss how reading and listening are similar and how they differ. Consider factors such as purpose, process, types of thinking, interference, recall, and retention. One student should record each group's findings and report them to the class. After each group has reported, the class should consider the question: Are some people better listeners than readers, and vice versa? Discuss why this may be true.

Activity II:
Each student should bring to class a notebook or a set of notes from a recent lecture. Working in small groups, students should exchange and evaluate one another's notes, using the checklist shown in Table 13.4.

Table 13.4
Note-Taking Checklist

	Yes	No
1. Notes are titled and dated.	❏	❏
2. A separate line is used for each key idea.	❏	❏
3. Less important ideas are indented.	❏	❏
4. Abbreviations and symbols are used.	❏	❏
5. The organization of the lecture is apparent.	❏	❏
6. Words and phrases (not entire sentences) are recorded.	❏	❏
7. Examples and illustrations are included.	❏	❏
8. Sufficient explanation and detail are included.	❏	❏
9. Adequate space is left for editing.	❏	❏
10. Marginal space is available for recall clues.	❏	❏

Interactive Chapter Review

Knowledge	List at least six techniques for effective listening.
Comprehension	What is active listening? Why is active listening important in taking effective notes? What does it allow you to do that you couldn't do by using a more passive approach?
Application	Before the next lecture you attend, take 15 minutes to review and respond to the "Thinking Critically" box on p. 236. Answer the listed questions before, during, and after the lecture. Then write a summary statement about what was most useful to you.
Analysis	Choose the class in which taking lecture notes is most difficult. Analyze the reasons for your difficulty. Take into account each of the following factors: the typical lecture format, the ways the instructor emphasizes main ideas, the lecturer's format, the lecturer's thought patterns, your learning style, and your usual way of taking notes. Which areas are creating difficulty?
Synthesis	Based on your analysis, develop your own creative note-taking system for this class. Be sure to address each difficulty you identified in your analysis.
Evaluation	For the next week, use the recall clue system as a final step to editing your lecture notes. Then evaluate the system as an aid to learning and memory. What changes to the system, if any, would make it even more effective for you?

Further Analysis

Figure 13.8 on p. 247 shows the notes a student took for a psychology lecture on stress. Review the notes and then critique them using the checklist shown in Table 13.4. Make specific suggestions for improvement.

Discussion

1. A student complains that her computer science professor spends each class reading his notes aloud. She is having difficulty taking notes and maintaining interest. What suggestions would you offer?

2. A classmate who missed all her classes last week due to a skiing injury has asked to borrow your notebook for your medical terminology course over the weekend. How would you respond?

3. Identify and list factors that interfere with effective listening. Then discuss how each can be controlled.

4. Discuss how listening to music differs from and is similar to listening to a lecture.

5. Table 13.1 lists common note-taking problems. Discuss additional problems and offer possible solutions.

Figure 13.8

Notes from a Psychology Class

Coping with stress is a problem solving activity done by direct action –
    behavior that masters it. Palliation – way of addressing symptoms of
    stress
    stress and your ability to cope is affected by cognitive appraisal –
    also by sympathetic support –

Predictability –
    – more stress if unpredictable advance notice helps

Control affects the intensity of stress
    experiment by Brady showed monkeys more stressed by control than
    non-control
    – used "executive monkey"

Relaxation involves muscle tension control
    – headaches, hypertension insomnia
    – at least 30 minutes/day progressive relaxation

The Work Connection

Learning by listening carefully and taking good notes can be a valuable skill not only in your education but also as you explore different careers by conducting *informational interviews.* When you interview people who have jobs that interest you, you can gain insight into whether you might like to have such a job. Listening closely as someone describes the career field, the organization, and his or her own career path can provide you with realistic details about what it would be like to work at a similar job. The same basic guidelines for understanding class lectures also apply to learning from informational interviews:

- Use the tips for effective listening (p. 225).
- Prepare for the interview by writing down questions you want to ask.
- Take notes of main ideas, important details, and important issues in the field.
- Review your notes immediately after the interview and fill in any missing information so you won't forget it.

1. List five people who have jobs that seem interesting. Choose one to interview. Contact the person to ask for a 10–15-minute interview.

2. Before the interview, write down questions about that person's career, typical careers in the field, and the types of skills needed to do the job. Leave blank spaces to fill in brief answers during the interview.

The Web Connection

1. Note-Taking Systems

   http://www.sas.calpoly.edu/asc/ssl/notetaking.systems.html

   This site from Cal-Tech, San Luis Obispo, describes five major note-taking systems along with information on when to use them and advantages and disadvantages of each.

2. Effective Note Taking

   http://www.dartmouth.edu/admin/acskills/success/notes.html

   The Academic Skills Center at Dartmouth College prepared this helpful Web site with note-taking tips.

3. Abbreviations in Note Taking

   http://www.und.nodak.edu/dept/ULC/rf-abbrv.htm

   Look over this list of abbreviations you can use in your note taking from the University of North Dakota, Grand Forks.

Go Electronic!
For additional readings, exercises, and Internet activities, visit the Longman Study Skills Web site at:
http://www.ablongman.com/StudySkills
If you need a user name and password, please see your instructor.

Chapter 14

College Textbooks and Electronic Resources

Each semester you will spend hours reading, reviewing, and studying textbooks and other information sources. The course textbook is often the focal point of a college course. Class lectures are often coordinated with reading assignments in the course text, written assignments require you to apply or evaluate ideas and concepts presented in the textbook, and term papers explore topics introduced in the text. Your instructor may refer you to electronic sources, as well—the Internet, CD-ROMs, video, and so forth.

This chapter presents strategies for using textbooks and electronic sources as efficiently as possible. It discusses organization of the textbook; describes its unique features; demonstrates how to preview textbook reading assignments; discusses the SQ3R reading/study system; presents strategies for studying graphs, tables, and diagrams; and discusses how to learn from visual and electronic sources and how to handle supplementary reading assignments.

Features of Textbooks

College textbooks are written by college professors who are experienced teachers. They know their subject matter, but they also know their students. Having taught the material, textbook writers know topics you may have difficulty understanding and know the best way to explain them. Because textbooks are written by teachers, they contain numerous features to help you learn.

Keys to Overall Textbook Organization

When you first purchase a textbook, it may seem like an overwhelming, unmanageable collection of facts and ideas. However, textbooks are highly organized, well-structured sources of information. They follow specific patterns of organization and are uniform and predictable in format and style. Once you become familiar with these structures, you will come to regard them as easy-to-use resources and valuable guides to learning. Various features of textbooks make their organization and purpose understandable and explicit.

Preface

Traditionally, a textbook begins with an opening statement, called a *preface,* in which the author describes some or all of the following:

◆ Author's reasons for writing the text
◆ Intended audience
◆ Major points of emphasis
◆ Special learning features
◆ Structure or organization of the book
◆ Distinctive features
◆ Suggestions on how to use the text
◆ Author's qualifications
◆ References or authorities consulted

Reading the preface gives you a firsthand impression of the author and his or her attitudes toward the text. Think of it as a chance to get a glimpse of the author as a person.

Some authors include, instead of or in addition to a preface, an introduction titled "To the Student." Written specifically for you, it contains information similar to that of a preface. The author may include an introduction "To the Instructor" as well. Although this section often may be quite technical, discussing teaching methodologies and theoretical issues, it may contain information of interest to students as well. Figure 14.1 on p. 251 presents an annotated portion of the preface of an introductory biology text.

Exercise 14.1	Read or reread the preface or introduction to the student in this book *and* in one of your other textbooks. Using the list above as a guide, identify the types of information each provides.

Table of Contents

The table of contents is an outline of the textbook's main topics and subtopics. It shows the organization of the text and indicates the interrelations among the topics. Often, it reveals thought patterns used throughout the text.

Besides using the table of contents to preview a text's overall content and organization, be sure to refer to it before reading particular chapters. Although chapters are

Figure 14.1

Sample Preface

Preface

About This Book

It seems like a long time ago since those dark ages when the first edition of *Biology: The World of Life* appeared. As I recalled, I was working on Ibiza, in the Balearic Islands, when I received word of its success from my editor, written in longhand on yellow legal paper. I have to admit I was elated. Now, all these years later, you're holding the seventh edition, and I'm just as proud of it. It doesn't look much like the first edition, which was slim and had only two colors, but I think the spirit of the first edition is still here. I remember, from the beginning, I didn't want to write anything from which ideas would have to be mined with a mental pickax. I wanted to write a book that students would enjoy reading, maybe get a laugh, as they warmed to the science called biology. I still feel that way, so I hope the "personality" and the student-friendly tone of the book haven't changed.

. . .

background about the text

author's purpose

About This Edition

I have retained the basic plan of earlier editions, in that we move from small (molecules) to large (ecosystems). This is done because, as someone has said, if you want to understand cathedrals, you must know something about stones. The chemistry of energetics is presented at two levels, *a poet's view* and *a closer view*, because I have often been reminded that the material is often taught on one level or the other. As usual, you can also expect to see more environmentalism in this book than in many others. I believe it's important to know how to build an energy-efficient home and to understand something about the price of gasoline, if the air you breathe is being changed. You will also notice I may have let an opinion slip through here or there. I don't worry about that if it stimulates good conversation. In fact, I believe it's time we begin to talk about the situation here on this planet, our home, to see where we stand and if we cannot do better.

You will probably not be surprised to learn that some new topics appear in this edition. For example, three new discussions of the origin of life, the biology of viruses, and human evolution. Also, I have increased the number of essays, which are brief asides intended to engage the reader and to provide special information that might enrich the narrative and promote discussion. As you would expect, all the other material has been updated, revised, and expanded to effectively reflect the status of biology today. The pedagogical aids, such as end-of-chapter materials, have received special attention.

. . .

basic plan and rationale

emphasis on environmentalism

new topics

organized as separate units, they are interrelated. To understand a given chapter, note what topics immediately precede and follow it.

Recent textbooks include a brief table of contents, listing only unit and chapter titles, followed by a complete table of contents that lists subheadings and various learning aids contained within each chapter. The brief table of contents is most useful for assessing the overall content and structure of the entire text, while the complete one is more helpful when studying individual chapters.

In the brief table of contents from a computer textbook shown in Figure 14.2, you can see that the text divides the subject of computers into three primary topics. The

Figure 14.2
A Brief Table of Contents

Brief Contents

Photo Essay: The Age of Information   1

Part 1

An Overview of Computers 15

CHAPTER 1
Computer Hardware: Meeting the Machine   17

CHAPTER 2
Computer Software: Productivity and Systems Software   41

Part 2

Hardware Tools   67

CHAPTER 3
The Central Processing Unit: What Goes on Inside the Computer   69

CHAPTER 4
Input and Output: The User Connection   95

CHAPTER 5
Storage and Multimedia: The Facts and More   125

Part 3

Internet Tools 157

CHAPTER 6
Networking: Computer Connections   159

CHAPTER 7
The Internet: A Resource for All of Us 195

CHAPTER 8
Security and Privacy: Computers and the Internet   223

APPENDIX A
History and Industry: The Continuing Story of the Computer Age   A-1

Glossary   G-1

Credits   C-1

Index   I-1

first section provides an overview of computer hardware and software. The second focuses on three basic categories of hardware tools, and the third considers three topics related to Internet tools. The thought pattern used to organize the textbook's contents is classification.

Figure 14.3 is an excerpt from a detailed table of contents from the same textbook. The chapter outlined examines the basic components of a network and how the different types of networks operate. Two thought patterns are evident: classification and order or sequence.

Figure 14.3
Excerpt from a Complete Table of Contents

Exercise 14.2	Turn to the table of contents of one of your textbooks. Choose a unit or part that you have not read. Use the table of contents to predict the thought pattern(s) for each chapter.

Appendix

The appendix of a textbook contains supplementary information that does not fit within the framework of the chapters. Often, the appendix offers valuable aids. For example, an American government text contains three appendixes:

Appendix 1   The Declaration of Independence
Appendix 2   The Constitution of the United States of America
Appendix 3   Beyond the Call of Duty: Data and Documents

The textbook includes appendixes 1 and 2 for the readers' convenience, since the text refers to each frequently. Appendix 3 lists and explains additional sources of information for each chapter.

Glossary

The glossary is a minidictionary of specialized vocabulary used throughout the text. Uses of the glossary are discussed in Chapter 11.

Index

At the very end of many texts, you will find an alphabetical subject index, listing topics covered in the text along with page references. Although its primary function is to allow you to locate information on a specific topic, it also can be used as a study aid for final exams. If you have covered most or all of the chapters in the text, then you should be familiar with each topic indexed. For example, suppose the index of an accounting textbook listed the following:

Purchases
    determining the cost of, 169–170
    of equipment for cash, 17–18, 36–37, 200
    of merchandise for cash, 201–202
    of merchandise on credit, 163–168

To review for an exam, look at each entry and test your recall. In the accounting textbook example, you would ask yourself: How is the cost of purchases determined? How are equipment purchases using cash recorded? What are the procedures for purchases of merchandise on credit?

Some texts also include a name index that allows you to locate references to individuals mentioned in the text. The checklist in Figure 14.4 is provided to help you quickly assess a textbook's content and organization.

Exercise 14.3	Use the checklist in Figure 14.4 to analyze the content and organization of one of your textbooks.

Figure 14.4

Assessing Your Textbook's Learning Features

Check "Yes" or "No" after each of the following statements.	Yes	No
Preface		
The purpose of the text is stated.	❏	❏
The intended audience is indicated.	❏	❏
The preface explains how the book is organized.	❏	❏
The author's credentials are included.	❏	❏
Distinctive features are described.	❏	❏
Major points of emphasis are discussed.	❏	❏
Aids to learning are described.	❏	❏
Table of Contents		
Brief table of contents is included.	❏	❏
The chapters are grouped into parts or sections.	❏	❏
Thought pattern(s) throughout the text are evident.	❏	❏
Appendix		
Useful tables and charts are included.	❏	❏
Supplementary documents are included.	❏	❏
Background or reference material is included.	❏	❏
Glossary		
The text contains a glossary.	❏	❏
Word pronunciation and meaning are provided.	❏	❏
Index		
A subject index is included.	❏	❏
A name index is included.	❏	❏

Learning Aids in Textbooks

In addition to its useful organizational features, a textbook contains numerous learning aids: chapter previews, marginal notes, special-interest boxes or inserts, review questions, lists of key terms, summaries, and references. A textbook is a guide to learning, a source that directs your attention, shows you what is important, and leads you to apply your knowledge. Learning will be easier if you use the textbook's learning aids to your best advantage.

Chapter Preview

Research in educational psychology indicates that if readers have some knowledge of content and organization of material *before* they begin to read it, their comprehension and recall increase. Consequently, numerous textbooks begin each chapter with some kind of preview. Previews take several common forms.

Chapter Objectives

In some texts, the objectives of each chapter are listed beneath its title. Objectives may appear as statements such as "To explain photosynthesis," or as questions, as is done in this book. The objectives are intended to focus your attention on important ideas and concepts. They are usually listed in the order in which the topics appear in the chapter, presenting an abbreviated outline of the main topics.

Chapter Outline

Other texts provide a brief outline of each chapter's contents. Formed from the headings and subheadings used throughout the chapter, the outline reflects both the content and organization of the chapter. A sample outline, from an American government text, is shown in Figure 14.5 on p. 257. As you study a chapter outline, pay attention to the sequence and progression of topics and look for thought patterns.

Chapter Overview

Some textbook authors provide a preview paragraph in which they state what the chapter is about, discuss why certain topics are important, focus the reader's attention on important issues, or indicate how the chapter relates to other chapters in the book. Overviews may be labeled "Chapter Preview," "Overview," or as in the sample shown in Figure 14.6 on p. 258 from an American government text, with a less obvious title such as "Memo."

Each type of preview can be used to activate and monitor your learning before, during, and after reading the chapter.

Before reading
◆ Use the chapter preview to activate your prior knowledge of the subject. Recall what you already know about the subject by trying to anticipate the chapter's main points.
◆ Use chapter previews to predict the predominant thought patterns.
◆ Use previews to anticipate which portions or sections of the chapter will be most difficult or challenging.

While reading
◆ Use the preview as a guide to what is important to learn.
◆ Mark or underline key information mentioned in the preview.

After reading
◆ Use the preview to monitor the effectiveness of your reading.
◆ Test your ability to recall the key information.
◆ Review immediately any material you were unable to recall.

Figure 14.5
A Chapter Outline

7   **The Mass Media and
            the Political Agenda**

THE MASS MEDIA TODAY

THE DEVELOPMENT OF THE MASS MEDIA
   The Print Media
   The Broadcast Media

REPORTING THE NEWS
   Defining News
   Finding the News
   Presenting the News
   Bias in the News

THE NEWS AND PUBLIC OPINION

THE POLICY AGENDA AND THE SPECIAL ROLE OF THE MEDIA

UNDERSTANDING THE MASS MEDIA
   The Media and the Scope of Government
   Individualism and the Media
   Democracy and the Media

**Exercise
14.4**

Refer to the chapter outline in Figure 14.5 to answer the following questions.

1. What role do you think the mass media should play in U.S. politics? Activate your prior knowledge by listing several recent world or national political events in which the media played a major role.

2. What predominant thought pattern(s) do you predict the chapter will use?

3. Which section do you feel will be the most difficult to read and learn? Justify your choice.

Figure 14.6

A Chapter Preview

10   Interest Groups

MEMO

Like parties and elections, interest groups are a linkage institution. And like these other linkage institutions, they have been dramatically reshaped by our high-technology politics. In this chapter, we will see how.

Interest groups—sometimes called special interests, pressure groups, or lobbies—seek favorable public policies from government and want to side-track unfavorable ones. No part of the government is immune from interest groups.

Frankly, interest groups these days have had bad press. People usually think of them as representing some narrow, special, and selfish interest. Press and public alike suspect that they exert a corrupting influence on our political system. I, for one, believe these charges are partially true but greatly oversimplified. There is a significant bias in the interest group system; not all groups are created equal. But interest groups are a vital part of our political system.

Keep the following in mind as we discuss groups and government:

■ The American political system teems with an amazing array of groups. Some of them will seem trivial to you, but they have interests and members work to achieve their policy goals.

■ Groups, unlike parties, view the whole political system as fair game. Lobbying, electioneering, litigation, and appeals to the public are major group strategies.

■ Small groups, curiously, have a distinct advantage over large ones.

■ We can try to understand interest groups by looking at them from the perspectives of democratic theory, elite and class theory, pluralism, and hyperpluralism.

297

Exercise 14.5   Refer to the chapter preview in Figure 14.6 to answer the following questions.

1. What do you know about interest groups? Activate your prior knowledge by listing several special-interest groups with which you are familiar.

2. What predominant thought pattern(s) do you predict the chapter will use?

Figure 14.7

Marginal Notations

There are other biases that lead us to make incorrect attributions about ourselves or others. One is called the **just world hypothesis,** in which people believe that we live in a world where good things happen only to good people and bad things happen only to bad people (Lerner, 1965, 1980). It's a sort of "everybody gets what they deserve" mentality. We see this bias (or fallacy) when we hear people claim that victims of rape often "ask for it by the way they dress and act." In fact, even the victims of rape sometimes engage in self-blame in an attempt to explain why in the world they were singled out for a crime in which they were the victim quite by chance (Janoff-Bulman, 1979; McCaul et al., 1990).

just world hypothesis the belief that the world is just and that people get what they deserve

Another bias that affects our attributions is the **self-serving bias.** It occurs when we attribute successes or positive outcomes to personal, internal sources and failures or negative outcomes to situational, external sources (Harvey & Weary, 1984; Miller & Ross, 1975). We tend to think that when we do well it is because we're able, talented, and work hard, whereas when we do poorly it is the fault of someone or something else.

self-serving bias the tendency to attribute our successes to our own effort and abilities, and our failures to situational, external sources

---

Marginal Notations

Textbooks used to have wide, empty margins, useful to students for jotting notes. Recently, some textbook authors have taken advantage of this available space to offer commentary on the text; pose questions based on the text; provide illustrations, examples, and drawings; or identify key vocabulary. Figure 14.7, excerpted from a psychology text, illustrates one type of marginal notation. In the excerpt, brief definitions of key terms are given in the margin next to the sentence in which the term is first introduced.

The best way to approach marginal notes is usually to refer to them once you have read the text to which they correspond. Often marginal notes can be used to review and check your recall. If the marginal notes are in the form of questions, go through the chapter, section by section, answering each question. Test your ability to define each key term in your own words.

Special-Interest Inserts

Modern textbooks may contain, at various points within or at the end of the chapters, brief articles, essays, or commentaries that provide a practical perspective or an application of the topic under discussion. Usually these inserts are set apart from the text using boxes or shaded or colored print. Usually, too, the inserts are consistently titled throughout the text, often suggesting their function, such as "Focus," "Counterpoint," or "Today's Problems." In a sociology textbook, in a chapter on drug abuse, a vivid narrative of the life of a drug addict may be included. Or, in an economics text, specific situations that apply key concepts may be included.

Make use of article inserts in the following ways:

◆ Read the insert *after* you have read the text material on the page.
◆ Determine the purpose of the insert and mark in the margin the concept or principle to which the insert refers.
◆ When reviewing for exams, especially essay exams, quickly review the chapter inserts, especially if your instructor has emphasized them.

Exercise 14.6

Read the box insert in Figure 14.8 on p. 261, which is taken from a marketing text chapter on investment opportunities. Then answer the following questions.

1. What marketing principle does this special-interest box illustrate?

2. How useful do you feel this insert would be in preparing for an exam?

3. Do you feel the example of the Bic Corporation will make the concept presented here come alive and seem real? Give reasons for your answer.

Questions for Review

Some textbook chapters conclude with a set of review questions. Read through these questions *before* you read the chapter. They serve as a list of what is important in the chapter. Usually the questions are listed in the order in which the topics appear in the chapter, forming an outline.

As you read and locate answers in the text, be sure to underline or mark them. Review questions are a useful but by no means a sufficient review. These questions often test only factual recall of specific information. They seldom require you to pull together ideas, compare, assess causes, or react to the information presented.

Lists of Key Terms

Lists of key terms are often found at the end of each chapter. Usually, only specialized terms that are introduced for the first time in that chapter are included. Glancing through the list before reading the chapter will familiarize you with them and make reading go more smoothly.

Chapter Summaries

Reading the end-of-chapter summary is useful both *before* and *after* you read a chapter. Before reading, the summary will familiarize you with the chapter's basic organization and content. After the chapter, it provides an excellent review and helps you tie together, or consolidate, the major points covered in the chapter.

Figure 14.8

A Special-Interest Insert

MARKETING IN ACTION ▰▰▰▰▰

Bic Corporation Sets Objectives

"Without a clear, concise statement of objectives, there can be no viable strategy," states Donald M. Wilchek, a marketing manager at the Bic Corporation. "At Bic, specific objectives are set before a project is undertaken." This is just as true for small projects such as the development of a selling sheet as it is for the major launch of a new product. The corporate philosophy is that if money is spent, the firm must know what it hopes to achieve by the expenditure. This has been true at Bic since the company first began with the introduction of simple stick pens.

The disposable "crystal" stick pen, still Bic's largest seller, was regionally launched in 1959 and nationally launched with a retail price of $.19 in 1964. The company's objective was clear and concise—dominate the ballpoint pen market. Utilizing a straightforward strategy of producing a product that draws a line as well or better than anything on the market, pricing it significantly lower than the competition, making it almost universally available, and letting consumers know about it, Bic has clearly succeeded in achieving its objective. Today, Bic accounts for about two of every three ballpoint pens sold at retail.

Suggested Readings or References

Many textbook authors provide a list of suggested readings at the end of each chapter or section. This list refers you to additional sources, both books and periodicals, that provide more information on topics discussed in the chapter. References given in this list provide a useful starting point when researching a topic discussed in the chapter.

The evaluation list shown in Table 14.1 on p. 262 will enable you to quickly assess the learning aids a chapter provides.

| **Exercise 14.7** | Use the evaluation list shown in Table 14.1 on p. 262 to analyze how the author of one of your current textbooks guides your learning. |

Table 14.1

Evaluation of Learning Aids

Chapter preview

> What preview format is used?
>
> What is its primary purpose?
>
> What thought pattern(s) is evident?
>
> How can you use it for review?

Marginal notes

> What format is used?
>
> How can you use them for study and review?

Special-interest inserts

> How do they relate to chapter content?
>
> How much importance should you place on them?

Review questions

> Do the questions provide an outline of chapter content? (Compare them with chapter headings.)
>
> What types of thinking do they require? Are they primarily factual, or do they require critical thinking?

Key terminology

> How many, if any, words are already familiar?
>
> How difficult do you predict the chapter will be?

Chapter summary

> Does it list the main topics the chapter will cover?
>
> Is a thought pattern evident?

Suggested readings

> What types of sources are listed?
>
> To which topics do they refer?

Previewing Your Textbooks

Familiarity with a task enhances your ability to perform it effectively. If you are familiar with a large city, driving to a destination there is relatively simple. Similarly, if you are familiar with a reading or class assignment before you begin, you will find that you can read or complete it more easily and retain more information. You can become familiar with your reading assignments by focusing on those features that convey the major ideas and how they are organized. *Previewing* provides a means of familiarizing yourself quickly with the content and organization of an assignment before you begin.

Working Together

Each student should bring two textbooks to class. Working in groups of three, students should complete each of the following activities.

1. Students should exchange texts and review each text using the lists on p. 262. Then each student should identify the text that provides the strongest learning aids and justify his or her choice to the group. Collectively the group should agree on the "best" textbook.

2. Each group should appoint a group spokesperson who will present and describe the group's choice to the class. Depending on class size, the class might also identify the text with the strongest learning aids from among those chosen by each group.

How to Preview Textbook Reading Assignments

Think of previewing as getting a sneak preview of what a chapter will be about. Use the following steps:

1. **Read the title and subtitle.** The title provides the overall topic of the article or chapter; the subtitle suggests the specific focus, aspect, or approach toward the overall topic.

2. **Read the introduction or the first paragraph.** The introduction or first paragraph serves as a lead-in to the chapter, establishing the overall subject and suggesting how it will be developed.

3. **Read each boldfaced (dark print) heading.** Headings label the contents of each section, announcing the major topic of the section.

4. **Read the first sentence under each heading.** The first sentence often states the central thought of the section. If the first sentence seems introductory, read the last sentence; often this sentence states or restates the central thought.

5. **Note any typographical aids.** Italics emphasize important terminology and definitions by using slanted (*italic*) type to distinguish them from the rest of the passage. Notice any material that is numbered 1, 2, 3; lettered a, b, c; or presented in list form.

6. **Note any graphic aids.** Graphs, charts, photographs, and tables often suggest what is important in the chapter. Be sure to read the captions for photographs and the legends for graphs, charts, or tables.

7. **Read the last paragraph or summary.** This provides a condensed view of the chapter, often outlining the key points in the chapter.

8. **Read quickly any end-of-article or end-of-chapter material.** This might include references, study questions, discussion questions, chapter outlines, or vocabulary lists. If there are study questions, read them through quickly since they will indicate what is important to remember in the chapter. If a vocabulary list is included, rapidly skim through it to identify terms that you will need to learn as you read.

Figure 14.9 illustrates how previewing is done. A section of a business communications textbook chapter discussing job application letters is reprinted there; the portions to focus on when previewing are shaded. Read only those portions. After you have finished, test the effectiveness of your previewing by answering the questions in Exercise 14.8.

Figure 14.9
Demonstration of Previewing

The Unsolicited Letter

Ambitious job seekers don't limit their search to advertised openings. The unsolicited, or "prospecting" letter is a good way of uncovering other possibilities. Such letters have advantages and disadvantages.

Disadvantages. The unsolicited approach does have two drawbacks: (1) You may waste time writing letters to organizations that simply have no openings, (2) Because you don't know what the opening is (if there is one), you can't tailor your letter to specific requirements as James Calvin did in his solicited letter.

Advantages. This cold-canvassing approach does have one important advantage for an advertised opening, you will compete with legions of qualified applicants, whereas your unsolicited letter might arrive just when an opening has materialized. If it does, your application will receive immediate attention, and you just might get the job. Even when there is no immediate opening, companies usually file an impressive application until an opening does occur. Or the application may be passed along to a company that has an opening. Therefore, unsolicited letters generally are a sound investment if your targets are well chosen and your expectations realistic.

The Aggressive Approach to Unsolicited Letters. If you've thoroughly researched a company and its needs, you might find that your specific qualifications can benefit a company. (For further discussion on how to research a company, see the following chapter, "Interviews.") Your unsolicited letter then becomes the means to achieve your end—getting a particular job with a particular company. Thorough research is the key, for, in effect, you ideally create your own position by showing a personnel director or executive how your particular qualifications, skills, and aptitudes match that company's needs. Even if you don't convince them that they need you for the position you want, they may consider you for another—or refer you to another company looking for a person such as yourself. After all, you have demonstrated your initiative and desire to accept responsibility. Employers actively seek candidates with such qualities.

Reader Interest. Because your unsolicited letter is unexpected, attract your reader's attention early and make him or her want to read further. Don't begin: "I am writing to inquire about the possibility of obtaining a position with your company." By now, your reader is asleep. If you can't establish a direct connection through a mutual acquaintance, use an interesting opening, such as:

Figure 14.9

(Continued)

```
Does your hotel chain have a place for a junior manager with a college
degree in hospitality management, a proven commitment to quality ser-
vice, and customer-relations experience that extends beyond text-
books? If so, please consider my application for a position.
```

Unlike the usual, time-worn, and cliched opening, this approach gets through to your reader.

The Prototype

Most of your letters, whether solicited to unsolicited, can be versions of your one model, the prototype. Thus, your prototype must represent you and your goals in the best possible light. As you approach your job search, give yourself plenty of time to compose a model letter and résumé. Employers will regard the quality of your application as an indication of the quality of your work.

Above all, your letter and résumé must be visually appealing and free of errors. One or two spelling or grammatical errors might seem minor. But look at these documents from the employer's point of view. An employer expects you to present yourself in the most favorable way. A candidate who doesn't take the time to proofread carefully doesn't project the qualities employers want. After all, if you aren't conscientious about such important documents as your own application letter and résumé, how conscientious will you be with the employer's documents? Businesses incur a good deal of expense projecting favorable images. The image you project must measure up to their standards.

Your Dossier

Your dossier is a folder containing your credentials, college transcripts, letters of recommendation, and any other items (such as a notice of scholarship award or letter of commendation) that testify to your accomplishments. In your letter and résumé, you talk about yourself; in your dossier, others talk about you. An employer impressed by what you've said will want to read what others think about you and will request a copy of your dossier.

If your college has a placement office, it will keep your dossier on file and send copies to employers who request them. In any case, keep your own copy on file. Then, if an employer writes to request your dossier, you can make a photocopy and mail it, advising your reader that the placement office copy is on the way. This isn't needless repetition! Most employers establish a specific timetable for (1) advertising an opening, (2) reading letters and résumés, (3) requesting and reviewing dossiers, (4) holding interviews, and (5) making job offers. Obviously, if your letter and résumé don't arrive until the screening process is at step 3, you're out of luck. The same holds true if your dossier arrives when the screening process is at the end of step 4. Timing, then, is crucial. Too often, dossier requests from employers sit and gather dust in some "incoming" box on a desk in the placement office. Sometimes, one or two weeks will pass before your dossier is mailed out. The only loser is you.

Exercise 14.8	Without referring back to Figure 14.9, answer the following questions.
	1. What is an unsolicited letter?
	2. What are its advantages?
	3. What is one disadvantage?
	4. What is a prototype?
	5. What is a dossier?

Most likely, you were able to answer all or most of the questions correctly. Previewing, then, does provide you with a great deal of information. Now, suppose you were to return to Figure 14.9 and read the entire section. You would find it to be an easier task than it would have been if you had not previewed it.

Why Previewing Is Effective?

Previewing helps you make decisions.   Just as a film preview helps you make decisions about whether you want to see a film, so does previewing help you make decisions about how you will approach the material in a book. Based on what you discover about the text's organization and content, you can determine which reasoning and thinking strategies will be necessary for learning the material.

Previewing activates your thought processes.   It puts your mind in gear and initiates your thoughts on the subject.

Previewing activates your prior knowledge of the subject.   It helps you connect new material with what you already know.

Previewing gives you a mental outline of the chapter's content.   It enables you to see how ideas are connected, and since you know where the author is headed, reading will be easier than if you had not previewed.

Thinking Critically
. . . About Previewing

While previewing a reading assignment, you can make predictions about its content and organization. Specifically, you can anticipate what an assignment will contain and how it will be presented. Ask the following questions to sharpen your critical thinking-previewing skills:

◆ How difficult is the material?

◆ How is it organized?

◆ What is the overall subject and how is it approached?

◆ What type of material is it (practical, theoretical, historical background, or a case study)?

◆ Where are the logical breaking points where you might divide the assignment into portions, perhaps reserving a portion for a later study session?

◆ At what points should you stop and review?

◆ How does this material connect to class lectures?

Exercise 14.9	Select a chapter in one of your textbooks that you have not read and preview it using the procedure described in this section. When you have finished, answer the following questions.

1. What is its overall subject?

2. What topics (aspects of the subject) does the chapter discuss? List as many as you can recall.

3. How difficult do you expect the chapter to be?

4. How is the subject approached? That is, is the material practical, theoretical, historical, research oriented, procedural?

Using the SQ3R Reading/Study System

Developed in the 1940s, the SQ3R system has been used successfully for many years and has proved effective in increasing retention of information. It is especially useful for textbooks and other highly factual, well-organized materials. Basically, SQ3R is a way of learning as you read. Its name is taken from the first letter of each step. First we will summarize the steps, and then we will apply the system to a sample selection.

Survey

Become familiar with the overall content and organization of the material. You already have learned this technique and know it as previewing.

Question

Formulate questions about the material that you expect to be able to answer as you read. As you read each successive heading, turn it into a question.

Read

As you read each section, actively search for the answers to your guide questions. When you find the answers, underline or mark the portions of the text that concisely state the information.

Recite

Probably the most important part of the system, "recite" means that after each section or after each major heading, you should stop, look away from the page, and try to remember the answer to your question. If you are unable to remember, look back at the page and reread the material. Then test yourself again by looking away from the page and "reciting" the answer to your question. This step is a form of comprehension and retention assessment that enables you to catch and correct weak or incomplete comprehension or recall. Here, you are operating primarily at the knowledge and understanding levels of thinking.

Review

Immediately after you have finished reading, go back through the material again, reading titles, introductions, summaries, headings, and graphic material. As you read each heading, recall your question and test yourself to see whether you still can remember the answer. If you cannot, reread that section. Once you are satisfied that you have understood and recalled key information, move toward the higher-level thinking skills. Consider applications, analyze, synthesize, and evaluate the material. Ask questions. Some students like to add a fourth "R" step—for "React."

Now, to get a clear picture of how the steps in the SQ3R method work together to produce an efficient approach to reading/study, let's apply the method to a textbook reading. Suppose you have been assigned in a communication class the article on p. 269 on nonverbal communication. Follow each of the SQ3R steps in reading this section.

Survey

Preview the article, noting introductions, headings, first sentences, and typographical clues. From this prereading, you should have a good idea of what information this textbook excerpt will convey and should know the general conclusions the authors draw about the subject.

Question

Now, using the headings as a starting point, develop several questions to which you expect to find answers in the article. Think of these as guide questions. You might ask such questions as:

What are the major types of nonverbal cues?
What are spatial cues?
What messages are communicated at each of the four distances?

Read

Now read the selection through. Keep your questions in mind. Stop at the end of each major section and proceed to the next step.

Recite

After each section, stop reading and check to see whether you can recall the answer to the corresponding question.

Review

When you have finished reading the entire article, take a few minutes to reread the headings, recall your questions, and write answers to your questions to see how well you can remember the answers.

Types of Nonverbal Cues

You now have a definition of nonverbal communication, you know how much nonverbal communication counts, you understand the characteristics most non-verbal cues share, and you know the functions and forms, so it is time to examine the types of nonverbal cues. In this section, spatial cues, visual cues, vocal cues, touch, time, and silence will be discussed.

Spatial Cues

Spatial cues are the distances we choose to stand or sit from others. Each of us carries with us something called informal space. We might think of this as a bub-ble; we occupy the center of the bubble. This bubble expands or contracts de-pending on varying conditions and circumstances such as these:

- Age and sex of those involved.
- Cultural and ethnic background of the participants.
- Topic or subject matter.
- Setting for the interaction.
- Physical characteristics of the participants (size or shape).
- Attitudinal and emotional orientation of partners.
- Characteristics of the interpersonal relationship (like friendship).
- Personality characteristics of those involved.

In this book *The Silent Language,* Edward T. Hall, a cultural anthropologist, identifies the distances that people assume when they talk with others. He calls these distances intimate, personal, social, and public. In many cases, the adjust-ments that occur in these distances result from some of the factors listed above.

Intimate distance. At an **intimate distance** (0 to 18 inches), you often use a soft or barely audible whisper to share intimate or confidential information. Physical contact becomes easy at this distance. This is the distance we use for physical comforting, lovemaking, and physical fighting, among other things.

Personal distance. Hall identified the range of 18 inches to 4 feet as **per-sonal distance**. When you disclose yourself to someone, you are likely to do it within this distance. The topics you discuss at this range may be somewhat confidential and usually are personal and mutually involving. At personal dis-

---

Continued

tance you are still able to touch another if you want to. This is likely to be the distance between people conversing at a party, between classmates in a casual conversation, or within many work relationships. This distance assumes a well-established acquaintanceship. It is probably the most comfortable distance for free exchange of feedback.

Social distance. When you are talking at a normal level with another person, sharing concerns that are not of a personal nature, you usually use the **social distance** (4 to 12 feet). Many of your on-the-job conversations take place at this distance. Seating arrangements in living rooms may be based on "conversation groups" of chairs placed at a distance of 4 to 7 feet from each other. Hall calls 4 to 7 feet the close phase of social distance; from 7 to 12 feet is the far phase of social distance.

The greater the distance, the more formal the business or social discourse conducted is likely to be. Often, the desks of important people are broad enough to hold visitors at a distance of 7 to 12 feet. Eye contact at this distance becomes more important to the flow of communication; without visual contact one party is likely to feel shut out and the conversation may come to a halt.

Public distance. **Public distance** (12 feet and farther) is well outside the range for close involvement with another person. It is impractical for interpersonal communication. You are limited to what you can see and hear at that distance; topics for conversation are relatively impersonal and formal; and most of the communication that occurs is in the public-speaking style, with subjects planned in advance and limited opportunities for feedback . . .

—Weaver, *Understanding Interpersonal Communications,* pp. 215–218

How SQ3R Helps You Learn

The SQ3R system helps you learn in three ways. It increases your comprehension, it enhances your recall, and it saves you valuable time by encouraging you to learn as you read.

Your comprehension is most directly improved by the Survey and Question steps. By surveying or previewing, you acquire an overview of the material that serves as an outline to follow as you read. In the Question step, you are focusing your attention and identifying what is important to look for as you read.

Your recall of the material is improved through the Recite and Review steps. By testing yourself while reading and immediately after you finish, you build a systematic review pattern that provides the repetition needed to promote learning and recall.

Finally, because you are learning as you are reading, you will save time later when you are ready to study the material for an exam. Since you already have learned the material through recitation and review, you will find that you need much less time to prepare for an exam. Instead of learning the material for the first time, you can spend the time reviewing. You also will have time to consider applications, to pull the material together, to analyze it, and to evaluate its usefulness.

Adapting the SQ3R System

To make the best use of SQ3R, you must adapt the procedure to fit the material you are studying. You also must adjust the system to suit how you learn and to fit the kind of learning that is expected.

Adapting SQ3R to Suit the Material

Your texts and other required readings vary greatly from course to course. To accommodate this variation, use the SQ3R system as a base or model. Then add, vary, or rearrange the steps to fit the material.

For example, when working with a mathematics text, you might add a Study the Sample Problems step in which you analyze the problem-solving process. When reading an essay, short story, or poem for a literature class, add a React step in which you analyze various features of the writing, including the writer's style, tone, purpose, and point of view. For textbooks with a great deal of factual information to learn, you might add Underline, Take Notes, or Outline steps.

Adapting SQ3R to Suit Your Learning Style

Throughout your school experience, you probably have found that some learning techniques work better for you than others. Just as everyone's personality is unique, so is everyone's learning style. Refer to the Learning Style Questionnaire discussed in Chapter 8, p. 128.

Try to use knowledge of your learning style to develop your own reading/study system. Experiment with various study methods and adapt the SQ3R system accordingly. For instance, if writing outlines helps you recall information, then replace the Recite step with an Outline step, and make the Review step a Review and Outline step. Or if you have discovered that you learn well by listening, replace the Recite and Review steps with Tape-Record and Listen steps, in which you dictate and record information to be learned and review by listening to the tape.

There are numerous possibilities for developing your own reading/study system. The best approach is to test variations until you find the most effective system.

Exercise 14.10	Get together with other students taking the same course (or courses within the same discipline or department). Discuss and prepare a list of modifications to the SQ3R system that would be appropriate for your course's content and learning requirements.

Exercise 14.11	Apply the SQ3R system to a chapter in one of your other textbooks. List your questions on a separate sheet, and underline the answers in your textbook. Evaluate the effectiveness of your approach and decide on any modifications needed.

Learning from Graphs, Tables, and Diagrams

Significant portions of textbooks in the sciences, economics, and business are devoted to graphs, tables, and diagrams. These graphics present a visual picture of a given situation and summarize a great deal of information in a relatively small space.

It is tempting to skip over graphs, tables, and diagrams; stopping to study a graph takes time and seems to break your flow. Because they do not present information in verbal form (there are no statements to underline or remember), some students think they are unimportant. Actually, graphics are often *more* important than the paragraphs that surround them. They are included to call your attention to, emphasize, and concisely describe a situation. Graphics require time and effort to prepare and are expensive to include in a text. Consequently, graphics often indicate what the author thinks is important.

How to Read Graphics

Here are some general suggestions for reading graphics:

Read the title or caption.   The title often tells you what situation or relationship is being described.

Determine how the graphic is organized.   If you are working with a table, note the column headings. For a graph, notice what is marked on the vertical and horizontal axes.

Note any symbols and abbreviations used.

Determine the scale or unit of measurement.   Note how the variables are measured. For example, does a graph show expenditures in dollars, thousands of dollars, or millions of dollars?

Identify the trend(s) or pattern(s) the graph is intended to show.   The following sections will discuss this step in greater detail.

Read any footnotes.   Footnotes printed at the bottom of a graph or chart indicate how the data was collected, explain what certain numbers or headings mean, or describe statistical procedures.

Check the source.   The source of data is usually cited at the bottom of the graph or chart. Unless the information was collected by the author, you are likely to find a research journal or publication listed from which the data were taken. Identifying the source is helpful in assessing the reliability of the data.

Identifying Thought Patterns in Graphics

All graphics describe some type of relationship. Not coincidentally, these relationships correspond to the thought patterns studied earlier, in Chapter 12.

Tables: Comparison and Classification of Information

Sociologists, psychologists, economists, and business analysts frequently use tables to organize and present statistical evidence. A table is an organized display of factual information, usually numbers or statistics. Its purpose is to classify information so that comparisons can be made between or among data.

Take a few minutes now to study the table in Figure 14.10, using the suggestions listed above. Then analyze the table, using the following steps.

Determine how the data are classified or divided.   This table compares, for males and females, the number of new cases and deaths per year attributed to 14 major types of cancer. Notice that this table contains both column (top to bottom) and row (left to right) headings. Note also that the footnote indicates the source of the data.

Make comparisons and look for trends.   This step involves surveying the rows and columns, noting how each compares with the others. For example, by looking at the

Figure 14.10

Example of a Table

Rates of Some Major Cancers

Site	Number of New Cancer Cases 1993		Number of Deaths 1993	
	Male	Female	Male	Female
Lung	100,000	70,000	93,000	56,000
Breast (invasive)	1,000	182,000	300	46,000
Colon and rectum	77,000	75,000	28,800	28,200
Prostate	165,000		35,000	
Cervix (invasive)		13,500		4,400
Endometrium and body of uterus		31,000		5,700
Pancreas	13,500	14,200	12,000	13,000
Lymphomas	28,500	22,400	11,500	10,500
Ovary		22,000		13,300
Stomach	14,800	9,200	8,200	5,400
Leukemia	16,700	12,600	10,100	8,500
Bladder and kidney	55,800	23,700	20,800	13,000
Mouth and throat	20,300	9,500	4,975	2,725
Skin (melanoma only)	17,000	15,000	4,200	2,600
Combined sites	509,600	472,200	228,875	209,325

horizontal column for colon and rectum cancer, we can see that males and females experience nearly the same number of new cases and deaths per year. Be certain to compare columns and rows, noting both similarities and differences and focusing on trends.

Draw conclusions.   This final step is to decide what the data presented are intended to show. You can conclude from Figure 14.10 on p. 273 that lung cancer is clearly the leading cancer cause of deaths for both sexes and that for all types of cancer, taken together, males and females are nearly equal in numbers of new cases and deaths per year. Often, you will find clues, or sometimes direct statements, in the paragraphs that correspond to the table. The portion of the text that refers you to the table often makes a general statement about what the table is intended to show.

Once you have drawn your conclusions, be sure to stop, think, and react. For example, you might consider what the data in Figure 14.10 suggest about the causes of cancers and the part played by environmental as opposed to genetic factors, or what we can do to prevent these types of cancer.

Exercise 14.12	Study the table shown in Figure 14.11 and answer the following questions.
	1. What change of direction or focus has community health nursing taken?
	2. How has the service emphasis changed?
	3. What thought patterns are evident in this table?

Figure 14.11

Example of a Table

Development of Community Health Nursing

Stages	Focus	Nursing Orientation	Service Emphasis	Institutional Base (Agencies)
District nursing (1860–1900)	Sick poor	Individual	Curative: beginning of preventive	Voluntary: some government
Public health nursing (1900–1970)	Needy public	Family	Curative: preventive	Government: some voluntary
Emergence of community health nursing (1970–present)	Total community	Population	Health promotion: illness prevention	Many kinds: some independent practice

HOW DO YOU SEE IT?

*"But is showing you this toy and telling about it the whole story?
Let's take a look at its sales record, as illustrated by this chart,
which compares it with other toys in its price class."*

Graphs and tables often show patterns that are not evident in isolated incidents. Keep a record for 24 hours, listing the occurrence of a specific behavior that you would like to change (smoking, snacking, fingernail biting, daydreaming, etc.) and what activity you are involved in when the behavior occurs (working, studying, watching TV, talking on the phones, etc.). Describe the pattern, or lack of a pattern, that you see.

Graphs: Relationships Among Variables

Graphs depict the relation between two or more variables, such as price and demand or expenditures over time. Put simply, they are pictures of relationships between two or more sets of information. As you read and study in various academic disciplines, you will encounter many seemingly different types of graphs. They are all variations of a few basic types: linear, circle, and bar.

Linear Graphs. For linear graphs, information is plotted along a vertical and a horizontal axis, with one or more variables plotted on each. The resulting graph allows easy comparison between the variables. From variables. A sample linear graph is shown in Figure 14.12 on p. 276. The line graph displays federal revenues from 1970 to 1998. It enables you to compare the amount taken in from four sources over a period of 28 years.

Figure 14.12

A Linear Graph

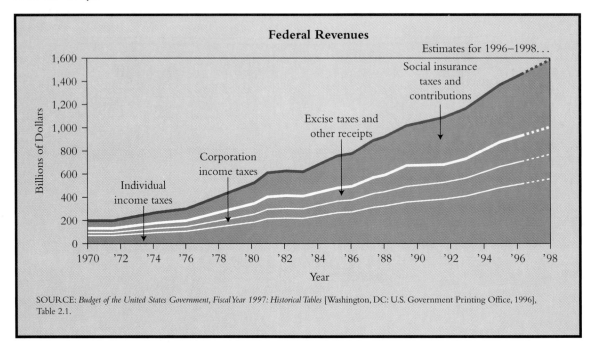

Federal Revenues

Estimates for 1996–1998 . . .

Social insurance
taxes and
contributions

Excise taxes and
other receipts

Corporation
income taxes

Individual
income taxes

Billions of Dollars

1,600
1,400
1,200
1,000
800
600
400
200
0

1970 '72 '74 '76 '78 '80 '82 '84 '86 '88 '90 '92 '94 '96 '98

Year

SOURCE: *Budget of the United States Government, Fiscal Year 1997: Historical Tables* [Washington, DC: U.S. Government Printing Office, 1996], Table 2.1.

In addition to yearly comparison, the graph also allows you to determine the general trend or pattern among the variables. Generally, this graph shows an overall increase in each of the four categories. You can see that social insurance taxes and contributions have increased most dramatically, while individual and corporation taxes and excise taxes have increased at a slower rate over the 28-year period.

A linear graph can show one of three general relationships: positive, inverse, or independent. Each of these is shown in Figure 14.13 on p. 277.

Positive Relationships. When both variables increase or decrease simultaneously, the relationship is positive and is shown on a graph by an upwardly sloping line. Graph A shows the relation between how long a student studies and exam grades. As the time spent studying increases, so do the exam grades.

Inverse Relationships. Inverse relationships occur when, as one variable increases, the other decreases, as shown in Graph B. Here, as exam grades increase, the amount of time spent watching television decreases. The inverse relationship is shown by the line or curve that slopes downward and to the right of the point of origin.

Independent Relationships. When the variables have no effect upon or relationship to one another, the graph appears as in Graph C. In this graph you can see that the amount of coffee drunk while studying had no effect upon exam grades.

Figure 14.13

Relationships Shown by Graphs

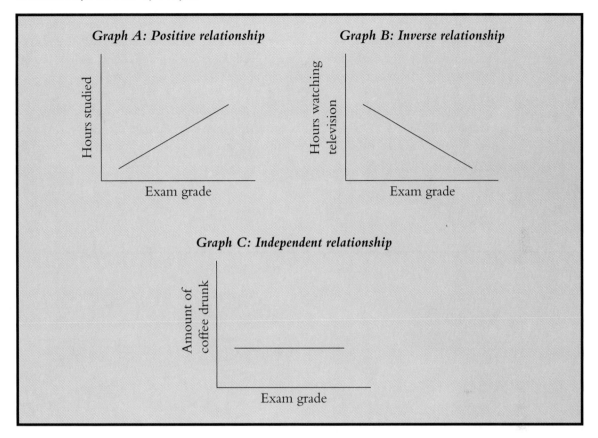

From these three relationships, you probably realize that linear graphs may suggest a cause and effect relationship between the variables. A word of caution is in order here: Do not assume that since two variables change, one is the cause of the other.

Once you have determined the trend and the nature of the relationship a linear graph describes, be sure to jot these down in the margin next to the graph. These notes will be a valuable time-saver as you review the chapter.

Exercise 14.13	What type of relationship (positive, inverse, or independent) would each of the following linear graphs show?

1. In a graph plotting effective use of study time versus college course grades, what type of relationship would you expect?

2. In a graph plotting time spent reading versus time spent playing tennis, what relationship would you predict?

3. What type of relationship would be shown by a graph plotting time spent checking a dictionary for unknown words versus reading speed?

Circle Graphs.   A circle graph, also called a pie chart, is used to show whole-part relationships, or to show how given parts of a unit have been divided or classified. Figure 14.14 shows a series of four circle graphs that present the characteristics of America's teachers in the year 2000. Each of these graphs is divided or classified into two or more categories. In the gender graph there are two categories represented; for race and ethnicity, five; for marital status, three; and for highest degree obtained, four. Circle graphs often are used to emphasize proportions or to show relative size or importance of various parts.

Bar Graphs.   A bar graph is often used to make comparisons between quantities or amounts. Figure 14.15 on p. 279 presents bar graphs that compare the responses of two age groups of workers to four statements concerning social security, health care, technology and computers.

Figure 14.14

Circle Graphs

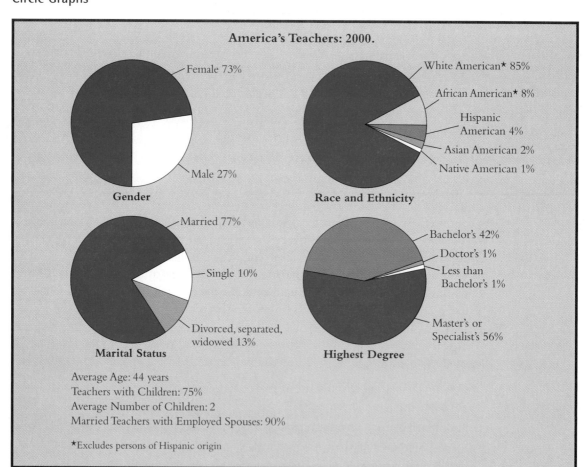

America's Teachers: 2000.

Gender — Female 73%, Male 27%

Race and Ethnicity — White American★ 85%, African American★ 8%, Hispanic American 4%, Asian American 2%, Native American 1%

Marital Status — Married 77%, Single 10%, Divorced, separated, widowed 13%

Highest Degree — Bachelor's 42%, Doctor's 1%, Less than Bachelor's 1%, Master's or Specialist's 56%

Average Age: 44 years
Teachers with Children: 75%
Average Number of Children: 2
Married Teachers with Employed Spouses: 90%

★Excludes persons of Hispanic origin

Figure 14.15

A Bar Graph

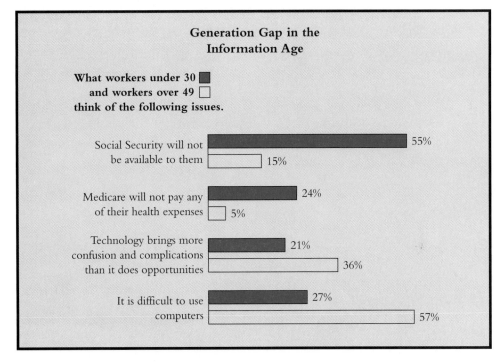

Diagrams: Explanations of Process

Diagrams are often included in technical and scientific as well as business and economic texts to explain processes. Diagrams are intended to help you visualize, see relationships between parts, and understand sequence. Figure 14.16 on p. 280, taken from a biology text, demonstrates how a portion of the sun's energy is used to heat the earth.

Reading diagrams differs from reading other types of graphics in that diagrams often correspond to fairly large segments of text, requiring you to switch back and forth frequently between the text and the diagram, determining to which part of the process each paragraph refers.

Often, the text presents an overview of the diagram, as in Figure 14.16. The underlined sentence summarizes what the diagram is intended to demonstrate. The text may also offer more detail about the process shown. The second paragraph, for example, explains the work accomplished by the 50 percent of solar energy that reaches earth.

Because diagrams of process and the corresponding text are often difficult, complicated, or highly technical, plan on reading these sections more than once. Use the first reading to grasp the overall process. In subsequent readings, focus on the details of the process, examining each step and understanding its progression.

Figure 14.16

A Process Diagram and Corresponding Text

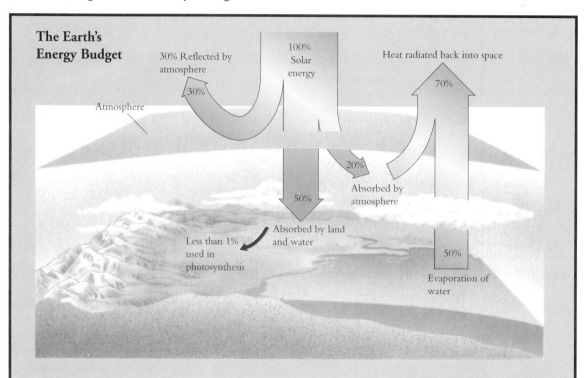

The relative constancy of conditions in the biosphere depends ultimately on an equilibrium between energy entering and energy leaving. Most of the absorbed energy reenters the atmosphere through evaporation from the earth's water. The thin arrow represents energy released by organisms.

SOLAR ENERGY

For the most part, the surface of the earth is heated by solar energy, energy from the sun. Only about half of the incoming solar energy ever actually reaches the earth's surface; about 30% is reflected back into space, while 20% is absorbed by the atmosphere. The 50% that does reach earth is absorbed by the land and waters, from which it radiates back into the atmosphere as heat (Figure 45.1). However, a great deal of work is accomplished during the time it interacts with the biosphere.

You are aware, of course (if all is going well), that photosynthesis drives much of the activity of life by enabling the energy of sunlight to be captured in the molecules of food manufactured by plants. However, you may be surprised to hear that on this green planet, less than 1% of incoming solar energy is used in photosynthesis. Actually, most of the solar energy reaching the earth is used to shuffle water around in the **hydrologic cycle,** which is the evaporation and condensation of the earth's waters. This cycle, of course, is responsible for the earth's rainfall pattern. In addition to distributing water more equitably over the earth's surface, the cycle redistributes heat.

One of the best ways to study a diagram is to redraw the diagram without referring to the original, including as much detail as possible. Or test your understanding and recall of the process explained in a diagram by explaining it, step-by-step in writing, using your own words.

| Exercise 14.14 | Study Figure 14.17 on p. 282. Then answer the following questions. |

    1. What is the purpose of the diagram?

    2. What control does the executive branch exert over the judicial branch?

    3. How does the judicial branch influence the legislative branch?

    4. If a president were convicted of a criminal act, what branch would handle his removal from office?

    5. Now test your knowledge of the procedure by drawing your own diagram without referring to the original.

Thinking Critically
. . . About Graphs and Statistics

Analyzing Statistics

The purpose of many graphs, charts, and tables is to display statistics in an easy-to-read format. A critical reader should look as closely at statistics as at any other type of information. While statistics may seem like hard facts, they can be misleading and deceiving.

Here is an example. Many graphics report averages—average salaries, average costs, average weights, or average educational levels. Did you know that an average can be computed three different ways with, at times, three very different results? The terms *median, mode,* and *mean* are all used to report averages. Let's say you want to report the average temperature for one week in your town or city. The daily temperatures are 69, 70, 70, 94, 95, 95, 96.

The mean temperature is 84.1.
The median temperature is 94.
The mode is 70.

These are very different numbers. Here's how they were calculated:

Mean: total the daily temperatures and divide by 7.
Median: arrange the temperatures from low to high and take the middle-most temperature (the one between three higher and three lower temperatures).
Mode: choose the temperature that occurs most frequently.

This is just one example of why caution is needed when interpreting statistics. There are many others. (In the example above, for instance, how was the daily temperature calculated? Was it the daily high, daily low, 24-hour "average"?)

Since statistics are subject to manipulation and interpretation, study graphics with a questioning, critical eye.

Figure 14.17

A Conceptual Diagram

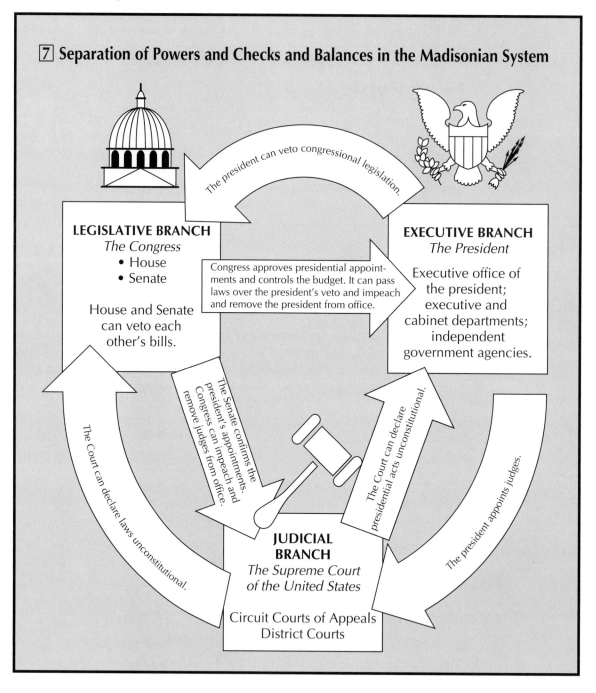

7 **Separation of Powers and Checks and Balances in the Madisonian System**

The president can veto congressional legislation.

LEGISLATIVE BRANCH
The Congress
• House
• Senate

House and Senate
can veto each
other's bills.

EXECUTIVE BRANCH
The President

Executive office of
the president;
executive and
cabinet departments;
independent
government agencies.

Congress approves presidential appointments and controls the budget. It can pass
laws over the president's veto and impeach
and remove the president from office.

The Senate confirms the
president's appointments.
Congress can impeach and
remove judges from office.

The Court can declare
presidential acts unconstitutional.

The Court can declare laws unconstitutional.

The president appoints judges.

**JUDICIAL
BRANCH**
*The Supreme Court
of the United States*

Circuit Courts of Appeals
District Courts

Learning from Visual and Electronic Media

Technology is playing an increasingly important role in education. College instructors use a wide variety of instructional media to supplement the information from textbooks and lectures. Your instructor may make assignments in nonprint materials such as videotapes, films, television documentaries, CD-ROMs, computer tutorials, or the Internet. In fact, some college texts are accompanied by computerized tutorials or CD-ROMs for your use outside the classroom. In some courses you may be encouraged or required to use Internet sources or to communicate with your instructor by e-mail. This section will provide suggestions for using and learning from visual and electronic learning sources and resources.

In general, you should approach assignments using visual and electronic media as you approach printed assignments. Be sure to determine your purpose and to take adequate notes at the time, since it is usually time consuming to review the material later. Taking notes on materials such as these is, in some ways, similar to taking notes on class lectures. Refer to Chapter 13 for suggestions on lecture note taking. In the case of films, dramatic re-creations, or performances, your notes should reflect your impressions as well as give a brief review of content.

Video, Film, and Television

One instructor might show a videotape, film, slide presentation, or television program segment in class. Another might assign it for viewing on your own time, requiring you to write a brief summary or critique. The most important step in viewing and learning from these sources is to determine what you are expected to learn from them. Instructors use visual media to accomplish a variety of purposes. They may use them to demonstrate principles, procedures, or causes and effects, to illustrate new or unfamiliar information, to make abstract ideas more concrete, or to explain difficult concepts. To learn more effectively from visual media, use the following suggestions:

1. **Determine the purpose of the visual.** Ask yourself, "Why am I looking at this?"
2. **Pay attention to your instructor's introduction.** Often an instructor will focus your attention on what you are to learn from the visual.
3. **Do not try to take extensive notes while viewing.** Instead, jot down brief words or phrases that will trigger your memory later.
4. **Pay attention to your instructor's comments following the presentation.** He or she may discuss important ideas, raise relevant questions, or suggest alternative viewpoints.
5. **As soon as possible after viewing, write a brief summary.** Include the main point of the visual, as well as striking or memorable details.

Exercise 14.15	From the courses you are taking this semester, choose at least one situation in which your instructor showed a film or videotape to enhance instruction. List the course and the type of media used, then explain the purpose or purposes it was intended to accomplish.

Electronic Learning Aids

Two types of electronic learning aids that are becoming increasingly common in college courses are computerized tutorials and CD-ROMs.

Computer Tutorials Some college textbooks come with computer tutorials in the form of floppy disks. These are usually provided by your instructor or found in the college's academic computer lab. They are mainly used for practice and application of the skills or concepts taught in your textbook. For example, software for an algebra text may contain review of the different algebraic functions, games and activities, and review quizzes. To learn best from this type of software, use the following suggestions.

1. **Keep a record of your progress on quizzes.** Many programs will do this for you and allow you to print a progress report. This record will enable you to see your strengths and weaknesses, plan further study, and review troublesome topics.

2. **Space out your practice.** Because many software programs are fun and engaging, some students work on them for hours at a time. To get maximum benefit from the time you are spending, limit your work to an hour or so. Beyond that, many activities become routine, your mind switches to "automatic pilot," and learning ceases to occur.

3. **Consolidate your learning.** When you finish a module or program segment, do not just exit and shut the computer off. Stop and reflect on what you have learned. If you worked on an algebra module about the multiplication of polynomials, then stop and recall the techniques you've learned. Write notes or summarize the process in a separate section of your course notebook reserved for this purpose.

CD-ROMs That Accompany Textbooks CD-ROMs may be included with your textbooks or they may be available in your college's academic computer labs. (Not all textbooks have CD-ROM accompaniments.) CD-ROMs contain an abundance of information, learning resources, and activities. A CD-ROM accompanying a psychology text might contain:

◆ Information on terms, concepts, etc.
◆ Demonstrations and experiments
◆ A review of key topics
◆ A glossary of key terms
◆ Games and other learning activities
◆ Review quizzes
◆ A student notepad (for recording your own ideas)
◆ Reference sources

The benefit of CD-ROMs is that they are interactive and interesting. The sound, dialogue, and visuals hold your attention and are well suited if you tend to be an auditory, spatial, or pragmatic learner. They also allow you to choose what and how you want to learn. If you need to review a topic, you can click on an icon and be guided through a learning sequence. You can easily find more information if you need it. When you've finished you can choose to take a review quiz to determine what you have learned. Also, since many of the activities are interactive, you become involved with the material by responding to it, rather than just reading it.

Here are a few guidelines for learning from CD-ROMs that accompany textbooks.

1. **Use them with but *not* in place of your text.** CD-ROMs are supplements. Although they are fun to use, you must still read your textbook.

2. **Use the CD-ROM as a chapter preview.** View the CD-ROM segment on a particular topic to get an overview of it before reading the corresponding text material.

3. **Use the CD-ROM for review and practice.** After you have read the text, use the CD-ROM to help you learn the material.

4. **Use the quiz or self-test modules when studying for an exam.** Use the quizzes to discover which topics you need to study further.

5. **If the CD-ROM has a notepad (a place where you can write your own notes), use it.** You will learn more efficiently if you express what you have learned in your own words.

Internet Sources

The Internet is a worldwide network of computers through which you can access a wide variety of information and services. Through the Internet, you can access the

World Wide Web (a network of networks), a service that connects this vast array of resources. Many instructors use the Internet and have begun requiring their students to do so. In many cases, the Internet has become a visual medium. Many sources use graphics and photographs to present and display information. Here is an overview of the services your instructor may ask you to access.

E-Mail (electronic mail)   E-mail (electronic mail) is a means of sending messages from one person or place to another by using your computer. A variety of computer programs are available that allow you to send and receive messages electronically, as well as to print them for future reference. E-mail is now being used in conjunction with many college courses. Students may collaborate on a class project or critique each other's papers using e-mail. Instructors and students may communicate through e-mail. In completing a research paper, it is possible to use e-mail to contact professors or other students doing research on the topic you are studying. It is also possible to transmit word processing files by attaching them to an e-mail message.

Most e-mail follows a consistent format and, consequently, is easy to read. Messages begin with a memo format in which the topic of the message, the date the message was sent, the name of the sender, and the name of the receiver are identified as "Subject" or "Re," "Date," "From," and "To." The message follows this introductory identifying information. Following the message is transmittal information that tracks the electronic path through which the message was sent. This information can be ignored unless you wish to verify the source of the sender.

The style of e-mail messages tends to be more casual and conversational than the traditional print forms of communication (letters and memos) but more formal than phone or in-person conversations. Because e-mail is intended to be a rapid, expedient means of communication, some formalities of written communication are relaxed. Expect to find a briefer introduction, more concise sentences, and few or no concluding remarks. Consequently, e-mail requires close attention; unlike print forms of communication, there is little repetition and fewer cues as to what is important.

Reading lengthy e-mail messages may be easier if you print them first. Figure 14.18 on p. 287 shows a sample e-mail message. Notice that the message is a concise yet effective form of communication.

Web Sites   A Web site is a location on the World Wide Web where you can obtain information on a particular subject. It is a collection of related pages stored together. You can move around the site from page to page by clicking on specially marked areas on the screen called *links*. Each page is called a *Web page* and includes a set of information. (It can be any length and is not restricted to a single screen or printed page.) The first page you see when you access a Web site is called its home page.

Major corporations such as Hertz, Burger King, and General Motors have Web sites, as do many universities, government agencies, and local businesses. Suppose you are researching the game of futebol played in Brazil for a sports and physical fitness class and the instructor referred you to the Nike Web site shown in Figure 14.19 on p. 288.

Figure 14.18

Sample E-Mail Message

Subj: Research on Dream Catchers
Date: 98–02–12 11:49:34 EST
From: JSantos@daemon.edu (Julia Santos)
Reply to: JSantos@daemon.edu
To: RichardApp@daemon.edu

Dear Richard,

In response to your request for information on the Native American craft of preparing dream catchers, I do know of one Web site that may be useful as a starting point. It includes both instructions and diagrams. Its URL is

http://www.nativeweb.org/NativeTech/dreamcat/dreminst.html

Good luck on your research project.

Julia

Web sites have recently been established by textbook publishers and authors to provide information and activities that supplement the text. A Web site for a biology text, for example, may contain reviews of recent research and discoveries not included in the text. A Web site for an English composition textbook may contain additional, current readings, up-to-date information on using and evaluating electronic sources, or exercises that relate to specific portions of the textbook. Web sites also provide interesting links, or connections, that direct you to other Web sites that offer related information. Web sites are useful sources of information when exploring a topic. If you have been asked to read about an issue related to biotechnology, you could access the Web site sponsored by Virginia Polytechnic Institute and State University, an excerpt of which is shown in Figure 14.20 on p. 289. Notice that it lists several subtopics related to biotechnology that you can explore.

Exercise 14.16   Visit a Web site sponsored by an educational institution and a Web site sponsored by a corporation. Then answer the following questions.

1. What is the purpose of each site?

2. In what ways are they similar and in what ways do they differ?

Figure 14.19

A Sample Web Site

Web Site Addresses Each Web site has its own address, known as its URL (Uniform Resource Locator). Here's how to read a URL for the *San Francisco Chronicle:*

transfer format host computer directory path

http://www.sfgate.com/chronicle

The transfer format identifies the type of server the document is located on and indicates the type of transfer format that is to be used. The second part names the host computer. The directory path is the "address" part of the Web site.

Many sites can be contacted using only the transfer format and the host computer address. Then once you've contacted the site, you can move to different directions and files within the Web site.

Anyone can place a Web site on the Internet. Consequently, you must be cautious and verify that the sources are reliable. See "Evaluating Internet Sources" on p. 290.

Examining a Web site address can help you evaluate the source. Commercial sources usually have <com> as part of the host computer address; colleges and universi-

Figure 14.20

A Sample Web Site

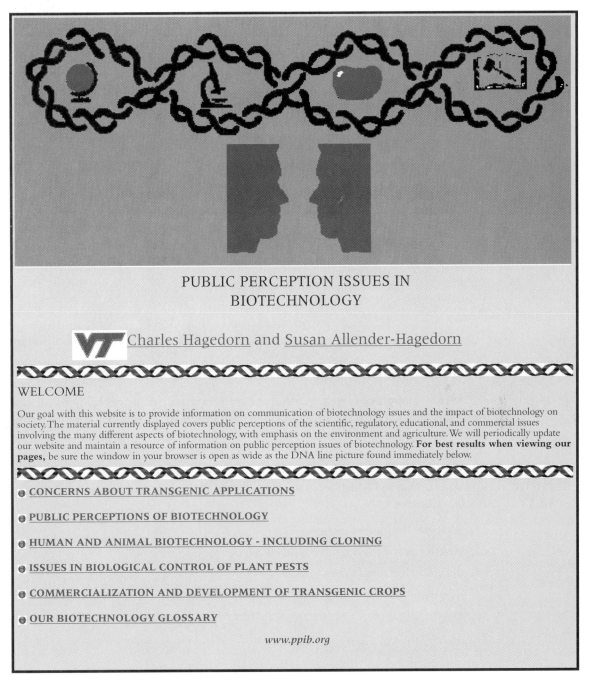

ties and other educational institutions are labeled <edu>; government agencies are identified by <gov>; <net> refers to a network; and <org> refers to an organization. Thus
the URL can help you distinguish educational, governmental, and commercial sources.

Reading a Web Site   The Web site's home page is your key to reading and using the site effectively. It is the master directory of the Web site. A home page may contain an identifying logo and will offer an overview of what you will find on other pages connected to the site and may suggest links to other Web sites.

Each page of a Web site usually contains a heading, called a header, that serves as a title for the information on that page. It usually appears in bigger, bolder type than the rest of the text on the page. These headers serve as valuable, concise descriptions of the contents of the page. Use them to decide whether the page contains the information you need and if it is worth reading.

Web sites are well suited for skimming. You can scroll through a Web page by using the down arrow or Page Down key.

Newsgroups   Newsgroups are collections of people interested in a particular topic or issue and who correspond and discuss it. Participants post messages on a given topic; other participants read and respond. Always read these postings with a critical mind-set. Remember that average people write most of these postings and that they represent their opinions. Postings such as these may be informative, but they may also contain incorrect information, bias, and unsubstantiated opinion. At times, you also may find postings that are mindless ranting and raving. Here are some tips for reading newsgroup postings.

- ◆ Separate fact from opinion. (See Chapter 16, p. 326.)
- ◆ Take into account the bias, motivation, and prejudices of the person posting the message.
- ◆ Verify any information you get from a newsgroup with a second source.

Usually newsgroups are open forums; anyone can lurk, or "listen in," to the discussion. Newsgroups can yield additional sources of information, as well as a variety of interesting perspectives on a topic.

Exercise 14.17   Visit a newsgroup and either "listen in" or participate in the discussion. Then answer the following questions.

1. What was the topic of discussion?
2. Were the postings largely fact or opinion?
3. Did you detect bias or prejudice?
4. How useful was the newsgroup as a source of information?

Evaluating Internet Sources

While the Internet contains a great deal of valuable information and resources, you need to be aware that it contains much rumor, gossip, hoaxes, and misinformation. In other words, not all Internet sources are trustworthy. You must evaluate a source before accepting it. Here are some guidelines to follow when evaluating Internet sources.

1. **Check the author.** For Web sites, look for professional credentials or affiliations. If no author is listed, you should be skeptical. For newsgroups or discussion groups, check to see if the author has given his or her name and a signature (a short biographical description included at the end of messages).

2. **Discover the purpose of the posting.** Many Web sites are written with an agenda such as to sell a product, promote a cause, advocate a position, and so forth. Look for bias in the reporting of information.

3. **Check the date of the posting.** Be sure you are obtaining current information. Web sites usually include the date on which they were last updated.

4. **Check the sponsoring organization of the site.** If a site is sponsored or provided by a well-known organization, such as a reputable newspaper like the *New York Times,* the information is apt to be reliable.

Learning from Supplemental Reading Assignments

In addition to the textbook, many professors assign supplemental readings. These assignments are drawn from a variety of sources: other textbooks, paperbacks, newspapers, periodicals, scholarly journals, and reference books. If the reading is not available as a paperback that you can purchase, a visit to the library is usually necessary. Often, your professor will place the required book or periodical *on reserve* in the library. This designation means the book is held at the reserve desk, where its use is restricted to a specified period of time.

Supplemental assignments present the following:

◆ New topics not covered in your text
◆ Information not covered in the text
◆ Updated information
◆ Alternative points of view
◆ Applications or related issues
◆ Realistic examples, case studies, or personal experiences

Reading supplemental assignments requires different skills and strategies from those for reading textbooks. Unless the assignment is from another textbook, you may find that the material is not as well or as tightly organized as in a textbook. It may also be less concise and factual.

Analyzing the Assignment

First determine the purpose of the assignment: How does it relate to existing course content? Listen carefully as your professor announces the assignment; important clues are often provided at this time. Next, determine the type and level of recall that is necessary. If, for example, the purpose of an assignment is to present new, important topics not covered in your text, then a high level of recall is required. If, on the other hand, an assignment's purpose is to expose you to alternate points of view on a controversial issue, then key ideas are needed, but highly factual recall is not. Or, if an assignment is given to help you understand real-life experiences, key ideas are all that may be necessary.

Choosing Reading and Study Strategies

Depending upon the purpose of the assignment and the necessary level and type of recall, you may need to read one assignment quite differently from another. Your choices range from a careful, thorough reading to skimming to obtain an overview of the key ideas presented. Before you begin, you need to select a study strategy to enable you to retain and recall the information. Table 14.2 lists examples of supplementary assignments and their purposes and suggests possible reading and study approaches for each. The table demonstrates that strategies vary widely to suit the material and the purpose for which it was assigned.

Table 14.2

Strategies for Supplemental Readings

Assignment	Purpose	Reading Strategies	Study Strategies
Historical novel (American history course)	To acquaint you with living conditions of the historical period	Read rapidly, noting trends, patterns, characteristics; skip highly detailed descriptive portions	Write a brief synopsis of the basic plot; make notes (including some examples) of lifestyle, living conditions (social, religious, political, as well as economic)
Essay on exchange in Moroccan bazaars for economics course	To describe system of barter	Read for main points, noting process, procedures, and principles	Underline key points
Article titled "What Teens Know About Birth Control" assigned in a maternal care nursing course	To reveal attitudes toward and lack of information about birth control	Read to locate topics of information, misinformation, and lack of information; skip details and examples	Prepare a three-column list: information, misinformation, and lack of information

Interactive Chapter Review

Knowledge	Name at least five main features of a textbook that you can use to analyze its content and organization.
Comprehension	When would the following features and learning aids in this book be useful to study? a. Do You Know questions at the beginning of the chapters b. Thinking Critically boxes within chapters c. Interactive Chapter Reviews at the ends of the chapters
Application	Preview a chapter of one of your textbooks. Then write brief answers to the following questions: What do you already know about this subject? What thinking strategies will you probably need to use to learn this material? How does this material connect to class lectures? Then use the SQ3R system to read the chapter.
Analysis	Refer to the circle graphs in Figure 14.14 and answer the following questions. Do the graphs indicate . . . a. that most teachers are male or female? b. how many female teachers are African-American? c. a positive relationship between race/ethnicity and highest degree obtained? Explain your answers.
Synthesis	List at least five ways the organization of textbooks and lectures are similar. Consult Chapter 13 if necessary.
Evaluation	Is learning to use the Internet important in reaching your goals? Consider your present and future life at college, work, and home to help you decide. Justify your answer.

Further Analysis

Analyze the following situation and answer the questions below.

A student attending the University of Manitoba is finding his ecology textbook overwhelmingly difficult and technical. He says he recognizes that the text contains numerous learning features, but despite these aids he is unable to master several assigned chapters per week. The student spends six hours per week on the assignment; he reads each chapter, then rereads and outlines it in detail. Then he studies the outline, memorizing portions of it. The student described his problem to his professor, and she advised him to take a more active approach to his study.

1. Using your knowledge of textbook learning and study and thinking skills, evaluate this student's learning strategy.

2. Suggest how the student might learn more actively. How might learning aids be used to promote more accurate learning?

Discussion

1. Explain why reading a chapter overview increases your comprehension and recall of chapter content.

2. What do you consider to be the primary difference between a textbook and any other type of nonfiction book?

3. Discuss whether the following student complaints are justifiable:

   a. A student criticized her business management professor because she assigned textbook chapters but did not discuss them in class.

   b. A student felt he had wasted money because he was required to purchase a textbook for a course in which the professor assigned fewer than half of the chapters.

   c. A student complained that she would not have had to purchase the text at all since all the material on the exam was discussed in class.

   d. Students in a sociology course were concerned when the instructor distributed a two-page supplemental reading list but did not make specific assignments. Instead, he advised students to "sample" as many readings as possible.

4. Six students in a physics class will be without textbooks for three weeks because the bookstore ran out of the text and has to reorder. How should these students handle this problem?

The Work Connection

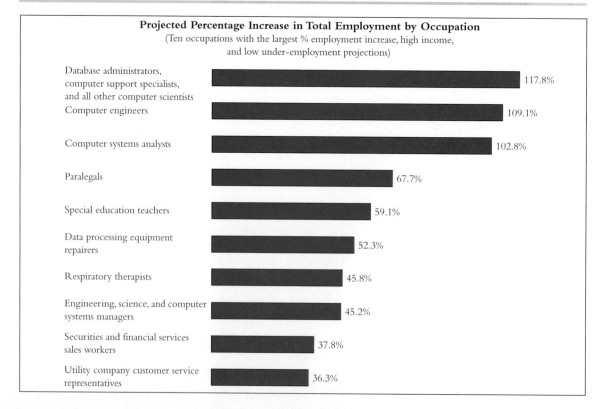

Projected Percentage Increase in Total Employment by Occupation
(Ten occupations with the largest % employment increase, high income, and low under-employment projections)

Occupation	Percentage
Database administrators, computer support specialists, and all other computer scientists	117.8%
Computer engineers	109.1%
Computer systems analysts	102.8%
Paralegals	67.7%
Special education teachers	59.1%
Data processing equipment repairers	52.3%
Respiratory therapists	45.8%
Engineering, science, and computer systems managers	45.2%
Securities and financial services sales workers	37.8%
Utility company customer service representatives	36.3%

This bar graph, based on data from the U.S. Bureau of Labor Statistics, shows excellent prospects for people entering certain careers during the 10-year period beginning in 1996. Of the top 10 high-growth opportunity, high-pay, low under-employment occupations listed, nine require two to four years of technical training or college to qualify for the positions.

1. List three factors in addition to growth opportunities, income, and steady employment that you have considered, or will consider, in choosing your career goals.

2. Does the information presented in this visual aid influence your thoughts and feelings about your chosen career path? Why or why not?

The Web Connection

1. Reading Textbooks: The Better Way

   http://www.cencol.on.ca/counselling/handouts/reading.html

   From Centenniel College, this site gives basic tips to making the most of your textbook.

2. Textbook Marking

   http://www.byu.edu/ccc/learning/text-mkg.shtml

   Learn some strategies and actual markings from this Brigham Young University site.

3. Web Page Evaluation Sheet

   http://www.duke.edu/~de1/evaluate.html

   Print out this page and use it to evaluate the Web sites you are using.

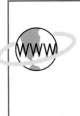

Go Electronic!
For additional readings, exercises, and Internet activities, visit the Longman Study Skills Web site at:
http://www.ablongman.com/StudySkills
If you need a user name and password, please see your instructor.

Chapter 15

Organizing and Synthesizing Course Content

DO YOU KNOW?

How can you reduce the amount of information you need to learn?

What techniques are useful for highlighting and annotating?

What strategies can you use to organize the information you have to learn?

When does it make sense to take outline notes or to make maps to organize information?

How can you use your computer to synthesize course content?

Have you ever wondered how you will learn all the facts and ideas your textbooks include and instructors present? The key to handling the volume of information presented in each course is a two-step process. First, you must reduce the amount to be learned by identifying what is important, less important, and unimportant to learn. Then you must organize and synthesize the information to make it more meaningful and easier to learn. This chapter describes two strategies for reducing the information—textbook highlighting and marginal annotation—and three means of organizing information—note taking, mapping, and computer integration.

Textbook Highlighting and Annotation

Both textbook highlighting and marginal annotation are useful ways to condense textbook material and emphasize what is important.

Textbook Highlighting

Textbook highlighting is an extremely efficient way of making textbook review manageable. Especially when combined with annotation, it is a quick and easy way to review so that you do not have to reread everything when studying for an exam. If you highlight 20 percent of a chapter, you will be able to avoid rereading 80 percent of the material. If it normally takes two hours to read a chapter, you should be able to review a highlighted chapter in less than a half hour. Highlighting by itself, however, is not a sufficient study method. The hour and a half you save, then, can be spent studying what you do not know, organizing and synthesizing the information, and preparing for your exam.

How to Highlight

To highlight textbook material most effectively, apply the guidelines below:

Begin by analyzing the task. Preview the assignment and define what type of learning is required. This will determine how much and what type of information you need to highlight.

Assess your familiarity with the subject. Depending on your background knowledge, very little or thorough highlighting might be necessary. Do not waste time highlighting what you already know. In chemistry, for example, if you already have learned the definition of a mole, then do not highlight it.

Read first; then highlight. Finish a paragraph or headed section before you highlight. Each idea may seem important as you first encounter it, but before you can judge its relative importance you must see how it fits with other ideas in the section.

Use the boldfaced headings. Headings are labels that indicate the overall topic of a section. These headings serve as indicators of what is important to highlight. For example, under the heading "Objectives of Economic Growth," you should be certain to highlight each objective.

Highlight main ideas and only key supporting details.

Avoid highlighting complete sentences. Highlight only enough so that your highlighting makes sense when you reread it. Notice that in Figure 15.1 on p. 298, an excerpt from a criminology text, only key words and phrases are highlighted.

Maintain a reasonable pace. If you have understood a paragraph or section, then your highlighting should be fast and efficient.

Develop a consistent system of highlighting. Decide, for example, how you will mark main ideas, how you will distinguish main ideas from details, and how you will highlight new terminology. Some students use a system of brackets, asterisks, and circles to distinguish various types of information; others use different colors of ink, or combinations of pens and pencils. The specific coding system you create is unimportant; what is important is that you devise some consistent approach to highlighting. At first, you will need to experiment, testing out various systems. However, once you have settled on an effective system, use it regularly.

Adopt a 15–25 percent rule of thumb. Although the amount you highlight will vary from course to course, depending on your purposes, try to highlight no more than between 15

Figure 15.1

Sample Highlighting

Losing Data Through Nonreporting

Much information on crime is lost because individuals simply do not bring suspicious events to the attention of police. Estimates in recent years indicate that even with serious crimes such as robbery, rape, and burglary, a considerable proportion of offenses are not brought to police attention—perhaps as high as 75 percent.[19] Most often cited are the figures compiled from a survey of 10,000 households conducted in 1965 and 1966 on behalf of the President's Commission on Law Enforcement and the Administration of Justice. Many more people responding to this survey reported having been victimized than official statistics would indicate should be the case. Apparently, many victims of crime do not report their experiences to the police. *Victimization rates* (the number of incidents in which persons are victims of crime per 100,000 people) were around 3 1/2 times the crime rate officially published for rape, triple the rate published for burglary, and about double the official rates for robbery and aggravated assault.[20] Other recent studies of victimization support the general findings of this first study, namely, that official rates are significantly lower than rates of victimization for most crimes. One exception is auto theft. Here, official rates and victimization rates are similar. This is largely because victims must report the offense to collect insurance. . . .

Why, of all people, do the victims of crime not report their victimization to the police? Two of the more common explanations given by the victims themselves are that they felt "nothing could be done anyway," or they felt that the police would not want to be bothered with their problems. Another reason often given is that the incident was a private matter, and the victim would rather keep it that way.[21] Can you think of other reasons why victims might not report offenses to the police?

---

and 25 percent of any given page. If you exceed this figure, you may not be sorting ideas as efficiently as possible. Remember, the more you highlight, the smaller your timesaving dividends will be as you review. Figure 15.1 provides an example of effective highlighting.

Overcoming Common Pitfalls

Highlighting, if done properly, is one of the biggest time-savers of all. However, if done incorrectly, highlighting can waste valuable time and leave you inadequately prepared to review for an exam. Here are a few common mistakes to avoid.

Highlighting without a defined purpose.   Some students highlight because they feel it will help them learn, rather than identify specific information for subsequent review. Consequently, their review is unfocused and does not produce results. Be certain, then, to carefully assess the nature of the material and what you are expected to learn. For example, in a political science course, are you focusing on trends, facts, solutions to problems, or making comparisons and contrasts?

Highlighting too much.   This is the most common problem that students face. Operating on mistaken ideas about "better safe than sorry" or "too much is better than too little," they tend to highlight almost every idea on the page.

Highlighting nearly everything is about as effective as highlighting nothing, since no sorting occurs: Key ideas are not distinguished from other, less important ones. Highlighting too much can become a way of escaping or postponing the issue at hand—determining what is necessary to learn and recall.

Highlighting too little.   Highlighting less than 10 percent per page may be a signal that you are having difficulty comprehending the material. Test your comprehension by trying to express the content of a given section in your own words. If you understand what you read but are highlighting very little, then you may need to refine or redefine your purpose for reading.

Thinking Critically
. . . About Highlighting

Highlighting, like any other learning strategy, deserves evaluation. To evaluate whether you are highlighting effectively use the following suggestions:

1. **Does your highlighting convey the key idea of the passage?**
2. **Can you follow the author's train of thought and progression of ideas by reading only the words highlighted?**
3. **Is the highlighting appropriate for your purposes?**
4. **How does your highlighting compare with that of a classmate?** While each set of words you're highlighting will be different, each should reflect the same key ideas.

The Added Benefits of Highlighting

Highlighting is beneficial for several reasons. The process of highlighting forces you to sift through what you have read to identify important information. This sifting or sorting is an active thought process; you are forced to weigh and evaluate what you read. Highlighting keeps you physically active while you are reading. The physical activity helps focus your concentration on what you are reading. Highlighting can help you discover the organization of facts and ideas as well as their connections and relationships. Highlighting demonstrates to you whether you have understood a passage you have just read. If you have difficulty highlighting, or your highlighting is not helpful or meaningful after you have finished reading, you will know that you did not understand the passage.

A word of caution: Do not assume that what is highlighted is learned. You must process the information by organizing it, expressing it in your own words, and testing yourself periodically.

Exercise 15.1	Choose a two- or three-page section from one of your textbooks and highlight it using the guidelines suggested above. Then evaluate the effectiveness of your highlighting as preparation for an objective exam on the material.

Marginal Annotation

In many situations, highlighting alone is not a sufficient means of identifying what to learn. It does not separate main ideas from examples or either of these from new terminology. Nor does it give you any opportunity to comment on or react to the material. Therefore, you may need to make marginal annotations as well as to highlight. Table 15.1 on p. 301 suggests various types of annotation used in marking a political science textbook chapter.

Figures 15.2 on p. 302 and 15.3 on p. 303 present two copies of the same paragraph. The first copy has been highlighted, while the second has been both highlighted and annotated. Notice how the second version (Figure 15.3) more clearly conveys the meaning of the passage.

Summary Notes.   Writing summary words or phrases in the margin is another valuable form of annotation. It involves pulling together ideas and summarizing them in your own words. This process forces you to think, monitor your comprehension, and evaluate as you read, and it makes remembering easier.

Figure 15.4 on p. 304 illustrates effective use of summary notes to annotate a sample passage. First read the passage, and then study the marginal summary clues.

Summary clues are most effectively used in passages that contain long and complicated ideas. In these cases, it is simpler to write a summary phrase in the margin than to highlight a long or complicated statement of the main idea and supporting details. To write a summary clue, try to think of a word or phrase that accurately states in brief form a particular idea presented in the passage.

Recall Clues.   In Chapter 13 you learned to write recall clues in the margin of your lecture notes (see p. 244). A similar system will work for studying textbook chapters. Recall clues are words, phrases, or questions that you can use to test yourself on the material. Each recall clue summarizes a particular section of text. To study your text using recall clues, cover up the page, exposing only the recall clues. Read the first recall clue and try to remember the information contained in the text. Continue working with the remaining recall clues on the page.

Table 15.1

Marginal Annotations

Types of Annotation	Example
Circling unknown words	...redressing the apparent (asymmetry) of their relationship
Marking definitions	*def* [To say that the balance of power favors one party over another is to introduce a disequilibrium
Marking examples	*ex* [...concessions may include negative sanctions, trade agreements...
Numbering lists of ideas, causes, reasons, or events	components of power include ① ② ③ self-image, population, natural resources, and geography
Placing asterisks next to important passages	* [Power comes from three primary sources...
Putting question marks next to confusing passages	? → war prevention occurs through institutionalization of mediation...
Making notes to yourself	*check def in soc text* power is the ability of an actor on the international stage to...
Marking possible test items	⌐ There are several key features in the relationship...
Drawing arrows to show relationships	↗ ...natural resources..., ...control of industrial manufacture capacity ↓
Writing comments, noting disagreements and similarities	*can terrorism be prevented through similar balance?* war prevention through balance of power is...
Marking summary statements	*sum* [the greater the degree of conflict, the more intricate will be...

Exercise 15.2	Review the textbook excerpt used in Figure 15.1 on p. 298 and add annotation.

Exercise 15.3	Highlight and annotate a five-page portion of one of your textbooks. Bring the text to class and exchange texts with a classmate. Reading only what you have highlighted and annotated, the classmate should, if your work is effective, grasp the key ideas of each section.

Figure 15.2

Highlighting

> **Influencing Public Opinion: Easy to Assume, Hard to Prove.**
>
> Common sense suggests that long exposure to anything is likely to influence opinion. The average American spends twenty-eight hours and twenty-two minutes weekly glued to "the tube." (Contrary to popular opinion, teenagers are the least frequent TV viewers.) Thus Americans spend more time watching television than in any other single activity besides sleeping and working! On the average night, 100 million Americans—more than half the adult population—will be watching television.
>
> Because of its pervasiveness, it is easy to *overestimate* the effects of the technotronic media on opinion change. For one thing, the vast majority of what people watch on television and read about in the papers is essentially nonpolitical. "Sitcoms," the NFL, *Hill Street Blues,* and *Star Search* are not exactly high political drama. Even watching television news produces only about as much information as a single newspaper page.
>
> In the early days of research on media impact, it was assumed that there would be direct, visible impacts of the media on public opinion, but efforts to prove such direct effects usually failed. Most media effects are subtle; the most obvious is on "agenda setting." People pay attention to what the media pays attention to; what the media says is important, we assume is important. Because the media sets our priorities, we tend to adopt its world view of political issues.[31]

Note Taking to Organize and Condense Information

Although highlighting is usually a fast and efficient method of identifying and locating key information to be learned, it does little to help you organize information and relate or pull together ideas. Highlighting is of limited use in situations such as the following:

◆ Texts that deal with presentation and subsequent analysis of literary works or other documents

◆ Collections of readings (for example, "Readings in Psychology")

◆ Anthologies of literature

◆ Texts in technical fields such as electrical engineering

◆ Courses in which the text is used very selectively with only specific pages or sections assigned

◆ Very difficult, complicated material

◆ Reference material that cannot be removed from the library

Figure 15.3

Highlighting and Annotation

Influencing Public Opinion: Easy to Assume, Hard to Prove.

amount of TV watching

Common sense suggests that long exposure to anything is likely to influence opinion. The average American spends twenty-eight hours and twenty-two minutes weekly glued to "the tube." (Contrary to popular opinion, teenagers are the least frequent TV viewers.) Thus Americans spend more time watching television than in any other single activity besides sleeping and working! On the average night, 100 million Americans—more than half the adult population—will be watching television.

TV watching nonpolitical little effect on public opinion

Because of its pervasiveness, it is easy to *overestimate* the effects of the technotronic media on opinion change. For one thing, the vast majority of what people watch on television and read about in the papers is essentially nonpolitical. "Sitcoms," the NFL, *Hill Street Blues,* and *Star Search* are not exactly high political drama. Even watching television news produces only about as much information as a single newspaper page.

major effects agenda setting

In the early days of research on media impact, it was assumed that there would be direct, visible impacts of the media on public opinion, but efforts to prove such direct effects usually failed. Most media effects are subtle; the most obvious is on "agenda setting." People pay attention to what the media pays attention to; what the media says is important, we assume is important. Because the media sets our priorities, we tend to adopt its world view of political issues.[31]

Note taking is a step that can either follow or replace highlighting and annotating, depending on the type of material and your purpose for reading. Note taking has a number of benefits. It provides a truer test of your understanding of the material than does highlighting. While highlighting requires you to *recognize* what is important, note taking requires you to *express* it in words—a more difficult task that involves a higher level of thinking. Note taking enables you to organize the material for easier learning.

Note taking forces you to decide at once what is important. Since you cannot possibly record everything, you are forced to be selective. As you write, you have time to reflect on the ideas you are recording. This is a form of rehearsal, and it facilitates learning.

The outline form is often used for note taking because it provides a visual representation of thought patterns and reflects the organization and development of ideas. When an outline is mentioned, many students react negatively, thinking of a rigid, formal, "Roman

Figure 15.4

Passage Annotated with Summary Notes

The Deepening Shadow of Joblessness

joblessness rose during economic growth periods

The specter of massive unemployment, as we saw in Chapter 3, is no stranger to American life. Even if we ignore the Great Depression and consider only the years since World War II, unemployment has been a perennial problem that has receded only to return again in disturbingly recurrent cycles. Even during what we now regard with some nostalgia (and some truth) as an era of unparalleled economic growth and promise in the 1940s, 1950s, and 1960s, the jobless rate rose to the neighborhood of 6 percent (and even beyond) in 1949, 1958, and 1961. In the latter two years, joblessness was higher than it was in 1978 and 1979, years we regard as ones of economic decline.

1980's highest rate

Nevertheless, by the 1980s it was apparent that the job problem had been worsening over time. The jobless rate reached levels higher than any since the Great Depression; in early 1983 the number of unemployed in the United States was roughly equal to the entire Canadian labor force. Moreover, the peaks of unemployment had become progressively higher, while economic recovery hadn't brought the jobless rates down as significantly as in the past. Each successive recession of the 1970s and 1980s began with a higher level of unemployment than the one before; the level of joblessness just *before* the 1981–1982 recession began was much higher than any experienced in postwar America in any recession year before 1975.

eco. recovery hasn't reduced rates

problems of definition and measurement

The severity of the job problem is hidden, as we've seen, by the conventions of measurement and definition. An unemployment rate of around 10 percent means that roughly 11 million individuals are officially counted as out of work. But the true number of the jobless also includes the more than 1.5 million "discouraged" workers and the several million others who are "out of the labor force" but want to work. And even the lower figure of 11 million individuals out of work means that *25 to 30 million people in families* are touched by the unemployment of one or more members.

numeral I, II, capital letter A, B . . ." structure. Actually, this is only one form of outline notes; an outline is an adaptable, versatile structure that can take a variety of shapes and forms. Outline notes may be highly detailed or consist of a brief list of items; they may exhibit careful organization or be loosely structured. The type you write depends on how and why you are writing it.

The purpose of outline notes is to reflect the shape of a subject. Think of it as a sketch or drawing that shows general features but lacks the exact detail of a photograph.

Developing Outline Notes

Classification is the primary thought pattern involved in preparing an outline. Developing an outline involves two steps: (1) identifying how ideas relate and (2) grouping ideas together according to their connections. An effective outline, then, accomplishes two things:

- ◆ It shows the relative importance of ideas.
- ◆ It shows the relationships among these ideas.

An outline uses a listing order and a system of indentation. A quick glance at the outline indicates what is most important, what is less important, and how ideas support or explain one another. When you write an outline for your own use, you do not necessarily follow the formal outline format of roman numerals, capital letters, and so forth (I., A., 1., a.). Instead you can use an informal system of indentation as shown in Figure 15.5 on p. 306. Here are a few suggestions for developing an effective outline.

Concentrate on the relative importance of ideas.   Do not worry about the numbering and lettering system. How you number or letter an idea, or whether you label it at all, is not as important as showing what other ideas it supports or explains.

Be brief.   Use words and phrases, never complete sentences.

Use your own words.   Don't lift most of the material from the text or lecture notes.

Make sure subentries are relevant.   All the information you place in sublists beneath a heading should support or explain the heading.

Align headings to reflect their relative importance.   Headings with the same indentation on the page should be of equal importance.

How Much Information to Record

Before you begin writing an outline, determine how much information you need to include. An outline can be very brief and cover only major topics, or, at the other extreme, it can be very detailed, providing an extensive review of precise, factual information.

Figure 15.5

Informal Outline Notes

Time Management
- Analyze your time commitments –
hours per week
  - ex. class, part-time job,
  transportation
- Analyze Your Efficiency
  - notice wasted time, duplication
  of effort.
  - notice time traps
      ex-making small decisions
- Principles of Time Management
  1) Use peak periods of concentration
  2) do difficult tasks first

How much detail you include in an outline should be determined by your purpose for making it. For example, you need include very little detail in the outline for a supplemental reading that your instructor has assigned to show you the author's viewpoint and general approach to a problem. On the other hand, your outline of a section of an anatomy and physiology text for an upcoming objective exam must be much more detailed. To find the right amount of detail to include, ask yourself questions such as "What do I need to know?" or "What type of test situation am I preparing for?"

When to Use Outline Notes

Outline notes are particularly appropriate and effective in the following situations:

Difficult Material.   Outlining difficult or confusing material forces you to sort ideas, see connections, and express them in your own words, and it thus aids comprehension.

Interpreting and Reacting.   When you are asked to write an evaluation of, reaction to, or critical interpretation of an article or essay, it is helpful to write a brief outline of the factual content. Your notes will reflect development and progression of thought and help you analyze the writer's ideas.

Order and Process.   In courses where order or process is important, outline notes are particularly useful. In data processing, for example, where sets of programming commands must be performed in a specified sequence, outline notes would organize the information.

Classification.   In the natural sciences, where classifications are important, outlining is a helpful way to record and sort information. In botany, for example, you can use outline notes to list plant subgroups within each botanical category and keep track of similar characteristics.

Exercise 15.4	Write a brief set of outline notes reflecting the organization and content of one or two pages of one of your textbooks.

Mapping to Show Relationships

Mapping is a process of drawing a diagram to picture how a topic and its related ideas are connected. It is a method of organizing and consolidating information, often to emphasize a particular thought pattern. The degree to which you find mapping useful will depend on the courses you are taking, since some types of information are more easily learned by using visual or organizational maps than others. The effectiveness of mapping will also depend on your individual learning style. Spatial learners will find it to be a particularly effective technique.

This section describes a general mapping procedure, called concept maps, and discusses five types of specialized maps: time lines, process diagrams, part and function diagrams, organization charts, and comparison and contrast charts. Each utilizes one of the thought patterns discussed in Chapter 12.

Concept Maps

A concept map of Chapter 13, on lecture note taking, is shown in Figure 15.6 on p. 308. Take a moment now to refer to Chapter 12 before studying the map.

Basically a concept map is a form of outline that presents ideas spatially rather than in list form. Use the following steps in constructing a concept map:

◆ Identify the topic and write it in the center of the page.
◆ Identify ideas, aspects, parts, and definitions that relate to the topic. Draw each on a line radiating from the central topic.
◆ As you discover details that further explain an idea already recorded, draw a new line branching from the idea it explains.

Figure 15.6

Sample Concept Map

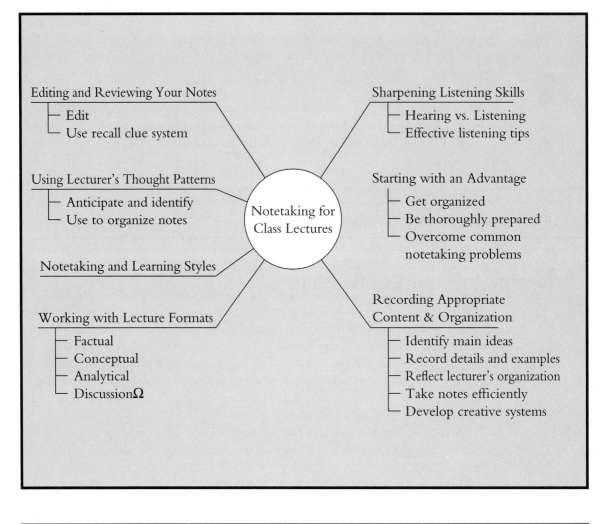

Exercise 15.5	Choose a section of a chapter in this text that you have already read. Draw a concept map reflecting its overall content and organization.

Concept maps can be drawn to organize any set of information. For example, you could draw a map to reflect chapter content. However, you can also draw maps to organize a section of a chapter, integrate several sets of lecture notes, or relate text and lecture notes on the same topic.

Concept maps can be simple or complex, brief or detailed, depending on the material you are mapping and on your purpose for mapping. Figure 15.7 on p. 309 shows a map an art student drew to integrate information on elements of design. Figure 15.8 on

Figure 15.7

A Sample Concept Map

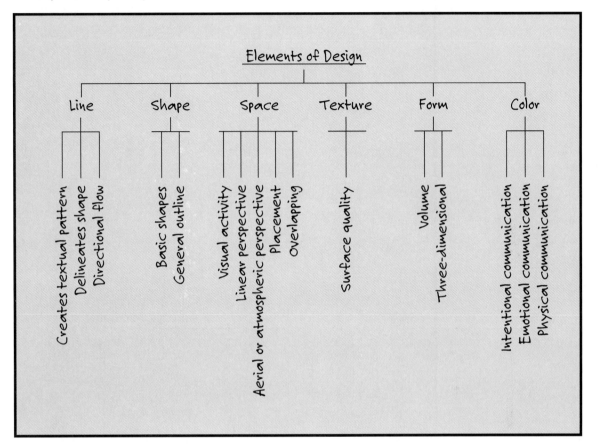

p. 310 shows a more detailed map of the cardiovascular system drawn for an anatomy and physiology course.

Specialized Maps

Each of the following maps relates to a specific thought pattern.

Time Lines. When studying a topic in which the sequence or order of events is a central focus, a time line is a useful way to organize the information. To map a sequence of events, draw a single horizontal line and mark it off in year intervals, just as a ruler is marked off in inches. Then write events next to the correct year. For example, the time line in Figure 15.9 on p. 311 was developed for a world history course in which the Napoleonic era was being studied. The time line shows clearly the sequence of events and helps you visualize their order.

Figure 15.8

A Sample Concept Map

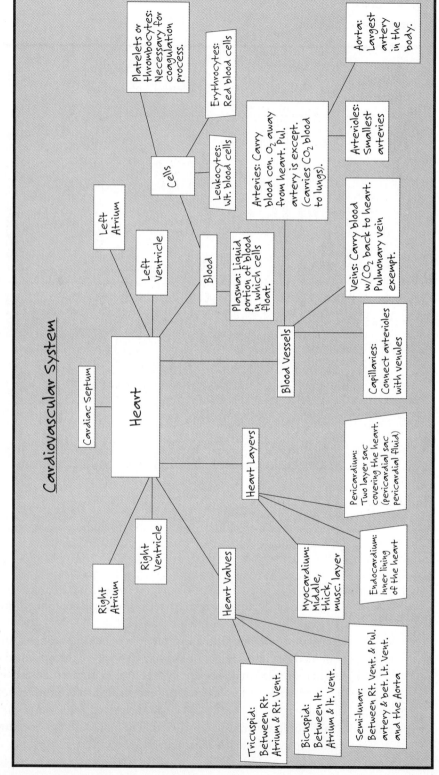

Cardiovascular System

Cardiac Septum

Heart

Left Atrium

Left Ventricle

Right Atrium

Right Ventricle

Cells

Blood

Blood Vessels

Heart Layers

Heart Valves

Platelets or thrombocytes: Necessary for coagulation process.

Erythrocytes: Red blood cells

Leukocytes: Wt. blood cells

Arteries: Carry blood con. O₂ away from heart. Pul. artery is except. (carries CO₂ blood to lungs).

Arterioles: Smallest arteries

Aorta: Largest artery in the body.

Plasma: Liquid portion of blood in which cells float.

Veins: Carry blood w/CO₂ back to heart. Pulmonary vein exempt.

Capillaries: Connect arterioles with venules

Pericardium: Two layer sac covering the heart. (pericardial sac pericardial fluid)

Myocardium: Middle, thick, musc. layer

Endocardium: Inner lining of the heart

Tricuspid: Between Rt. Atrium & Rt. Vent.

Bicuspid: Between lt. Atrium & lt. Vent.

Semi-lunar: Between Rt. Vent. & Pul. artery & bet. Lt. Vent. and the Aorta

Figure 15.9

A Time Line

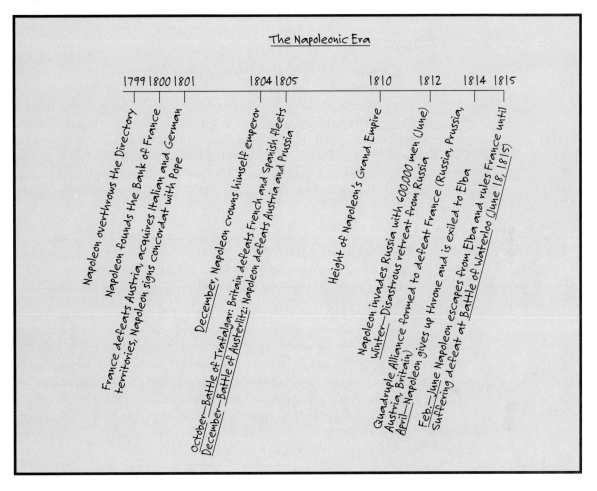

Exercise 15.6	The following passage reviews the ancient history of maps. Read the selection and then draw a time line that will help you visualize these historical events. (Remember that B.C. refers to time before Christ and that numbers increase as time moves back from history.)

In Babylonia, in approximately 2300 B.C., the oldest known map was drawn on a clay tablet. The map showed a man's property located in a valley surrounded by tall mountains. Later, around 1300 B.C., the Egyptians drew maps that detailed the location of Ethiopian gold mines and that showed a route from the Nile Valley. The ancient Greeks were early mapmakers as well, although none of their maps remain for us to examine. It is estimated that in 300 B.C. they drew maps showing the earth to be round. The Romans drew maps to tax land and to plan military tactics. The Romans drew the first road maps, a few of which have been preserved for study today.

Claudius Ptolemy, an Egyptian scholar who lived around A.D. 150, drew one of the most famous ancient maps. He drew maps of the world as it was known at that time, including 26 regional maps of Europe, Africa, and Asia.

Process Diagrams

In the natural sciences as well as other courses such as economics and data processing, processes are an important part of the course content. A chart that depicts the steps, variables, or parts of a process will make learning easier. For example, the diagram in Figure 15.10 might be used by a biology student. It describes the food chain and shows how energy is transferred through food consumption from lowest to highest organisms. Notice that this student included an example as well as the steps in the process in order to make the diagram clearer. Figure 15.11 shows a more complicated process diagram. It describes the process for a person charged with a misdemeanor. Alternatives at each step are shown.

Exercise 15.7   The following paragraph describes the process through which malaria is spread by mosquitoes. Read the paragraph and then draw a process diagram that shows how this process occurs.

Malaria, a serious tropical disease, is caused by parasites, or one-celled animals, called protozoa. These parasites live in the red blood cells of humans as well as in the female anopheles mosquitoes. These mosquitoes serve as hosts to the parasites and carry and spread malaria. When an anopheles mosquito stings a person who already has malaria, it ingests the red blood cells that contain the malaria parasites. In the host mosquito's body, these parasites multiply rapidly and move to its salivary glands and mouth. When the host mosquito bites another person, the malaria parasites are injected into the victim and enter his or her bloodstream. The parasites again multiply and burst the victim's blood cells, causing anemia.

Figure 15.10

A Process Diagram

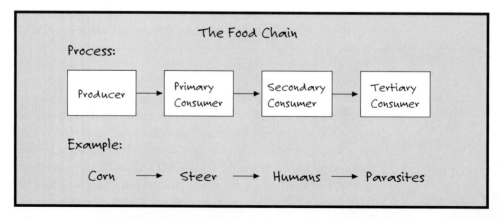

Figure 15.11

A Process Diagram

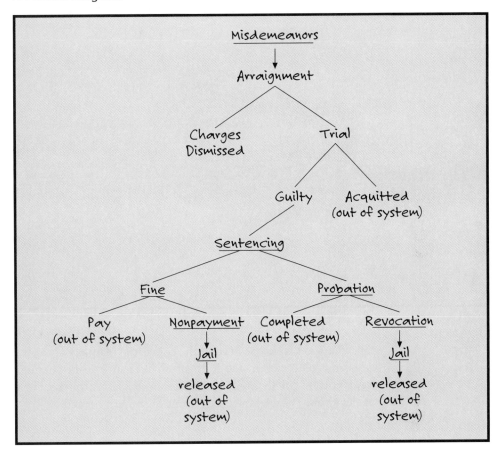

Part and Function Diagrams: Classification

In courses that deal with the use and description or classification of physical objects, labeled drawings are an important learning tool. In a human anatomy and physiology course, for example, the easiest way to learn the parts and functions of the inner, middle, and outer ear is to draw the ear. To study, sketch the inner ear, and test your recall of each ear part and its function. A sample drawing is shown in Figure 15.12 on p. 314.

Exercise 15.8	The following paragraph describes the earth's structure. Read the paragraph and then draw a diagram that will help you visualize how the interior of the earth is structured.

At the center is a hot, highly compressed inner core, presumably solid and composed mainly of iron and nickel. Surrounding the inner core is an outer core, a molten shell primarily of liquid iron and nickel with lighter liquid material on the

Figure 15.12

A Sample Part and Function Diagram

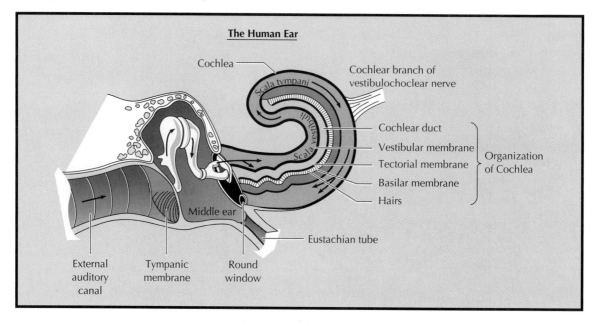

top. The outer envelope beyond the core is the mantle, of which the upper portion is mostly solid rock in the form of olivine, an iron-magnesium silicate, and the lower portion chiefly iron and magnesium oxides. A thin coat of metal silicates and oxides (granite) called the crust, forms the outermost skin.[1]

Organizational Charts

When reviewing material that is concerned with relationships and structures, organizational charts are useful study aids. In a business management course, suppose you are studying the organization of a small temporary clerical help firm. If you drew and studied the organizational chart shown in Figure 15.13, the structure would become apparent and easy to remember.

Exercise 15.9	The following paragraph describes one business organizational structure that is studied in business management courses. Read the paragraph and then draw a diagram that will help you visualize this type of organization.

It is common for some large businesses to be organized by place, with a department for each major geographic area in which the firm is active. Businesses that market products for which customer preference differs from one part of the country to another often use

Figure 15.13

An Organizational Chart

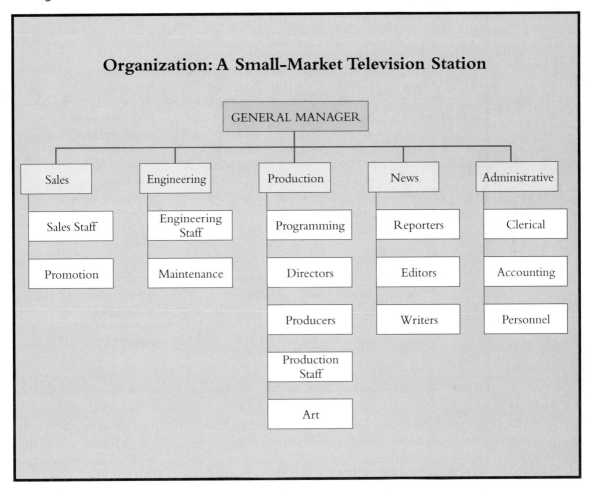

this management structure. Departmentalization allows each region to focus on its own special needs and problems. Often, the president of such a company appoints several regional vice-presidents, one for each part of the country. Then each regional office is divided into sales districts, each supervised by a district director.

Comparison and Contrast Charts

A final type of visual aid that is useful for organizing factual information is the comparison and contrast chart. This method of visual organization divides and groups information according to similarities or common characteristics. Suppose in a business course

Figure 15.14

A Comparison and Contrast Chart

Market Survey Techniques			
Type	Cost	Response	Accuracy
Mail	usually the cheapest	higher than phone or personal interview	problems with misunderstanding directions
Phone	depends on availability of 800 number	same as personal interview	problems with unlisted phones and homes w/out phones
Personal interview	most expensive	same as phone	problems with honesty when asking personal or embarrassing questions

on marketing and advertising you are studying three types of market survey techniques: mail, phone, and personal interview surveys. You are concerned with factors such as cost, level of response, time, and accuracy. To learn this information in an efficient manner, you could draw a chart such as the one shown in Figure 15.14.

Exercise 15.10

The following passage describes the major physical differences between humans and apes. Read the selection and then arrange the information into a map that would make the information easy to learn.

Numerous physical characteristics distinguish man from apes. While apes' bodies are covered with hair, man's body has relatively little hair. While apes often use both their hands and feet to walk, man walks erect. Apes' arms are longer than their legs, while just the reverse is true for man. Apes have large teeth, necessary for devouring coarse, uncooked food, and long canine teeth for self-defense and fighting. By comparison, man's teeth are small and short. The ape's brain is not as well developed as that of man. Man is capable of speech, thinking, and higher-level reasoning skills. These skills enable man to establish culture, thereby placing the quality and level of man's life far above that of apes.

Man is also set apart from apes by features of the head and face. Man's facial profile is vertical, while the ape's profile is *prognathous,* with jaw jutting outward. Man has a chin; apes have a strong lower jaw, but no chin. Man's nostrils are smaller and less flaring than those of the ape. Apes also have thinner, more flexible lips than man.

Man's upright walk also distinguishes him from apes. Man's spine has a double curve to support his weight, while an ape's spine has a single curve. Man's foot is arched both vertically and horizontally, but, unlike the ape's, is unable to grasp objects. The torso of man is shorter than that of apes. It is important to note that many of these physical traits, while quite distinct, differ in degree rather than in kind.[4]

Using a Computer to Synthesize Course Content

Colleges vary widely in the computer services available to students. Some colleges encourage students to purchase their own computers. Many have computer labs located in classroom buildings and dormitories. Others may also have restricted-use labs, with use limited to students taking certain courses. Find out what services are available on your campus. Visit your college's computer facilities or computer lab. Ask what is available and when someone is available to assist you. Some colleges offer workshops; others offer assistance by student aides who are familiar with computers.

A computer's word processing capability makes it a useful study and learning aid. The following sections offer suggestions for using the computer to organize your study. To make the most of these suggestions, you will need access to a computer on a daily basis.

HOW DO YOU SEE IT?

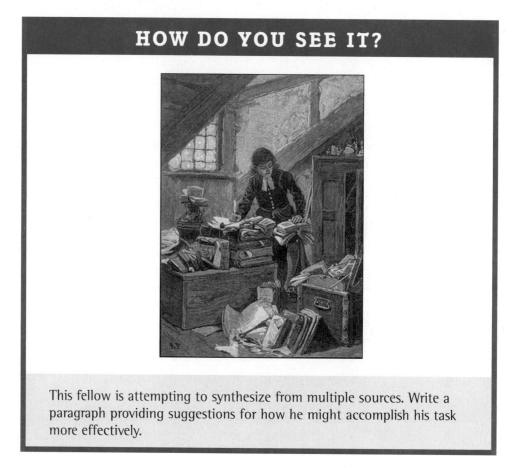

This fellow is attempting to synthesize from multiple sources. Write a paragraph providing suggestions for how he might accomplish his task more effectively.

Organizing Notes from Textbook Reading

As you take notes from readings, your notes tend to follow the organization of the text. That is, the order of ideas in your notes parallels the order of ideas presented in the text. At times, it is useful to reorganize and rearrange your notes. (See "Thematic Study" in Chapter 17). For example, you may want to pull together information on a certain topic that is spread throughout one or more chapters.

With a computer, you must type your notes initially, and you can edit and review them as you type. Then, the computer's word processing program's cut-and-paste functions enable you to rearrange and reorganize the notes or outlines easily without retyping.

Organizing Lecture Notes

Lecture notes are, of course, recorded by hand as you listen to the lecture, unless you are using a laptop computer. Typing your notes into the computer is a means of editing and review, as well as of reorganizing them.

Integrating Text and Lecture Notes

A continual problem students wrestle with is how to integrate lecture and textbook notes or outlines. Some try leaving blank space in their lecture notes to add textbook notes; others try a two-column approach, taking lecture notes on half the page and leaving the remaining column blank for textual notes. Neither system works extremely well, though, since one never knows how much space to leave, and some space is always wasted, since lectures and text do not always parallel one another.

The computer offers an ideal solution to the integration of textual and lecture notes. The cut-and-paste option allows you to move sections of your notes to any desired place in the document. Thus, you can easily integrate text and lecture notes on each major topic. In Chapter 17, you will discover how to use these sets of notes to prepare for exams.

Interactive Chapter Review

Knowledge	What are two ways to reduce the amount of information you need to learn in a course?
Comprehension	In which of your courses would it make sense for you to use outline notes? Explain each situation.
Application	Draw a concept map for one of your courses that shows the relationships between the ideas in a recent reading assignment and the corresponding lecture.
Analysis	Analyze the methods you used for condensing and organizing course content before you read this chapter. Which methods were effective, and which were ineffective? What changes do you need to make in the ineffective strategies? When will you begin?
Synthesis	Summarize what you have learned in this chapter by writing a letter to a senior in high school (real or imaginary). Discuss at least three major points about organizing and synthesizing course content that you think he or she should know at the beginning of a first college class. Give examples from your own early experience in college if appropriate.
Evaluation	There is an emphasis on organizing throughout this book: organizing your study area, your time commitments, how you approach your courses, and, in this chapter, how you organize the ideas of a course. Evaluate whether your life in general and your study skills in particular have benefited from this continued emphasis. First, make a list of the organizational advice from this book that you have actually put into practice. Second, consider how you would know whether you have benefited from the changes you have made. Third, evaluate the benefits. Is it "worth it" to be organized? Why or why not?

Working Together

Working in groups of three, students should complete the following steps.

1. Each group should choose one academic discipline and read the corresponding section in Chapter 10 of this text. Assume this material will be included on an exam.

2. One group member should highlight and annotate the section; another should make outline notes; the third member should draw a map of its content.

3. Group members should review and critique one another's work and discuss the following questions:

   a. Which of the three methods used seemed most effective for this material?

   b. Might your answer to the above question depend on the type of exam you would have (objective or essay)?

   c. What advantages did each method seem to offer? What were its limitations?

   d. Make a generalization about situations in which each can be used most effectively.

Further Analysis

Analyze the following situation and answer the questions below.

A student who is taking a course in human anatomy and physiology failed the first multiple-choice exam. She describes her main problem by saying, "I can't concentrate. Besides, the text is difficult and uninteresting." She also says that everything seems important, and if she used highlighting, she would have most of each page highlighted. The text already contains a detailed outline at the end of each chapter, so she feels she would be wasting her time by making outline notes.

1. Do you agree that highlighting is not an effective strategy?

2. Should the student make outline notes? If so, what use, if any, should she make of the end-of-chapter outline?

3. What additional learning strategies do you recommend?

4. What strategies will help this student concentrate?

Discussion

1. For which of your current courses do you think mapping would be most effective? In what types of courses would the technique be ineffective?

2. Outlining is a process of organizing information. In what nonacademic situations might outlining be a useful technique?

3. How is the method you choose to organize information related to your learning style? (See Chapter 8, pp. 136–139.)

4. In what career or job-related circumstances might the skills presented in this chapter be important?

The Work Connection

How can you use the techniques you have learned in this chapter to market yourself to prospective employers? One way is to organize and synthesize information about yourself so you can respond effectively to help wanted ads. To gain an interview with a prospective employer, you first need to figure out what the job requires and then demonstrate in a resumé that you have the needed knowledge, skills, and accomplishments. Since most employers spend only about 20 to 30 seconds reading a resumé,[5] you need to be able to organize and synthesize all your best points in a succinct format that directly responds to the points in a help wanted ad. Try the following steps.

1. Find a help wanted ad in a newspaper that lists at least three qualifications a successful job candidate should have. (An example of a qualification is "excellent written and verbal communication skills.") For each qualification, list experiences that demonstrate that you have the desired skills. List four to seven examples—from work, school, home, and extracurricular activities—that show you possess that qualification.

2. Which of your examples relate most directly to the qualification? Organize your examples from most important to least important. If some examples don't seem relevant, replace them with examples more closely related to the qualification. Stop when you have three solid examples for each qualification.

The Web Connection

1. Visual Organizers

   http://www.bucks.edu/~specpop/visual-org.htm

   Explanations and examples of various ways to graphically represent information are presented at this site created by Bucks County Community College.

2. How to Read a Textbook

   http://www.uwmc.uwc.edu/freshman_seminar/read.htm#how

   Visit this site to find more tips on highlighting and margin notes from the University of Wisconsin, Marathon County.

3. Concept Maps

http://www.fed.cuhk.edu.hk/~johnson/misconceptions/concept_map/concept_
maps.html

See some examples of concept maps from the biology department at the Chinese
University of Hong Kong.

Go Electronic!
For additional readings, exercises, and Internet activities, visit the Longman Study Skills
Web site at:
http://www.ablongman.com/StudySkills
If you need a user name and password, please see your instructor.

Chapter 16

Critical Analysis of Course Content

DO YOU KNOW?

How can you synthesize a number of different sources?
How do you sort subjective content from factual information?
How do you evaluate subjective content?
What critical questions can you ask to sort reliable information from unreliable information?
How can you evaluate the logic of an argument?

Textbooks and class lectures typically contain large numbers of facts, definitions, statistics, examples, dates, places, and events. It is easy to become overwhelmed by the sea of factual information. You fall into a rote learning mode, trying to absorb as much information as possible and, as a result, neglect other, more important aspects of study. In fact, many multiple-choice and essay exam questions are designed *not* to measure your factual recall, but to test your ability to think about and use what you have learned—to analyze, synthesize, evaluate, and apply course content.

In many introductory courses, you rely on your textbook as the primary source of written information. However, when you take more advanced courses, you will find yourself working with many new kinds of material: research articles, essays, critiques, reports, and analyses. To these, you will be expected to respond critically by discussing, criticizing, interpreting, and evaluating the authors' ideas. You may need to assess the accuracy and completeness of information, identify persuasive techniques, or evaluate an argument. The overall purposes of this chapter are to encourage you to pull together course content, to evaluate what you are reading and learning, to grasp implications, and to make applications.

Synthesizing Information

Many writing assignments require you to synthesize, or pull together, information from a variety of sources. Synthesis is often required for in-class assignments, essay examinations, and term papers. Synthesizing is creating something new from a number of sources. Synthesizing information is a process of examining and inferring relationships among sources and then making those relationships explicit, usually in writing. Synthesis is also a process of combining information and ideas to create or develop a new idea, focus, or perspective.

Synthesis is required in a variety of academic situations:

- ◆ Integrating text and lecture notes on the same topic
- ◆ Summarizing information from several sources
- ◆ Reading several magazine articles on the same controversial issue and discussing pros and cons
- ◆ Answering an essay exam question based on notes, lectures, and class discussion of the same topic

Here are a few more specific examples of assignments that require synthesis. Notice that each implies a thought pattern.

Mass Communications

Discuss how the use of television may have affected public opinion toward the Vietnam War. Refer to at least three sources.

Literature

Select two 20th-century American writers whose work you feel was influenced by the liberal attitudes of the 1960s. Discuss how this influence is evident in their writings.

Each of these assignments requires you to combine information or ideas to produce a unified, coherent response. Each assignment, too, focuses on a type of relationship or thought pattern. The mass communications assignment asks you to infer a cause and effect relationship between television and public opinion. The literature assignment requires comparison and contrast between two writers.

The thought patterns you learned in Chapter 12 will be useful in synthesizing information. If, for example, you are synthesizing two or more articles that explain cultural differences in the status of women in the Middle East as compared to the United States, you can expect each article to use a comparison-contrast and possibly a cause-effect pattern. The articles will contrast women's status in the two regions and possibly explain why the differences exist. One effective way to integrate the information, then, is to use patterns. You might make a comparison-contrast chart of differences and then rearrange it by grouping the differences according to categories such as public/social behavior, role in the family, dress, legal rights, and so forth. If the articles detail reasons for the differences, you might add a third column titled "Why?" or "Reasons."

The thought patterns most helpful in synthesizing are cause-effect, comparison-contrast, problem-solution, and classification. Figure 16.1 lists suggestions for using each of these four patterns to synthesize information.

Figure 16.1
Synthesizing Information Using Patterns

Pattern	Suggestions
Cause-effect	1. Is the same cause-effect relationship described in all sources?
	2. Can you construct a chain of events or happenings, each dependent on one another?
	3. How do sources differ in attributing cause or describing effects?
Comparison-contrast	1. Identify ideas that are similar. Discover points of similarity.
	2. Look for differences. Determine how and why the ideas or information differs.
	3. Draw charts outlining similarities and differences.
Problem-solution	1. Is the problem defined the same way in each source?
	2. What are the similarities and differences among solutions?
Classification	1. Organize information into broad types or categories.
	2. Look for similarities and differences among ideas. How are members of a group similar? How are they distinguishable from one another?
	3. Look for overlap among categories.
	4. List features of each category.

Exercise 16.1   Analyze the following assignment by identifying the thought pattern(s) and note-taking strategies to use in synthesizing the information:

> Using the periodical collection in the campus library, read three reports of a current national news event in *Time, U.S. News and World Report,* and one other periodical of your choice. Examine each, identifying factors such as completeness of coverage, political or social viewpoint, amount of detail. Write a one-page paper evaluating the completeness and accuracy of each source.

Recognizing and Evaluating Subjective Content

Textbooks are generally reliable, trustworthy, and accurate sources of information. You cannot assume the same for all other print materials. Many articles and essays are not written to present information clearly and directly; instead, they may be written to persuade you to accept a particular viewpoint, offer an opinion, or argue for one side of a controversial issue. Consequently, you must often recognize and separate factual information from subjective content. Subjective content is any material that involves judgment, feeling, opinion, intuition, or emotion rather than factual information. For example, "It is raining outside" is a fact. "It will rain before sundown" is a subjective statement. The second statement involves judgment, based on some evidence, while the first is verifiable.

Suppose a business management professor assigns a portion of *Iacocca: An Autobiography* in which Lee Iacocca, president of the Chrysler Corporation, describes how he attained his leadership position. In such a book you might expect to find a blend of personal experience, opinion, and reminiscence, as well as theories about and insights into corporate management strategy. Or suppose you are doing research for a term paper on the political career of former President Ronald Reagan. As you consult various sources, you will observe that some are factual, concise, and well documented, while others make general statements for which little or no support or documentation is provided. You will also encounter conflicting viewpoints on the Reagan era. Authors may also propose theories or hypotheses that explain Reagan's actions or decisions.

Recognizing and evaluating subjective content involves distinguishing between fact and opinion, identifying generalizations, evaluating viewpoints, understanding theories and hypotheses, weighing data and evidence, and being alert to bias.

Distinguishing Between Fact and Opinion

Facts are statements that can be verified—that is, proven to be true or false. *Opinions* are statements that express feelings, attitudes, or beliefs and are neither true nor false. Here are a few examples of each.

Facts:

1. Martin Luther King, Jr., was assassinated in 1968.
2. Native Americans in the Great Plains were primarily meat eaters; herds of buffalo provided their main source of food.

Opinions:

1. If John F. Kennedy had lived, the United States would have made even greater advancements against the spread of communism.
2. By the year 2025, food shortages will be a major problem in most Asian countries.

Exercise 16.2

Identify each of the following statements as either fact or opinion.

1. Between 1945 and 1990, 203,432 persons were arrested for homicide in Mexico.
2. Job orientation should begin before an employee starts to work.
3. All the states have developed laws that require hospitals and health care workers to report each incidence of communicable or infectious disease.
4. A major step in developing assertive behavior is evaluating your own strengths and weaknesses.

5. The immune deficiency in AIDS (Acquired Immune Deficiency Syndrome) results from a decreased number of certain white blood cells called T-helper lymphocytes.

6. People caught in the throes of romantic love are drawn to thoughts of marriage as moths are drawn to light.

7. The state should curtail the liberty of the individual.

8. An infection is an illness produced by the action of microorganisms in the human body.

9. Virtue is its own reward.

10. A prominent theory among biologists is that humans are by nature instinctively aggressive.

A special case within the realm of fact and opinion is that of *expert opinion* or testimony, the opinion of an authority. Dr. Ruth represents expert opinion on human sexuality, for example. Textbook authors, too, often offer expert opinion, as in the following statement from an American government text.

> Ample evidence indicates voters pay attention to economic conditions in making up their minds on election day: not only to their personal circumstances— whether they are employed or how secure their job is—but also to national economic circumstances.[1]

The author of this statement has reviewed the available evidence and is providing his expert opinion as to what the evidence indicates.

The ability to distinguish between fact and opinion is an essential part of critical thinking. Factual statements from reliable sources can be accepted and used in drawing conclusions, building arguments, and supporting ideas. As you write papers, participate in class discussions, and answer exam questions, you will use facts to support your ideas. Opinions, however, must be considered as one person's point of view that you are free to accept or reject. With the exception of expert ones, opinions have little use as supporting evidence. Still, they are useful in shaping and evaluating your own thinking. Exposure to both contradictory and supporting opinions provides background against which you can evaluate your own thinking.

A goal in many courses is to enable students to reexamine their existing beliefs, attitudes, and opinions. Expect your professors to ask challenging questions such as Why do you think so? What evidence do you have to support that opinion?

Exercise 16.3	For each of the materials listed below, discuss and predict whether it will contain primarily fact or opinion.

1. A book titled *Move Your Shadow: South Africa, Black and White*, written by Pulitzer prize-winning reporter Joseph Lelyveld, who lived in South Africa in the 1960s and again in the 1980s

Continued

2. An article titled "Advertising in the Year 2010"

3. A book titled *The Nazi Doctors: Medical Killing and the Psychology of Genocide* by Robert Lifton

4. An article in the *New England Journal of Medicine* titled "Control of Health Care Costs in the Next Decade"

5. A book titled *Secrets of Strong Families* by Nick Stinnett, which describes how to keep a family happy and together.

Evaluating Differing Viewpoints

College widens your horizons. It provides you with an opportunity to encounter new ideas and viewpoints. Some of these ideas may force you to reexamine your own values and beliefs and to reevaluate how you think about a particular issue. Within the structure of a course, an instructor may examine a controversial or current topic or issue by asking you to examine or compare differing viewpoints. A sociology professor may, for example, assign several supplementary readings, each of which takes a different stance on capital punishment. Or, in a modern fiction class, you may consider various interpretations of Kurt Vonnegut's *Slaughterhouse Five*.

In examining differing viewpoints, try the following suggestions:

◆ Deliberately put aside or suspend temporarily what you already believe about a particular issue.

◆ Discover what similarities and differences exist among the various viewpoints.

◆ Identify the assumptions on which each view is based.

◆ Look for and evaluate evidence that suggests the viewpoint is well thought out.

◆ To overcome the natural tendency to pay more attention to points of view with which you agree and treat opposing viewpoints superficially, deliberately spend more time reading, thinking about, and examining ideas that differ from your own.

◆ To analyze particularly complex, difficult, or very similar viewpoints, write a summary of each. Through the process of writing, you will be forced to discover the essence of each view.

Evaluating differing viewpoints is an essential critical thinking skill because it enables you to pull together divergent ideas and integrate differing, even contradictory, sources. The skill is valuable as you research topics, examine social and political issues, and resolve controversy.

Exercise 16.4	Determine how the three viewpoints on gun control expressed in statements 1 to 3 differ. 1. Guns don't kill people, people kill people. Gun laws do not deter criminals. (A 1976 University of Wisconsin study of gun laws concluded that "gun control laws have no individual or collective effect in reducing the rate of violent crime.") A mandatory

sentence for carrying an unlicensed gun, says Kates, would punish the "ordinary decent citizens in high-crime areas who carry guns illegally because police protection is inadequate and they don't have the special influence necessary to get a 'carry' permit." There are fifty million handguns out there in the United States already; unless you were to use a giant magnet, there is no way to retrieve them. The majority of people do not want guns banned. A ban on handguns would be like Prohibition—widely disregarded, unenforceable, and corrosive to the nation's sense of moral order. Federal registration is the beginning of federal tyranny; we might someday need to use those guns against the government.[2]

2. People kill people, but handguns make it easier. When other weapons (knives, for instance) are used, the consequences are not so often deadly. Strangling or stabbing someone takes a different degree of energy and intent than pulling a trigger. Registration will not interfere with hunting and other rifle sports but will simply exercise control over who can carry handguns. Ordinary people do not carry handguns. If a burglar has a gun in his hand, it is quite insane for you to shoot it out with him, as if you were in a quick draw contest in the Wild West. Half of all the guns used in crimes are stolen; 70% of the stolen guns are handguns. In other words, the supply of handguns used by criminals already comes to a great extent from the households these guns were supposed to protect.[3]

3. [Statement by Edward Kennedy] We all know the toll that has been taken in this nation. We all know the leaders of our public life and of the human spirit who have been lost or wounded year after year. My brother, John Kennedy, and my brother, Robert Kennedy; Medgar Evers, who died so that others could live free; Martin Luther King, the apostle of nonviolence who became the victim of violence; George Wallace, who has been paralyzed for nearly nine years; and George Moscone, the mayor of San Francisco who was killed in his office. Last year alone, we lost Allard Lowenstein, and we almost lost Vernon Jordan. Four months ago, we lost John Lennon, the gentle soul who challenged us in song to "give peace a chance." We had two attacks on President Ford and now the attack on President Reagan.[4]

Evaluating Generalizations

Each of the following statements is a generalization:

◆ College freshmen are confused and disoriented during their first week on campus.
◆ Typewriter keyboards and computer terminal keyboards are similar.
◆ The courts, especially those in large cities, are faced with far more criminal cases than they can handle.

A generalization is a statement made about a large group or class of items based on observation or experience with a portion of that group or class. By visiting campuses and observing and talking with freshman students, you could make the generalization that freshmen are confused and disoriented. However, unless you observed and talked with *every* college student, you could not be absolutely certain your generalization is

HOW DO YOU SEE IT?

"Once upon a time, there was a frozen pizza, and inside the pizza some very bad monsters lived. Their names were refined white flour, reconstituted tomato, and processed cheese. But the worst monster of all was called pepperoni!"

You can readily recognize this storyteller's subjective opinion. Write an interesting but unbiased paragraph describing the ingredients in a pizza or some other popular food.

correct. Similarly, unless you contacted each large city court, you could not be certain of the accuracy of the third statement. A generalization, then, is a reasoned statement about an entire group based on known information about part of the group. It involves a leap from observed evidence to a conclusion that is logical but unproven.

In many courses you will be expected to read and evaluate generalizations, as well as to make them yourself. Often, generalizations are followed by evidence that supports them, as in the following excerpt from a sociology text:

An act considered deviant in one time period may be considered nondeviant in another. Cigarette smoking, for example, has a long history of changing normative definitions. Nuehring and Markle (1974) note that in the United States between 1895 and 1921, fourteen states completely banned cigarette smoking and all other states except Texas passed laws regulating the sale of cigarettes to minors. In the early years of this century, stop-smoking clinics were opened in several cities and antismoking campaigns were widespread. Following World War I, however, cigarette sales increased and public attitudes toward smoking changed. Through the mass media, the tobacco industry appealed to women, weight-watchers, and even to health seekers. States began to realize that tobacco could be a rich source of revenue, and by 1927 the fourteen states that banned cigarettes had repealed their laws. By the end of World War II, smoking had become acceptable, and in many contexts it was thought socially desirable.[5]

The excerpt begins with two generalizations. The second generalization (sentence 2), which is supported throughout the remainder of the paragraph, is made in support of the first generalization, stated in the opening sentence.

Because writers do not always have the space to describe all available evidence on a topic, they often draw the evidence together themselves and make a general statement of what it shows. Generalizations that stand alone without any evidence to attest to their accuracy appear to be unsupported. The following paragraph makes numerous generalizations about the elderly.

The lifestyles of the elderly vary greatly, depending on their social class and income. Women and blacks are the groups most likely to live in poverty. The most common source of income for the aged is Social Security. A minimal income is available to those not on Social Security through the Supplemental Security Income program. Income and class level greatly influence the health of the elderly.[6]

Without supporting evidence, you cannot evaluate the accuracy of the generalizations unless you research the topic yourself. You are left to rely on the credibility of the author to make accurate generalizations. In textbooks, where the author is an authority in his or her field, credibility is seldom a problem. However, when reading other information sources, do not assume automatically that all generalizations are supportable.

In many courses, you will be required to make generalizations by applying your knowledge to related, similar situations. Generalizing is an important skill—one that makes your learning usable and relevant in a variety of situations. Here are a few instances that require you to generalize:

- Solving math problems similar to sample problems solved in class
- Summarizing your experience with part-time jobs to make a generalization about the benefits of work experience
- Applying methods you learned in child psychology to control your niece's temper tantrums

Your generalization is usable and relevant when your experiences are sufficient in number to merit a generalization.

Exercise 16.5	Indicate which of statements 1 through 10 are generalizations. Then indicate what support or documentation would be necessary for you to evaluate their worth and accuracy. 1. McDonald's is the largest owner of real estate in the world. 2. John Lennon's last book, *Skywriting by Word of Mouth,* will be hailed as a work of literature by those who appreciate brilliant, innovative writing. 3. Big money can be made in every corner of the world, including the world of legitimate drug consumption. 4. Floor space in department stores is valued at $1,000 per square foot. 5. Creative products including paintings, engineering design plans, and Monty Python skits are revised and revised again until they take final shape. 6. Intimacy is established through effective verbal communication. 7. Criminal law is divided into felonies and misdemeanors. 8. The kidney produces an enzymelike substance known as renin that raises blood pressure. 9. Quackery refers to the use of unproved or disapproved methods or devices to diagnose or treat illnesses. 10. Heroin costs the addict more than $100 a day.

Testing Hypotheses

Suppose you arrive three minutes late to your data processing class and find the classroom empty. You notice that the instructor's notes are on her desk and that most of the students have left their jackets or notebooks behind. So you form a hypothesis, a supposition to account for the observed circumstances and explain the absence of the class and instructor. You might hypothesize that the class went across the hall to the lab, for instance. A hypothesis, then, is a statement based on available evidence that explains an event or set of circumstances.

Here are a few examples of situations involving formulation of hypotheses:

◆ A nursing student is asked by her supervisor why she thinks patient X refuses to take his medication.

◆ A chemistry student must explain in her laboratory report why her experiment failed to produce expected results.

◆ A literature professor assigns a paper that requires you to develop and support a consistent theory explaining the symbolism used throughout a short story.

It is important to recognize that hypotheses are simply *plausible* explanations. They are always open to dispute or refutation, usually by the addition of further information. Or their plausibility may be enhanced by the addition of further information.

As you read textbook assignments, participate in class discussions, and conduct library research, you will frequently encounter hypotheses. In a political science course, for example, you might be asked to evaluate a theory or hypothesis that ex-

plains Stalin's popularity in Russia after Lenin's death. Or in a business and finance course, a class discussion may center on theories by Keynes and Friedman that explain why people choose to hold on to and not spend money. As a critical reader, you must assess the plausibility of each hypothesis. This is a two-part process. First, you must evaluate the evidence provided. Then you must search for information, reasons, or evidence that suggests the truth or falsity of the hypothesis. Ask questions such as these:

◆ Does my hypothesis account for all known information about the situation?
◆ Is it realistic—that is, within the realm of possibility and probability?
◆ Is it simple, or less complicated than, its alternatives? (Usually, unless a complex hypothesis can account for information not accounted for by a simple hypothesis, the simple one has greater likelihood of being correct.)
◆ What assumptions were made? Are they valid?

Exercise 16.6	Develop hypotheses to explain each of situations 1 through 3.

1. Bill Cosby's book *Fatherhood* appeared on the *New York Times* best-seller list for several months.

2. McDonald's has expanded its operations to numerous foreign countries. It has become England's largest food service organization.

3. There has been a recent increase in the number of children per couple in the United States.

Weighing the Adequacy of Data and Evidence

Many writers who express their opinions, state viewpoints, make generalizations, or offer hypotheses also provide data or evidence in support of their ideas. Your task as a critical reader is to weigh and evaluate the quality of this evidence. You must look behind the available evidence and assess its type and adequacy.

In assessing the adequacy of evidence, you must be concerned with two factors: the type of evidence being presented and the relevance of that evidence. The following can be considered evidence:

- ◆ Personal experience or observation
- ◆ Statistical data
- ◆ Examples, particular events, or situations that illustrate
- ◆ Analogies (comparisons with similar situations)
- ◆ Informed opinion (the opinions of experts and authorities)
- ◆ Historical documentation
- ◆ Experimental evidence

Each type of evidence must be weighed in relation to the statement it supports. Evidence should directly, clearly, and indisputably support the case or issue in question.

Here are a few examples of situations that would require you to assess the adequacy of evidence:

- ◆ In an exam you are asked to write an essay to defend or criticize President Clinton's decision of the United States taking military action against Iraq.
- ◆ For a business retailing class you are asked to evaluate three interior store design proposals and rationales submitted by three contractors and recommend the best in terms of sales productivity.
- ◆ For a nursing course you are required to criticize three alternate nursing plans for the care of a patient whose postsurgical condition you just viewed on videotape.

Exercise 16.7   Indicate the type(s) of evidence that would be appropriate to support each of the following assignments.

1. An editorial in a community college campus newspaper opposing the building of a rifle range for training local police cadets

2. A term paper for a business management course on theories of leadership

3. An essay exam response to the following question: Discuss whether public financing of campaigns should be extended to include congressional candidates

4. A critique of a film shown in a criminal justice course

5. A psychology class assignment to visit the snack bar to monitor and observe body language in a student conversation for 10 minutes

---

Asking Critical Questions

Suppose you received a phone call from someone saying you had just won a new car, and all you need do is pay a $200 claim fee to take ownership. Would you immediately write a check, or would you be suspicious and question the caller? Perhaps you would hang up, knowing it couldn't be true. As consumers we tend to be wise, alert, and critical—even suspicious. As readers, however, we tend to be much more tolerant and accepting. Many readers readily accept information and ideas presented in written form. This section of the chapter suggests questions that will help you become a more critical reader and thinker.

What Is the Source of the Material?

Determine from what book, magazine, reference book, or newspaper the material you are reading was taken. Some sources are much more reliable and trustworthy than others; knowledge of the source will help you judge the accuracy, correctness, and soundness of the material. For example, in which of the following sources would you expect to find the most accurate and up-to-date information about word processing software?

◆ An advertisement in *Business Week*
◆ An article in *Mademoiselle*
◆ An article in *Software Review*

The best source would be *Software Review,* a periodical devoted to the subject of computers and computer software. *Mademoiselle* magazine does not specialize in technical information, and the advertisement in *Business Week* is likely to present only the advantages of a particular brand of software.

Suppose you were conducting research for a term paper on the effects of aging on learning and memory. Articles from professional or scholarly journals, such as the *Journal of Psychology,* would be more useful and reliable than articles in newsstand periodicals.

To evaluate a source consider the following:

◆ Its reputation
◆ The audience for whom the source is intended
◆ Whether references or documentation are provided

What Are the Author's Credentials?

Not everything that appears in print is accurate and competently reported. Also, there are varying levels of expertise within a field. Consequently, you must assess whether the material you are reading is written by an expert in the field who can knowledgeably and accurately discuss the topic. In some materials, the author's credentials are footnoted or summarized at the end of the work. In journal articles, the author's college or university affiliation is often included. Authors also may establish their expertise or experience in the field within the material itself.

Why Was the Material Written?

As you read, try to determine why the author wrote the material. In textbooks, the author's primary purpose is to inform (present information). However, other material may be written to entertain, amuse, or persuade. If the author's purpose is to persuade or convince you to accept a particular viewpoint or take a specific action (such as to vote against an issue), then you will need to evaluate the reasoning and evidence presented.

Is the Author Biased?

Read each of the following statements and determine what they have in common:

◆ How can a sportsman, solely for his own pleasure, delight in the mutilation of a living animal?
◆ Laboratory experiments using live animals are forms of torture.
◆ The current vitamin fad is a distortion of sound medical advice.

Each statement reflects a *bias*—a partiality, preference, or prejudice for or against a person, object, or idea.

Much of what you read and hear expresses a bias. In many newspapers and magazine articles, nonfiction books, advertisements, and essays you will find the attitudes, opinions, and beliefs of the speaker or author revealed. As you listen to a history lecture, for example, you may discover the professor's attitude or bias toward particular historical figures, political decisions, or events. As you read biased material, keep two questions in mind: What facts has the author omitted? What additional information is necessary?

Some writers reveal their attitudes directly by stating how they feel. Others do so less directly, expressing their attitudes through the manner in which they write. Through selection of facts, choice of words, and the quality and tone of description, they convey a particular feeling or attitude.

Biased material is one-sided. Other facts, such as the advantages of using animals for laboratory research, or research that has confirmed the value of taking vitamins, are not mentioned. Notice, too, the use of emotional words such as "mutilation" and "torture."

As you read or listen to biased materials, keep the following questions in mind:

◆ What facts were omitted? What additional facts are needed?
◆ What words create positive or negative impressions?
◆ What impression would I have if different words had been used?

**Exercise
16.8**

In each of the following statements, underline the words and phrases that reveal the writer's bias. Indicate what additional information you would need to evaluate each.

1. Now you can have room and comfort as well as a world-class road car for under $10,000.

2. The country has wasted a lot of money on purposeless space exploration.

3. The drunken behavior of sports fans at play-off games is a disgrace and insult to players and fans alike.

4. Shakespeare exhibited creative genius far beyond his contemporary playwrights by revealing insights into human behavior and its motivation.

5. Highgate University offers competitive, athletic opportunities in football and basketball; its focus on academic excellence is unyielding; its emphasis on scholarship, outstanding; its commitment to equal opportunity, admirable.

Does the Author Make Assumptions?

An assumption is an idea or principle the writer accepts as true and makes no effort to prove or substantiate. Usually, it is a beginning or premise upon which he or she bases the remainder of the work. For example, an author may assume that television encourages violent behavior in children and proceed to argue for restrictions on watching TV. Or a writer may assume that abortion is morally wrong and suggest legal restrictions on how and when abortions are performed.

Does the Author Present an Argument?

An argument is a logical arrangement and presentation of ideas. An argument addresses an issue and takes a position or makes a claim. The writer supports his or her position by offering reasons and supporting evidence. It is reasoned analysis, a tightly developed line of reasoning. Arguments are usually developed to persuade the reader to accept the claim or take a particular action. You will encounter arguments in various forms in various types of courses. Here are a few examples:

◆ An astronomy professor argues that extraterrestrial life is a statistical probability.
◆ An editorial in the college newspaper proposes that all grades be eliminated for first-semester freshmen.
◆ A supplementary reading assignment for a political science course argues that terrorism is a necessary and unavoidable outgrowth of world politics.

Analyzing arguments is a complex and detailed process to which major portions of courses in logic are devoted. As a starting point, you might use the following guidelines as you encounter and analyze arguments:

◆ Analyze the argument by simplifying it. Reduce it to a list of statements or draw a map.
◆ What is the issue?
◆ What is the claim?
◆ What reasons are offered in support of the claim?
◆ What types of evidence support each reason?
◆ Are the terms used clearly defined and consistently applied?
◆ Is the reasoning sound? (Does one point follow from another?)

◆ Are counterarguments recognized and refuted or addressed?
◆ What persuasive devices or emotional appeals does the author use (examples: appeal to sense of patriotism, appeal to authority)?

Exercise 16.9

Analyze each of the following arguments by identifying the issue, the claim, and the reason(s) offered in support of the claim.

1. Capital punishment deters crime. It also makes certain that the killer will never commit another crime. Therefore, capital punishment should be widely and consistently applied.

2. Voluntary euthanasia, permitting a person to elect to die, should never be legalized. First of all, our religious and cultural traditions and principles oppose it. Also, providing a terminally ill patient with the option to make a death decision adds to the person's pain and anguish. Finally, death decisions are irreversible, and we all have heard of cases in which unexpected, miraculous recoveries occur.

3. Sex education classes in public schools should be banned. They create interest in sex where it did not previously exist. Further, they encourage sexual deviance by making everything about sex seem natural. Also, these filthy classes detract from parental authority and autonomy.

4. Once the emotionalism surrounding abortion is lessened, and abortion is examined in a rational manner, it would seem apparent that abortion can be morally justifiable. Prior to the time of viability, the mother's right to autonomy and self-determination about her own body supersedes the rights of an unborn, potential human being.[7]

Thinking Critically
. . . About Arguments

While an argument is a reasoned presentation of facts, it does require close scrutiny and evaluation by the reader. Most importantly, you must evaluate the author's logic. You must also be alert for persuasive techniques he or she may use and for errors in reasoning he or she may make. Here are a few questions to ask:

1. **Is circular reasoning used?** Circular reasoning occurs when an author supports a conclusion by giving a reason that says the same thing. Here is an example of circular reasoning. Conclusion: Gun control legislation needs serious and drastic revision. Supporting Reason: Our country cannot afford to continue without legislative revisions. Notice that this writer did *not* answer the question "Why is revision needed?"

2. **Does the author make emotional appeals?** Writers often attempt to appeal to the readers' emotions in order to persuade them to accept a conclusion. For ex-

ample, an author may argue against animal fur coats by describing an animal's face or behavior.

3. **Does the author use testimonials?** An author may argue in part that a conclusion is correct because a famous or well-known person endorses it. For example, a writer may cite a former U.S. senator's opinion on cancer research. However, unless the famous person is an authority on the issue at hand, the person's endorsement is not relevant to the argument. Unless the U.S. senator is an expert on cancer research, his opinion is not relevant.

4. **Does the author assume false cause?** This reasoning error occurs when one incorrectly assumes that two events are causally related just because they follow each other in time. If a drop in unemployment occurs immediately following a mayor's election, for example, a writer may attribute the decrease to the mayor's election. Unless the mayor took specific action to create jobs, the two events, although close in time, may be unrelated.

Interactive Chapter Review

Knowledge	What are four thought patterns useful in synthesizing a number of different sources?
Comprehension	Are generalizations always logical opinions?
Application	Get a copy of your campus or local newspaper and choose a news story to read. Referring to the list of types of evidence on p. 334, make a list of each piece of evidence the writer uses, and label it according to type.
Analysis	Generalize from your experiences on campus in each of the following areas: (a) friendliness of library staff, (b) ease of course registration, (c) availability of computers for word processing, (d) interactions with fellow students. Now examine each generalization. How many specific situations did you consider before deciding you had enough information to make the generalization? Would that number of examples convince someone else your generalization is accurate? Find out by asking a friend or classmate.
Synthesis	Use any relevant patterns of thought from Figure 16.1 on p. 325 to synthesize your textbook and lecture notes for the last two weeks' worth of classes and assignments from one course. When you are finished organizing the information, reread your synthesis. What do you discover that you hadn't realized before? What new questions do you have?
Evaluation	Is it important to reexamine your own values and beliefs? Why or why not? What benefits result in either case? Write a statement about the value or lack of value of reexamining values and beliefs, and support it with reasons and evidence from your experiences.

Working Together

Each student should write a one-page response to the following assignment.
Assignment: Agree or disagree with the following statement:
Any person on welfare for more than a year lacks motivation and initiative.
Working in pairs, students should complete each of the following steps:

1. Students should exchange and read each other's papers.

2. Students should identify or evaluate the paper using the following questions:

    a. Does the writer express opinions?
    b. Does the writer's viewpoint differ from your own? If so, how can you objectively evaluate the viewpoint?
    c. Does the writer make generalizations? If so, highlight them.
    d. What types of evidence does the writer provide to support his or her ideas?
    e. Is the writer biased?
    f. Evaluate the writer's argument. Is it logical and consistent?

Further Analysis

Analyze the following situation and answer the questions below.

An English instructor gave his class the following assignment:

Locate three articles on a current controversial issue. One of the three must express a different viewpoint from the other two. Write a two-page paper that critically evaluates each article.

One student in the class located three articles on censorship but did not know how to approach the assignment. He summarized each article and then wrote a paragraph describing how one article differed from the other two. The instructor refused to accept and grade this student's paper, saying that he had not completed the assignment.

1. Why was the student's paper unacceptable?

2. How should he have approached the assignment?

3. On what bases or using what criteria might the student have evaluated the articles?

Discussion

1. Critical analysis involves evaluation and judgment. What occupations and professions rely heavily upon these skills? Should courses in critical thinking be required for degrees in these fields?

2. Select an editorial from your local or campus newspaper. Analyze it carefully, answering the following questions:

a. Is the article primarily fact or opinion?

b, What types of evidence, if any, does the author use to support his or her position?

c. Identify any generalizations.

d. Identify instances of bias.

e. Evaluate the writer's argument.

f. What alternative viewpoints could be taken on this subject?

The Work Connection

Your ability to organize, synthesize, and evaluate information will assist you in diverse ways throughout your entire life, whether you are choosing which field to major in, which car to buy, or which health insurance to select. Any complex decision requires knowing how pieces of information relate to one another. Choosing a career that you will enjoy involves making multiple decisions based on any number of variables. You can practice your skills of synthesizing and evaluating while doing career-related research on the World Wide Web. Try the following steps.

1. Go to the three Web sites listed below:

"Career Development Manual" by Marlene Bryan at the University of Waterloo. Its Internet address, or URL, is:

http://www.adm.uwaterloo.ca/infocecs/CRC/manual-home.html

"Conducting an Effective Job Search" at the Career Resource Home page at Rensselaer Polytechnic Institute. URL:

http://www.cdc.rpi.edu/Calendar_Workshops/jobsearch.html

"Career Planning Process" by Pam Allen and Ellen Nagy at Bowling Green State University. URL:

http://www.bgsu.edu/offices/sa/career/process/index.html

2. Read and compare the information about self-assessment (assessing your skills, values, and interests). Take notes or make maps about the self-assessment information at each site. Then synthesize the information in a paragraph or two so that you will remember the information that seems most important to you.

The Web Connection

1. Try these online "Fact or Opinion" quizzes:

http://cuip.uchicago.edu/www4teach/97/jlyman/default/quiz/factopquiz.html

http://dhp.com/~laflemm/RfT/Tut2.htm

2. Charts and Graphs

   http://www.kcmetro.cc.mo.us/longview/ctac/GRAPHS.HTM

   From Longview Community College, this site explains how charts and graphs can be used to distort the truth.

3. Critically Analyzing Information Sources

   http://www.library.cornell.edu/okuref/research/skill26.htm

   This site from the Cornell University Library provides a well-organized, clear overview of evaluation techniques.

Go Electronic!
For additional readings, exercises, and Internet activities, visit the Longman Study Skills
Web site at:
http://www.ablongman.com/StudySkills
If you need a user name and password, please see your instructor.

PART FIVE

Chapter 17

Preparing for Exams

DO YOU KNOW?

How do you organize your review so you will do your best on exams?
What is thematic study, and why is it effective?
What are helpful study strategies for particular types of exams?
What kinds of study strategies can you use in specific academic disciplines?
How can you control test anxiety?

Quizzes, midterm examinations, and finals are important aspects of most college courses. Practically, they are often the basis on which grades are awarded. However, they are also valuable thinking and learning experiences. Quizzes or frequent tests force you to keep up with reading and assignments and provide regular feedback on the quality of your learning. Longer examinations require you to consolidate and integrate concepts and information. Final exams force you to step back and retrace the direction of the course, noticing overall trends and patterns and integrating your learning.

Many students spend a great deal of time preparing for an exam, yet never seem to earn top grades. Some report that they spend more time studying than students who do earn the highest grades. Grades, however, have little to do with the *amount* of time spent studying. What is important is *how* study time is spent. The strategies and techniques you use to prepare for an exam primarily determine the quality of your learning. The purpose of this chapter is to show you how to prepare for exams and earn the largest dividends for the time you spend.

Organizing Your Review

The following suggestions will help you approach your study in an organized, systematic manner.

343

Organize Your Time

The amount of time you will need to spend is determined by your familiarity with the material and the amount of material the exam covers. In general, the longer the interval between exams, the longer you will need to spend in preparation. Organize your review sessions, using the following suggestions:

Review at least one week in advance of the exam.   Set aside specific times for daily review. If the exam is in a difficult or troublesome subject, schedule extra study time.

Spend time organizing your review.   Make a list of all chapters, notes, and instructor's handouts that need to be reviewed. Divide the material by topic, planning what you will review during each session (see Thematic Study, p. 346).

Review again the night before the exam.   Reserve time the night before the examination for a final, complete review. Do not study new material during the session. Instead, review the most difficult material, testing your recall of important facts or information for possible essay questions.

Attend the Class Before the Exam

Be sure to attend the class prior to the exam. Cutting class to spend the time studying, although tempting, is a mistake. During this class, the instructor may give a brief review of the material to be covered or offer last-minute review suggestions. Have you heard instructors make statements such as, "Be sure to look over . . ." or "Pay particular attention to . . ." prior to exams? Listen carefully to the instructor's answers to students' questions: These answers may provide clues about what the exam will emphasize.

Find out whether the examination will be objective, essay, or a combination of both. Also check your notes from the first several classes; some instructors describe their exams as part of their course introduction. If your instructor does not specify the type of exam, ask during or after class.

Find out as much as possible about what the examination will cover. Usually, your instructor will either announce the exam topics or specify the time span that the exam will cover. Some instructors expect you to recall text and lecture material; others expect you to summarize using their perspective on a particular subject; still others encourage you to think, discuss, recall, and disagree with the ideas and information they have presented. You can usually tell what to expect from quizzes and how classes have been conducted.

Attend Review Classes

For final exams, particularly in mathematics or the sciences, professors occasionally offer optional review sessions. Be sure to attend these sessions: Time spent there is likely to be more productive than time spent studying alone.

Exercise 17.1	Plan a review schedule for an upcoming exam. Include material you will study and when you will study it.

Identify What to Study

In preparing for an exam, use all sources of information, as shown in Table 17.1.

Assess Your Preparedness

Once you have collected and briefly looked over the materials listed in Table 17.1, you can establish how well prepared you are and how much review and study time is necessary. If you are not caught up in your reading, highlighting, and homework assignments, make a list of what you have to do. Using this list, decide how to spend the first portion of your remaining study time. Try to get caught up as quickly as possible; double or triple your efforts to do so. Keep in mind that this is work you should have completed by now and, at this point, it is diminishing the time you have left for review.

Table 17.1
Review Strategies

Type of Material	Suggestions for Review
Textbook chapters	Reread highlighting and marking. Review chapter summary. Use your outlines, notes, summaries, or maps.
Lecture notes	Reread and mark important information. Use recall clues to self-test.
Supplementary assignments	Review purpose and relationship to course content. Review highlighting or summary notes.
Previous tests and quizzes	Mark all items you missed and look for a pattern of error. Identify types of questions you miss. Identify topics you need to study further. (See Thinking Critically About Returned Exams, p. 397.)
Instructor's handouts and class assignments	Note purpose of each item and to which lecture they correspond. Identify key points emphasized.

Also try to identify your strengths and weaknesses. Identify topics for which you feel unprepared and lack confidence as well as those that you have mastered thoroughly. For example, a student taking Western civilization identified several topics in history that she felt were her weakest: the Protestant Reformation, exploration and colonization, and absolutism. Then she concentrated on these periods, organizing and consolidating events and trends for each.

Thinking Critically
. . . About Group Study

Studying with friends or classmates is an option that you should weigh seriously. Some students find it highly effective; others report that it is time consuming and does not produce results. Use the following questions to decide whether group study would be effective for you:

1. Will group study force me to become more actively involved with the course content?

2. Will talking about, reacting to, and discussing the material help me learn?

3. Can I learn by explaining ideas to someone else? Does explaining an idea force me to think and test my own understanding?

4. What are the strengths of my learning style as discovered in Chapter 8? Am I strong in auditory or social learning, for example?

5. Can I prevent group study sessions from turning into social events where very little study occurs?

6. Can I avoid studying with the wrong people—those who spread negative attitudes? (The "None of us understands this and we can't all fail" attitude, for example?)

7. Can I avoid studying with poorly prepared students—those who have not read the material carefully or attended class regularly?

Exercise 17.2	For an upcoming exam, assess how well you are prepared by making a list of topics about which you feel confident and another list of those that will require further study.

Thematic Study

Most students approach their study and review for exams in convenient but arbitrary units. During a study session, they may review a specific number of pages or a given number of lecture notes. While this approach is systematic, it is not the most conducive to learning. A more meaningful approach is to integrate text and lecture material using a method called *thematic study*.

In thematic study, you focus on topics, or themes, rather than on an arbitrarily chosen number of pages or chapters. You pull together all available material on a given topic and learn it as an organized body of information. In essence, thematic study means studying by topic. For instance, for a macroeconomics test, a student's topics included aggregate demand and aggregate supply, real and nominal GNP, and indexes to measure price changes.

Why Thematic Study Is Effective

Thematic study forces you to think in the following ways:

◆ It forces you to decide what topics are important, to sift and sort and make decisions about course content.
◆ It forces you to integrate information, recognize similarities, and reconcile differences in approach and focus between text and lecture.
◆ It forces you to organize the information from a variety of sources into a meaningful set.
◆ It forces you to practice the skills that you are required to use when you take exams. Exams require you to draw upon information from all sources. Thematic study forces you to do this in advance; consequently, you are better prepared when you take an exam.

Selecting Themes

The key to selecting worthwhile, important themes is your ability to grasp an overview of the course and understand how and where specific pieces of information fit into the big picture. To get an overview of the course, try the following suggestions:

Think about how and why the material was covered in the order it was presented.   How does one class lecture relate to the next? To what larger theme are the lectures connected? For class lectures, check the course outline or syllabus that was distributed at the beginning of the course. Since it lists major topics and suggests the order in which they will be covered, your syllabus will be useful in discovering patterns.

Focus on the progression of ideas in the textbook.   Study the table of contents to see the connection among chapters you have read. Often, chapters are grouped into sections based on similar content.

Study relationships.   Ask yourself: "Where is the information presented in this chapter leading?" and "How does this chapter relate to the next?" Suppose in psychology you had studied a chapter on personality traits; next, you were assigned a chapter on abnormal and deviant behavior. In this situation, the chapter on personality establishes the standard or norm by which abnormal and deviant behavior are determined.

Do not let facts and details camouflage important questions, issues, and problems. Remember to ask yourself, "What does this mean? How is this information useful?

How can this be applied to various situations?" Once you have identified the literal content, stop, react, and evaluate its use, value, and application.

Identify predominant thought patterns.   Evident in both text and lecture material are patterns that point directly to key topics. For instance, in chemistry, a student identified problem-solution as a key pattern; then he made a list of types of problems and systematically reviewed and practiced solving each type.

Exercise 17.3	Assume you were to have an examination based on the first four chapters of this book. List the major topics you would review during thematic study.

Exercise 17.4	For an upcoming exam in one of your courses, identify several topics for thematic study.

How to Prepare Study Sheets

The study sheet system is a way of organizing and summarizing complex information by preparing mini-outlines on each topic. It is most useful for reviewing material that is interrelated and needs to be learned as a whole rather than as separate facts. Several types of information should be reviewed on study sheets:

- ◆ Theories and principles
- ◆ Complex events with multiple causes and effects
- ◆ Controversial issues—pros and cons
- ◆ Summaries of philosophical issues
- ◆ Trends in ideas or data
- ◆ Groups of related facts

The sample study sheet in Figure 17.1 was made by a student preparing for an exam in a communications media course. You will notice that the study sheet organizes the advantages and disadvantages of the various types of media advertising and presents them in a form that invites easy comparison of the various media types.

To prepare a study sheet, first select the information to be learned. Then outline the information, using as few words as possible. Group together important points, from both your text and lecture notes, that relate to each topic. Try to use one or more thought patterns as a means of organization.

The computer is an excellent aid to thematic study. If, as suggested in Chapter 15, you are able to type both your textbook and lecture notes into a computer file, then the preparation of study sheets is easily done. Using the word processor's copy function, you can compile information from various sets of text and lecture notes on a given topic.

Exercise 17.5	Prepare a study sheet for one of the themes you identified in Exercise 17.3.

Figure 17.1

A Sample Study Sheet

Forms of Media Advertising

Media form	Advantages	Disadvantages
1. Newspapers	- widely read - regional flexibility - offer use of inserts	- little buyer selectivity
2. Magazines	- better appearance than newspapers - longer life - people do reread	- advance commitment required - may have to buy entire national circulation
3. TV	- reaches 95% of households - can produce favorable product images - can choose stations to carry the ad	- commercial clutter (must compete with other ads)
4. Radio	- inexpensive - can afford high level of repetition - geographic selectivity - can change ads frequently and easily	- short lived (can't reread) - people don't listen to the ads
5. Outdoor Advertising	- large amount of repetition - low cost per exposure	- copy must be short

Review Strategies

Once you have developed study sheets, the next step is to develop effective review strategies. Many students review by rereading their notes and text highlighting. Rereading is a passive, inactive approach that seldom prepares you well for any exam. Instead, review for an exam should be a dress rehearsal for the exam itself. Think of a theater company preparing to perform a play. In rehearsal they simulate, as closely as possible, the conditions of their actual performance. Likewise, in preparing for an exam you should simulate the actual exam situation. You must, in effect, test yourself by asking questions and answering them. Since the exam is written, it is helpful to *write,* not just to mentally construct, answers.

Asking the Right Questions

As you review, be sure to ask questions at each level of thinking, especially those at the critical thinking levels of application, analysis, synthesis, and evaluation. Refer to Chapter 2 for a review of each of these levels. Refer to Table 17.2 for sample questions you could ask at each level if you were preparing for an exam on the media advertising material covered in Figure 17.1.

Knowledge and Comprehension Questions.   These levels require recall of facts; remembering dates, names, definitions, and formulas falls into these categories. The five "W" questions—Who? What? Where? When? and Why?—are useful to ask.

Application Questions.   This level of thinking requires you to use or apply information. The two following questions best test this level:

◆   In what practical situations would this information be useful?
◆   What does this have to do with what I already know about the subject?

Table 17.2

Sample Questions Based on the Study Sheet in Figure 17.1

Level of Thinking	Sample Questions
Knowledge and comprehension	What percentage of households does TV reach?
	Which media offer regional flexibility?
Application	What types of products could be most effectively advertised in each media form?
Analysis	Why don't people listen to the ads on the radio?
Synthesis	What are the similarities between radio and newspaper advertising?
Evaluation	How did the author decide what is low cost?

Analysis Questions.   Analysis involves seeing relationships. Ask questions that test your ability to take ideas apart, discover cause-effect relationships, and discover how things work.

Synthesis Questions.   This level involves pulling ideas together. Ask questions that force you to look at similarities and differences.

Evaluation Questions.   This level involves making judgments and assessing value or worth. Ask questions that challenge sources, accuracy, long-term value, importance, and so forth.

How to Test Yourself

To test yourself, follow these steps.

- Review each study sheet several times, asking questions at the various levels of thinking.
- As you find information that is difficult, unclear, or unfamiliar, mark it for later reference and further study.
- Jot appropriate questions in the margin or on the back of the study sheet. You may wish to refer to these as you predict questions for essay exams (see p. 354).
- Write answers to each of your questions. The process of formulating a written response clarifies your thinking and helps you learn the information.
- Critique your answers. First verify the correctness and completeness of factual information. Then analyze and think about your response. Did you really answer the questions? What related information might you have included? What are the implications of what you have said?
- Review both questions and answers periodically.

Some students find it useful to write their questions using a computer. Each question is entered in a test preparation file, and answers are typed on a separate line below. Some information can be copied from lecture and/or textual note files to save time. Review of questions and answers is simple using the scroll function. You can position each question at the bottom of the screen, without the answer showing. Then test your recall by writing the answer (on paper) or through mental review. Finally, to check your recall, scroll ahead to review the answer.

| **Exercise 17.6** | Choose a textbook chapter on which you are currently working. Write questions at each level for several main topics covered. |

Strategies for Particular Types of Exams

While basic study and review strategies are the same for all types of examinations, there are specific techniques to use as you prepare for objective exams, essay exams, open-book exams, take-home exams, problem-solution exams, and final exams.

Preparing for Objective Exams

Objective exams are those that require a brief right or wrong answer. These include multiple choice, true/false, matching, and fill-in-the-blank.

Objective tests often require mastery of a great deal of factual data—information at the knowledge and comprehension levels. Often, too, test items require you to apply, analyze, synthesize, and evaluate these facts. An effective way to prepare for an exam in which a large amount of factual learning is required is to use an index card system.

Using Index Cards

Step 1. Using 3-x-5-inch index cards (or small sheets of paper), write names of terms, laws, principles, or concepts on the front of the card and facts and details about them on the back. To review the significance of important events in a history course, for example, write the event on the front of one card and its importance on the back. To learn definitions, record the word on the front and its meaning on the back. The sample index cards shown in Figure 17.2 were prepared for an economics examination.

Step 2. To study each of these cards, look at the front and try to recall what is written on the back. Then, turn the card over to see if you were correct. As you work, sort them into two stacks—those you know and those you cannot remember.

Step 3. Go back through the stack that you did not know, study each, and retest yourself, again sorting the cards into two stacks. Continue with this procedure until you are satisfied that you have learned all the information. Review the index cards several times a day on each of the three or four days before the exam. On the day of the exam, do a final, once-through review so that the information is fresh in your mind.

This index card system has several advantages. Writing helps you learn, so preparing the cards is also a learning process. You spend time learning what you do not know and avoid wasting time reviewing already learned material. Cards are more effective than lists of material. If you study a list of items, you run the risk of learning them in a fixed order. When a single item appears out of order on the exam, you may not remember it. Sorting and occasionally shuffling your index cards eliminates this problem. You can carry cards in a pocket or purse and study them in spare moments.

| Exercise 17.7 | Choose a course in which you expect to take an objective examination. Prepare a set of index cards for one chapter you have studied. |

Figure 17.2
Sample Index Cards

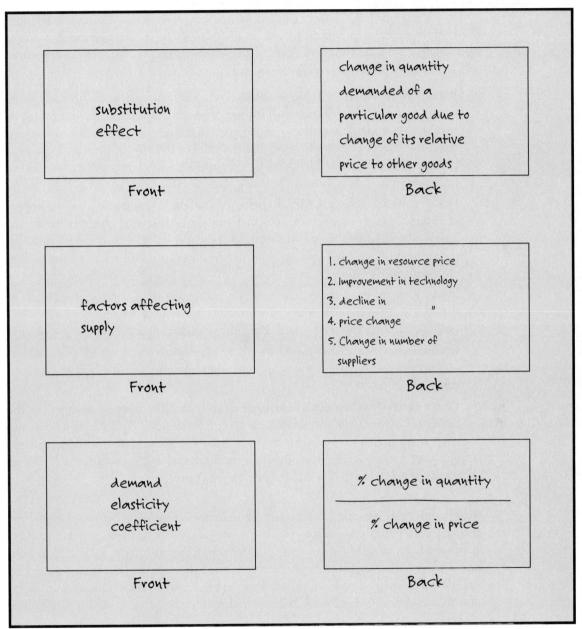

Preparing for Essay Examinations

Essay examinations demand complete recall; you begin with a blank sheet of paper on which you must answer the question. Reviewing for an essay exam is a process of concentrated thematic study.

Predict possible questions.   You have already learned how to identify important themes or topics. The next step is to formulate actual questions that might be asked about each theme. Predicting essay questions is a process of analyzing the relationships that exist within the material (see Chapter 12) and writing questions that concern these relationships. As you predict questions, be sure to include all course material; avoid trying to second-guess the instructor as to the content of the exam. The following suggestions will assist you in predicting possible essay questions:

1. **Reread your course syllabus or objectives.** These are often distributed on the first day of class, and the major headings or objectives refer to the important issues. For example, a sociology course objective might be "Students will understand the concept of socialization and the roles of the family, peer, and reference groups." This objective identifies the key topic and suggests what you need to know about it.

2. **Study your textbook's table of contents and the organization of individual chapters.** Notice important topics that run through several chapters. In a marketing textbook, you might discover that chapters on the impact of technology, federal regulations, and consumer-protection legislation all relate to the market environment.

3. **Study your notes.** Identify lecture topics and group them into larger subjects or themes. In a psychology course, for example, individual lectures on retardation, creativity, and IQ could be grouped together under mental abilities.

4. **Evaluate previous exams to see what key ideas were emphasized.** For example, in a history course you may find on each exam questions on the historical significance of events.

5. **Listen carefully when your instructor announces, discusses, or reviews for the exam.** He or she is likely to reveal important information. Make detailed notes and study them later. Your biology instructor might say, "Be sure to review the structure of plants, as well as their reproduction, development, and growth cycles." This remark indicates that these topics will be on the exam.

Write rough draft answers.   Once you have identified possible exam questions, the next step is to practice answering them. Do not take the time to write out full, complete sentences. Instead collect and organize the information you would include in your answer and record it in brief note or outline form, listing the ideas you would include. Form these ideas from information in your textbook and class notes that relates to the question. Figure 17.3 shows a sample essay question and a rough draft answer.

Use key word outlines.   As a convenient way to remember what your draft answer includes, make a key word outline of your answer. For each idea in your draft, identify a key word that will trigger your memory of that idea. Then list and learn these key words. Together, these words form a mini-outline of topics and ideas to include in an essay on this topic. A key word outline is shown in Figure 17.4 on p. 356.

Figure 17.3

Sample Essay Question and Answer

Question: Discuss the organized social life of monkeys and apes.

Rough draft response:

Social Structure developed for following advantages:
- group can spot predators & rally a defense
- foraging for food is more efficient if done in groups
- access to opposite sex is assured for reproduction
- groups permit socialization and learning from elders

Social structure organized according to following principles
- infants and young are dependent on mother
  longer than most animals
  allows for learned behavior to occur
  " " juvenile play - imp't for
    social bonds as adults
- adults hold social rank in group
  males dominate
  hierarchy often more significant among
    males than females

Sexual bonding occurs among mating adults
- breeding occurs only during specific seasons
- males are aware of estrous cycle of female

Grooming - acceptable form of social contact
- functions 1. remove parasites
             2. establish and maintain social relationships

Predicting and answering possible examination questions is an effective technique for several reasons. Predicting forces you to analyze the material, not just review it. Drafting answers forces you to express ideas in written form. Through writing you will realize relationships, organize your thoughts, and discover the best way to present them.

Figure 17.4

Sample Key Word Outline

> Advantages
>   Defense
>   Food
>   Reproduction
>   Learning
> Principles
>   Dependency
>   Social Rank
>   Sexual Bonding
>   Grooming

You will save time while taking the exam. If you have already collected and organized your thoughts, then you can use the time those processes would have taken to prepare a more complete, carefully written answer.

The computer is a useful tool for predicting and answering essay exam questions. The word-processing function enables you to rearrange information, thereby experimenting with various means of organizing and consolidating it. The various typographic features (boldfaced print, italics, underlining) enable you to add visually striking (and easy to remember) points of emphasis. For example, you might highlight key points or place key words in boldfaced print.

Exercise 17.8	Select a course in which you expect to have an essay examination or an essay question on your next exam. Predict and record possible essay questions. Then choose one question and prepare a rough draft answer and key word outline.

Preparing for Open-Book Exams

Open-book exams are those that allow you to refer to your textbook or lecture notes during the exam. At first, this type of exam may seem easy, almost a giveaway. Some students make the mistake of doing little or no preparation. Actually, an open-book exam is often an essay exam in which the instructor will assess your ability to interpret, evaluate, react to, or apply a given body of information. The focus is on your ability to think about and use available information.

Organization of information is the key to preparing for open-book exams. Time is usually limited and often a key factor in taking an open-book exam. If you have to waste time on an exam searching for a piece of information, it can affect the quality of your answer. Study sheets (see pp. 348–351) are effective because they draw together and organize information by topic. One useful addition to your study sheets is page references, from both your texts and lecture notes, allowing you to check your source for information on a particular topic, if needed.

Preparing for Take-Home Exams

Take-home exams are a variation of the open-book exam. However, instead of requiring you to complete the exam within a specific class time, the instructor allows you to leave the classroom and work on it for a specified period of time, usually several days. Usually, more extensive, complete answers are expected. Some instructors may expect research as well. A more carefully written, concise, and clear response is expected than for in-class writing. Be sure at the time the exam is distributed to clarify, as best you can, what is expected in terms of length, sources to be used, and format. If the exam consists of only one question, the take-home exam closely resembles the assignment of a paper in terms of what is expected.

Preparing for Problem-Solution Exams

Exams in mathematics and in some of the sciences, such as chemistry and physics, consist primarily or exclusively of problems to solve. Here are a few suggestions on how to prepare for such exams:

◆ Organize problems by types, and outline strategies for solving each type. Anticipate possible variations on each type.
◆ Prepare study sheets that include formulas and principles. Also include conversions and constants.
◆ Review by practicing solving problems—not by reading through sample problems and their solutions.
◆ Identify types of problems with which you have had trouble either on homework assignments or on quizzes, and spend extra time with these. Try to identify at what stage or step in the solution process your difficulty occurs.
◆ Give yourself a practice exam, selecting items from homework or previous quizzes. Complete the exam within the same time limit you expect to take the actual exam.

Preparing for Final Exams

Final exams differ from other types of exams in two respects: They are longer and more comprehensive, covering a larger body of material. What is more important, however, is that they often emphasize the integration of course content. To prepare for final exams, use the following suggestions:

Begin your study well in advance.   Finals all occur roughly within a one-week time period, usually immediately following the last class of the term.

Condense all course materials.   Prepare a master study sheet from your individual study sheets, drawing together and relating various topics.

Focus on large ideas.   Concentrate on concepts, trends, historical perspectives, principles, methods, patterns, and long-range effects—instead of individual facts. Try to identify themes that run through much or most of the course content. The theme of self-identity, for example, may pervade a Native American history course; a theme of revolution and change may be the focus of a course on 18th-century American literature.

Review outlines of course content.   Refer once again to your course syllabus or outline and your textbook's table of contents to reestablish an overview of the course. In preparing for a final exam, recall the "big picture" in order to avoid the mistake of becoming lost or overwhelmed by detail.

Anticipate essay questions.   If your final will include essays, try to predict and answer these questions. Essays on finals often are targeted to areas of major emphasis. As a starting point, ask yourself these questions:

What key ideas, themes, or processes has the professor been discussing all semester? Where does everything seem to be leading?
What long-lasting, beneficial ideas, processes, or principles have we learned?
To what topics has the professor devoted considerable time in class lectures or discussions?

Review previous exams and quizzes.   Identify topics and your areas of weakness for more intensive review. Look for patterns, trends, types of questions, and areas of emphasis.

Exercise 17.9	Using all the material you have covered up to this point in one of your courses, predict several essay questions that might appear on a final examination in that course.

Strategies for Specific Academic Disciplines

A key to becoming a top student is to study for each exam differently. Since each course, each instructor, and each lecture is different, each exam will also be different and require slightly different types of preparation. An examination in a literature course is quite unlike an examination in business management; an exam in mathematics is very different from one in political science. Table 17.3 offers suggestions for preparing for examinations in various academic disciplines. As you read this table, keep in mind that these strategies are general guidelines, not rules to follow. They may not always work, depending on the specific course, how the professor conducts it, and the types of exams given.

Table 17.3

Tips on Studying for Exams in Various Academic Disciplines

Academic Discipline	Emphasis/Focus of Study
Social sciences	Exams often contain both objective and essay questions. Objective exams test basic knowledge of theories, principles, concepts; essay questions may be on applications or a case study. Learn specialized vocabulary. Focus on relationships: comparisons and contrasts, cause and effects, sequences.
Sciences	Make lists of themes and principles covered; consider various situations in which these may be applied. Identify types of problems you expect to be covered and practice solving them. In the life sciences, be certain to learn and understand classifications.
Mathematics	Practice solving problems. Identify troublesome problem types and concentrate on them. Try to anticipate variations on general problem types. Memorize formulas.
Literature and the arts	Focus on trends and patterns demonstrated through series of works. Be certain to learn full names of works and the correct spelling of authors' or artists' names. Compare and contrast various works and authors or artists. Expect most exams to require essay answers. Note characteristics and features of particular works as well as themes and significant issues.
Career fields	Focus on applications: How is the information to be used? Anticipate questions that apply information to hypothetical situations or case studies. Learn procedures and processes and distinguish when each is appropriate.

Exercise 17.10	List the courses in which you are currently enrolled. For each course, predict the next type of exam you will have and the major topics it will cover. Then describe how you will approach each, emphasizing how you will modify your approach to suit the subject matter.

Controlling Test Anxiety

Do you get nervous and anxious just before an exam begins? If so, your response is perfectly normal; most students feel some anxiety before an exam. In fact, research indicates that some anxiety is beneficial and improves your performance by sharpening your attention and keeping you alert.

Research also shows that very high levels of anxiety can interfere with performance on a test. Some students become highly nervous and emotional and lose their concentration. Their minds seem to go blank, and they are unable to recall material they have learned. They also report physical symptoms: Their hearts pound, it is difficult to swallow, they break out in a cold sweat.

Test anxiety is a very complicated psychological response to a threatening situation. It may be deep rooted and related to other problems and past experiences. The following suggestions are intended to help ease your test anxiety. If these suggestions do not help, the next step is to discuss the problem with a counselor.

Be Sure Test Anxiety Is Not an Excuse

Many students say they have test anxiety when the truth is that they have not studied and reviewed carefully or thoroughly. The first question, then, that you must answer honestly is this: Are you really *unprepared* for the exam and therefore justifiably anxious?

Get Used to Test Situations

Psychologists who have studied anxiety use processes called "systematic desensitization" and "simulation" to reduce test anxiety. Basically, these processes allow you to become less sensitive or disturbed by tests by putting yourself in testlike conditions. Although these are complicated processes used by trained therapists, here are a few ways you can use them to reduce your own test anxiety:

Become familiar with the building and room in which the test is given.   Visit the room when it is empty and take a seat. Visualize yourself taking a test there.

Develop practice or review tests.   Treat them as real tests and do them in situations as similar as possible to real test conditions.

Practice working with time limits.   Set an alarm clock while taking practice or review tests and work only until it rings.

HOW DO YOU SEE IT?

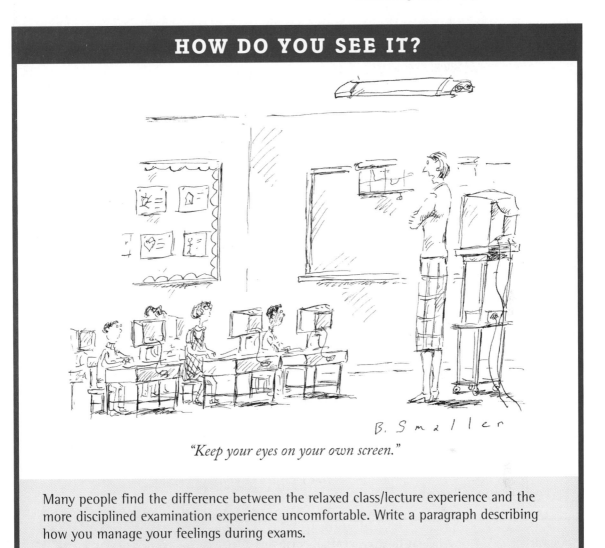

"Keep your eyes on your own screen."

Many people find the difference between the relaxed class/lecture experience and the more disciplined examination experience uncomfortable. Write a paragraph describing how you manage your feelings during exams.

Take as many tests as possible, even though you dislike them. Always take advantage of practice tests and in-chapter exercises. Buy a review book for the course you are taking, or a workbook that accompanies your text. Treat each section as an exam and have someone else correct your work.

Control Negative Thinking

Major factors that contribute to test anxiety are worry, self-doubt, and negative thinking. Just before and during an exam, anxious students often think such things as, "I won't do well," "I'm going to fail," or "What will my friends think of me when I get a failing grade?" This type of thinking is a predisposition for failure; you are telling yourself that you expect to fail. By doing this, you are blocking your chances for success. One solution to this problem is to send yourself positive rather than negative messages. Say to yourself, "I have studied hard and I deserve to pass" or "I know that I know the material" or "I know I can do it!"

Compose Yourself Before the Test Begins

Before you begin the test, take 30 minutes or so to calm yourself, to slow down, and to focus your attention. Take several deep breaths, close your eyes, and visualize yourself calmly working through the test.

Working Together

Suppose that your study skills instructor has just announced that in three weeks there will be a major exam of all the material you have learned so far in his course. Form groups of four students each to answer the following questions:

1. Based on the chapters of this book (and any other books) you have studied and your instructor's lectures, identify at least three to five topics for thematic study.

2. What type of exam seems appropriate for the material?

3. List topics, definitions, and types of problems that would make good exam questions.

4. Predict possible essay questions, if appropriate.

5. Discuss how you should schedule your study over the next three weeks.

Interactive Chapter Review

Knowledge	What are three elements of organizing effectively for a review of course material before an exam?
Comprehension	How do study sheets aid thematic study for an exam?
Application	Select three to four themes that have been important in your study skills course so far this term.
Analysis	Which specific study strategy or strategies from this chapter require you to use skills of analysis to study for an exam? Justify your response.
Synthesis	Suppose you were given the following essay question as an open-book exam in your study skills course: "Throughout this course, several patterns of thinking have been discussed as important during different study situations. Describe these patterns and give examples of when it is effective to identify and use them." Write a rough draft answer and then a key word outline of your response.
Evaluation	What is the long-term value to you of learning to study effectively for exams in college? What will it help you achieve or gain that is important to you? Write a paragraph in response.

Further Analysis

A freshman student is carrying a normal load of four courses: English composition, calculus, psychology, and first-year accounting. He works part time at a nearby convenience store. Throughout the semester he has maintained a low C average in each course. He has done little with the textbook assignments except to read each once, quickly, spending about two hours a week on each course. He owes his barely average grades to a verbal-auditory learning style that enables him to take good lecture notes and to a good memory of what was said in class, which allowed him to pass hour-long exams.

Now it is the week before final exams. In calculus, he knows the exam will be composed entirely of problems to solve. In psychology, he expects multiple-choice and short-answer questions and one essay question. In English, he will have a take-home final, and in accounting, he expects some multiple-choice but more emphasis on practical problems. He realizes that he can no longer recall each lecture, especially those from the first half of the course, and that he cannot rely on memory to handle final exams.

Eight days remain until finals begin, and the student is scheduled to work 20 hours at his job. He thinks he is best prepared for calculus and least prepared for psychology.

1. What serious changes should the student consider making to his daily schedule?

2. What study and review schedule would you recommend to give him the best chance of passing each of his courses?

3. What study and review strategies would you recommend for *each* course?

Discussion

1. Explain why you agree or disagree with the following strategy for preparing for an exam: "Learn everything that the professor particularly emphasized, and become familiar with the remainder as best you can."

2. You should have a fairly good idea of the grade you will earn on an exam before you take it. Agree or disagree.

3. Describe a situation in which you found group study particularly effective or particularly ineffective.

4. What types of exams do you handle best? Which are most difficult? Explain these differences in reference to your learning style (see Chapter 8).

5. How do you know when you are well prepared for an exam?

6. How can you improve your performance on exams?

The Work Connection

How does practicing effective study techniques for exams prepare you to win the job you want? Just as an exam in a college course shows your instructor that you have studied and thought about the course material, a job interview showcases your careful preparation and interest in the job for which you are applying. Career specialists recommend the following steps to prepare for a successful interview:

◆ Learn about the organization.

◆ Have a specific job or jobs in mind.

◆ Review your qualifications for the job. (See "Thinking Ahead" in Chapter 15, p. 321.)

◆ Prepare answers to broad questions about yourself such as "Tell me a little about yourself." and "What do you consider your strong and weak points?"

◆ Review your resumé.

◆ Practice an interview with a friend, relative, or career counselor.

1. Review this chapter. List five specific ideas that will help you organize your interview preparation.

2. Respond in writing (five to seven sentences) to the two broad questions given as examples in the list above. Think about how you can use your responses to demonstrate your competence and self-confidence to an interviewer.

The Web Connection

1. Preparing for Exams

   http://www.adm.uwaterloo.ca/infocs/Study/exam_prep.html

   The University of Waterloo presents suggestions for successful studying.

2. Ten Traps of Studying

   http://www.unc.edu/depts/unc_caps/TenTraps.html#Ten%20Traps

   Avoid these studying traps with help from the University of North Carolina at Chapel Hill.

3. Dealing with Test Anxiety

   http://www.iss.stthomas.edu/studyguides/tstprp8.htm

   Try some of these simple ways to avoid and deal with test anxiety, presented by the University of St. Thomas.

Go Electronic!
For additional readings, exercises, and Internet activities, visit the Longman Study Skills Web site at:
http://www.ablongman.com/StudySkills
If you need a user name and password, please see your instructor.

Chapter 18

Reasoning Skills for Objective Exams

DO YOU KNOW?

How can you approach exams with an advantage?
What reasoning skills should you develop to excel in objective exams?
How should you prepare for and take standardized tests?

Taking exams demands keen thinking and reasoning skills. These skills often distinguish top students from hardworking, above-average ones, or the A students from the B students. This chapter is intended to show you how to approach all types of exams with an advantage and how to apply thinking and reasoning skills to objective exams. The next chapter will focus on taking essay exams. If you follow the suggestions offered, your performance on examinations should improve, and you will approach them more confidently. Rate your present level of skill in taking exams by completing the questionnaire shown in Figure 18.1 on p. 366.

Starting with an Advantage

One key to success on any type of examination is to approach it in a confident, organized, and systematic manner. Unless you feel as if you have the situation under your control, you will probably not do well on the exam, regardless of how much you have prepared or how well you think and reason. Here are several useful tips to give you an important advantage.

Bring the Necessary Materials

When going to any examination, be prepared to take along any materials you might be asked or allowed to use. Be sure you have a watch, an extra pen, and take several number two pencils in case you must make a drawing or diagram or fill in an electronically scored answer sheet. Take paper—you may need it for computing figures or writing essay answers. Take along anything you have been allowed to use throughout the semester, such as a pocket calculator, conversion chart, or dictionary. If you are not sure whether you may use them, ask the instructor.

Figure 18.1

Rate Your Test-Taking Strategies

Respond to each of the following statements by checking "Always," "Usually," or "Never."

	Always	Usually	Never
1. Do you preview your entire exam paper before beginning?	❏	❏	❏
2. Do you allocate and keep track of time while taking the exam?	❏	❏	❏
3. Do you review the exam once you've finished?	❏	❏	❏
4. Do you avoid changing answers frequently unless you are certain that your first answer is wrong?	❏	❏	❏
5. Do you always read all of the choices on a multiple-choice exam before choosing the answer?	❏	❏	❏
6. Do you use the point value of short-answer questions as a guide to how much information to provide?	❏	❏	❏
7. Do you read the directions before beginning the exam?	❏	❏	❏
8. Do you avoid reading too much into a test question?	❏	❏	❏
9. Do you look for key words that qualify the meaning of true/false items?	❏	❏	❏
10. Do you look for clues in the question that suggest how to answer it?	❏	❏	❏

If you answered "Usually" or "Never" to more than one or two of the items, this chapter will help you improve your objective test-taking skills.

Time Your Arrival Carefully

Arrive at the examination room a few minutes early, in time to get a seat and get organized before the instructor arrives. If you are late, you may miss instructions and feel rushed as you begin the exam. If you arrive too early (15 minutes ahead), you risk anxiety induced by panic-stricken students who are questioning each other, trading last-minute memory tricks, and worrying about how difficult the exam will be.

Sit in the Front of the Room

The most practical place to sit for an exam is in the front. There, you often receive the test first and get a head start. Also, it is easier to concentrate and avoid distractions, such as a student dropping papers, someone whispering, or the person in front who is already two pages ahead of you.

Listen Carefully to Your Instructor's Directions

Your instructor may give specific instructions that are not included in the exam's written directions. If these are detailed instructions, and the instructor does not write them on the chalkboard, jot them down on your exam paper or on scrap paper. Note any changes in the questions you were given or in the point value of questions or sections. Listen critically to any instructions or comments your instructor adds; you might detect valuable hints about what your instructor considers to be an important focus or about specific information to include in your answers.

Preview the Exam

Before you start to answer any of the questions, quickly page through the exam, noticing the directions, the length, the type of questions, the general topics covered, the number of points the questions are worth, and where to put your answers. Previewing provides an overview of the whole exam and helps reduce anxiety.

Plan Your Time

After previewing, you will know the number and types of questions included. The next step is to estimate how much time you should spend on each part of the exam, using the point distribution as your guide. If, for example, an exam has 30 multiple-choice questions worth one point each and two essay questions worth a total of 70 points, you should spend twice as much time on the essay questions as on the multiple-choice items. If the point distribution is not indicated on the test booklet, ask the instructor. As you plan your time, allow four to five minutes at the end of the exam to read through what you have done, answering questions you skipped, and making any necessary corrections or changes. To keep track of time, always wear a watch.

If you are taking an exam with the question and point distribution shown below, how would you divide your time? Assume the total exam time is 50 minutes.

Type of Question	Number of Questions	Total Points
Multiple-choice	25	25
True/false	20	20
Essay	1	55

You probably should divide your time as indicated.

Previewing	1–2 minutes
Multiple-choice	10 minutes
True/false	10 minutes
Essay	25 minutes
Review	3–4 minutes

Avoid Reading Too Much into the Question

Most instructors word their questions so that what is expected is clear. A common mistake students make is to read more into the question than is asked for. To avoid this error, read the question several times, paying attention to how it is worded. If you are uncertain of what is asked for, try to relate the question to the course content, specifically the material you have studied. Do not anticipate hidden meanings or trick questions.

Exercise 18.1   For each of the exams described below, estimate approximately how you would divide your time:

1. Time limit: 75 minutes

Type of Question	Number of Questions	Total Points	Minutes
Multiple-choice	20	40	____
Matching	10	10	____
Essay	2	50	____

2. Time limit: 40 minutes

Type of Question	Number of Questions	Total Points	Minutes
True/false	15	30	___
Fill-in-the-blanks	10	30	___
Short-answer	10	40	___

Skills for Objective Exams

The most common types of objective exam questions are multiple-choice and true/false, although some instructors include matching and fill-in-the-blank items as well.

General Suggestions

Before we examine particular types of objective exams, here are a few general suggestions to follow in approaching all types of objective exams:

Read the directions.   Before answering any questions, read the directions. Often, an instructor will want the correct answer marked in a particular way (for example, underlined rather than circled). The directions may contain crucial information that you must be aware of in order to answer the questions correctly. In the items below, if you did not read the directions and assumed the test questions were of the usual type, you could lose a considerable number of points.

> *True/False Directions:* Read each statement. If the statement is true, write a T in the blank to the left of the item. If the statement is false, add and/or subtract words that will make the statement correct.

> *Multiple-Choice Directions:* Circle all the choices that correctly complete the statement.

Leave nothing blank.   Before turning in your exam, check through it to be sure you have answered every question. If you have no idea about the correct answer to a question and there is no additional penalty for wrong answers, guess. You might be right! On a true/false test, your chances of being correct are 50 percent; on a four-choice multiple-choice question, the odds are 25 percent. The odds improve if you can eliminate one or two of the choices.

Students frequently turn in tests with some items unanswered because they leave difficult questions blank, planning to return to them later. Then, in the rush to finish, they forget them. To avoid this problem, when you are uncertain, choose what looks like the best answer, and mark the question number with an X or checkmark so you can return to it; then, if you have time at the end of the exam, give it further thought. If you run out of time, you will have an answer marked.

Look for clues.   If you encounter a difficult question, choose what seems to be the best answer, mark the question with an X or checkmark so that you can return to it, and keep the item in mind as you go through the rest of the exam. Sometimes you will see some piece of information later in the exam that reminds you of a fact or idea. For example, a psychology student could not recall a definition of behaviorism for a short-answer question. Later in the examination, a multiple-choice item mentioned the psychologist Skinner. The student remembered that Skinner was a behaviorist and knew enough about him to reason out an answer to the short-answer item. At other times, you may notice a piece of information that, if true, contradicts an answer you had already chosen.

Write your answers clearly.   If your instructor cannot be sure of the answer you wrote, he or she will mark it wrong. Answer with capital letters on multiple-choice and matching tests to avoid confusion. Write or print responses in fill-in-the-blank tests legibly. Be sure that your answers to short-answer questions are not only written neatly, but are also to the point and express complete thoughts.

Check over your answers before you turn in the exam.   As mentioned earlier, reserve some time at the end of the exam for reviewing your answers. Check to be sure you didn't use the same matching-test answer twice. Be sure your multiple-choice answers are written in the correct blanks or marked in the correct place on the answer grid. One answer marked out of sequence could lead to a series of answers being in error. If there is a separate answer sheet, verify that your fill-in-the-blank and short answers correspond with the correct question numbers.

Don't change answers without a good reason.   When reviewing your answers during an exam, don't make a change unless you have a reason for doing so. Very often your first impressions are correct. If clues from a later test item prompt your recall of information for a previous item, change your answer.

True/False Tests: Making Judgments

True/false tests require you to make judgments, based on your knowledge and information about the subject, about the correctness of each item. The following suggestions will help you make more accurate judgments and reason the answer with a higher degree of accuracy:

Watch for qualifying words and phrases.   Watch for words that qualify or change the meaning of a statement; often, just one word makes it true or false. Consider for a moment a simplified example:

- ◆ All students are engineering majors.
- ◆ Some students are engineering majors.

Of course, the first statement is false, whereas the second is true. While the words and statements are much more complicated on most true/false exams, you will find that one word often determines whether a statement is true or false.

- ◆ *All* paragraphs must have a stated main idea.
- ◆ Spelling, punctuation, and handwriting *always* affect the grade given to an essay answer.
- ◆ When taking notes on a lecture, try to write down *everything* the speaker says.

In each of the examples above, the word in italics modifies—or limits—the truth of each statement. When reading a true/false question, look carefully for limiting words such as *all, absolutely, some, none, never, completely, only, always, usually, frequently,* and *most of the time.* Close attention to these words may earn you several points on an exam.

Read two-part statements carefully.   Occasionally, you may find a statement with two or more parts. In answering these items, remember that both or all parts of the statement must be true in order for it to be correctly marked "True." If part of the statement is true and another part is false, as in the following example, then mark the statement "False."

> The World Health Organization (WHO) has been successful in its campaign to eliminate smallpox and malaria.

While it is true that WHO has been successful in eliminating smallpox, malaria is still a world health problem and has not been eliminated. Since only part of this statement is true, it should be marked "False."

Exercise 18.2	Read each of the following statements and underline the portion that is *not* true:

1. Although thinking is a single-dimensional skill, most students can improve their thinking skills.
2. Patterns are difficult to recognize in most college lectures, but it is important to record as many key points as possible.
3. Problem solving and decision making are similar processes; each depends on the other for success.
4. Because textbooks are highly structured, it is usually possible to learn efficiently by rereading.

Look for negative and double-negative statements.   Test items that use negative words or word parts can be confusing. Words such as *no, none, never, not,* and *cannot* and prefixes such as *in-, dis-, un-, il-,* or *ir-* are easy to miss and always alter the meaning of the statement. Make it a habit to underline or circle negative words as you are reading examination questions.

Statements like the following that contain two negatives are even more confusing:

It is not unreasonable to expect that some welfare applicants feel that their privacy has been violated.

In reading such statements, remember that two negatives balance or cancel each other out. So "not unreasonable" can be interpreted to mean "reasonable."

Make your best guess.   When all else fails and you are unable to reason out the answer to an item, use these three last-resort rules of thumb:

◆   **Absolute statements tend to be false.** Since very few things are always true, with no exceptions, your best guess is to mark statements that contain words such as *always, all, never,* or *none* as false.
◆   **Mark any item that contains unfamiliar terminology or facts as false.** If you have studied the material thoroughly, trust that you would recognize as true anything that was a part of the course content.
◆   **When all else fails, it is usually better to guess true than false.** It is more difficult for an instructor to write plausible false statements than true statements. As a result, many exams have more true items than false.

HOW DO YOU SEE IT?

Unlike many questions in life, most objective exam questions have one right answer. Write a paragraph expressing your opinion as to whether or not objective tests accurately measure competence in the academic discipline that interests you most.

Exercise 18.3

The following true/false items are based on content presented in this text. Read each item; then locate and underline the word(s) or phrase(s) which, if changed or deleted, could change the truth or falsity of the statement. Indicate whether the statement is true or false by marking T for true and F for false.

_____ 1. Decision making is primarily a process of discovering alternatives.

_____ 2. A table never displays more than two sets of data.

_____ 3. Critical thinking is often defined as the careful, deliberate evaluation of ideas and information for the singular purpose of establishing their importance.

_____ 4. Most students avoid taking responsibility for their grades by shifting the blame to others.

_____ 5. Previewing rarely enables you to focus your attention on a reading assignment.

_____ 6. Process and procedure are usually important in mathematics courses.

_____ 7. A study sheet is most useful for reviewing material that is interrelated.

_____ 8. Falling behind on reading assignments is often a sign of academic difficulty.

_____ 9. Active learning is primarily a discrimination task.

_____ 10. Retrieval of information from memory depends exclusively upon its relevance and meaningfulness.

Matching Tests: Discovering Relationships

Matching tests require you to select items in one column that can be paired with items in a second column. The key to working with matching tests is to discover the overall pattern or relationship between the two columns. Begin by glancing through both columns before answering anything to get an overview of the subject and the topics the test covers. Are you asked to match dates with events, terms with meanings, people with accomplishments, causes with effects? In the following excerpt from a literature test, determine the relationship that exists:

Column 1	Column 2
1. Imagery	a. "One short sleep past, we wake eternally and Death shall be no more; Death, thou shalt die."—Donne
2. Simile	b. "We force their [children's] growth as if they were chicks in a poultry factory." —Toynbee
3. Personification	c. "And many a rose-carnation feeds with summer spice the humming air." —Tennyson

Use the following suggestions to answer matching items:

Answer the items you are sure of first, lightly crossing off items as they are used. This process of elimination will make it easier to match the remaining items. Try each item that remains with each of the remaining answers in the other column. Each time you eliminate another item, repeat this procedure.

Don't choose the first answer that seems correct; items later in the list may be better choices. Often, there are several possible matches for each item. You must choose the *best* match. In order to do this, you need to look at all possible matches, not just the first good match.

Make a list with the longer choices your starting point. If the first column consists of short words or phrases and the second is lengthy definitions or descriptions, save time by reverse matching; that is, look for the word or phrase in column 1 that fits each item in column 2.

Use clues to narrow down the possible matches. Match terms with definitions or synonyms that are the same part of speech. Look for a synonym for a term among the possible definitions. Key in on the meanings of familiar word parts in unknown terms to help you make a match. Try to "think outside the box" by applying your powers of logic and your everyday knowledge.

Short-Answer Tests: Listing Information

Short-answer tests require you to write a brief answer, usually in list or brief sentence form, such as asked by the following example:

List three events that increased U.S. involvement in the Vietnam War.

In answering short-answer questions, keep the following in mind:

Use the point distribution as a clue to how many pieces of information to list. For a nine-point item asking you to describe the characteristics of a totalitarian government, give at least three ideas.

Plan what you will say before starting to write.

Use the amount of space provided, especially if it varies for different items, as a clue to how much should be written. If you are asked to list three causes or to describe four events, number your answers so each point is clear and easy to identify.

Write your answer in sentence and paragraph form. Unless you are specifically directed to "list," express your answer in complete sentences. If the answer requires more than one sentence, structure it as a paragraph with a topic sentence and supporting details.

Fill-in-the-Blank Tests: Factual Recall

Test questions that ask you to fill in a missing word or phrase within a sentence require recall of information rather than recognition of the correct answer. Therefore, it is important to look for clues that will trigger your recall. Here are a few suggestions:

Look for key words in the sentence. Use them to determine what subject matter and topic are covered in the item. Here is a sample item: "Kohlberg devised a _____ to chart the course of 'moral development'". In this item you should focus on "Kohlberg," "chart," and "moral development."

Decide what type of information is required. Is it a date, name, place, new term? In the above item, a name or title is needed.

Use the grammatical structure of the sentence to determine the type of word called for. Is it a noun, verb, or qualifier? In the above item you must supply a noun. The correct answer is "stage theory," a noun phrase. If the blank is preceded by "an," the answer should be a noun beginning with a vowel.

Multiple-Choice Tests: Recognizing Correct Answers

Multiple-choice is the most frequently used type of exam and often the most difficult to answer. The following suggestions should improve your success in taking this type of exam:

Begin by reading each question as if it is a fill-in-the-blank or short-answer question. Cover up the choices and try to answer the question from your knowledge of the subject. In this way, you will avoid confusion that might arise from complicated choices. After you have formed your answer, compare it to each of the choices, and select the one that comes closest to your answer.

Read all choices first, considering each. Do not stop with second or third choices, even if you are certain that you have found the correct answer. Remember, on most multiple-choice tests your job is to pick the *best* answer, and the last choice may be a better answer than any of the first three.

Read combination choices. Some multiple-choice tests include choices that are combinations of previously listed choices, as in the following item:

The mesodermal tissue layer contains cells that will become

    a. skin, sensory organs, and nervous systems
    b. skin, sensory organs, and blood vessels
    c. bones and muscle
    d. stomach, liver, and pancreas
    e. a and c
    f. b, c, and d
    g. a, c, and d

The addition of choices that are combinations of the previous choices tends to make answers even more confusing. Treat each choice, when combined with the stem, as a true or false statement. As you consider each choice, mark it true or false. If you find more than one true statement, then select the choice that contains the letters of all the true statements you identified.

Use logic and common sense.   Even if you are unfamiliar with the subject matter, you can sometimes reason out the correct answer. The following test item is taken from a history exam on Japanese-American relations after World War II:

> Prejudice and discrimination are
> a. harmful to our society because they waste our economic, political, and social resources.
> b. helpful because they ensure us against attack from within.
> c. harmful because they create negative images of the United States in foreign countries.
> d. helpful because they keep the majority pure and united against minorities.

Through logic and common sense, it is possible to eliminate choices *b* and *d*. Prejudice and discrimination are seldom, if ever, regarded as positive, desirable, or helpful since they are inconsistent with democratic ideals. Having narrowed your answer to two choices, *a* or *c*, you can see that choice *a* offers a stronger, more substantial reason why prejudice and discrimination are harmful. The attitude of other countries toward the United States is not as serious as a waste of economic, political, and social resources.

Examine closely items that are very similar.   Often, when two similar choices are presented, one is likely to be correct. Carefully compare the two choices. First, try to express each in your own words, and then analyze how they differ. Often, this process will enable you to recognize the right answer.

Pay special attention to the level of qualifying words.   As noted for true/false tests, qualifying words are important. Since many statements, ideas, principles, and rules have exceptions, be careful in selecting items that contain such extreme qualifying words as *best, always, all, no, never, none, entirely,* and *completely,* all of which suggest that a condition exists without exception. Items containing words that provide for some level of exception, or qualification, are more likely to be correct. Here are a few examples of such words: *often, usually, less, seldom, few, more,* and *most.* Likewise, numerical answers that are about in the middle of a range of choices are probably correct.

In the following example, notice the use of the italicized qualifying words:

> In most societies
>
> a. values are *highly* consistent.
> b. people *often* believe and act on values that are contradictory.
> c. *all* legitimate organizations support values of the majority.
> d. values of equality *never* exist alongside prejudice and discrimination.

In this question, items *c* and *d* contain the words *all* and *never*, suggesting that those statements are true without exception. Thus, if you did not know the answer to this question based on content, you could eliminate items *c* and *d* on the basis of the level of qualifiers.

Some multiple-choice questions require application of knowledge or information. You may be asked to analyze a hypothetical situation or to use what you have learned to solve a problem. In answering questions of this type, start by crossing out unnecessary information that can distract you. In the following example, distracting information has been eliminated.

> Carrie is comfortable in her new home in New Orleans. When she gets dressed up and leaves her home and goes to the supermarket to buy the week's groceries, she gets nervous and angry and feels that something is going to happen to her. She feels the same way when walking her four-year-old son Jaxon in the park or playground.

Carrie is suffering from
a. shyness.
b. a phobia.
c. a personality disorder.
d. hypertension.

Jot down the essence. If a question concerns steps in a process or order of events or any other information that is easily confused, ignore the choices and use the margin or scrap paper to jot down the information as you can recall it. Then select the choice that matches what you wrote.

Avoid the unfamiliar. Avoid choosing answers that are unfamiliar or that you do not understand. A choice that looks complicated or uses difficult words is not necessarily correct. If you have studied carefully, a choice that is unfamiliar to you or contains unfamiliar terminology is probably incorrect.

Eliminate choices that are obviously false. Treat each choice in a troublesome question like you would a statement on a true-false test. Follow the procedures on pp. 370–373 to pare down the number of probable answers.

Choose the longest or most inclusive answers. As a last resort, when you do not know the answer and are unable to eliminate any of the choices as wrong, guess by picking the one that seems most complete and contains the most information. This is a good choice because instructors are usually careful to make the correct answer complete. Thus, the answer often becomes long or detailed.

Be careful of "all of the above" and "none of the above" questions. This type of question can be particularly difficult, since it usually involves five choices and can lead to confusion. To make it easier, first try to eliminate "all of the above." If even *one* choice is incorrect "all of the above" will be incorrect. If you think that at least *one* of the choices is correct, you can eliminate "none of the above." If you think two choices are correct but you are unsure of the third one, you should choose "all of the above." When questions such as these occur only a few times in a test, "all" or "none" is probably the correct choice.

Make educated guesses.   In most instances, you can eliminate one or more of the choices as obviously wrong. Even if you can eliminate only one choice, you have increased your odds on a four-choice answer from one in four to one in three. If you can eliminate two choices, you have increased your odds to one in two, or 50 percent. Don't hesitate to play the odds and make a guess—you may gain points.

Exercise 18.4

The following multiple-choice items appeared on an exam in psychology. Study each item and use your reasoning skills to eliminate items that seem incorrect and then, making an educated guess, select the best answer.

1. Modern psychological researchers maintain that the mind as well as behavior can be scientifically examined primarily by
   a. observing behavior and making inferences about mental functioning.
   b. observing mental activity and making inferences about behavior.
   c. making inferences about behavior.
   d. direct observation of behavior.

2. Jane Goodall has studied the behavior of chimpanzees in their own habitat. She exemplifies a school of psychology that is concerned with
   a. theories.
   b. mental processes.
   c. the individual's potential for growth.
   d. naturalistic behavior.

3. If a psychologist were personally to witness the effects of a tornado upon the residents of a small town, what technique would he or she be using?
   a. experimentation
   b. correlational research
   c. observation
   d. none of the above

4. A case study is a(n)
   a. observation of an event.
   b. comparison of similar events.

c. study of changes and their effects.

d. intense investigation of a particular occurrence.

5. Events that we are aware of at a given time make up the

a. unconscious.

b. subconscious.

c. consciousness.

d. triconscious.

6. Unlocking a combination padlock

a. always involves language skills.

b. always involves motor skills.

c. never involves imaginable skills.

d. seldom involves memory skills.

Thinking Critically
. . . About Practicum Exams

Often, exams in technical fields such as computer science, accounting, nursing, computer-assisted drafting, engineering, and medical technology take the form of practicums. In this type of exam, you are required to perform a task or solve a problem that simulates one you might encounter on the job. For example, a computer science student might be required to "debug" a faulty computer program. A nursing student might be required to install a number of intravenous devices. In preparing for practicum exams ask yourself the following questions:

1. **What tasks will I probably be asked to perform?** Consider any classroom demonstration your instructor presented. Review any lab assignments or class projects you carried out.

2. **What procedures are involved with these tasks?** Determine the process or steps you were taught for each task. Review your class notes on them. Prepare a summary sheet listing the steps in order. Write out an index card for each step, shuffle the cards, and then practice arranging them in the right order. Rehearse the steps mentally or write them out from memory to test yourself. Draw diagrams or sketches depicting the process. Picture yourself carrying out these procedures.

3. **How can I improve my performance of the task?** Repeatedly carry out the task while you review the steps or procedures you learned. Work with another student so that you can observe and evaluate each other's techniques.

Achieving Success with Standardized Tests

At various times in college, you may be required to take standardized tests. These are commercially prepared; they are usually lengthy, timed tests that are used nationally or statewide to measure specific skills and abilities. Your score on these tests compares your performance to that of large numbers of other students throughout the country or state. The SAT and ACT are examples of standardized tests you may have already taken. Many graduate schools require one or more standardized tests as part of their admission process. The most common is the Graduate Record Examination (GRE). Others are the Medical College Admission Test (MCAT), the Law School Admission Test (LSAT), and the Graduate Management Admission Test (GMAT). Licensing and certification exams are also a form of standardized test. Tests you take to obtain credentials as a CPA, nurse, or public school teacher are examples. Standardized tests are also given as admission tests for specialized training or employment: police, firefighters, and postal employees often take qualifying written exams.

Preparing for the Test

Find out as much as possible about the test.   Meet with your advisor or check the career center to obtain brochures and application forms. Find out about its general contents, length, and timing. Determine its format and the scoring procedures used. Know when and where the test is given.

Take a review course.   Find out if your college offers a preparatory course of review sessions to help you prepare for the test.

Obtain a review book.   Review books are available to help you prepare for many standardized tests. Purchase a review book at your college bookstore, a large off-campus bookstore, or through the Internet. Or, you may be able to borrow one from your college library or the public library if you cannot purchase it.

Begin your review early.   Start to study well ahead of the exam, so that you can fit the necessary review time into your already hectic schedule.

Start with a quick overview of the test.   Most review books contain a section that explains the type of questions on the test and offers test-taking strategies. If a brief review of the subject matter is offered, read through it.

Take practice tests.   To become most comfortable with the test, take numerous timed practice tests and score them. Make your practice tests as much like the actual test as possible. Work at a well-lighted desk or table in a quiet setting and time yourself carefully.

Review your answers.   Thoroughly review the questions you answered incorrectly. Read through the explanations given in your review book and try to see why the indicated answer is best.

Keep track of your scores. Keep a record of both your total score and subtest scores on practice tests. This will help you judge your progress and can give you insights into areas of weakness that require extra review.

Taking the Test

Arrive prepared at the exam room. Get to the testing site early so you can choose a good seat and become comfortable with the surroundings. Wear a watch, bring two sharpened pencils with erasers (in case one breaks), and two pens (in case one runs out of ink).

Get organized before the timing begins. Line up your answer sheet and test booklet so you can move between them rapidly without losing your place. Carefully fill out your answer sheet.

Skim the instructions. This can save you valuable time. If you have prepared yourself properly, you should be very familiar with the format of the test and the instructions. A quick reading of the directions will be all that is necessary to assure yourself that they have not changed.

Work quickly and steadily. Most standardized tests are timed, so the pace you work at is a critical factor. You need to work at a fairly rapid rate, but not so fast as to make careless errors.

Don't plan on finishing the test. Many of these tests are designed so that most people do not finish. So work on the easier questions first and put a mark next to the harder ones, so you can return to them if time permits.

Don't expect to get everything right. Unlike classroom tests or exams, you are not expected to get all of the answers correct.

Find out if there is a penalty for guessing. If there is none, then use the last 20 or 30 seconds to randomly fill in an answer for each item that you have not had time to do. The odds are that you will get one out of every five correct. If there is a guessing penalty, guess only if you can narrow the answer down to two choices. Otherwise, leave it blank.

Check your answer sheet periodically. If you have skipped a question, make sure that later answers match their questions. If the test has several parts, check to see that you are marking answers in the correct answer grid.

Don't just stop, if you finish early. If you have time left over, use it. Redo marked questions you skipped. Review as many answers as you can. Check over your answer sheet for stray marks and darken your answer marks.

Working Together

The class should first complete the chapter review quiz for this chapter or another chapter in this book. Working in pairs, students should review the quiz, comparing their reasoning for each item, and identify the level of thinking each item required.

Interactive Chapter Review

Knowledge	What elements of an exam should you preview, and why?
Comprehension	Answer the following true/false question: Instructors usually like to ask trick questions on exams.
Application	Circle each word or phrase in the following questions that probably indicates the answer is False:
	Cinnamon always grows on the north-facing side of mountains.
	All the economic indicators point to a depression starting in this country by the year 2005.
	Adults abused as children never completely recover from the experience.
Analysis	Analyze the following multiple-choice question and then answer it.
	José is a student with a lot of ambition and drive to succeed. Even before he started attending this university, José borrowed college textbooks from friends and read them on his own. He wrote down answers to all the questions the author asked. Then he went back and checked to see if he had them right. Once he had earned enough money, he registered for classes at the university. He takes 12 credit hours per term. Currently, José normally studies four hours each night after he returns home from his part-time job at the grocery store. He thinks through his reasons for studying before each study session. José has decided he wants to start his own business after college.
	Which choice best describes José?
	1. José is a social learner and a hard worker.
	2. José is a self-motivated person and independent learner.
	3. José is a weakly goal-directed but hardworking learner.
	4. José is an auditory learner and a hard worker.
	5. All of the above.
	6. None of the above.
Synthesis	Name at least three strategies you can use to figure out any type of objective question.
Evaluation	Think about the last objective exam you took. Consider how you prepared for the test, how you began the test, how you answered the questions, and how you used the time you had. Compare what you did with the recommendations in this chapter for taking objective tests. How can you improve your chances for excelling on your next objective exam?

Further Analysis

1. Use the following information about a history final exam to estimate the maximum amount of time you should spend on each part. Write your answers in the column labeled "Time Allotted."

Time limit: 2 hours, 50 minutes (Ten minutes have already been deducted from 3 hours to allow for prereading, time budgeting, and reviewing the exam.)

Type of Questions	Number of Questions	Percent	Time Allotted
Multiple-choice	30	30%	_____ minutes
True/false	5	5%	_____ minutes
Matching	10	10%	_____ minutes
Fill-in-the-blank	5	5%	_____ minutes
Essay	5	50%	_____ minutes

2. Each question below, taken from a psychology exam, contains a "hint" which helps you eliminate incorrect choices and, therefore, to determine the answer. Explain what this hint is AND give the correct answer to the question.

True/False Questions:

1. A psychology test always measures behavior.

   Explanation of hint: _____

   Answer: _____

2. All babies are able to say at least a few words by the time they are two years old.

   Explanation of hint: _____

   Answer: _____

3. Thomas Jefferson was the primary author of the Declaration of Independence and the first president of the United States.

   Explanation of hint: _____

   Answer: _____

Fill-in-the-Blank Questions:

4. The type of memory which contains information for only a short period is called _____ memory.

   Explanation of hint: _____

   Answer: _____

5. Information that is condensed and organized with headings indented to reflect their relative importance is known as an _____.

   Explanation of hint: _____

   Answer: _____

Multiple-Choice Questions:

6. You can *best* improve your memory by

   a. reading about memory

   b. taking a lot of courses at one time

   c. practicing saying, seeing, and hearing the information you want to remember

   d. listening more attentively to lectures

   Explanation of hint: _____

   Answer: _____

7. Information can be transferred from your short-term to your long-term memory by

   a. repeating it.

   b. elaborative rehearsal.

   d. taking notes on it.

   e. all of the above.

   f. none of the above.

   Explanation of hint: _____

   Answer: _____

8. Which is the best estimate of the percentage of Americans suffering from a psychological disorder?

   a. 5 percent

   b. 10 percent

   c. 20 percent

   d. 40 percent

   Explanation of hint: _____

   Answer: _____

9. If learning is "latent," it is

   a. of *no* value to the organism.

   b. revealed *only* in social situations.

   c. shown in *later* behavior.

   d. *not* remembered.

   Explanation of hint: _____

   Answer: _____

10. When squirrels bury nuts for use in the winter, they

    a. create a mental map and remember where they were buried.

    b. make little markers on the ground to guide them later.

    c. usually have no idea where to find them when they need them.

    d. hide so many nuts they can always manage to find a few by chance.

Explanation of hint: _____

Answer: _____

Discussion

1. Some students leave the exam room as soon as they finish the exam; others stay until the end, rereading and rechecking their answers. Discuss the advantages and disadvantages of each approach.

2. Discuss which type of objective exam is most difficult: multiple-choice, matching, fill-in-the-blank, or true/false.

3. Discuss the levels of thinking each type of objective test can and is most likely to require.

The Work Connection

Becoming familiar with the format of objective exams may prove useful when you apply for a job. Some employers give a variety of tests as part of their preemployment process. *Aptitude tests* measure your ability to perform job functions; *integrity tests* predict your attitudes, work ethic, and personality; and *psychological tests* provide in-depth information about you. Hunter and Hunter (1984) found that how applicants do on ability tests predicts future job success better than job interviews, previous employment history, education, or reference checks.[1] Familiarity with objective exams will be an advantage if your prospective employer uses objective tests to measure, for example, such basic skills as the ability to solve problems, use words precisely, or do basic math.

1. If you were to take a test now on your mastery of basic language and math skills, how well do you predict you would do? Why?

2. Aside from the study skills course in which you are currently enrolled, what other courses or campus services can help you learn how to do well on objective tests? List two or three ways you can improve your test-taking skills.

The Web Connection

1. Practice Test Made by Students

   http://www.mtsu.edu/~studskl/practest.html

   Students from Middle Tennessee State University created this practice test that reviews how to take true/false and multiple-choice exams.

2. Special Suggestions for Problem Tests

http://www.unc.edu/depts/unc_caps/TestTake.html#Problem%20Tests

The University of North Carolina, Chapel Hill, offers some useful tips for taking exams that involve solving math or science problems.

3. Guessing Suggestions for Tests

http://www.ulc.arizona.edu/online_materials/test_taking/guess.html

Sometimes you need to guess on an exam. The University Learning Center at the University of Arizona offers tips for making the best guess.

Go Electronic!
For additional readings, exercises, and Internet activities, visit the Longman Study Skills Web site at:
http://www.ablongman.com/StudySkills
If you need a user name and password, please see your instructor.

Chapter 19

Taking Essay Exams

DO YOU KNOW?

What are four steps to writing effective essay exam answers?
How can you succeed at writing competency tests and essay exams?

To many students, essay exams present a greater challenge than objective exams. Objective exams such as multiple-choice and true/false tests require primarily that you *recognize* correct answers, whereas essay exams require you to demonstrate higher-level thinking skills. Essay exams provide a greater opportunity to demonstrate your learning and to distinguish yourself as an excellent student. Your essays reveal a great deal about your level of mastery of the course content as well as your ability to organize, synthesize, and apply it. Essay exams measure your ability to think about the subject and communicate those thoughts in written form.

The manner in which you approach an essay exam, and how carefully you read the questions and organize and write your answers, can influence your grade by as much as 10 or 15 points. The primary purpose of this chapter is to discuss each of these aspects of taking essay exams. Suggestions for achieving success on writing competency tests and exit exams are also presented.

Writing Effective Essay Exams

Essay answers are usually rated on two factors: content and form. It is not enough, then, simply to include the correct information. The information must be presented in a logical, organized way that demonstrates your understanding of the subject. There can be as much as one whole letter grade difference between a well-written and a poorly written essay even though both contain the same basic information. This section offers suggestions for earning as many points as possible on essay exams.

Writing effective essay answers involves three stages: (1) organizing your approach, (2) constructing your answer, and (3) writing your answer.

Organizing Your Approach

Here are a few suggestions to help you approach essay exams in an organized, systematic manner:

Read the directions.   Before reading any of the essay questions, be certain to read the general directions first. They may tell you how many questions to answer, how to structure your answers, what the point distribution is, or what the minimum or maximum length for your answer should be.

Plan your time.   If you have to answer two essay questions in a 50-minute class session, allot yourself 20 to 25 minutes for each one. There is a strong tendency to spend the most time on the first question, but you should guard against it. Keep track of time so that you are able to finish both questions. Allow a few minutes at the end of an in-class exam to check and proofread your answers. Allow more time for a final exam.

Know the point value of each question.   If that information is not included on the exam, ask the instructor. Use this information to budget your time and to decide how much to write for each question. Suppose you are taking an exam that has three questions with the following values:

> Question 1: 20 points
> Question 2: 30 points
> Question 3: 50 points

Because question 3 is worth half the total points, you should spend approximately half of your time on it. Divide the remaining time nearly equally on questions 1 and 2. Point distribution can suggest how many ideas to include in your answer. For a 20-point question, your instructor probably expects four or five main points ($4 \times 5 = 20$), since most instructors don't work with fractions of points. If you can think of additional ideas to include and time permits, include them because point distribution is only an indicator, not a rule for length.

When you have to make a choice.   When the directions specify a choice of questions to answer, select those on which you will be able to score the most points. Some essay questions are more difficult than others; some require specific, exact information, while others call for a reasoned, logical interpretation or evaluation. Take time to make a careful choice. A few moments spent at the beginning may well save you the time it takes to switch from one question to another should you realize midway that you are not able to prepare an adequate response.

Answer the easiest question first.   Assuming the questions are of equal point value, answer the easiest question first. Knowing you are doing well will build your self-confidence and help you approach the remainder of the exam with a positive attitude. You will be able to complete the easiest question fairly quickly, leaving the remainder of time to be divided among the more difficult questions.

Make notes as you read.   As you read a question the first time, you may begin automatically to formulate an answer. Jot down a few key words that will bring these thoughts back when you are ready to organize your answer.

Analyze the question. Well-written essay questions define the topic and suggest what kinds of information to include, as shown in the following item.

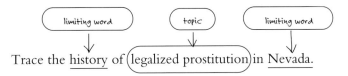

Trace the history of (legalized prostitution) in Nevada.

Here the topic, legalized prostitution, is clearly defined, and it is limited or restricted in two ways: (1) you are concerned only with its history—not its status today, or its effects; and (2) you are concerned only with the state of Nevada. Also notice the word "trace." It suggests the method of development to use in writing this essay. Since *trace* means to track something through time, you should use chronological order to develop your answer.

Here are a few more examples: The topics have been circled and the restricting or limiting words have been underlined.

List several (categories of speeches) and describe their primary functions and uses.

Describe the basic differences between the reproductive cycles of angiosperms and gymnosperms.

Compare the purpose and function of (analytical reports and research reports.)

Develop the habit of looking for and marking or circling key words as you analyze essay questions.

Watch for questions with several parts. Students often fail to answer all parts of an essay question. Most likely, they become involved with answering the first part and forget to complete the remaining parts. Questions with several parts come in two forms. The most obvious form is as shown in the following example:

For the U.S. invasion of Panama, discuss the (a) causes, (b) immediate effects, and (c) long-range political implications.

A sample of a less obvious form that does not stand out as a several-part question is shown below:

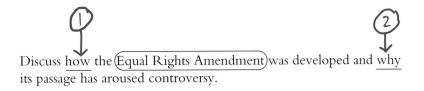

Discuss how the (Equal Rights Amendment) was developed and why its passage has aroused controversy.

When you find a question of this type, circle the topic and underline the limiting words (as in the example) to serve as a reminder.

Use thought patterns as clues to content and organization.   Essay questions contain one or more clue words that indicate the predominant thought pattern(s) to use in organizing, constructing, and writing your answer. These words specify what approach you are to take in answering the question. They indicate whether you are to make comparisons, summarize, explain, or answer in some other way. Here is a sample essay question:

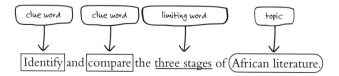

The topic of this essay question, African literature, is limited to a consideration of its three stages. The clue words "identify" and "compare" specify what type of response is called for. They tell you *what* to say about the stages of African literature. First you are to identify—that is, name and briefly describe—each stage. Then you are to compare the three stages, describing their similarities. The most commonly used clue words, and the thought patterns they often suggest, are summarized in Table 19.1.

Exercise 19.1	Read each of the following essay questions. In each question, underline the topic, circle the limiting word(s), and identify the thought pattern(s) the question suggests.

1. Discuss the long-term effects of the trend toward a smaller, more self-contained family structure.

2. Trace the development of monopolies in the late 19th and early 20th centuries in America.

3. Explain one effect of the Industrial Revolution upon each of three of the following:
   a. transportation
   b. capitalism
   c. socialism
   d. population growth
   e. scientific research

4. Discuss the reason why, although tropical plants have very large leaves and most desert plants have very small leaves, cacti grow equally well in both habitats.

5. Describe the events leading up to the War of 1812.

6. Compare and contrast the purposes and procedures in textbook marking and lecture note taking.

7. Briefly describe a complete approach to reading and studying a textbook chapter that will enable you to handle a test on that material successfully.

8. List four factors that influence memory or recall ability, and explain how each can be used to make study more efficient.

9. Summarize the techniques a speaker or lecturer may use to emphasize the important concepts and ideas in his lecture.

10. Explain the value and purpose of the previewing technique, and list the steps involved in prereading a textbook chapter.

Table 19.1
Essay Exam Questions

Thought Pattern	Clue Word	Example	Information to Include
Chronological	Trace	Trace the history of the foreign exchange market.	Describe the development or progress of a particular trend, event, or process in chronological order.
Process	Describe	Describe how an advertisement is produced and prepared.	Tell how something happened, including how, who, where, and why.
Comparison	Compare	Compare the causes of air pollution with those of water pollution.	Show how items are similar as well as different; include details or examples.
Contrast	Contrast (differentiate)	Contrast the health care systems in the United States with those in England.	Show how the items are different; include details or examples.
Cause and effect	Prove	Prove that ice is a better cooling agent than air when both are at the same temperature.	Give reasons or evidence, or establish that a concept or theory is correct, logical, or valid.
	Justify	Justify the decision to place economic sanctions on Iraq.	Give reasons that support an action, event, or policy.
	Criticize	Criticize the current environmental controls to combat air pollution.	Make judgments about quality or worth; include both positive and negative aspects, explaining or giving reasons for your judgments.
	Evaluate	Evaluate the strategies our society has used to treat mental illness.	React to the topic in a logical way. Discuss the merit, strengths, weaknesses, advantages, or limitations of the topic, explaining your reasons.
Listing	Discuss	Discuss the effectiveness of drug rehabilitation programs.	Consider important characteristics and main points.
	Enumerate (list)	Enumerate the reasons for U.S. involvement in the Persian Gulf War.	List or discuss one by one.
	State (illustrate)	State Boyle's Law and illustrate its use.	Explain, using examples that demonstrate or clarify a point or idea.

Continued

Table 19.1 (Continued)			
Listing	Summarize	Summarize the arguments for and against offering sex education courses in public schools.	Cover the major points in brief form; use a sentence and paragraph form.
Definition	Define	Define thermal pollution and include several examples.	Give an accurate meaning of the term with enough detail to show that you really understand it.
Classification	Diagram	Diagram the stamen and pistil of a lily.	Make a drawing and label its parts.

Constructing Your Answer

As soon as they have finished analyzing the question, many students begin immediately to write the answer. A far better technique is to take a few moments to think about, plan, and organize your ideas. Since you are working within a time limit, you might not be able to revise your answer. Consequently, it is even more important than usual to plan your essay carefully before you begin.

Outline.   Make a brief word or phrase outline of the ideas you want to include in your answer. After you have read and marked each question, jot down ideas you'll include in your essay on the back of the exam, or on a separate sheet of paper that you won't turn in. If the question is one that you predicted, jot down the outline of your draft essay, making adjustments and additions to fit the actual question. Arrange your ideas to follow the method of development suggested in the question. Number them to indicate the order in which you'll present them in your essay. Keep in mind, too, the point value of the essay, and be sure to include sufficient ideas and explanations.

One student made these notes in response to the following question:

Identify the stages of sleep and describe four sleep disorders.

Stages	Disorders
1 wakefulness	4 hypersomnia
2 quiet sleep	1 insomnia
3 REM sleep (active)	2 sleepwalking
	3 night terrors

As you write your essay, other ideas may occur to you. Add them to your list so they won't slip from your mind.

Rearrange the outline.   Study your word outline and rearrange its order. You may want to put major topics and important ideas first and less important points toward the end. Or you may decide to organize your answer chronologically, discussing events early in time near the beginning of the essay and mentioning more recent events near the end. The topic you are discussing will largely determine the order of presentation.

If the point value of the essay is given, use that information as a clue to how many separate points or ideas may be expected. For example, for an essay worth 25 points, five major points may be expected.

If you are having difficulty recalling needed information or if you should suddenly "go blank," try a technique called brainstorming. Basically, it involves writing a list of everything and anything you can think of related to the topic. Then review your list; you are likely to find some ideas you can use in your answer.

Exercise 19.2	For a course you are currently taking, predict an essay question you think your instructor is likely to include on a midterm or final exam. Underline the limiting word(s), circle the topic, and box in the clue word(s); then construct and revise an outline of your answer to this question.

Writing Your Answer

The appearance, organization, and correctness of your essay influence your grade. Numerous experiments have been done; most indicate that well-organized, correctly written papers receive nearly one letter grade higher than papers that express the same content but do so in a poorly organized, error-filled manner. An effective essay answer should adhere to correct paragraph form, use complete sentences, and clearly present ideas in a logical format. You should begin your answer with a thesis statement, and then explain and support it in several paragraphs.

Write a clear thesis statement. The thesis statement you write for essay tests should be simple and straightforward. It should clearly state the main point your essay is intended to explain. Often, simply rephrasing the question is sufficient. Here are two examples:

Essay Question	Thesis Statement
Explain how advertising differs from publicity.	Advertising differs from publicity in three primary ways.
Discuss the practical applications of Newton's three laws of motion.	Newton's laws of motion have many practical applications.

Other times, it might be appropriate to include additional information. In the following example, the questions provided a structure to which the writer added more information.

Essay Question	Thesis Statement
Explain the differences between primary and secondary groups.	Primary groups differ from secondary groups in their purpose, membership, level of interaction, and level of intimacy.

Always make your thesis statement as direct, concise, and specific as possible. Your goals should be to announce to your instructor that you know the answer to the question and to indicate how it will be organized.

Exercise 19.3

Write a thesis statement for each of the following essay questions.

1. Discuss how books differ from other print media in communicating to the public.
2. Describe the types of long-term memory.
3. Criticize the current state of mental health services in the United States.
4. Explain how communication is affected by the Internet.
5. Compare Thurstone's model of intelligence with Guilford's.

Make your main points stand out.   You can do this most easily by writing a separate paragraph for each major supporting detail. Begin each paragraph with a topic sentence that introduces its main point. For example, your thesis statement might be:

There are four social factors that may affect the consumer buying process.

Your topic sentences could then read as follows:

Paragraph 1: First, social role and family influence are factors that affect consumer decisions.

Paragraph 2: Reference groups are a second social factor.

Paragraph 3: Social class also affects the consumer's purchase decisions.

Paragraph 4: Finally, cultures and subcultures affect buying decisions.

Due to the large volume of essays that many instructors must read in a short period of time, they tend to skim for the key ideas rather than to read everything. Therefore, it is best to make your main points easy to find, at the beginning of each paragraph. For lengthy answers or multipart questions, you can use headings, the numbering from the question, or space between the different parts of your answer, to make your key points obvious.

Develop your main points.   Instructors often criticize essay answers because they fail to explain or to support ideas fully. If you include only one major idea per paragraph, you will avoid this danger and force yourself to explain the major points. Also, if you answer an essay question with the intent of convincing your instructor that you have learned the material, then you are likely to include enough explanation.

You should take care to provide relevant and sufficient explanation of the topic sentence of each paragraph. In other words, each detail you include should directly support your topic sentence and there should be enough details to make your topic sentence understandable and convincing. Providing too much information is better than including too little. For the sample above on consumer buying, you should explain or define each social factor and then discuss how it affects buying behavior.

Refer to the sample essay answer shown in Figure 19.1 to see how the thesis statement, main points, and supporting details come together in an essay answer.

Write a brief conclusion. A concluding sentence is an effective way to reemphasize your main points in a lengthy essay.

Figure 19.1
A Sample Essay Question and Answer

ESSAY QUESTION
Crime is a human act that violates criminal law. Identify the various categories of crime. Describe and provide an example of each.

ANSWER
There are five categories of crime. Each violates one or more — Thesis Statement
aspects of criminal law. The first of these categories is Index Crime. — Main Point #1
Index Crimes are those identified by the Federal Bureau of
Investigation as serious crimes. They include criminal homicide, rape, } Supporting Details
robbery, burglary, aggravated assault, larceny, auto theft, and arson.

The second type of crime is white-collar crime. These crimes may — Main Point #2
be committed by corporations or individuals, usually within the course
of daily business. The criminals are often affluent and respectable } Supporting Details
citizens. Some examples are embezzlement and income tax evasion.

A third type of crime is professional crime. Professional crimes — Main Point #3
are committed by criminals who pursue crime as a day-to-day
occupation. They often use skilled techniques and are respected by } Supporting Details
other criminals. Shoplifters, safecrackers, or cargo highjackers are
examples of professional criminals.

Organized crime is a fourth type of crime. Organized crime — Main Point #4
involves the sale of illegal goods and services and is conducted by
criminals who organize into networks. Organized crime is often
transmitted through generations and does not depend on particular } Supporting Details
individuals for its continuation. Organized crime often involves
political corruption. Examples of organized crime are gambling,
narcotics sales, and loan sharking.

A fifth type of crime is victimless crime. These crimes involve — Main Point #5
willing participants; there is no victim other than the offender. } Supporting Details
Examples include drug use, prostitution, and public drunkenness.

Table 19.2

Tips and Techniques for Presenting Essay Answers

Tips	Techniques
Use correct paragraph form.	Explain one idea per paragraph.
Begin your answer with a thesis statement.	Write a sentence that states what the entire essay will discuss.
Make your main points easy to find.	State each main point in a separate paragraph; use headings; number ideas; use blank space to divide ideas.
Include sufficient explanation.	Provide several supporting details for each main point.
Avoid opinions and judgments.	Include only factual information unless otherwise requested.
Make your answer readable.	Use ink; use 8½-×-11-inch paper; number your pages; write on one side; leave margins and spaces between lines.
Proofread your answer.	Read through your answer to check only grammar, spelling, and punctuation.

Proofread your answer.   Be sure to leave enough time to proofread your answer. Check for errors in spelling, punctuation, and grammar. If time permits, make minor revisions. Pay attention to sentences that do not make sense, and write your changes as neatly as possible. If you think of an important fact to add, do so.

Table 19.2 summarizes these and further suggestions for presenting a correctly written essay answer.

If You Run Out of Time

Despite careful planning, you may run out of time before you can finish writing one of the essays. If this happens, try to jot down the major ideas that you would discuss fully if you had time. Often, your instructor will give you partial credit for this type of response, especially if you mention that you ran out of time.

If You Don't Know the Answer

Despite careful preparation, you may be unable to answer a particular question. If this should happen, do not leave a blank page; write something. Attempt to answer the question—you may even hit upon some partially correct information. However, the main reason for writing something is to give the instructor the opportunity to give you at least a few points for trying. If you leave a completely blank page, your instructor has no choice but to give you zero points. Usually losing full credit on one essay automatically eliminates one's chances of getting a high passing grade.

| Exercise 19.4 | Use the outline you constructed in Exercise 19.2 to write an answer to the essay question you predicted. |

| Exercise 19.5 | Exchange essays with another student and evaluate the essays by discussing how well each achieved the following criteria. |

1. Use of complete sentences and paragraph form
2. Clarity of thesis statement
3. Ease of locating main points
4. Quality of supporting details
5. Organization of the essay

Thinking Critically
. . . About Returned Exams

Most students do not pay enough attention to returned exams. If you usually file away returned exams for future reference once you have noted your grade, STOP. You can learn a lot by analyzing a returned exam. Use the following questions to guide your analysis:

1. **Where did you lose your points?** Make a list of topics on which you lost points. Do you see a pattern? Can you identify one or more topics or chapters that were particularly troublesome? If so, review that material now, and make a note to review it again before your final exam.

2. **What type of questions did you miss?** If the exam had several parts, where did you lose the most points (essay or multiple-choice, for example)? Adjust your study and review strategies accordingly, using the suggestions in Chapter 17.

3. **What level of thinking (see Chapter 2, p. 36) was required in the questions you missed?** Did you miss knowledge and comprehension questions? If so, you will need to spend more time on factual recall. If you missed questions that require analysis, then you should adjust your study plan to include more thought and reflection. If you missed questions that require synthesis, then you should devise study strategies that force you to pull information together. If you missed application questions, spend more time looking at practical uses and applications of course content. If you missed evaluation questions, ask more critical questions about course content.

Achieving Success with Competency Tests and Exit Exams

Your college may require that you pass competency tests in such skill areas as reading, writing, and mathematics. You should think of tests such as these as readiness tests, since they assess the skills required in more advanced college courses. Competency tests and exit exams are intended to ensure that you will not be placed in courses for which you are inadequately prepared or that are too difficult for you. You should, of course, try your best with these types of tests, but you shouldn't be upset if you don't score at the required level. It is best to be sure you possess the necessary skills before you attempt more difficult courses.

The suggestions given in this section focus on competency tests and exit exams in writing, but also apply to other tests.

Find Out About the Test

Find out as much as possible about the test ahead of time, so you will feel confident and prepared for the test. You'll want to know

- what skills the test measures.
- what kinds of questions are included (for example, will you write an essay or correct errors in paragraphs?).
- the number of questions there are.
- if there is a time limit and, if so, what it is.
- how the test is scored (do some skills count more than others?).
- if you are to write an essay, whether you are expected to revise or recopy it.

Your instructor should be able to answer many of these questions. In addition, talk with other students who have taken the test. They may be able to offer useful tips and advice.

Make Your Final Preparations for the Test

Since competency tests and exit exams in writing are usually taken right after you have finished a writing course, you should be well prepared for them already. Only a few last-minute matters remain.

Essay tests.   If your test requires you to write an essay, the following suggestions will help:

1. Review all papers your instructor has graded in order to identify and make a list of your most common errors. When you revise and proofread your competency-test answers, check for each of these errors.

2. Before you go into the exam, construct a mental checklist that you can use for revising your essay. If time permits, jot your list down on scrap paper during the exam and use it to revise your essay.

3. Plan how to divide your time if your test is timed. Estimate how much time you will need for each step in the writing process. Gauge your time on a practice test. Wear a watch to the exam, and check periodically to see that you're on schedule.

4. Take a practice test. Ask a classmate to make up a topic or question for you to write about that is the same type as the questions that will be on the test. Observe the time limit that will be used on the test. Finally, ask your classmate to evaluate your essay.

Error-correction tests.   If your test requires you to edit or correct another writer's sentences or paragraphs, do the following:

1. Review your graded papers from the course. The errors you made when you wrote them are likely to be those you'll have difficulty spotting on the test.

2. If time permits, read each sentence or paragraph several times, looking for different types of errors each time. For example, read it once looking for spelling errors, another time to evaluate sentence structure, and so forth.

3. Practice with a classmate. Write sample test items for each other. Pay attention to the kinds of errors you fail to spot; you're likely to miss them on the test as well.

4. If you are taking a state exam, practice manuals or review books may be available. Check with your college bookstore. Take the sample tests and work through the practice exercises. Note your pattern of errors and, if necessary, get additional help from your instructor or your college's academic skills center.

HOW DO YOU SEE IT?

You may envy the students who have already left this picture. Write a paragraph describing how you know when to consider an essay exam completed.

Interactive Chapter Review

Knowledge	What are the four main stages of writing effective essay answers?
Comprehension	Describe what the following terms related to essay exam questions mean: *topic, limiting word, clue word*. Give an example of each.
Application	Refer to Table 19.1 on p. 391 to describe which thought pattern each of the following essay questions requires: 1. Compare and contrast each pair of the five elements of a person's learning style. 2. Describe the development of the vaccine for polio. 3. Discuss the social and legal effects of Anita Hill's testimony in the Clarence Thomas nomination hearings.
Analysis	Examine any tests that your instructors have returned to you within the last month. Using the list in "Thinking Critically . . . About Returned Exams" on p. 397 as a guide, analyze each exam. In each of your class notebooks, jot down notes to yourself about what you need to do before your next exams to avoid the same mistakes.
Synthesis	What patterns, if any, did you notice among the returned exams you just analyzed? Are there any repeating errors—for example, types of questions that you tend to do poorly with? If so, how can you improve in this area? Can you point to any particular levels of thinking that seem to present a problem in more than one class? How can you improve your thinking at this level?
Evaluation	Assume the following question is on the final exam in your study skills course. The question is worth 50 percent of your exam grade. Analyze the question, construct your answer, and write your answer. Take no more than 30 minutes to do so. Describe Bloom's taxonomy of thinking skills, providing an example of each level of thinking. Which levels are considered "critical thinking"? Then determine whether or not your own critical thinking skills have developed and improved this term. Illustrate your answer. Now evaluate your answer by rereading pp. 33–37. (See the index for other places where critical thinking is discussed.) What grade do you think you should receive on your answer?

Further Analysis

Given below is an essay question and one student's response to that question. The question was worth 30 points on an examination totaling 100 points; total test time was 75 minutes. Read and analyze the question and the essay answer and then respond to each question listed below:

Discuss each stage of the memory process, and identify and explain several strategies for improving the effectiveness of each stage.

Working Together

Each class member should write a response to the following essay question. Then, form groups of four or five students and follow each step listed below:

Problem solving is a vital and important skill. Describe the problem-solving process and illustrate its use in a particular academic situation.

1. Group members should read and evaluate each other's answers. Specifically, they should rate each answer and award it a grade of A, B, C, or D based on each of the following criteria:
   a. Correct and complete information (refer to Chapter 17)
   b. Sufficient detail and explanation
   c. Clear organization of ideas
   d. Effectiveness of thesis statement
   e. Grammatical correctness and readability
2. Group members should defend, compare, contrast, and discuss each other's ratings.

Essay Answer

Memory is important in everyone's life because it is the means by which we store and remember information. Psychologists have identified three stages: encoding, storage, and retrieval. In the encoding stage you put facts and ideas into a code, usually words, and file it away in your memory. Encoding can be improved by defining your purpose for learning and using various sensory modes. Storage involves keeping information in your permanent long-term memory.

The effectiveness of storage can be improved by immediate review of material you have just read or heard. Organizing or recording the information is also useful because it allows you to store the information in chunks. Developing retrieval clues is also an effective storage strategy.

Retrieval, the third stage of the memory process, is the ability to get back information that is in storage. You can improve retrieval by practice, by learning beyond mastery, and through elaboration.

1. Evaluate the accuracy of the information presented by referring to Chapter 9.
2. Evaluate the effectiveness of the writer's thesis statement.
3. Comment on the writer's organization.
4. Did the writer include sufficient explanation and detail?
5. What additional information might the writer have included?
6. What specific suggestions would you make to help this student improve his skill in answering essay questions?

Discussion

1. Some students find one type of examination question easier to handle than others. What factors could explain these differences?

2. If a student is 10 minutes late for a class in which an hourly exam is being given, what should he or she do?

3. Some colleges operate on the honor system: A student is obligated to report another student whom he or she observes cheating on an exam. Students who fail to report cheating are also considered guilty. What is the policy on your campus for students who have been found cheating on exams? Agree or disagree with this policy.

4. Suppose that you wake up the morning of an important exam feeling queasy and feverish. You realize you have caught the flu. What should you do?

The Work Connection

What personal characteristics and skills have been identified as vital to a person's employability? From 34 studies of the qualities employers desire most in employees, the following are the top five characteristics for getting and keeping a job:

1. Dependability/responsibility

2. Positive attitude toward work

3. Conscientiousness, punctuality, efficiency

4. Interpersonal skills, cooperation, working as a team member

5. Self-confidence, positive self-image

In a review of the studies, Kathleen Cotton noted that "virtually *all* of the employers in these studies cited 'dependability', 'responsibility', and 'positive attitude toward work' as vital."[1]

Analyze one of the following essay questions and make notes about how you would answer it:

1. Choose one of the traits listed above and illustrate its importance to employers.

2. As an employer, how would you know if your employee had a positive attitude toward work? Explain.

The Web Connection

1. Answering Essay Questions

   http://www.coun.uvic.ca/learn/program/hndouts/essayq.html

   This site from the University of Victoria presents more tips for approaching essay questions on exams.

2. Reasons to Review Tests

   http://www.mtsu.edu/~studskl/rtrned.html

   Middle Tennessee State University offers a dozen practical reasons to look over your returned tests.

3. Planning the Final Exam Period

   http://www.conestogac.on.ca/stserv/html_pages/preparing_for_exams.html#Planning%20the%20Final%20Exam%20Period

   This site from Conestoga College provides advice on how to deal with finals week.

 Go Electronic!
For additional readings, exercises, and Internet activities, visit the Longman Study Skills Web site at:
http://www.ablongman.com/StudySkills
If you need a user name and password, please see your instructor.

References

Barker, Larry, R. Edwards, C. Gaines, K. Gladney, and F. Holley (1980). "An Investigation of Proportional Time Spent in Various Communication Activities by College Students." *Journal of Applied Communication Research* 8: 101–109.

Sylvan Barnet, *A Short Guide to Writing About Art.* Boston: Little, Brown, 1989.

Shirley K. Bell, "Is Abortion Morally Justifiable?" *Nursing Forum,* Vol. XX, No. 3.

Bettina Lankard Brown, "Career Resilience." *ERIC Clearinghouse on Adult, Career, and Vocational Education,* Digest 178, 1996.

Louis Berman and J. C. Evans, *Exploring the Cosmos, 2nd ed.* Boston: Little, Brown and Co., 1977.

Careers and Employment Online, "The Use of Psychological Tests in Candidate Selection: An Overview." www.careers.unsw.edu.au/careered/Vocational%20Assessment/psych_testing.html.

Sabra Chartrand, "Employees Devise New Strategies to Test Job Applicants," *The New York Times,* December 14, 1997.

Sabra Chartrand, "A World Where Language and 'Soft Skills' Are Key," *The New York Times,* April 6, 1997.

Carolyn Corbin and James D. Henry, "Conquering Career Codependence." At http://www.cweb.com/21stcentury/welcome.html.

Carolyn Corbin, "Employment in the 21st Century." Speech to the National Association of Colleges and Employers, May 29, 1998. At http://www.jobweb.org/nace/nm98/may29.shtml.

Kathleen Cotton, "Developing Employability Skills," *School Improvement Research Series.* Portland: Northwest Regional Educational Laboratory School Improvement Research Series, (SIRS) Close up #15. At http://www.nwrel.org/scpd/sirs/8/c015.html

DeVry Institute of Technology, a division of DeVry University, "Survival of the Fittest." *Directions* newsletter, 1997.

Rebecca J. Donatelle, *Access to Health, 7th ed.* San Francisco, CA: Benjamin Cummings (Pearson), 2002.

Robert B. Ekelund and Robert D. Tollison, *Economics.* Boston: Little, Brown and Co., 1986.

J. Ross Eshleman and Barbara G. Cashion, *Sociology: An Introduction.* Boston: Little, Brown and Co., 1985.

Walter S. Jones, *The Logic of International Relations, 5th ed.* Boston: Little, Brown and Co., 1985.

Brenda Kemp and Adele Pilitteri, *Fundamentals of Nursing.* Boston: Little, Brown and Co., 1984.

Edward M. Kennedy, "The Need for Handgun Control." *Los Angeles Times,* April 5, 1981.

Robert L. Lineberry, *Government in America, 3rd ed.* Boston: Little, Brown and Co., 1986.

Elaine P. Maimon, *Writing in the Arts and Sciences.* Cambridge, MA: Winthrop Publishers, 1981.

George Miller, "The Magic Number. Seven Plus or Minus Two: Some Limits on Our Capacity for Processing Information," *Psychological Review 63* (1956).

Kenneth J. Neubeck, *Social Problems: A Critical Approach.* Glenview, IL: Scott, Foresman, 1979.

Robert C. Nickerson, *Fundamentals of Structured COBOL.* Boston: Little, Brown and Co., 1984.

Edward M. Reingold and Wilfred J. Hansen, *Dale Structures.* Boston: Little, Brown and Co., 1983.

Carl E. Rischer and Thomas A. Easton, *Focus on Human Biology, 2nd ed.* New York: HarperCollins, 1995.

Rosemary A. Rosser and Glen L. Nickolson, *Educational Psychology.* Boston: Little, Brown and Co., 1984.

Frederick A. Russ and Charles A. Kirkpatrick, *Marketing.* Boston: Little, Brown and Co., 1982.

Adam Smith, "Fifty Million Handguns." *Esquire,* April, 1981.

Star Tribune, "Part III: The coming trauma" of "On the Edge of the Digital Age." *Star Tribune,* 1996. At http://startribune.com/stonline/html/digage/main3.html

H. F. Spitzer, "Studies in Retention." *Journal of Educational Psychology* 30 (1939): 641–656.

Richard L. Weaver, *Understanding Interpersonal Communication, 6th ed.* New York: HarperCollins, 1993.

Endnotes

Chapter 2
1. Weaver, p. 283-84; 2. Neubeck, p. 247; 3. Corbin and Henry; 4. Corbin.

Chapter 3
1. http://jobtrak.com.

Chapter 4
1. Donetelle, p. 285, adapted.

Chapter 5
1. Chartrand. The New York Times, December 14, 1997.

Chapter 6
1. Barker, et.al., p. 101-109; 2. Chartrand. *The New York Times*, April 6, 1997.
Chapter 7
1. DeVry.
Chapter 8
Ekelund and Tollison, p. XXV.
Chapter 9
1. Miller, pp. 81-97; 2. Spitzer, pp. 641-56; 3. Brown.
Chapter 10
1. Maimon, pp. 4-5; 2. Barnet, pp. 21-22.
Chapter 11
1. Reingold and Hansen, p. 334; 2. Russ and Kirkpatrick, p. 5; 3. *Star Tribune*;
4. *Star Tribune*; 5. *Star Tribune*.
Chapter 12
1. Lineberry, p. 316; 2. Kemp and Pilitteri, p. 194; 3.

Nickerson, p. 121; 4. Lineberry, p. 276; 5. Jones, p. 183; 6. Jones, p. 185; 7. Jones, p. 364; 8. Jones, p. 278; 9. Jones, p. 5; 10. Rosser and Nickolson, p. 81; 11. Jones, p. 376; 12. Jones, p. 390; 13. Lineberry, p. 564; 14. Lineberry, p. 610; 15. Jones, p. 370.
Chapter 15
1. Berman and Evans, p. 145.
Chapter 16
1. Lineberry, p. 547; 2. Smith; 3. Smith; 4. Kennedy; 5. Eshleman and Cashion, p. 165;
6. Eshleman and Cashion, p. 313; 7. Bell.
Chapter 18
1. http://www.careers.unsw.edu.au/careered/ Vocational%20Assessment/psych_testing.html
Chapter 19
1. Cotton.

Credits

Figure 1-2: Spokane Community College home page. Reprinted by permission of Spokane Community College.
Chapter 2, p. 35: From *Understanding Interpersonal Communication*, 6th ed. by Richard L. Weaver II. Copyright © 1993 by HarperCollins College Publishers.
Chapter 2, p. 38: "Indipreneur" is trademarked by Carolyn Corbin. Used by permission.
Chapter 2, p. 38: From speech "Employment in the 21st Century" by Carolyn Corbin.
Chapter 5, p. 96: From "Employees Devise New Strategies to Test Job Applicants," by Sabra Chartrand, *The New York Times*, December 14, 1997.
Chapter 6, p. 190: From "A World Where Language and 'Soft Skills' Are Key" by Sabra Chartrand, *The New York Times*, April 6, 1997. Web site at: http://www.nytimes. com/library/jobmarket/121497sabra.html
Chapter 7, p. 124: From "Survival of the Fittest" from *Directions* newsletter, 1997. Used by permission of DeVry Institute of Technology, a division of DeVry University.
Chapter 9, p. 163: From "Career Resilience" by Bettina Lankard Brown from *ERIC Clearinghouse on Adult, Career, and Vocational Education, Digest* 178, 1996. Web site at: http://www.uncg.edu/edu/ericcass/career/digests/dig178. htm
Chapter 11, p. 192–193: From Edward M. Reingold and Wilfred J. Hansen, *Data Structures*. Copyright © 1983 by Edward M. Reingold and Wilfred J. Hansen. Reprinted by permission of Little, Brown and Company.
Chapter 11, p. 195: From Frederick A. Russ and Charles

A. Kirkpatrick, *Marketing*. Copyright © 1982 by Frederick A. Russ and Charles A. Kirkpatrick. Reprinted by permission of Little, Brown and Company.
Chapter 11, p. 204: From "Part III: The coming trauma" of "On the Edge of the Digital Age" from the *Star Tribune*. Copyright © 1996 Star Tribune. Web site at: http://www. startribune.com/stonline/html/digage/main3.htm
Figure 14-1: From Robert A. Wallace, *Biology: The World of Life*, 7th ed. Copyright © 1997 by Addison Wesley Educational Publishers Inc. Reprinted by permission of Addison Wesley Educational Publishers Inc.
Figures 14-2 and 14-3: From H.L. Capron, *Computers*, Brief Edition, © 1998 Addison Wesley Longman Inc. Reprinted by permission of Addison Wesley Longman.
Figure 14-5: From George C. Edwards III, Martin P. Wattenberg and Robert L. Lineberry, *Government in America: People, Politics and Policy*, 7th ed. Copyright © 1996 by Addison Wesley Educational Publishers Inc. Reprinted by permission of Addison Wesley Educational Publishers Inc.
Figure 14-6: From Robert L. Lineberry, *Government in Amercia*, 3rd ed. Copyright © 1986 by Robert L. Lineberry. Reprinted by permission of Little, Brown and Company.
Figure 14-7: From Josh R. Gerow, *Psychology: An Introduction*, fifth edition. Copyright © 1997 by Addison Wesley Educational Publishers Inc. Reprinted by permission of Addison Wesley Educational Publishers Inc.
Figure 14-8: From Thomas C. Kinnear, Kenneth L. Bernhardt and Kathleen A. Krentler, *Principles of Marketing*, 4th ed. Copyright © 1995 by Addison Wesley Educational

Publishers Inc. Reprinted by permission of Addison Wesley Educational Publishers Inc.

Figure 14-9: From Raymond A. Dumont and John M. Lannon, *Business Communications.* Copyright © 1985 by Raymond A. Dumont and John M. Lannon. Reprinted with permission of Little, Brown and Company.

Figure 14-10: Figure "Information on Some Major Cancers" from *Cancer Facts and Figures,* 1993. New York: American Cancer Society. Used by permission of the American Cancer Society.

Figure 14-11: From Barbara Walton Spradley, *Community Health Nursing,* 2nd ed. Copyright © 1985 by Barbara Walton Spradley. Reprinted by permission of Little, Brown and Company.

Figure 14-12: Reprinted from the summer 1997 issue of the *Journal of Career Planning & Employment,* with permission of the National Association of Colleges and Employers, copyright holder.

Figure 14-14: From Joseph W. Newman, *America's Teachers: An Introduction to Education,* 3rd edition. Copyright © 1998 by Addison Wesley Longman, Inc. Reprinted by permission of Addison Wesley Educational Publishers Inc.

Figure 14-15: Source: US News/Bozell poll, 1996. "Generation Gap in the Information Age" from *Sociology,* 5/e, by Thio. Copyright © 1998, p. 406.

Figure 14-16: From Robert J. Ferl, Robert A. Wallace and Gerald P. Sanders, *Biology: The Realm of Life,* 3rd ed. Copyright © 1996 by Addison Wesley Educational Publishers Inc. Reprinted by permission of Addison Wesley Educational Publishers Inc.

Figure 14-17: From Robert L. Lineberry, *Government in America,* 3rd ed. Copyright © 1986 by Robert Lineberry. Reprinted by permission of Little, Brown and Company.

Figure 14-19: "Brasil Futebol" screen capture from Nike website. Reprinted with permission of Nike, Inc.

Figure 14-20: "Public Perception Issues in Biotechnology" by Charles Hagedorn and Susan Allender-Hagedorn. Web site at: http://fbox.vt.edu:1002/cals/cses/chagedor/index/html

Chapter 14, p. 294: Information from U.S. Bureau of Labor Statistics.

Chapter 15, p. 298: From Hugh D. Barlow, *Introduction to Criminology,* 3rd ed. Copyright © 1984 by Hugh D. Barlow. Reprinted by permission of Little, Brown and Company.

Chapter 15, p. 302: From Robert L. Lineberry, *Government in America,* 3rd ed. Copyright © 1986 by Robert L. Lineberry. Reprinted by permission of Little, Brown and Company.

Chapter 15, p. 283: From Elliot Currie and Jerome H. Skolnick, *America's Problems.* Copyright © 1984 by Elliot

Currie and Jerome H. Skolnick. Reprinted by permission of Little, Brown and Company.

Figure 15-1: From Hugh D. Barlow, *Introduction to Criminology,* 3rd ed. Copyright © 1984 by Hugh D. Barlow. Reprinted by permission of Little, Brown and Company.

Figures 15-2 and 15-3: From Robert L. Lineberry, *Government in America,* 3rd ed. Copyright © 1986 by Robert L. Lineberry. Reprinted by permission of Little, Brown and Company.

Figure 15-4: From Elliott Currie and Jerome H. Skolnick, *America's Problems.* Copyright © 1984 by Elliott Currie and Jerome H. Skolnick. Reprinted by permission of Little, Brown and Company.

Figure 15-12: From *Focus on Human Biology, 2nd ed.* by Carl E. Rischer and Thomas A. Easton. Copyright © 1995 by HarperCollins Publishers Inc.

Chapter 16, p. 329: From Adam Smith, "Fifty Million Handguns." Copyright © 1981 by Adam Smith. Reprinted with permission of *Esquire.*

Chapter 16, p. 329: "The Need for Handgun Control" by Senator Edward Kennedy in the *Los Angeles Times,* April 5, 1981. Reprinted by permission of Senator Edward Kennedy.

Chapter 16, p. 338: From Shirley K. Bell, "Is Abortion Morally Justifiable?" *Nursing Forum,* Vol. XX, No. 3. Reprinted by permission of Nursing Forum.

Chapter 19, p. 402: From "Developing Employability Skills" by Kathleen Cotton from *School Improvement Research Series.* Reprinted by permission of the Northwest Regional Educational Laboratory School Improvement Research Series, Portland, Oregon.

Photo Credits

Page 4: Courtesy of Spokane Community College; p. 12: © The New Yorker Collection 1994 Bernard Schoenbaum from cartoonbank.com. All Rights Reserved; p. 26: © The New Yorker Collection 1994 Liza Donnelly from cartoonbank.com. All Rights Reserved; p. 31: Kevin Horan/Tony Stone/Getty Images; p. 41: © Randy Faris/CORBIS; p. 68: Hulton-Deutsch Collection/CORBIS; p. 87: © Genevieve Naylor/CORBIS; p. 93: Bob Collins/The Image Works; p. 102 © The New Yorker Collection 2001 Robert Weber from cartoonbank.com. All Rights Reserved; p. 106: Rick Baker/Unicorn Stock Photos; p. 116: Bruce Ayers/Tony Stone/Getty Images; p. 121: © The New Yorker Collection 1993 Robert Weber from cartoonbank.com. All Rights Reserved; p. 134: © The New Yorker Collection 1998 Tom Cheney from cartoonbank.com. All Rights Reserved;

Index